Millennium Sunset:

Reflections on God's Word and my Faith Journey

Eugene W. Etheridge, Ph.D.

Order this book online at www.trafford.com
or email orders@trafford.com

Most Trafford titles are also available at major online book retailers.

Print information available on the last page.

ISBN: 978-1-4269-7050-4 (sc)
ISBN: 978-1-4269-7051-1 (hc)
ISBN: 978-1-4269-7052-8 (e)

Library of Congress Control Number: 2011916089

Trafford rev. 11/10/2015

 www.trafford.com

North America & international
toll-free: 1 888 232 4444 (USA & Canada)
fax: 812 355 4082

INTRODUCTION

I had always known since my college days that our calendar was wrong by five or six years. It didn't seem to matter much when I thought about it late in 1999, just before the triple-witching hour was to hit us. I tried to work up enthusiasm for the event. What could be rarer than experiencing a new year, a new century and a new millennium all in the same split second? But then—on New Year's Eve, I think it was—from some obscure corner of my memory I recalled a prophecy coming from one of those books that didn't quite make it into the Canon. Its author, Enoch, prophesied that there would be two millennia from Adam to Abraham, another two from Abraham to Christ, then a final two from Christ to his Second Coming. The prophecy went on to say that a final segment would be the Eternal Age. So here was a prophecy that presented a week of millennia as God's scheme of things. A week, I noted, that had already entered its seventh day.

This scheme wouldn't seem strange to a Bible-loving Christian, for Scripture has many like uses of symbolic numbers. Jesus referred to one of them in Daniel, that of 70 weeks. Following Daniel's directions, we would multiply 70 times 7 and come up with 490 days, which we are instructed to change to 490 years. From the start of the count in Daniel's day until the fall of Jerusalem would be 490 years. Jesus warned his listeners in Matthew 24 that the time would end very soon. The prophecy was indeed fulfilled when Titus laid siege to Jerusalem in 68 AD. The siege ended two years later, and by 72 AD with the fall of Masada, the Diaspora of the

Jewish nation began. I had always used these dates when talking about the matter, but I wondered why nobody seemed to be interested in adjusting the calendar backward five years to make it more accurate. I asked myself why scholars didn't remind us that the year 1995 was the bi-millennial anniversary of Christ's birth. I didn't see anything in the newspapers or hear anything from the pulpit. When New Year's Day came in 999 AD, people then were certainly more aware of the end of the first millennium since Christ's birth than we were of the second. Cults arose, and people gathered on their housetops to be nearest the Lord as he descended on that New Year's Day, 1000 AD. I continued to muse—Christ's Second Coming didn't occur either at the end of the first millennial anniversary of his birth, or in 1995 at the end of the bi-millennial anniversary.

It was then that the subject for this book, *Millennium Sunset*, opened up before me like a mighty scroll. Perhaps Christ will descend in glorious clouds, accompanied by an infinitude of heavenly beings singing to the music of the trumpet, if not on the anniversary of his birth, then at the anniversary of some other event in his life—all of which occurred 2,000 years ago, and could also occur at various dates during this present century.

I know that some of my readers might think I border on superstition or sensationalism—not so! I have the highest authorities on my side—Peter, Daniel and Jesus. Peter himself said a day with the Lord is as a thousand years, and a thousand years as one day. So in dealing with celestial events, we must turn away from our secular calendar. Of interest to us all, a prophecy in the Dead Sea Scrolls says that Jerusalem would be destroyed "about 40 years" after the death of the Great Teacher. Christ was crucified in 28 AD on Passover. Titus laid siege to Jerusalem on Passover, 68 AD, because the number of people in the city would be three times larger than usual. Titus knew he could then more rapidly drive them into submission by starvation! The Dead Sea Scroll prediction was fulfilled on the same day of the Hebrew year, and possibly on the exact 40th anniversary of Christ's crucifixion. Let us not minimize either the importance of this Dead Sea Scroll or the millennial-week prophecy of Enoch simply because they did not make it into the Canon. Recall that the Magi also had some non-canonical books at hand to announce the celestial sign of the Nativity Star at Christ's birth.

The triple-witching hour came and went and, frankly, I didn't feel a thing. I expected some sort of a thrill—anything that suggested this particular New Year's Day was a bit above the rest. I anticipated a thrill at least as great as what the Venetian lads in the Middle Ages felt when they arched over their watery streets using pole vaults, but there was no such thrill for me. In fact, I remember most the New England minced clams on the half shell and the stuffed mushroom caps we had for our midnight snack. I suppose my inability to rise to the occasion is due to the fact that we humans don't really experience time at all—age, yes, but not the intellectual construct called time. Philosophers refer to present time as the "specious moment."

Over the next few months, this triple-witching hour kept coming back to mind. I thought of it and the Second Coming of Christ, what theologians call the Parousia, a Greek word meaning "appearance." I want to be alive when he returns to start God's Seventh Day. I love Jesus, and I want to see him in person—the sooner, the better. He says through Paul that he has prepared a "crown of righteousness" for each of us who love his appearing. Might I be alive at his return? We are told by Christ Himself that we should always be ready for his return because it will come as a surprise to all mankind. So I probably should not even bother making an intelligent prediction. Still, I decided to do a little bit of arithmetic. It wouldn't do any harm, and given my present age, it is unlikely that I will be alive for any of the bi-millennial events that come during this century. Yet some of my readers will be. So I got out my Paschal lunar chart and came up with the following interesting information. I will adjust the calendar back five years (and forward 2,000 years) to be as accurate as possible.

Arguing from the farthest to nearest, I chose the finishing of the New Testament Canon, with the final contribution of St. John's Apocalypse at approximately 2085 AD. This would be a logical choice, for that year 2,000 years ago, men were first thoroughly furnished for every good work. The year 2065 relates to the fall of Jerusalem; it also might be a likely choice. I am especially persuaded by the date of the Macedonian call, when Paul first entered Europe on his second missionary journey and preached to the ancestors of European Christians. Its bi-millennial anniversary will be around 2050, depending on what dating scheme is used for Paul's missionary journeys. But the year we would be most likely to choose is 2028, the bi-millennial for Christ's crucifixion, resurrection and ascension into heaven. We must also include the day of Pentecost. All these history-shattering events happened during the first century AD. Will Christ come on the bi-millennial anniversary of one of these? Of course, just as Jesus said, we are not to know for sure.

Some of you may see that my figures differ from those of others. This is because we cannot be precise about these dates. If we say Christ was born in 5 BC but cannot give the exact day, his birth could have been closer to a year before or a year later. This partly explains the differences. Then I suppose old habits are hard to break, and scholars use the customary dates for our calendar, forgetting to adjust them backwards.

I realized at the time that I could use the Paschal moon chart even to determine the actual days when Christ was crucified, rose from the dead and ascended into Glory. Yet after all this calculating, I realized I would have nothing before me but an exercise in futility. Christ still comes as a thief in the night. Christ has told us that his return will be sudden, secret and unexpected. My task is to live ready, to be prepared for my part in these eschatological events that are on their way even now.

I refer to two sets of Last Things—mine and the world's—and given the law of probability, mine will come first. I have always thought that when I leave the planet, I go into a timeless suspension of reality, where all other people are also waiting. Perhaps I will be near Adam and Eve when the trumpet fanfare sounds. After that split-second sleep, that twinkling-of-an-eye moment, we shall rise into the supreme ecstasy of God's presence. So in effect, nothing changes for me once I begin my own part in the series of Final Things. In fact, Paul tells us those who are alive at the Second Coming of Christ will not precede those who died at an earlier time. So my eschatological experiences and those of all others will be simultaneous. It stands to reason then that I must get ready, for my departure is quite near. I haven't any time to lose. I must stop thinking of the Parousia as remote, for it is as near as my natural death. We Christians need to shift our gears, get out of "future-overdrive" and into the ever-living present. I met Christ this morning, and will every day until the shadows flee away and I first see him face to face.

So I decided to take inventory, make changes, to add and subtract, and to fine-tune my ranking of priorities. I recall an excellent story coming from an ancient Jewish commentary. It was about the First Passover, when the angel of death was to fly over Egypt and kill the firstborn of each family, except for those who had put lamb's blood on their doors. That night, a young girl asked her father if he had put the blood on the door. He assured her that one of the servants had been told to tend to the matter. As the night went on, the girl decided to make absolutely sure her father's orders had been followed. She was especially concerned because, after all, she was the family's firstborn. She went outside to find out for herself and discovered that the servant had failed to put the blood on the door. Her father rushed to make amends and finished his task just minutes before midnight. Of course, the moral of the story is that we all should tend to our personal worship ourselves, and not expect someone else to do it for us.

In the spirit of this Hebrew girl who lived over 3,000 years ago, I want to make doubly sure that the road ahead is clear—and the one behind, too, so that others (including you) may see The Christian Road ahead more clearly. Maybe I have let Georgia's fabulous kudzu vine grow across the path behind in just a short time. It could slow the progress of others who are trusting me to show the way, not to hide a pitfall beside the narrow, difficult path. I have my double-edged machete. With it I intend to hack through the jungle of ignorance that lies ahead. I can hear you ask, "Why do you call it a jungle, since you are so close to the Last Things, with heaven so clear in your vision?" I do so because the faster our world changes, the more quickly the jungle grows. I read a compelling ad in a periodical the other day. It was about patriotism, and it began with this in large letters: "Before freedom can be defended, it must be defined." This is why religious issues, especially ethics, are an ongoing, never-ending challenge. My main objective is to give Christian answers to problems that are new in the 21st century. This includes civil, social and scientific problems. There are new ways of sinning against God, in addition to those common to man since his sojourn on earth first began. What's more, there are important doctrines that need new definitions, or at least a refinement of existing ones. On the abortion issue, I say you have to define life before you can defend it. The definition I learned in college fifty years ago is definitely out of date.

Though truth itself never changes, our vocabulary does. New enemies appear, and we must not give them names that camouflage their true nature. Since we are living in a communication renaissance, and given the growing symbiotic nature of the world economy, I noticed that optimism was running high among the television pundits for the UN to become a world government. Then one day in September suddenly stunned us into silence on that subject—possibly forever. It was then that one of the major bridges of hope we had built to other cultures collapsed with the fall of the towers of the World Trade Center, and the murdering of 3,000 innocent souls. Jesus Christ interpreted a like event for the city of Jerusalem, and we must apply it to our country, our personal lives, and modify anew what we mean by the term "world government."

Television itself needs a moral definition—is it a one-eyed monster, the exponent of cultural mediocrity, or a worthy guest in our homes? Is it a valid mode for spreading the Gospel of Jesus Christ? Does the "electronic church" meet the Bible's definition of a church? We also must include the role of the personal computer in our society. How does it relate to our moral development and spiritual enlightenment? In addition, what about "prosperity theology?" Seemingly, it links temporal to spiritual prosperity—is this a justifiable nexus?

We must hone our machetes well, so we can hack into another gadding vine on the road ahead. It is the presumption that there is no such thing as an ethical carry-through from faith to works. The natural brother of our Lord, James, tells us that the devils also believe . . . and tremble, and that faith without works is dead. I have to share with these naïve folk entangled in this vine that Christ not only instantly saves our souls from hell, but he saves our lives progressively from sinning and also from the nebulous regions of unexamined behavior and self-centered orientation.

The Christian Road is made for walking. The Bible is our atlas and also our dictionary.

I assure you in spite of what I have just said about keeping our definitions up to date and asking new questions about newfangled intruders into our status quo, I have absolutely nothing new to say. Rather, I want to be like the merchant who brings from his bag things both new and old. Jesus meant not two kinds of things, the old and the new, but things being old, yet newly seen. I will not neglect Scripture at all, but will make a different emphasis. Instead of using a horizontal, proof-text approach to popular and controversial doctrines, I will choose fewer verses and dig deeply into their meaning. Recently, there has arisen a fad in Bible study, the prayer of Jabez (I Chron. 4:10). Whole books recently have been written about this one brief biblical prayer. I do not wish to add this to our repertoire of devotional material. Rather, I will choose one line from the Lord's Prayer, dig into it as though for oil, and hope for an exciting gusher that will obliterate the rote doldrums and mindless cant that usually infects our overuse of the most famous prayer the world has ever known. Now, wouldn't that be better than praying with Jabez for more real estate?

My approach is devotional and not in scholarly format—no footnotes or bibliography. I have no time for adding these things. Time is running out for me. I am in my sunset years. But as the Psalmist says, "God makes the outgoing of the morning and evening to rejoice," one of my favorite quotes. By "outgoings," the Psalmist means sunrise and sunset, or the beginning and end of one's life. I hear the distant siren of tinnitus in my ear, urging me to "cut the fat," as it were. Besides, ten years ago I gave away my library of about 1,000 volumes—the religious books to a small, struggling seminary in Mississippi, and the secular ones to a new church college in Iowa. So this is not a book for professionals—I am sure they already have enough scholarly books. I write for the young in the faith, and especially for the veterans who are ahead of me on the Christian Road.

I have insisted that I maintain an ecumenical spirit throughout. I have no axe to grind, nor time for disputations. I promise to be liberal enough in the non-essentials so that the essentials will be neither affected nor neglected. I will stay close to the contents of the Nicene Creed. I am far more excited about it than about the modes of baptism, or whether we ought to allow statues in the sanctuary. I remind you that wars have been fought and blood has been let over such non-vital issues.

I do not believe in one church organization any more than I believe in one world government. Given human frailty and what I have learned from the Bible, experience and history, I have come to the conclusion that the more countries and the more churches we have, the better. Yet I look forward to the time when all Christians cross love's bridge to one another. Others must agree with me about this, and are doing things to build this bridge. I hear of impromptu gatherings in homes for special speakers or regular Bible-study groups, of weekend retreats, women's or men's weekday meetings at all sorts of hours, luncheon prayer meetings, and of ecumenical gatherings to hear gifted speakers. I understand that even street preachers are organizing to discover more effective ways to present their "confrontational evangelism." New periodicals have emerged that are wholly devoted to helping Christian scholars cross over to one another. It is critical that we get together. By this I do not mean to get doctrinally closer, but spiritually. We will have to mute our differences, and magnify the cardinal truths to hitherto unachieved heights. I dedicate these pages to that very end.

Trouble in our nation argues for such a higher unity. A great falling away from critical doctrines is cause for alarm. Look also at the new role America has spontaneously assumed now that the USSR has fallen. This is not all good news for us Americans, for we are becoming for the whole world what the Jews once were for Hitler's Germany. The kings of the earth cry out for a whipping boy, and we are it. The sunset is upon our bi-millennial world. Christ's return is upon us. A strange and hungry god is rising in the East, whose stated purpose is to devour Western culture. We must get together. After all, Whom we have in common is so great that what we have in difference should never keep us apart.

Finally, I want to share a new definition with you, a fine-tuning of what we usually call "growth in grace." I call it cumulative grace. It is also the only expression I know of that effectively refutes the fallacious notion of "progress in history." We will discuss this fully in a later chapter, but for now I see all my education, my decades of teaching, my writing and preaching as contributing to this very moment. With this same sweeping view of history, Mordecai said to Queen Esther, "What do you know but that you are come to the Kingdom at such a time as this?" *Millennium Sunset* is a work of cumulative grace. I hope you will find something new and life-saving in each chapter. My cumulative grace is at your disposal to this very end.

Just a couple of technical points. I use the masculine pronoun as generic, solely for stylistic ease. Also, since God has chosen the masculine for himself, may all my female readers please consider that we honor him, and not the masculine gender. God and the limitations of language leave me no better choice. When I quote from the New Testament or from the Greek Old Testament, I take the liberty of making my own translation.

Well, I see the sun is rising. I am prepared to leave the caravansary. This is my last oasis. My Expert Guide has told me that home is just beyond the horizon. But first, I must make a final check to be sure all my camels are in the right order and that I have left nothing behind. Would you care to join me?

Eugene W. Etheridge, Ph.D.
Professor Emeritus of English
Indiana State University

Chapter I:
Questions At Sunset—
This Dying Millennium

I am beginning to understand what Pascal meant by "These infinite spaces frighten me." I must confess that this has not always been the case. In my youth, I led the unexamined life, which gives rise to few questions, especially questions without answers—the kind Pascal refers to. Youths see no infinite spaces; the term means nothing to them. Yet as the years pass, I find that the more I learn, the more I am aware of what I do not yet know. Pascal was one of the world's great thinkers, a pre-eminent mathematician and one of the world's great Christian apologists. Pascal spoke of infinite spaces, which rose not only from mathematics, but from the Bible and life in general. They are frightening to us, too, when we make serious efforts to ply reality in quest of Ultimate Value. En route, we learn that each new answer asks a dozen new questions. We learn from scientists that each deeper penetration into nature's detail argues for the possibility of deeper penetration, yet with the same degree of detail in what we observe. Indeed we join the first astronomer who looked through Mt. Palomar's new telescope as he answered the question, "What do you see?" He said, "More stars!"

As I near the end of my earthly travels, the nagging questions continue about infinite spaces, many of which suggest God's frown. I am taught by the Good News of Jesus Christ that the time is near when I will see that the frown has really been a smile. Still, I want all who hear my testimony to know that, even at this late hour, I am no closer to knowing HOW and WHY than I was when I met God at 18, who first changed my WHO and WHAT from an egocentric universe of my own creation into a theocentric universe with Jesus Christ as its center. I must face the fact that, with my increase of knowledge, I have an increase of distance between God and me. Solomon had it exactly right: "He who increaseth knowledge, increaseth sorrow." I see our problem as having a perimeter of understanding less than the circumference of our awareness of God's governance of the universe. I call this overlap the Tragic Zone, for it is here where so many determine their eternal destination. Consider with me the dimensions we speak of. If the earth is the center of the universe, and if the shape of the universe is globular, then with our present knowledge of distances involved, the universe has a radius of 100,000,000 light years. In miles it would be a 5.85 x 10 40 diameter. But if we do not know our distance from the perimeter of the universe, how then can we know that we are in the center? We also certainly guess when we speak of shape. The universe could be round or oblong, even square or doughnut-shaped—perhaps even flat. Its horizontal dimension could exceed its vertical dimension so greatly that it could appear as a sheet of five-ply.

In his infinite wisdom, God put us in a universe where our awareness and his involvement in our universe overlap. We live in this tragic zone where we know the earth and use its sciences, but at the outer fringes we see the dawning of the eternal day. We see it as through the use of a polished oval of copper, which Paul meant when he said we see through a glass darkly. In this tragic zone, God whispers to us about the bright Morning Star still shining when all other luminaries have faded, because the eternal day is dawning upon our dying millennium. This star, the Eternal *Logos*, led the way of the magi of long ago, and speaks to us again after his resurrection from the dead.

When I first came out of the Tragic Zone a new creature, I hesitated calling my cataclysmic experience a mere religion. Most religions I had examined seemed no more than a book of how-to's for adjusting to the world. In contrast, I found that my experience was more of a kidnapping.

Others came out of this zone with a bag of tools. I came out a new person without any regard for tools. No, what had happened was a new birth, not a choice of one religion from among all others. I found in the Gospels the name I was hunting for—"Way." My resurrected life would be for me the Christian Way. Those distracting daughters of Jerusalem who ask, "What is thy beloved more than another beloved?" I told to hush up. Their question was irrelevant.

Why not call the place where Christ kidnapped me the Heroic Zone? If I did, some might suggest I believed in humanism, that man can save himself through some heroic act. Also, such a name would completely ignore the vast majority of fatalities that occur there. There is nothing heroic about people who end up there and cast their souls into hell. This includes those who bring out of the mist a bag of tools that help them to adjust to this world, and those who come out with machine-guns and rifles with the notion that the only way to salvation is to kill everyone who doesn't agree with them.

Let me pause here for an "edifying aside," as I often tell my students when I can't resist sharing with them some impromptu blessing. Early on the Christian Way, I learned two often neglected truths of great value. One is that the Bible does not contain all the truth. I do not refer just to scientific facts (which, I am told, compound daily at a geometric ratio), but to spiritual truths—ethics I do well to live by. A friend tells me that he has found ten versions of the Golden Rule outside Scripture, all of which were written before the time of Jesus Christ. We must accept these and live by them, for we can see they are wholly consistent with Scripture. Second is the realization that the main religions of the world contain some important truths, or they would never have achieved the popularity and impetus to achieve worldwide influence. It would be strange, indeed, if we did not find some representation of these truths in the Bible itself.

In my defense of the Tragic Zone, I would draw our attention to Greek religion of ancient times. Their religion was not founded by given individuals like Gautama, Mohammed or Confucius; theirs was a folk religion that rose from many sources over long periods of time. It made no claim of coming from divine inspiration—just from wise and talented men. It was a religion of the imagination and concerned itself with helping people to lead better lives in this world. It was a one-way religion, from the gods down to men, with no movement in the other direction whatsoever. The greatest of its thinkers was Socrates, who died a martyr to education for denying the plurality of the gods. You will recall the narrative of his death, so inspirational that I take pleasure in repeating it here. He was pronounced guilty at his trial, guilty of corrupting the youth of Athens by implying the gods did not exist. He was given two choices—give up teaching or death. He chose death rather than not being allowed to seek, learn and share what he learned with others. He said, "The unexamined life is not worth living." His other teachings are recorded in the works of Plato. One of his students was Aristotle, and these two took opposite views on what has proved the most controversial question ever raised, a question which has never been satisfactorily answered until this day, yet philosophers cannot escape asking it. How do we begin recognizing what we see? Plato said cognition is stamped on our minds from eternity—he became the founder of idealism. Aristotle said cognition comes from the environment about us—he is the founder of realism.

Greek religion came from sources tracing back to a time before King David, whose contemporary, Homer, wrote of the pantheon of gods in his folk epics, *Iliad* and *Odyssey*. In these works we find summarized stories about the Greek gods, who were wholly anthropomorphic in nature, i.e., had dispositions and actions common to all men. That is to say, they were not ideal in nature. This approach also applies to the Roman Pantheon, which so parallels the Greek to the extent that some of their gods have the same name in both languages. The Romans heard their Greek slaves pray to their king of the gods, Zeus: "*O Zeu Pater* . . . ." Soon, the Romans started imitating their slaves. Because they did not have Z in their alphabet, they substituted its nearest equivalent, the "J" sound, and the enunciation became Jupiter. The Romans actually changed the name of the king of their gods, Jove, to the Greek Jupiter. Surely, eclecticism could go no further!

I will pass those colorful narratives about quarrels in the royal household between Zeus and Hera, the deceptions, battles and many other similarities to human plots. There is but one relating to our subject, the concept of incarnation. Many of the gods visited the human race, often leaving bastard offspring for humans to raise. Achilles was one of these, the son of a sea goddess and a Greek named Peleus. But the greatest of them all is Zeus falling in love with a beautiful young girl named Leda. He flew down in the form of a swan and raped her, from which union were born twin girls, Helen and Clytemnestra, no doubt the two most important women in the prehistory of Greece. One inadvertently caused the war between the Greeks and the Trojans, and the other murdered her husband, king of the ancient Greeks. These are the kinds of incarnations the Greeks imagined. There is no virtuous example for us in Zeus, that's for sure. In fact, the Greeks were fond of addressing him as "Zeus, Deceiver."

Returning to a consideration of the Tragic Zone, I prefer the term "tragic" because those who coined the term did not always end the lives of their tragic heroes with the finality of death, like Shakespeare's Hamlet, Lear, Romeo and Juliet. Rather, we see Oedipus very much alive, walking slowly offstage to face life henceforth as a blind leader in disgrace. From then on, he would face the truth that he had murdered his father and married his mother, by whom he sired four children. You see, the Greeks thought of their tragic hero as one born to a high position (the potential of our youth), who was average in morality (all have sinned and come short of God's excellence), and who brought about his own downfall through a fault in his character (the human condition). From this fall, which is commonly attributed to *hubris* (i.e., pride), most die violently. Yet some get up and keep going with a catalytic modification of their lives that enters into the conversion process in a positive way. Recall that it was not until after he was blind that Milton was able to compose the greatest description of Paradise ever to come from a human pen. Bach's hands, by which he praised God every Sunday playing the church organ as none had ever played it before, became so gnarled with arthritis that his script became illegible as he wrote perhaps the greatest major composition in all the annals of music, the Mass in B Minor. Indeed, arthritis, blindness and other forms of infirmity can enter most subtly, and yet so profoundly, into God's plans for some of us.

I have yet one more item from ancient Greece I must share with you before we press on, one that helps equip us for the Tragic Zone ahead of us. In addition to defining the tragic hero, Aristotle said the tragic hero must never be helped by any deity who dumps a lapful of goodies upon him. That would ruin the dimensions of our heroic subject. No, he must struggle upward by great effort. No shortcuts from above, no *deus ex machina*, no "god in a machine," as Aristotle put it. Some poorly written dramas of Aristotle's day did end with a god perched on a catapult onstage, who solves the subject's problem for him.

The Christian doctrines are clearly discerned in this shadowy matter. We all know God is Omnipotent; nothing is beyond his ability. His arm is not so short that it cannot save, but that is not the whole message. This same Omnipotent God also requires that we participate in the lifelong process of salvation. So God will not come up with the cash every time we need financial help. We must not expect a *deus ex machina*. These wise Greeks also share this bit of wisdom with us: "The gods shower gifts on those they want to destroy." This means that people can handle adversity better than they can prosperity. We have the daily newscast to convince the doubter, as well as examples we have seen closer to home. Having a "god in a machine" would be the worst thing for us to experience. It would make our faith unnecessary and keep us always as infants. The only satisfying solution to our problems would be accepting the blood shards of our broken dreams, and holding on to the hope of finding some way to fabricate those shards into a future life. Here's the heroic part of the tragic hero we all admire and wish to be; here is true beauty. Again, this from the Greeks and for our scrapbook of memories: "Beauty is the goddess that hovers over adversity."

The year 2002 AD brought New York City back to my mind. I lived there one summer while attending chaplain's school on David's Island. I recall attending the Riverside Church every Sunday. I especially remember the organist playing those huge pipes. Their forzando sounded extraterrestrial, to say the least. It is probably like the voice of God, which I am hearing more often now that I find two dying millennia coming to my life—my own and that of the world I live in. I need to hear that voice.

I need it to help mute my severe case of tinnitus, that perpetual ringing in the ears that comes to old folks. The bitter tears gather again in my eyes, which strangely wash my vision clearer as I conclude that man is too intelligent to keep from asking questions, and too stupid to comprehend the answers. This Pascal concluded about life, as did Job when adversity washed his eyes clear. He declares, as the theophany comes to its end, "I have asked questions seeking answers—both are too wonderful for me to understand, and so I cannot say a word. I will shut my stupid mouth and bow in ashes before thee."

We have often heard that before we get new answers, we must have new questions. However, we must ask the right questions and distinguish them from pseudo-questions and non-questions, i.e., questions that have no possible answers. Two of these are WHY and HOW, the rightful purlieu of scientists. I am fond of calling these my "biceps of pride." We have found that Scripture often answers the questions WHO and WHAT. "Come and let us reason together, saith the Lord." Our Omniscient Lover thus invites us to appetizers of the coming feast, although we all will probably get a zero on the questions he intends to ask us. A student once asked during one of my lectures how I could believe in a universe ruled by a loving God in light of the coexistence of good and evil. I told him I would answer his question if he would first answer one of mine. He said he would, and so I asked, "Why do you tolerate the co-existence of good and evil in your own life?" He chuckled a bit and sat down.

We are—or ought to be—concerned with WHO and WHAT. Both these have one clear, bold answer for us living spirits (as distinguished from being scientists in lab smocks), viz., "And we know that for those loving God, all things work together for good" (Rom. 8:28). Yet how good will these things be when I am nearer God than ever, as I end my earthly pilgrimage knowing nothing about WHY and HOW? I understand there is a part of me up in heaven now waiting to clothe me, whom Paul calls "that man which is from above." I imagine this union to be something like the miracle that weaves together a coherent picture for me to view on a television screen, or perhaps some kind of chambray cloth, with me being the warp and God the woof. Other comparisons can be made; poetry is full of as many metaphors as unanswered HOW can imagine. My temptation to join the scientists with their ready-made answers makes me sort of a control freak. Again, I seem so much like Job, who believed without any reservation whatsoever that knowing WHY God had wrecked such devastation on him would satisfy his questioning, and fortify his shaky hope that God didn't really hate him after all. Like Job, I too want to know WHY and HOW; I want to use the biceps of pride, when I should be quite satisfied to know WHO and WHAT. Maybe I think knowing the answers to these questions would put me partially in control of the outcome of my life just now, while I still have time to effect some improvement. Yet this is ridiculous, I know. Maybe I just want to intensify my worry about the inevitable, thinking my suffering may partially atone for the sins that still plague me where I am just now, after Skull Place, there on Har Megiddo, where I first came face to face with my Divine Lover. This will not do either, for it smacks of salvation by works. It is a ridiculous notion, yet I am looking toward the end of life as did John Calvin. He said on his deathbed, "Lord, thou bruiseth me, but it is enough to know that it is Thou."

I must be ever careful about these biceps of pride, especially as I read again the Great Prologue to life, the Creation Hymn, Genesis 1-3. I bring all the science I know to bear on the matter. In fact, I cannot help but bring all knowledge-about into full focus on what God says about the creation of the universe. What I see is like approaching a door with a doorknob plate that has a keyhole through which I see the universe. The plate is as ornate as any from an 18th-century palace. It is so polished that it dazzles my view through the keyhole. This plate is science and the keyhole is my understanding, through which I look into the wonders of the Creation Hymn.

What is it that I see? WHO and WHAT, absolutely nothing more. What I do not see is HOW and WHY. Those mischief-makers, those faithless scientists in their lab smocks, for whom faith is their greatest enemy, always end up with the cowardly "straw man fallacy," of supererogating the Creation Hymn, i.e., making it say more than it does, so they can prove it in error. A careful examination of the whole biblical Canon reveals very few answers to the WHY and HOW questions. No matter how elaborate we make the doorknob plate, the keyhole remains the same size. And what we see has nothing whatever to do with the scientists' world; there is a Grand Canyon between us and them, the only nexus being the tragic lament that so many see science as their savior and that the North Rim of the Canyon doesn't even exist. The achievements of scientists are as gladly admitted as they are enjoyed. We almost daily come to benefit from some new breakthrough. At present, we are experiencing the Renaissance of Communication, which opens a whole new world to every household via the personal computer. It is grand living in this renaissance. Still, we know profoundly that before we can communicate, we must have a subject matter to share. This brings me to the matter of faith, a faith for the twilight of our passing millennium. This we must have, for man shall not live by bread alone, a fact Satan once hoped Christ would forget and which many scientists are hoping we will ignore. I will attempt to give a satisfying definition of faith. I say "satisfying" definition, for I believe many laymen need to be disabused of false or misleading definitions of this vital word—it is vital, for we are saved by faith. I can hear Martin Luther echo from heaven, *"Pistis sola!"*

I maintain that we must first define who is to receive this definition—man himself. There is great controversy raging in academic circles about exactly who man is. In our quest, we must go to the first page of Genesis. We are told that man was made in the image of God, not the other way around. It is certainly erroneous to imagine, as a certain modern cult avers that "as man is, God once was." Recall Robert Browning's poem, "Caliban upon Setabos," in which a character taken from Shakespeare's *The Tempest* tells us what he thinks God is like. We end up with a recapitulation of the pantheon of ancient Greece. Of course, we all (including the Bible) liken God to man. What other comparisons are possible? As Jesus wept over Jerusalem, he went beyond this by using a zoomorphism, likening himself to a mother hen. However, we must be careful to avoid man's fallen nature as part of any mythological use in our description. This blasphemous error is what the author of Psalm 50 had in mind when he said, "Thou thoughtest that I was *altogether* such a one as thyself" (Ps. 50:21). No, the opposite is true; man was made in the image of God. The first attribute we gave to God intuitively as children is that God is a Spirit, exactly what Jesus told the Samaritan woman who came to draw water from Jacob's well. So we are spirits and we are like God, qualitatively speaking. Every attribute we know of him, we also have. It is true that we have bodies, but we are not bodies per se, or psychosomatic organisms (bodies plus spirits), but spirits with all the attributes of God. We must be cautious here to distinguish between Old Testament and New Testament meanings of "spirit." Paul uses "spirit" to mean the opposite of carnal. He says, "to be carnally minded is death, but to be spiritually minded is life and peace." However, when we use "spirit" as it is used in Genesis, we refer not to orientation, but as to nature.

My readers will probably shudder at the implications involved in our being gods, as indeed they ought. We all ought to shudder, for we all are gods, with the responsibilities tantamount to the privileges and destinies. Men know this, and so they would rather forego the honor to avoid the responsibility. They rush to invoke the notions of Freud and Darwin, pronouncing animal forms and animal destinies upon us all. Thereby, too, they gain an option to mitigate their more than brutish behavior that would make animals (if they could) blush for shame. But gods cannot be beasts, though they may be devils imitating beasts in their pitiless acts of violence. How often we must cry out, "Oh, the inhumanity of man to man." But Genesis 1 demands that we acknowledge our divinity, that each of us is working with God through faith to perfect his godliness, or with the only other supernatural power known to us, the Devil, and his progressive deterioration of our godhead toward demonization. This is harsh language, but to say less is to join the Enemy.

We must see saints and demons en route everywhere. We must recognize that Judas lives in our block, Herod just around the corner; Hitlers, Stalins and bin Ladens can be anywhere. They lack only the time and occasion to rise to such bad eminence. Introspection may indeed cause many to conclude with Goethe, who once claimed his inner potentials were in such precarious balance that, given the slightest change in his personality, there is not a crime he would be incapable of committing. This may be more poetry than truth, but better Goethe than the Pharisee who regarded that his tithe made him superior to the evil tax collector who knelt at the same altar rail, so possessed with bitter disappointment that he could not look up to heaven as he prayed.

Men have two options, only two—to be gods or demons. Christ's advent has given us no other choice. When he came, he defined what man ought to be. He was the Personification of Virtue, the Second Adam, the *Logos*. Now comes Skull Place. The Second Adam meets the descendants of the First Adam. Both enter into mortal conflict, and the Second Adam wins! This outcome he proved three days later when he spontaneously resuscitated from the dead. We gods must join him or go off into the oblivion God has prepared for the Devil and his angels.

There is a second thing Scripture teaches us, just as neglected and unwelcome as the divinity of man. It is the fact that all men have a religion. We all pursue what we conclude is "ultimate value." It is indeed "funnel vision" for us to look at the historical superstructures of the Christian religion and suppose that here is religion. I do not say all are followers of the Christian Way, but merely what each accepts as ultimate value is his religion, whether he be following a Loving Heavenly Father, and being guided by the earthly life of his Son, or be running after some phantom floating around in his egocentric universe. I am certain some—if not many—will be totally unaware they have any ranking of values in their lives that lead upward to some ultimate value. Indeed, some may never give values a second thought. Yet even though they stoutly deny the ranking of any values in their lives, they might as well deny they exist at all. Their ranking of values must be recognized as devotion to their own ultimate value.

Another observation we must make is that all men are experts in religion. This at first seems like a left-handed compliment, but it may actually be a reckless exaggeration. However, one should note that I did not say man was an expert in theology or one of its related academic fields. If we define religion as ultimate value, wouldn't everyone be an expert in precisely that? In addition, we must not leave out the offices of the Holy Ghost, who begins in our earliest years wooing us with thoughts, guiding us toward the God who loves all men and wants none to perish. Then in these rare hours when the contemplation of infinity teases us into the Tragic Zone, we start arriving at conclusions. This Tragic Zone, what the poet David called "the valley of deadly shadows," opens ways for us to go. It is not long before some start bringing tool kits out of the mist. By the time I was 14, I was an atheist, and I surely regarded myself an expert in what I believed in. I would be surprised if many of my readers will disagree with me about this.

Man is a spirit—a spirit in a machine. He has his own religion or accepts the religion of someone else. He is involved in an ongoing process of ranking his values and yielding priority to them. This ranking must include and exclude values held by others.

With these matters before us, let me come to a definition of faith—*revealed perception*. Let us look briefly at these two words. First is *perception*. This term means more than mere seeing. One modern philosopher speaks of the exclusionary element of perception as a selection of certain sensa from a larger number that exist. This is to say that we see more than we perceive. Perception is a limited view of what the eye sees, or any other of the senses are stimulated by. I went to church last Sunday and I remember the sermon well, but I cannot recall what tie I wore, or the color of the ceiling in our sanctuary, though I must have seen it dozens of times. These things are not important to me, so I do not include them in my memory.

Here's another example, a bit more serious in its implication. I once called on a man to invite him to church. I note that he didn't have the courtesy to shut the television off, but watched it with one eye. I conversed with him as best I could for about ten minutes. The program then ended and the news came on. He jumped up and changed channels. I found out later that he never read about the news in the paper, and never watched news programs on the television. There were two things he said he would not "argue" about—politics and religion. This anecdote illustrates two points I have been making. Each of us has his own religion, and each is involved in the ongoing process of ranking its priorities.

We come now to a mysterious word—*revelation*. We are able to reveal something about ourselves to each other, either intending to do so, or inadvertently. But there is also supernatural revelation, which comes in two distinct parts. God can reveal to you things you would never be able to arrive at by thinking about any given subject. One reason Jews reject Jesus as their Messiah is that it is unthinkable that God would allow Christ's earthly life to end on a Roman cross. I agree with them; it is unthinkable. However, that doesn't mean the unthinkable is impossible, or that it didn't happen. The other matter is the supernatural disclosure of data you could understand but have not the ability to foresee. This involves what we call prophecy. The Virgin Mary had revealed to her the nature of her pregnancy.

Now we come to the revelation of the Divine Person. There is nothing we can do to reveal Christ to others. True, we can demonstrate his virtues to them and thereby help God create a contextual impellent toward revelation. We can bring them to church, where the context is richest, especially after they have attempted to pray and read the Bible. We create an environment in which revelation is most likely to take place. We can hope that supernatural selection of impressions will take place and that Christ will reveal himself to them, but we cannot reveal Christ to them. Christ Himself says, "If I be lifted up, I will draw all men unto me." From this promise, it seems that revelation of the Divine Person—not the historical Jesus—is universal, dependent only on one's willingness to seek it.

Revelation comes directly from Latin. Its meaning is "from hiding." The Greek word is *apocalypse*, a word our last century made popular by such titles as *The Four Horsemen of the Apocalypse* and *Apocalypse Now*. Some scholars hold that "apocalyptic expectancy" is one of the characteristics of the great Renaissance that swept across Europe from the 14th to the 17th centuries, and has come back to haunt us in the twilight of our millennium. In a popular sense, apocalypse means the things to occur at the end of the human race, especially the bad things—doom literature, as some have called it. This false meaning is due to the fact that so many of the last things are described in the Apocalypse itself, another name for the book of Revelation. But the Greek word means exactly what the Latin one does—to be called from hiding.

It must be obvious that, if something has to be revealed, it must be very special—something not available to someone who is attempting to get it on his own. What is hid, and from whom? In our context as Christians, the answer is the identity of Jesus, that it is hidden from all mankind because man would never recognize Jesus on his own. In fact, he is in flight from God. He does not want to believe his own universe (no matter how small it may be) is founded on someone else. He does not want to believe that someone else is God Himself and that he sent his Son to set our thinking in the right direction. Jesus says few will ever find salvation, and if they do, it must be revealed to them by God Himself.

This is exactly what happened to Peter when the revelation came to him. Miraculously, he perceived that before him stood, not superstition's choice, John the Baptist; not logic's choice, Jeremiah or one of the other prophets; but the very Messiah for whom Israel had been languishing, lo, these many centuries. Jesus responds to this Great Confession that God had given to Peter by changing his name from the Hebrew, *Simon (Simeon)*, to the Greek name, *Peter*. He says, "Blessed art thou, Simon bar Jonah, for flesh and blood hath not revealed it unto thee, but my father which is in heaven." So we must tell the world what we ourselves have already experienced, that men must seek a special revelation from heaven. This is knowledge that only God can give. I will not try to prove this statement or to justify it. I will take Christ's word for it.

What is revealed to us? Christ and his Holy Gospel, the Good News that God will give the respondent to his revelation of Christ a cure for his crippled epistemology (i.e., Adamic nature), will set his thinking aright, forgive all iniquity, and will allow him to share in the resurrection from the dead and eternal life. Now comes the difficult part—sharing the Good News with others. We will have to speak of the information sent us from heaven using earthly terms, and so many begin with the word *belief.* When we do so, our audience will start thinking about what one learns in school. One believes knowledge. *Belief* and *knowledge* so often go together that we can separate them only with consistent effort. One believes in certain knowledge, such as that very exciting discovery which some have called the greatest since the invention of the wheel—the Pythagorean Theorem. When Pythagoras finally proved that the square upon the hypotenuse of a right triangle is equal in area to the squares upon its two sides, he was ecstatic. He was so aware of his great accomplishment that he went to the temple and sacrificed a bull to Zeus. Now, ask him, "Pythagoras, do you believe in this theorem?" He will reply, "Oh, yes, and with all my heart." So do we all believe, but we also believe that faith is infinitely more than belief.

Biblical scholars realize the inadequacy of *belief* as the right word to describe the verb form of faith, the crown jewel of Christian theology. They tell us philosophy has saved the word for us by distinguishing between two kinds of knowledge—knowledge by acquaintance and knowledge by description. The latter is quite obviously the language of science, or belief *that,* and the former is a synonym for faith, or belief *in.* All this is well and good, but the distinction hardly exists in the pedestrian mind. Scholars go from believe *in* to such limited forms as believe *on,* trust *in* or rely *on.* These are improvements, but fall short of what is needed. Also consider that the verb form *trust in* cannot avoid ambiguity. One meaning is found in the sentence, "I trust in the Constitution of the United States." Now contrast that with the sentence, "I trust you will not forget your promise to me." Here the usage means hope, not faith. I have faith that I am saved; I could never be content only hoping I am saved. Hope always relates to the future, and faith to a present reality.

These expressions are not quite adequate. Our trouble is with the limitations of the English language, which has no verb form for faith. I can say "I love," "I hope," but not "I faith." The point before us cannot be stressed too much. We are dealing with the very means of our salvation. We are saved by faith, and the just shall live by faith. When we get right down to it (as we will in a later chapter), faith is also that which neutralizes Adamic nature, which must be brought in tow if anyone ever expects to have revealed to him that omnipotent achievement of the lowly Nazarene carpenter, who with his calloused hand opens to us the gate of Paradise.

Our solution is to find a word to express faith as a verb. The Greek word for faith is *pistis.* It is used often in the New Testament, occurring as a verb 214 times. We must avoid the alternate translations as listed above. The problem of translating *pistis* as *belief* began with the formulators of the Latin creeds, called Apostles Creed and Nicene Creed. Indeed, each begins with *Credo,* I believe, rather than *pistis,* which is also a Latin word transliterated directly from Greek. Of course, *I believe* is the correct translation of the Latin term. It has been in use in English ever since. It seems clear to me that since there is no verb form for *faith*, we will have to settle for the expression *have faith.* Nothing else is available to us.

Recall the event in Acts when Paul and Silas in the depths of the Philippian jail were in joyful dialogue about their salvation, and then sang hymns. You can be sure the jailer heard this witness. Then at midnight an earthquake opened the jail's door. Seeing this, the jailer prepared to fall on his own sword to avoid a worse execution he knew he would receive if the prisoners escaped. Paul yelled out for the man to do himself no harm because the prisoners had not escaped. The man then cried out to Paul, "What must I do to be saved?" Paul was swift to answer, but did he say in Greek, "Believe on" or "Have faith in the Lord Jesus Christ"? Of course, the latter is the Greek expression.

A final illustration of the inadequacy of these expressions is found in Heb. 11:6. It is especially bad because it is translated as *believe that,* an expression reserved for the scientists in pursuit of knowledge by description. Read it now with its correct translation:

> For he that cometh to God must *have faith* that he exists
> and is the rewarder of them that diligently seek him.

Now let us come to the only definition of faith given in the New Testament and compare it with what I suggest faith is, viz., *revealed perception.* We will begin with the King James Version (KJV) of Heb. 11:1.

> Faith is the substance of things hoped for, the evidence of
> things not seen.

Right away we are in trouble, for we must wade through abstract nouns to define faith, which also is an abstract noun. I point out at the outset that this is not a conceptual definition as one would find in the dictionary, but a dynamic definition. That is, it tells us how something works, not exactly what it is. This same difficulty confronts us as we read I Cor.

13, one of the most sublime passages of prose ever written. Paul gives a dynamic definition of love. After all, life overflows logic. It has taught us that some things lie too deep for the discursive mode, requiring rather the presentational mode, exchanging the straight line of writing in prose for the sunburst effect, comparable to what we would find in a lyric poem. So Paul uses a dynamic definition of love, and the world of religion and literature are the richer for it. Since life does overflow logic, you cannot find God at the end of a syllogism. Perhaps in the final analysis, faith is an overflow of our cup of salvation. Now consider my translation of Heb. 11:1.

> Faith involves the Personification of the things we are
> hoping for, who is the proof of things not seen.

Heb. 11:1, as it stands in the KJV, is such a poor translation that no subsequent translation lets it stand as it is. I offer my translation, which is quite different, as you see. I present a full defense of the changes, which appears in the next chapter for those who wish to dig a little deeper into the matter.

Recall that Paul reminds us that heaven and all eschatological glories awaiting us are not available to the eye or ear——or even to the imagination. We must not think about material things like rocking chairs, fishing poles, solar heaters for our swimming pools, or the best cars to drive "because God wants his children to have the very best." We must not dream of ruling a planet in some distant solar system, as one minister recently suggested. Instead, we must make a leap of faith beyond the limitations of things.

We come at last to the *Civitate Deo,* and learn that there is no night there, for God and his Son are the light of the City of God. What would all these be—transparent walls, streets of pure gold, gates of a single pearl each, the size of which has never been seen on the face of this planet—without any light to see them by? Here's the secret: Heaven is a Person, the Lord of Lords and the King of Kings, the *Logos,* the Word, the Essential Nature of

God. Fix your hopes on Him, the focus of your faith. It is the monumental task facing us all to transform the desire for things into an adoration of the Person of Christ. He has boldly told us he is the Light of the World, the Bread of Life, the Water of Life, the Good Shepherd, the Way, the Truth, and the Life. Stretch your faith to make him the climax of reality.

Now our definition of faith rises clearly, soaring upward through the painful limitations of language and human ignorance. Faith is *revealed perception* of him who becomes the embodiment of our greatest hopes. It takes a miracle to reach heaven, the eternal reality that begins now and never ends. Paul experienced Christ on the Road to Damascus. He was blinded by the vision of Christ, so his eyes were not involved, yet he perceived with his soul, which gave him a perception clearer than what eyes could see. So must be our perception, too intense for seeing. We have all experienced times when the eyes were seeing, but we were not there—we were perceiving something revealed. At times, we transcend this ortholinear mode of thought that proceeds in the shape of a line like the free association of ideas in reverie. Christ comes to us when our wandering steps have brought us to Har Megiddo. We see Emmanuel. He shows us his love, and all the eye sees and ear hears disappear. Revelation is taking place. Our ortholinear awareness perceives the consequence of our sin, the crucifixion we take part in, and then his love in spite of all. We "see" nothing else but, in rapt attention, the sunburst glory of Him, the Perfect Adam with the miracle interlacing of his destiny with our own. We see that this revelation is the antecedent prerequisite of faith, and he becomes the reality of our faith in quest of his own glorious person. My faith involves the personification of all I am hoping for, whose daily companionship becomes the evidence of the universe that is not yet seen.

Paul never ceased praising the Christ of the Damascus Road. He took every opportunity to narrate the particulars of his conversion every chance he had. He mentioned Christ once every four verses in his letters. Faith is revealed *perception*. We deal not with things seen, but things perceived, which come from sources other than mere eyes.

In the millennium sunset before me, I am quite uneasy about my personal task of transferring the satisfaction things give me to Christ, who is the personification of everything I hope for. These things are few in number, but wide enough to include all that I dream of having in heaven. What are they? I know so little about the nature of heaven that my answers will be incomplete. In a word, I want to live in a world "wherein dwelleth righteousness," where the very things I want most are what Christ most wants me to have. I want a repleteness of being to exchange for my aging body that grows weaker as my soul grows stronger. I want to fall down at the feet of Christ Himself, to see him as he is in his post-incarnate glory, and to ask for the last time his forgiveness for my sins—that's all. Having these is having everything.

Yet I must confess that one thing still troubles me now—the matter of further improvement in my spirituality. Frankly, I don't see how I could fit into the *Civitate Deo* in my present condition. I surely must have further castigation before I am ready. God is a faithful Father, and so he must yet chastise me, or so I feel about myself.

In such twilight meditation, I have come up with a few ways God may yet use to get me ready for heaven. They are not found in the Bible, but I am exhorted by Paul to "work out my own salvation with fear and trembling." So I consider what might happen, i.e., circumstances that do not contradict any Scripture I am aware of. I share them hoping some of my readers will be comforted or encouraged by them.

First, I consider an existential extension of time—that God may compress, say, ten years of experience for me into a month of clock time. After all, clock time and existential time are never the same. Five minutes on a roller coaster is not the same as five minutes in a dentist's chair. That would add considerable time for me to continue getting ready.

Second is what I call a quantum leap, or genetic jump. There may be something working inside me to effect a great change for the better, though it might not be perceived as such by my limited judgment. This consideration always puts Beethoven in mind, who was an old man and totally deaf before he composed his final quartets. Maybe his deafness, like Bach's crippling arthritis and Milton's blindness, gave him the impetus for a quantum leap into a higher greatness than he had ever known. When I speak of a genetic jump, I draw an analogy from atheistic evolutionists (the evolutionists that I have met have all been atheists, though I am sure there must be some theistic evolutionists). They say that evolutionary changes do not occur gradually, but suddenly. Let's say that everyone had tails three feet long. In movement toward having no tail at all, this tail does not decrease an inch in each generation. Rather, there builds up in the genetic message within the cell the tendency toward shorter tails. This tendency is latent until the time comes when, suddenly, a child is born without any tail at all. Even so, there may be in my psychosomatic makeup some growing tendency toward the person I hope to be, whom I know I must become, before my earthly life is over. Of course, I do not know what it is, or how and when it will surface. After all, I am a stranger to myself. I don't even know how to pray as I ought, just like Paul. All I know is that I need spiritual improvement in my life, and this may be the shape it will take.

Third is what I call concurrent castigation. Given my self-ignorance, it is altogether possible that I am even now experiencing some castigating force that moves me closer than I think. Suddenly—tomorrow perhaps—I may reap the benefit of such a force in my life. The heat and pressure that I have felt so long may crystallize into some gem. How much time passed, we all wonder, between Paul's composing of his final letter in the Canon, II Timothy, and his death? The question comes to me because of one thing he said, which I give you in my own translation, "This is a faithful saying, and worthy of being accepted by everybody, that Christ Jesus came into the world to save sinners, of whom I myself am chief." This self-evaluation was correct for Paul, as it is for us all. He was to die soon after writing it. Maybe concurrent castigation was the means whereby he grew to the stature required by God.

Or it could be perhaps a combination of two or all of the above, or maybe something I haven't yet dreamed of. Mature people (a euphemism for "old") ought to use their God-given minds to find deeper meaning in their often lackluster and quite lonely days. We "chief of sinners" ought to want more time to get ready for heaven, not less.

Let us visit again Pascal's infinite spaces. He wrote in the 17th century as a Christian mathematician. He could not have anticipated the grand discoveries known to us today, many of which have profound implications for theologians. Pascal could never have dreamed of computing the value of *pi* to ten million decimals via sophisticated computers. He did, however, rightly predict *pi* to the millionth decimal to be exactly 5. What of our telescopes that have discovered galaxies 100 million light years away, and atomic scientists who have discovered that atoms do not always obey the laws of Newton? Pascal would certainly have relished turning his skill to the new math of quantum mechanics! What of the strange conclusion urged upon us by our electron microscopes that nature does not reduce to simplicity, but rather maintains a constant degree of complexity, no matter how small the object examined nor how deep the penetration? There is also a spatial matter to consider—that of the distance between the proton and electron of a hydrogen atom, which has a comparative distance of that between our sun and the planet Mars. Surely, the infinite spaces science speaks of are enough to move Pascal and us all into absolute silence and awe as we see into the mysteries we now know of, and then to anticipate those mysteries at such a time in the future as now exists between us and Pascal. What does God want us to think about a universe that is more space than matter? Space that is so full of neutrinos that a million of them pass through me in my small slot of existence during the writing of this one sentence? What, indeed!

I am certain that Pascal had deeper matters in mind than scientific measurements, which is of questionable significance to us who prefer to join Abraham in seeing the dimensions of life as terminating in Eternity. Abraham was born just about 4,000 years ago, and he died without receiving the promise God made to him 75 years before. Recall, the promise was a country of his own and innumerable descendants. Or did he receive it after all? Or did he even die? Jesus has him in his parable of Dives and Lazarus as being seated in heaven watching his progeny proliferate to immeasurable numbers. I am sure, though, during his pilgrimage on earth, Abraham was frightened by one question—WHEN? As he bid this world good-bye, he had only three legitimate descendants—Isaac and the twins, Jacob and Esau. But WHEN? All in good time, Father Abraham, all in God's time.

WHEN involves frightening spaces. We see many examples in the Psalms when teary-eyed poets lament the seeming indifference of God.

"How long, O God, will the wicked prosper? How long will the righteous suffer?" This expresses not only our Adamic impatience, but our selective memory. Each sums up his own microcosmic review using his own measuring stick (always shorter than it ought to be), and comes up with a lopsided view of God's governance of his universe. Also, he fails to see the great advantage God has in such delay. In Eccles. 8:11, we read, "Because sentence against an evil work is not executed speedily, therefore the heart of the sons of men is fully set in them to do evil." Men act wickedly, and God seems indifferent to their act, allowing the righteous sufferers from that wickedness to see the wicked prosper because of that wickedness. Still, Solomon sees that wicked men must have the opportunity to deny God's Providential care of the world. So God delays his response to wickedness to such a time when they can say of whatever adversity comes to them, "God had nothing to do with it." Had they a proximate cause for every act of wickedness rather than a remote one, they would find it virtually impossible to commit evil. If an angel with a huge club on his shoulder heeled a foul-mouthed blasphemer and whacked him over the head every time he took God's name in vain, it would not be long until his vocabulary would improve dramatically—but entirely for the wrong reason. For virtue to exist, the possibility of evil must be present. Let us put WHEN away. Let us never imagine the Lord of time will wear a lab smock and confine himself to the strict law of universal causation, even to the point of limiting himself to using only the proximate cause. Nothing could be worse for building a life of faith. Our Eternal Lover sometimes improves our patience and further degenerates the wicked by his omniscient delays.

By far, the greatest infinite spaces are summarized by the questions of HOW and WHY. This is what the book of Job is all about. Job told God repeatedly that he would be satisfied if God would tell him why he suffered such unspeakable adversity at the hand of a Loving Heavenly Father, and he was the most righteous man in the entire world. Just think of it—loss of ten children, all livestock and fields of grain, and then inflicted with smallpox in one single diurnal day! But does God answer? He does not. Given the limitations of Job, God could not reduce his answer to Job's understanding, and God also knew the answer would not satisfy him.

Job could not even understand the answer if God were to give it. What's more, Job had no way of knowing about the existence of an antecedent question, the answer to which he could understand and be satisfied as to why this horrendous calamity came upon him. God speaks, however. First, he comes at Job with a long list of questions mostly about nature, not one of which Job could answer. It was exactly then when God's appearance and the unanswered questions revealed to Job the antecedent question and its answer, "God, do you love me?" God says so by interrupting his governance of the great universe and paying Job a personal visit, just as God did two thousand years later when Emmanuel became our answer at Skull Place. "Does God love me?" cries out Adam within, to which the answer comes with a voice that human desperation will never let die:

> God so loved the world that he gave his son, his only
> begotten, that whosoever has faith in him will not perish
> but have life from now on. (John 3:16)

So Job begins to see the cause of his problem, which is not his calamity at all, but his own ignorance and overestimation of his natural talents. I am sure this sounds quite familiar to us all. Here is a lesson all men should learn before their pride sends them to hell. It is this: Man is too intelligent to keep from asking questions he is too stupid to understand.

Yet the greatest question facing us all is HOW. How is it that God will grant us entrance into his eternal kingdom when our progress toward the virtues apparent in our Lord Jesus Christ seem to crawl at a slower rate than the speed at which our lives gallop toward their natural end? At times, we could rightly feel that our knowledge of the excellence that is in Christ Jesus increased at a geometric ratio, while our conquest of sin increases only arithmetically. I have long since given up the notion of progress in history. There is no such thing. What we see is a progressive proliferation of technology disguised in liberal minds as "progress." We could speak of progress, of course, if we meant our present standard of living compared to that of our grandparents. Or might I not see personal progress by comparing the beginning of my Christian life to my life today?

But that's not allowed—the Christian Way has no rearview mirror. We have the Absolute Measure up there ahead of us, raised up high so all can see, which all men do see, though few perceive. It is He, the *Logos*, our Hypostasis, the Son of Man, God-with-us. Measure yourself by him and put away this nonsense about "progress in history."

In this regard, we must not overlook Paul's evaluation of himself. It has been rightly said that, at the beginning of his ministry, he called himself "the last of the apostles," in the middle of his ministry "the least of all saints," then in the last letter he wrote "the chief of sinners." Let me share with you again my translation of that quotation:

> This is a faithful saying and worthy of being accepted by everybody, that Christ Jesus came into the world to save sinners, of whom I myself am chief.

How comfortable are you admitting you are in that class of sinners known as "chief "? I am not at all comfortable, and the harder I try to escape, the more entrenched I become. Why? Because my knowledge of Christ increases at a greater rate than my conquest of sin. In fact, I have given myself a new name, which I often use in prayer. It is "Protamarty," which combines the two Greek words for "first" and "sinner." I am quite comfortable with this name, though I never use it in public, or as a *carte blanche* for sin. Never this. My answer for the abundant life is the same as Job's. I see that God loves me, though I cannot see HOW he would save me when I can discern no way to get ready in time. He loves me! More than this I cannot know, and need not know.

I must cling to this love, for there comes a time when I make my final trip to *Har Megiddo*, which translated means "Mount of Rendezvous." This final trip is what Kierkegaard meant when he said, "There comes a midnight hour when we all must unmask." The time is coming for the final battle when my own body and even the crippled logic of my foggy brain will join the confederation of the world and the Devil. I see the sinewy biceps of pride, HOW and WHY, draw the bowstring back to shoot its final quiver-full of fiery darts, and my only shield is that of the faith whereby I will quench those darts. HOW and WHY will mean nothing to me then, when I have the WHO drawing me onward and upward beyond the din of battle into eternal light.

I must ever reject the temptation to finish the name of God with any subject complement other than God Himself. You will recall that twice Jesus used the sacred name, I AM, once before his doubting Pharisees, for which they tried to stone him, and once before the soldiers in Gethsemane, when they tumbled backward, overawed by the voice that once said, "Be light!"—and there was light. Notice the name, I AM, which is at once both the most inconclusive and all-inclusive thing that could be said. It is also a sentence fragment, leaving the need to finish his name. Yet there are voices abroad, braying like asses that cannot find their stalls. They want you to finish God's name with "castles in Spain," or "the best automobile," or the name of some planet in some other solar system, say, in the newly discovered Galaxy of Linda, 100 million light years away, which God has chosen for you to rule. Do not listen to these voices broadcasting daily on the television and, I do fear, in many of our pulpits. Remember that we are after a person, The Person, as the author of the Hebrew Epistle has it, "the express image of the personification of all we hope for."

The closer we draw to the Person, the greater becomes our ignorance of how he does what he does. I am now close enough to smell the cedar of his garments, but no nearer as to how he will effect Romans 8:28, the greatest historiographical statement in the whole of Scripture. I can see the prismatic halo of its promise as it clusters around every object I behold, but I am made the more aware of the dying embers of this foul world of ours. I can never erase from my memory the smoking twin towers of the World Trade Center—never. I taste the honey under his tongue, but the sweet fruits of anticipation yet elude me. I hear his sandal scrape on a rocky spot as we walk along, but I cannot see the path ahead—even one day or one step. He is as the Shulamite sings in the Song of Songs, "a sachet of myrrh that lieth all night between my breasts." Yet having him so near, and my dying machine going so fast in the opposite direction toward the final battlefield, frightens me. I recall many of the some 50,000 promises in the Bible, and yet I have memories of failed living, my fascination with the world and its allurement, the wasted time and effort, the dishonesty of excuses, the mindless ingratitude, the pride of office, the uncharitable response, the neglect of spiritual development, the acts of rebellion and all else that join to widen the gap between Christ and me. I tell him I am a spiritual ragamuffin, that I mourn because I am, that I hunger and thirst after doing the right thing—even about the wrong things still in my life—and he tells me it will be all right. He loves me, you see, and this love so moves me that HOW no longer matters, and I even welcome the final battle.

CHAPTER II:
A DEEPER LOOK AT FAITH

I would like to pause a moment and ask my readers to join me in taking a deeper look into Scripture, one that biblical scholars are usually reluctant to take with laymen. Most often, Bible instruction goes no further than to travel in the horizontal plane, comparing verses of Scripture with other verses. This approach is what we call *exposition*. Many make this approach all their lives, some by preference and some because there is no other choice. Whatever their motives, they usually end up with a sound understanding of the Christian Way. The beginning student of God's Word will also soon discover that some passages are more important than others. I do not mean they are more inspired, for there is no degree possible as regards inspiration. Some passages are more important because they are wider in their scope (John 3), more universal in their appeal (Ps. 23), or deal with matters that are often repeated by other canonical writers, by which we infer their greater importance. It may be, on the other hand, some extremely important matters are rare in Scripture. For example, only two New Testament chapters treat the pre-incarnate life of Christ, John 1 and Phil. 2. It stands to reason that we must dig more deeply into these Scriptures than satisfying ourselves with the horizontal approach. In some cases this approach is not even possible. Before us is a verse, the only one in the entire Bible, that gives us a definition of faith—Heb. 11:1. It is also controversial as it stands translated from Greek to English.

> Faith is the substance of things hoped for, the evidence of
> things not seen. (KJV)

This brings us to that deeper scholarly approach called *exegesis*. This always means a definitive study—"cutting apart" as its word parts mean—every sentence, even each word, tracing it if necessary back to the Hebrew language. I invite you now to join me as I attempt to cross the linguistic barrier with those of you who do not know Greek. Will you join me just this one time? If you know Greek, of course, the journey will be quite familiar, so bear with me as I slow my pacing a bit. You may see something hitherto overlooked. If classical literature and music have such surprises for you as you repeatedly expose yourself to their greatness, how much more so Scripture, the greatest classic of them all? None other than God is its author, and he speaks miraculously and perfectly through the imperfections of men directly to us. You who do not know Greek may learn much indeed from our uncommon effort. If this does not prove so, at least you will appreciate the dedication of scholars, and the painstaking effort of exegesis as you gain insight into how difficult it is, as Pilate once implied to Jesus, to arrive at the truth.

As we look at Heb. 11, before long we see three things of critical importance to its meaning. First, we do not see a conceptual definition, but a dynamic one. We also see the author uses a compound form, one item with two items relating to the noun. Faith is substance and evidence. In lexicography, we would call this an impossibility, for the two objects would have to relate to a common antecedent if a conceptual definition is to take place. Second, those who are familiar with Greek discover two words that have found dignified places in the English language—*hupostasis* and *pragma*. In English, they become "hypostasis" and "pragmatic" or "pragmatism." Students of Greek are often delighted when they see so many of our English words expressed in Greek. For example, in Heb. 11:1-3, I have located no fewer than seven words that are direct ancestors of modern English words. Scholars, especially etymologists and lexicographers who should know better, erroneously tell us that more words come into English from Latin than from any other language. This is not exactly true. If you count all those Latin words that the Romans borrowed from the Greeks and subtract them from all Latin words that have come into English, you would plainly see that Greek, not Latin, has made the greatest contribution to English. The third thing we see is the very strange word order, quite elliptical in construction. The only verb is "is" itself, followed by two participles, "being hoped for" and "being seen." English words will have to be added to piece out the sentence.

Before we proceed further in this exegesis, we should pause and consider at least one problem facing translators, that being how liberal or conservative should one be? Some translators are so conservative that their translation appears awkward, hence, difficult to read. At the other end of the spectrum is the liberal who is so free and loose with his material that he turns out a paraphrase, not a true translation, though his work will appear in a most readable form. It has been said of the KJV that it best strikes a balance between truth and beauty of all translations that have ever appeared in English. I have read them all, and am in complete agreement with this view. To determine this for yourself, just read several versions of the text under discussion. While you are at it, trying reading several translations of Psalm 23. None comes even near the beauty of the KJV's rendition. Truly, it is a literary masterpiece. It strikes the closest balance between truth and beauty that has ever been achieved by any other translation into our language. However, there are errors in this work— some excusable, some tolerable, and a few that ought to be changed. Indeed, three new editions have corrected most of these errors. We must be careful not to count as errors the addition of words not found in the Greek text; usually, they are italicized. But others are not, such as two instances in this verse of the word "things." You see, the participles are spelled to express plurality and possession as well. So, we have "things of which we have hope" and "not things being seen."

Examine several translations of Heb. 11:1. You will note that rarely do all translators choose the same English equivalents for Greek words. I know of two translations of Psalm 23 that have only two nouns in common. Abstract nouns, especially, admit greater latitude in meaning than concrete nouns and other parts of speech. The KJV translation of the verse before us adds two words not found in the Greek, two instances of the word "things," as we have just noted. This is correct, but not so the translation of *hupostasis,* for which they choose "substance"—far too broad a meaning for this Greek word. Modern dictionaries define it transliterated into English as "hypostasis" or "essential nature," distinguishing it from attributes. Let me illustrate: Jesus says to the Samaritan woman at the well, "God is a spirit." Here is what we call a hypostatic statement, unlike other biblical descriptions of God, viz., "God is good" or "God is love," which are attributes of this "essential nature." The Greek word for hypostasis is comprised of two common Greek root words, meaning "stand" plus "under." "Foundation" is what is meant, whether in the concrete sense as a real foundation of a building, or in the abstract sense as we say of Christ, that he is the foundation of the Church. You will agree that this meaning is far afield of the word chosen by the KJV translators, "substance." Now we see the meaning emerging in the first line of my tentative translation:

> Faith is the essential nature of the things we are hoping
> for.

Note that it is not the things themselves, but their nature. We find the author of Hebrews conceding that he is not giving us a conceptual definition at all, but a dynamic one. His definition begs the antecedent question: What is the essential nature of what we are hoping for?

Remember that God speaks to us through silences from "infinite spaces" in sound. Let me ask you to answer this question for yourselves. I have a hunch you will arrive at the same answer this silence urges me to choose.

I remember a line from one of C. S. Lewis' books that goes something like this. God doesn't answer our most urgent questions, because in the sight of his glorious countenance, the questions disappear.

Now we turn to our second line, which completes the couplet form we often see in Hebrew poetry, especially in Proverbs. The second line is parallel in form to the first and is intricately related in thought to it. Any student of philosophy (and several other disciplines, for that matter) knows that *pragma* refers to pragmatic, or pragmatism. The word is plural by implication, and refers to some sort of activity, such as matters, affairs, pursuits—even things. It also names a branch of philosophy, pragmatism, which judges the value of a thing by the value of what it accomplishes. Another word, the one translated "proof," is an obscure, seldom-used word in the New Testament. It also means "conviction" and "evidence." Now we bring the two lines together:

> Faith involves the essential nature of what we are hoping
> for, the origin of matters not being seen.

It is evident from this working definition that we must never get our foundation confused with our superstructure, which is the core error of that heresy, "prosperity theology," raging like a wildfire across our nation. In truth, it interprets the trappings of wealth and luxury as proof of God's care of us, hypnotizing us with "the things hoped for" and ignoring "the essential nature of things." Here comes into play gratification from things of this world, like rocking chairs and fishing poles. St. Paul speaks emphatically against such heresies by raising our vision, as God raised Abraham's vision with the spiritual nature of future events. I remind the reader that I include in my translation something the KJV and other translations ignore.

> Things that eye has not seen, ear has not heard, neither
> have entered into the heart of man, things God has
> prepared for them who are loving him.

Please note that Paul uses the word "things" twice. Here Paul speaks of two categories of things—sensuous and spiritual—the very distinction found in Heb. 11:1. God is a spirit, man is a spirit, and so are heaven and eternal life spiritual matters. Though we indentured slaves of this carnal world must often use concrete examples to share the Good News, we must never reify the spiritual as mundane. Any future prepared for us by God that can be described in human terms is too little to satisfy my needs that themselves defy human solution. So I turn to the ineffable God, who calls himself I AM, and his son who echoes this I AM on a Roman cross.

Let us look further at the Greek word *hupostasis* as it appears elsewhere in the New Testament. Actually, it appears five times. Three times it has the remote translation of "confidence," as we see in II Cor. 9:4, 11:17, and Heb. 3:14. The English equivalent seems remote when elsewhere it becomes "essential nature," a synonym for *Logos,* the term coming from Plato and used by St. John in the Prologue to his Gospel. In his concept of ideas, Plato called the ideal man *Logos.* But how did "confidence" become the meaning for this word? There were no lexicographers in those days, so we will probably never know, but we can hazard a guess. I opine that "confidence" has something to do with buildings. In those days, stone was the preferred medium. Only kings like David could afford dwellings of cedar wood, so stone was used for most buildings. These had walls close enough to each other so that a single tree trunk could serve for ceiling rafters. In fact, many buildings had no roofs at all. So these ancients were not as concerned about ceilings falling as they were about foundations sinking and, subsequently, walls falling. Of paramount concern was the foundation, the *hupostasis.* This word is a blend of two common Greek words meaning "under" plus "stand," as we have already noted. It reminds us of the anecdote Jesus used at the end of his Sermon on the Mount. It is easy, then, to see a transfer of meaning, making *hupostasis* an everyday Greek word. These people believed the walls and floors would not collapse, so they had "confidence" the building would maintain its integrity because the walls and foundation were sound.

However, there are two other translations of *hupostasis* to be reckoned with. In Heb. 1:3, we see that it means "person." We read that Christ is "the brightness of his [God's] glory and the express image (*charaktir*) of his person (*hupostasis*). Here is a definition of God's essential nature. Of course, in our text it is translated in the KJV as "substance," which is a very long way from "person." It should be quite clear to my readers that the translation is in error.

One word more about the definition of faith found in Heb. 11:1. As previously noted, the KJV has "things" appearing twice, as implied by the two participles involved. Why not have "being hoped for" and "being seen" apply to the person of Jesus Christ instead of to "things," just exactly as it is used in Heb. 1:3? With this one final change, return with me to the translation of faith. I trust it will not alarm you that faith is the quest, not for rocking chairs or monarchies of planets elsewhere in the Milky Way, but for Christ, our *Logos*, our hypostasis, who died on the cross that we might live forever. Surely, it is better to have him waiting for us at the end of our lifelong stretch of faith than mere things. As we have seen, the author of Hebrews uses *hupostasis* as meaning Person of God, and if so, it can also mean Personification. Here is a faithful translation of Heb. 11:1.

A final word about hypostasis. It has yet one more meaning, which we must not let pass without comment. It is the term used in systematic theology, as distinguished from biblical theology. The former speaks about the study of God based on a logical outline. We must not minimize the accomplishments of such an approach to biblical subjects, for some of the greatest theologians have used the systematic approach. However, there is always the possibility of error when the predominant direction is not toward a biblical sequencing of subjects. Some systematic theologians ask non-biblical questions and end up with anti-biblical answers. Examples include modern fads such as neo-orthodoxy, "God is dead" theology, and now the so-called "prosperity theology." Then there are the post-moderns who do not believe in anything but a "new morality." What is next, we often wonder. Men have been trying to bury the resurrected Christ for nearly two thousand years, and they are still trying after two millennia.

Regarding the theological use of hypostasis, systematic theologians have been considering the non-biblical notion of Christ having two natures—a study, sadly enough, they call hypostasis. Now where did they get that notion? Where in the Bible can it be found? Christ's nature is the same as ours. This is not a boost to the human ego, but an accusation, for we are sorely pressed to see his likeness in ourselves. We are gods, as he is God. Similar to this non-biblical distinction are the secular categories of "human" and "animal." This distinction is necessary for the biologist, who more likely than not wants to keep us reminded that "We are Apes," as goes the title of a lecture given at my university by Dr. Watson, one of the two formulators of the DNA model. Scripture is not concerned with such a distinction, though we enjoy knowing that an early 20th-century scientist said that there is more difference between a man and an ape than between an ape and an amoeba. Evolution opens the door to another erroneous category, which I speak of as "the devil option." Men rationalize their cruel behavior toward others as a product of the vestigial remains of the creatures our ancestors were in the previous geological age, if not early in this age, swinging through the trees with the aid of prehensile tails. As spirits, humans cannot go to an animal grave. They are made in the image of God and, as gods, they cannot return to the dust. However, they can imitate animal behavior and become devils, unless they begin and continue in the process of regeneration.

So the crown of Divine Royalty rests upon our heads, and it is heavier than the one that crowns the British monarch. You say I surely must be wrong in this. You draw my attention to church history where so many pages are sprinkled with the blood of martyrs; blood shed not by the rulers of the world who take council together against the Lord and his Christ, but by the very church itself. The bloodbath starts openly with the crucifixion of Christ—the priests, politicians and professors of his day leading the pack. Then hypocrisy and willful ignorance soil Christ's reputation during the slow convolutions of the ages. No, we might think, we cannot be gods.

If we are not gods, why do we daily join Jesus in calling God our Father who is in heaven? Yes, there is a church history, but it holds only a faint adumbration of the transparent gold of the New Jerusalem. Where is the place and the names of those giants on whose shoulders Newton stood? Rarely, but surely, we see glimpses of the cloud of witnesses no man can number, though the names of 99.9% of them never made it into print. History is an indictment of the churches of this world, but history is also a silent friend of the unheralded saints who are merely yeast, as Jesus says, that moves the world along. It is evident that sins not committed never get into print. Adamic nature would rather hear bad things about people, and these make headlines. One conservative friend of mine said a political history must necessarily be a history of liberal politics. Whoever makes headlines for holding prodigal spending from the national treasury in check? It's the spending programs that loom large in print. So it is with the saints in history. They hold society together, their sentiment prevented wars from happening. So God's true church goes silently alone, making no headlines—indeed, often having no news to offer at all. A communist leader once boasted all he needed to conquer a democratic nation was to have only six percent of its citizens strategically placed. If six percent could do it for communism, what can the true Ruler of this age, the Holy Ghost, do among those on the Christian Way?

Do we still feel unworthy? Indeed, and so we should! But what effect does this royalty have on us? Recall that I spoke of the Greek hero who did not die but got up from his knees and changed his downfall into a catalytic modification of his life. This is what we Christians call "growth in grace." It was *hubris*, pride, arrogance against God that flung Satan from the ramparts of heaven to the depths of hell. We must accept the heavy crown and we must feel its weight in the streets and alleys, as well as in the private chambers of our homes. Just as the clerical collar often served to keep English clergymen from yielding to temptation, so does the crown of royal divinity help us turn our downfalls into victories.

There is yet another blessing. We have often heard that if you have an employee whom you treat as though you approved of who he was, he is likely to become lower than he is in your and his own expectations. However, if you treat him as though he were what you hoped he would someday become, you have acted as a catalyst on his potential. In kind, Almighty God sent his own son to raise us to the privileged heights of divinity as royal sons. He treats us royally, and we find our hearts strangely warmed, and the power of a new affection raises us upward. As we are drawn upward by God's view of our potential, we divinities go into the throne room where he sits with his son beside him. We may stay as long as we wish. It is no wonder we are reluctant to wear the crown—but wear it we shall, by His grace.

CHAPTER III:
RED AND JEAN

The Bible begins where no other book can begin—at the beginning; it ends where no other book could possibly end—at the end of this spatial-temporal continuum. The Bible is more than the world's first history. Written by the Hebrew people (who invented history), it is more than their literary and cultural history. Because they were a sanctified race, the Bible has to be a history of God using his communicable attributes. Inspired by God, the Lord of Canon and the Bible's editor, holy men of old wrote his message to us. Indeed, we are amazed at the miracle before us. God used a primitive language that had not yet even developed a way to separate consonants from vowels, proper nouns from common ones, or had not even achieved a precise way of giving tense to its verbs—this language smudged with human fingerprints—to tell us his message about his creation of all things. Yet we must disabuse ourselves of pride's crippling notion that to be primeval means to be primitive. The language may be primitive, but not the minds of men who used the language. We are looking at a document written by some unknown hand over three thousand years ago. The hand had no paper, not even a pen, only a twig with a strip of leather tied to it that inked syllabics upon animal skins. God is speaking to us, and we must listen humbly, inquiringly and awestruck, lest the Book, like the gates of Paradise, close against our understanding as they did behind Red and Jean, the parents of the human race.

The first thing we hear is not some theological proof for the existence of God, but the voice of God Himself. We need no proofs; we are the people of faith. We have come to terms with the challenging fact that life overflows logic. Like Red and Jean, we recognize the voice immediately.

It soon becomes evident to us that we have two stories of creation. As we examine the contents of the first few chapters of Genesis, we find these are not, as some superficial reading might suggest, two accounts of the same creation, but accounts of two different creations. Chapter one is the preamble of the entire library of books, 66 in all. It is rightly called the Creation Hymn because it celebrates in stanza form what God has done. It is he who has made us and not we ourselves. We are ultimately responsible to him for how we respond to his creation. God does, and the geologists agree, separate his creation into six periods of undesignated duration. How long each day lasts is not given, but he labors perhaps for billions of our years, this Divine Lover of ours. What then is it that this Omnipotent Lover does? He rests! Not because he is tired, but as an example for us. He gives us on the first page of his Book the greatest cultural gift imaginable, one day's rest in seven. God knows what man needs and he proves it by this gift, which comes from no other culture on earth, and is so perfectly adaptable to man that it has extended without resistance throughout the entire world. It would be four millennia later that he would split the heavens, come down himself and give us an additional day. So dearly does he love us and so keenly does he desire us to worship him that he sees to it we will have time to do so.

Therefore, the Creation Hymn is the preamble for the entire Bible. What then is the function of the chapters that immediately follow it? They deal with the creation of the Holy Family, the special creation starting with one man and one woman, God's own family, through whom he would reveal his will to the rest of mankind. The events beginning with Gen. 2 I will call the Garden Narrative. But what about the other people in the world at this time? We are not told about them—this is a matter for others to discover. When we come across such questions, we must never lose sight of the divine inspiration of Scripture. Since God is Omniscient, what is not included in Scripture is left out for a reason, and never because the author was ignorant of it or forgot to include it. We conclude then that where other antediluvian people came from is of no importance to the Garden Narrative. There is, of course, room for us to include them in the Creation Hymn and even some versions of evolution, and plenty of room for galaxies whose light, seen by the Hubbell telescope, started for earth around 14 billion years ago.

TWO PRELIMINARY CONSIDERATIONS

Before attempting an analysis of Gen.1-3, we must answer two perennial questions. First, is the Creation Hymn a myth? A mature response to this question would be to determine first what one means by the word "myth." I define it as "a popular explanation of a psychological, social or natural phenomenon." The buzzword here, of course, is "popular," by which we mean non-scientific. When you say, "The rose is red," or "The sun rose at 0600," you use myth, for neither of these statements is scientifically accurate, though everyone understands exactly what you mean. If you say, "The stoplight just turned green," you are again being mythical, for the stoplight, being inanimate, cannot do anything at all, and it is every color but green, the color it rejects. So in a strict sense, we use myth all the time. We cannot help but use it. The only exception would be when we are required to speak scientifically about a subject.

Even the scientist rarely uses scientific language. When his wife orders him to take the garbage can to the curb in three feet of snow, and during a chill factor of -30 degrees F, she does not use scientific language, nor does he when he argues for a more convenient time or a more available member of the family to perform the task. In truth, for most communication, the scientist prefers the more economical, colorful and effortless use of language—the mythopoeic use—and not the scientific.

It seems unreasonable, then, for scientists to expect the author of the Creation Hymn, who produced this document well over 3,000 years ago, to be "scientifically accurate." After all, they complain, if Scripture is divinely inspired, God should make sure the author wrote free of error. I point out that Moses, or whoever wrote the Creation Hymn, did not intend to tell us how God created the universe, or how long it took him to do so. He invites us to join him in breathless adoration as we examine divinely inspired words that tell us why we should be in perpetual praise of our Maker.

What exactly is the scientific error they find in the Creation Hymn? Of course, the Hymn is not in agreement with the theories of some scientists. The Big Bang Theory may well fit in quite handily, but the person who holds to the spontaneous generation of life cannot agree with fiat creation as is emphatically stated in the Hymn. The atheist balks at the very first verse of Genesis, but as regards scientific fact—not theory, but fact—the Creation Hymn is scientifically accurate.

But was the universe made in six 24-hour days? Hebrew, like every other language, uses the word for day—*yom*—to mean periods of time, depending on the context for the duration intended. When Jesus said, "Abraham saw my day and rejoiced," he meant a much longer period of time than a diurnal day, just as Eleanor Roosevelt did when she titled her over 12 years of experiences in the White House as *My Day*. It is nonsense for scientists to interpret the word "day" in a strictly literal sense. This misunderstanding is partly based on the use of Bishop Usher's dating of 4,004 BC for the events in the Creation Hymn. Had he used this date only for the Garden Narrative, he would have been in perfect agreement with biblical scholars. They estimate that Red and Jean were created on the eighth day of creation, 4005-4006 BC. This is why a male Hebrew child is circumcised on the eighth day of his life. St. Paul, as you will recall, told us that this is what happened to him.

Some who fail to discern a different function for the Garden Narrative from that of the Creation Hymn see a conflict in Gen. 2:19, which seems to say (contrary to Gen. 1) that Red and Jean were created before the animals. Such doubters should consider that, had there been such a flagrant contradiction in the Hebrew text as they suppose, scholars would long since have corrected the matter. The only error here is in the minds of the doubters themselves—they do not know the Hebrew language. You see, Hebrew verbs do not express tense in the same way we do in modern languages. The verse in question refers back in time to the creation of the animals. Plainly, there is no disagreement here at all. We are correct in reading the text using the perfect tense: "And the Lord God *had formed* every beast of the field . . . ."

Is the Creation Hymn a myth? Well, if one insists that only two choices are available—myth and science—the answer would be quite obvious. However, calling the Creation Hymn myth would start us thinking about fiction, for most myth is indeed fictional, if not downright fantastic, literature. This is what we find in most of the world's religions. I have read all the cosmogonies and theories of creation found in their holy books, and they are beyond doubt non-scientific. Here is where the Creation Hymn rises high above them all. I repeat, not one scientific fact is in contradiction to what it boldly proclaims, and yet it is not meant to be a book about science at all. It fully intends to capture the minds and souls of more than scientists, and to do this, it must on occasion make a mythopoeic use of language. To say the Creation Hymn must be either scientific or mythic is like saying we must decide which is right and wrong between two descriptions of God's place of worship, either Ezekiel's measurement of the temple or Ps. 84, "How amiable are thy tabernacles, O Lord of Hosts." The Creation Hymn is neither science nor myth. It belongs not at the end of a syllogism, but in the human heart.

Turning now to the Garden Narrative, we are confronted with the second preliminary question—is the account of one day in the life of Red and Jean allegory or fact? The argument for allegory goes something like this. Here we have a seemingly casual and unconscionably brief account of such a cataclysmic event. Too much is compressed into too small a space. So much has been left out. Each event gives rise to haunting questions that go without answers. Indeed, many books have pondered at length these few events. How could all the violence in man's history be traced back to this cookie-jar peccadillo, which didn't seem as bad as the time St. Augustine and boyhood friends had an apple fight with fruit stolen from a neighbor's orchard? At least our Primogenitor did not waste the fruit, but ate it. Anyone pondering Gen. 2-3 cannot help but come away with more questions than answers, and in the resulting frustration, suppose some deeper meaning is intended.

Yet what is an allegory? One might think of it as a symbolic story, like John Bunyan's *Pilgrim's Progress* or Dante's *Divine Comedy*. There is one in the Bible, the Song of Songs, in which the natural love between a man and a woman is likened to the love between God and the one who worships him. The allegory is a popular genre in modern fiction, especially in the short story. It requires the reader to shift his imagination into high gear and to help the author create the meaning of the narrative.

Is the Garden Narrative an allegory? If it is so, it is indeed a poor one. In order for an allegory to do its work of illuminating its disguised subject, it must be far enough away from it so that contrast can enrich the insight it gives, and also so confusion from overlapping and mixing of the two sets of ideas will not confuse the message. This is the reason I cannot accept the Song of Songs as an allegory about the love between Christ and the Virgin Mary, as some medieval scholars suppose. The subjects are too close to do the work intended. Those who consider the Garden Narrative as allegory always settle on likening it to the coming-of-age theme, or as some have called it, the rite of passage. They apply it to the individual person passing into adulthood, or to the entire history of the human race struggling toward maturity, or even to both. It is my opinion that these interpretations are too close to the Narrative. Also, I have another problem. There is nothing in the Narrative to urge me to believe the author used this fictional device. There is no doubt that the reader can see similarities between this day in the life of Red and Jean and a youth reaching the age of accountability. Like them, we also are tempted to blame others for our mistakes. Perhaps we all at one time or another have sought companions to enrich the pleasure of sin. In retrospect, can't we all recall times we disobeyed just for the thrill of opposing an authority figure—our parents, for example?

The power of the Garden Narrative to capture the consciences of us all does not mean that this day in the life of Red and Jean is a full-blown allegory. I find no challenge to a literal interpretation of this narrative. I find no difficulty in believing Satan spoke through a snake's mouth or that our primal parents really ate a *de facto* fruit. In fact, this cookie-jar transgression gains even more significance from its trivial nature and the effortless bravado that attends their feasting upon it.

I regard the Narrative as an example of what I call "didactic history." Of course, it may well be argued that history is always didactic, but I refer to a matter of degree—events that really happened, but are so compressed that they leave out details we would naturally expect to find in historical accounts in order to give maximum emphasis to the little that remains. It is true that history does not include all the detail available. If it did, it would no longer be true history, but rather a diary or chronicle, such as the writings of a first-century Jew named Josephus, who gave us the only eyewitness account of the fall of Jerusalem to the Romans forty years after the crucifixion of Christ. As valuable as it is, his writing is not really good history because he does not organize his material in a thematic way and limit his choice of detail. Ideally, what we would like to have is a visit with the past, such as we would experience when reading biographies or autobiographies. That is, indeed, the purpose of history. The word itself is actually a Greek word meaning "to visit." We experience such satisfying visits when we read the Joseph Narrative (Gen. 37-50), or the book of Ruth. These historical biographies are so perfectly written that they teach us and satisfy us aesthetically at the same time, as short stories do.

However, what if you were forced, as Moses was, to reduce an extremely important event to one page? How could you summarize the life of Abraham Lincoln in, say, 300 words? So very much would have to be excluded. No time to describe his imposing physical figure. No time for any of the anecdotes for which he was famous. No time for that remarkable letter he wrote Dennis Hanks, not even for the Gettysburg Address—not in 300 words!

So we have the creation of the universe and an explanation of why God made life such a bittersweet experience. As Milton puts it, Moses writes "to justify the ways of God to men." All this in three short chapters? One of the objectives of writers is to create unique, believable characters. Three especially come to my mind, and hardly a day passes but I meet someone who reminds me of one of them. I speak of Chaucer's Wife of Bath, Browning's duke in "My Last Duchess," and Eliot's Prufrock as he strolls along the beach talking to himself. Yet we will never meet anyone like Red and Jean. Moses' task was to shrink his detail to absolute minimum. He knew how to create satisfying characters. This literary genius wrote the Joseph Narrative, which we almost forgot as we contemplate the starved detail in the Garden Narrative. Of course, we will never meet the two-dimensional characters, Red and Jean. The message is that we are not supposed to because we are they.

NEW NAMES FOR OUR PARENTS

Writers sometimes use the technique of renaming a person to get a fresh, new look at him. This is a significant motif in the Bible, as even a casual reader knows. Abraham and Sarah were given new names by God Himself, and Jacob's name was changed from the less-than-flattering "Supplanter" to "Prince of God," or Israel. Jacob was displeased with the name the dying Rachael gave her second child, "Son of My Birth Pangs," or "Benoni," so he changed it to "Son of My Right Hand," or "Benjamin." Giving someone a new name suggested to the Apostle John an appropriate way to express a new life. In the Apocalypse, he tells us that we all will have new names when we arrive in our eternal home. We see special significance in this promise to the Negro slave who wrote the spiritual, "I told Jesus it would be all right if he changed my name."

When we come to translating the Bible into modern languages, scholars are always confronted with the sometimes-perplexing option of either translating a word as a common noun or transliterating it as a proper name. The choice is further exacerbated by the fact that biblical languages never developed a way of expressing proper nouns. Indeed, they did not even come to the use of upper-case and lower-case letters, and the convenient use of cursive writing, i.e., writing words without lifting the pen from the page between letters. These convenient features in writing did not arrive until several hundred years after the Holy Canon was complete. We are amazed as we look at the earliest manuscripts of the New Testament, those written early in the fourth century AD, and discover not only the exclusive use of printed capital letters, but also the absence of spaces between words.

We must not get too deeply into the fascinating study of the history of orthography, but we do need a little insight into this significant problem confronting translators. Did you ever wonder why the Old Testament did not speak more often about the Messiah? We notice, in fact, that Christ (the Greek name for "Messiah"), is called by his prophetic title only twice in the English Old Testament, in Dan. 9:25-26. However, in the Hebrew text, the Messiah is named several times! Look at just one example from Ps. 2 in which I transliterate as a proper noun the word meaning "anointed":

> The kings of the earth set themselves, and the rulers take counsel together, against the Lord, and against his Messiah, saying, Let us break their bands asunder, and cast away their cords from us.

I assure you that the word in question is exactly the same in both Daniel and Ps. 2. Why, then, would the translators make this change? Quite possibly because they did not want to appear arbitrary and give needless offence to the Jews, who do not accept Jesus as their Messiah. In this, the translators erred because the Jews themselves regard this passage as definitely Messianic. But if we go through the Old Testament and transliterate the Hebrew word for "anointed" as a proper noun, instead of translating it as a common noun, we will indeed find the Messiah's visibility more in keeping with that degree of visibility befitting his Advent into the world.

Not only would I like for us to take a fresh look at Adam and Eve by calling them Red and Jean, but we thereby occasion a fresh look at our Beloved Lord Jesus Christ. Let me show you how. Maybe you have pondered, as I have, about the strange new name or nickname Christ gave himself—Son of Man. Searching into the subject, I was amazed to discover 11 words for "man" in the Hebrew Old Testament. Which of them did Jesus use when he spoke to his Hebrew audiences? Recall that the Jews did not speak Greek, the only language in which his words are preserved for us, but rather Aramaic, a language quite similar to Hebrew. So when we read our Greek text, we see *Hwios Anthropou,* Son of Man in English. The Hebrew expression, Son of Man, occurs in only two Old Testament writers, Daniel and Ezekiel. They also use the same word as Moses to designate the progenitor of the Holy Family, each referring to him as Ben-Adam. So Jesus, speaking in Aramaic, calls himself often by his nickname, Ben-Adam. Adam also means "ruddy" or "red," the same name as a nickname for Jacob's twin brother, only we spell the names using different vowels. Edom and Adam looked alike in ancient Hebrew.

Indeed, in the language of the day, Jesus called himself Son of Red, identifying himself with Red, the father of the Sanctified Family. Paul says Adam was a "figure of him who was to come," or a prototype of Christ. In this case, the type is an antitype, for Christ, though like Adam in one respect, is overwhelmingly his opposite. The argument of Paul is in Rom. 5. By calling himself Son of Red, Jesus is proclaiming that he comes from Eternity to give humanity a second chance. In my youth, I often heard ministers sternly warn sinners that there is no second-chance religion. More correctly put, they really meant no third-chance religion after death at the Judgment Seat of Christ. Look at the special insight we get from presenting the good witness of Jesus before Caiaphas, using the original Aramaic for his nickname:

> Thou hast said. Nevertheless, I say to you, hereafter shall you shall see the Son of Red [Ben-Adam] sitting on the right hand of power, and coming in the clouds of heaven.

It is little wonder that the high priest rent his robes and called for Christ's crucifixion. Nothing could be worse, you see, than that Jesus the carpenter from Nazareth should in the same breath identify himself with the arch sinner, Red himself, and a seat beside Almighty God amidst the glorious clouds of the eternal sunrise. How could this be anything less than the grossest blasphemy? Or so he thought.

"Jean" is itself a Greek word, but is so common in English that it functionally belongs in our language. The root word is *gen,* and occurs in many English words. Incidentally, the LXX gives Eve the name *Zoe,* which means "life," but I prefer the name Jean, "the source of life."

POINT OF VIEW

Before we get into the text itself, we must say a brief word about what writers call "point of view." By this, they mean the position the writer himself takes as he proceeds with his narrative. First is the exciting and highly subjective first-person point of view, in which the author speaks directly to his readers using the personal pronoun (the point I am now making). He is narrating about something that happens to himself or tells you how he feels about another matter. We see this in Solomon's treatise called Ecclesiastes. The most frequently used point of view is the exact opposite of this approach, called the third-person. This abounds in our newspapers and periodicals, except on the editorial page. The omniscient point of view gives the reader the additional insight into what the protagonists are thinking. Finally is the dramatic point of view, so called because it presents to the reader only what he would get if he were watching a play. Three areas are treated: visible scenery, direct action and dialogue—nothing more. No asides, flashbacks or other background material; no pauses for character-building facts or omniscient adventures into the protagonists' inner thoughts. This is a favorite point of view of modern short-story writers and novelists. Steinbeck and Hemingway used this approach almost exclusively. They all had a good example to follow— the Holy Bible itself. Indeed, most of the historical sections of the Old Testament, the Gospels and Acts in the New Testament use the dramatic point of view.

Of course, there are times when our curiosity and even nobler motives wish it had been otherwise. What went on in the mind of Abraham during that long night before the intended sacrifice of Isaac? Two millennia later, the author of the New Testament book of Hebrews tells us that Abraham during that sleepless night concluded that God, who cannot lie and who cannot break his promises, absolutely must raise Isaac from the dead.

Another event that tantalizes us is the night after Paul's Damascus Road vision of Christ, which left him blind. What thoughts must have tortured David during the many months of Bathsheba's first pregnancy? There are many other insights we wish we had. In addition, what of physical appearances? We do not have descriptions to any satisfying degree of specificity for any of the major figures of the Bible, including Jesus. We know more of what Goliath looked like than of the youth who slew him. The colossus of Michelangelo comes to mind. We look at that giant in white marble and wonder whether he really looked like that. Perhaps he did. I imagine that Michelangelo made it several feet taller than Goliath to remind us that, spiritually speaking, David was by far the taller of the two. Perhaps God wants each of us to remember that the physical appearance is not what we should consider, and that we had best create a David of our own. That same freedom generates from the dramatic point of view for a visualization of Jesus, the Christ. Therefore, by denying us detail, Scripture invites—even requires—us to supply our own. The dramatic point of view forces us to participate in creating the meaning of Scripture.

The artists participate, too. I repeat, since our Omnipotent and Omniscient Heavenly Father is the Lord of Canon, what he precludes from us is just as deliberate and significant as what he chooses to tell us. As we review again the events of that day in the life of Red and Jean, we cannot help but recall Milton's great work, *Paradise Lost.* How biblical is its message? A more satisfying answer would come to us if we asked, How anti-biblical is its message? The answer is, not at all; every detail of plot is possible, and enjoyed by those who like being led by his great talent into the realms of the God-given imaginations with which we are blessed. Of course, we must accept the obvious fact that we are not dealing with what happened, but with what could have happened. Frankly, I had always wondered why Satan still persists in his opposition to Almighty God, knowing in the end that he will end up in the Lake of Fire. Milton gives us his answer, which I regard as quite insightful. Satan believes that he and God both spontaneously generated, and the contest between them is by no means over. He believes he will win out over God, and he has the statistics to shore up his confidence, too. This seems a satisfying answer to a non-biblical question. The only criticism any biblical scholar ever leveled against Milton is that his own marital problems gave him a bias against women. On the whole, however, Milton's treatment is quite harmless as far as classical biblical theology is concerned.

The dramatic point of view is never totally adhered to. There will be exceptions, especially when the subject is as grand in scope, and yet so compact in its pacing, as we find in the Creation Hymn. Moses pauses for a sentence or two to stress our bisexuality. He speaks directly to us on page one to get married, have children, and fill the earth with our offspring. Then note this very strange invisible part of the scenery, invisible at least to Red and Jean—the Tree of Life. It is located in the middle of the Garden, apparently next to the Tree of the Knowledge of Good and Evil, yet Red and Jean are not told of the existence of that tree, though it is beyond doubt the most important tree in the Garden. In fact, we learn that our first parents did not even know the name of the other tree. God sees to it that we know of the existence of the Tree of Life, and that Red and Jean do not! This holy tree casts its benign shadow over the events of that entire day. We are on tenterhooks as we wait for our Progenitor and his spouse to discover that wonderful tree. However, Red and Jean are preoccupied. They are wondering why God did not want them to eat of the prohibited tree—the Tree of the Knowledge of Good and Evil.

Let us assume Moses is the author of Genesis. Surely, he had a hand in shaping it into its present form. We can see from what we have just been talking about that he writes with an air of expectancy; he envisions the world audience, of which we ourselves are a part. He speaks directly to us. Note another thing Red and Jean do not know—that Satan is in the snake. He wants us to ask why we have such information, and why those who seemingly would be most affected by the knowledge do not get it at all. It is easy for us to imagine that Moses invites us to get in a time machine and speed back around 15 billion years, ascend into some balcony, some vantage point where we behold the glory of the Almighty God as he begins a creation that has never ended.

THE CREATION HYMN

The sixth millennium since the creation of Red and Jean is fast drawing to its end, and my time is especially short. As any momentous journey nears its end, we always tend to take a mental journey back to its beginning. So I must in my millennial safari return once more to the Paradise of Eden. The Apostle John did exactly that in the last chapter of the Bible; he returned to the Garden of Eden. As a student of science, I must confess that I am almost paralyzed with frustration as I visit biblical beginnings once again. It is here more than anywhere else in the Old Testament that I definitely do not need to prime the pump, but rather to shore up the floodgates. Still, there's no time to discuss the longevity of the antediluvian patriarchs. No time for the Great Deluge and the Canopy Theory that gives a rationale to its massive rainfall. No time to scold scientists who mix a witch's brew of science and religion. No time for the origin of peoples outside the Holy Family of Red and Jean. No time for comparing cosmogonies in the world's religions with the Creation Hymn. Regrettably, I pass by all these exciting subjects. I have time just to repeat the only conclusion possible: the Creation Hymn is the world's only viable cosmogony coming from a religious source. The more science you know, the more you will agree that this is so.

As I have already said, Genesis begins assuming the existence of God. Most people believe in some sort of supernatural power. But as James reminds us, "even the devils believe—and tremble." To this day theologians have come up with only four proofs for the existence of God, and philosophers have neutralized them all. So we still cannot prove the existence of God, neither can the seculars deny it. The human mind is utterly frustrated on this subject. However, I would like to pause a moment to give credit to a coterie of brave scientists who recently have done new work as regards the teleological argument for the existence of God. I refer to such lonely pioneers as William Dembski, Michael Behe, and the jurist Philip Johnson, who speak of intelligent design and irreducible complexity. Yet though I am satisfied with their arguments, I predict that the naysayers will come up with a way to neutralize these descriptions of reality, and we will end up with the existence of God still eluding proofs conceptualized by the mind. God is a subject too big for the human brain. I am surrounded by transcendence on all sides. My problems are too big for me, my immediate future is unknowable, my loved ones have difficulties I cannot talk them through, the world seems headed for destruction, and

I cannot do a thing about it. I need a God as big as these things—yes, bigger, one who invites me into a heaven that itself reaches beyond the eye, ear and even my "heart"—the mysterious, synergistic, holistic me. Amidst such proportionality, I find it quite acceptable—even preferable—to live with a God who is beyond my puny logic.

Listen with me as our Loving Heavenly Father thunders through the lifeless night before him, "Be light!" This is in the imperative mood in Hebrew, which we English-speaking people do not have in our grammar. But what he wills happens. He wills nature into existence, with its infinity of design, complexity, variety and beauty. Now he will share with us as best he can the creation of man. It will not be easy for him, for he created man capable of understanding only so much. God must reduce his thought to human language, share with us a description of us that we are able to understand. See how clumsily it inks the page:

> And God (sing.) said, Let us (pl.) make man (sing.) in our (pl.) image (sing.) after our (pl.) likeness (sing.), and let them (pl.) have dominion. (Gen. 1:26)

> And the Lord God formed man from the dust of the ground and breathed into his nostrils the breath of life, and man became a living soul. (Gen. 2:7)

Before we get into the puzzling mechanics of these sentences, please note with me that two nouns are necessary to describe the creation of man: image and likeness. Image refers to the components of man's personhood; he has all the components in his nature that God also has. Likeness refers to the quality of being, or spirituality. We are spiritual beings, having all the components of God.

Let's look at the mechanics. Perhaps God is using what we call the "plural of majesty," such as is used by monarchs when speaking to their subjects, thereby reminding themselves and their hearers of the multifarious involvement and grandeur of their public selves. This must be part of the reason here for this seesaw construction. In fact, the plural of majesty was used here a long time before it was appropriated by earthly kings and their minions. The plural for God, or *el,* becomes *Elohim,* which is always used by biblical writers when they spoke of God. It is interesting to note that in times before Moses, the term used was a dual form, *Elohai.* I suppose this usage comes from the fact that man is a bilateral creature. He has two of almost every part of his body. Therefore, the canonical writers expressed their similarity to God by using the "dual of majesty."

By the time of Moses, a truth then on the distant horizon began to emerge—that of the Holy Trinity. God did indeed reveal to Moses, as Jesus says, that he who makes man like himself will someday come to man as his redeemer. He will, as John says, "pitch his tent among us." Even Abraham saw Christ's advent in the future and rejoiced. Moses here, by using this strange interweaving of grammatical numbers, expresses the Trinity of God as best he can in the ortholinear mode of written communication. Is God our creator? Yes. Is Christ our creator? Yes. Is the Holy Ghost our creator? Indeed. We meet him in the Bible's third sentence: "And the Spirit of God moved upon the face of the water."

This dialogue argues for an audience. There are angels, archangels, cherubim and seraphim. These are the "morning stars" and "sons of God" Job speaks of. Moses anticipates the "cloud of witnesses" among whom we ourselves are included.

So God is Ultimate Being, beyond singularity (though singular), beyond plurality (though a Trinity), beyond the limitations of language that seesaws between opposites into oxymoronic babblings. We are made in the image of God. This expression itself is an oxymoron, for "image" relates to icons, idols and other statues in this spatial-temporal continuum. Yet God is a spirit, just as Jesus told the Samaritan woman at the well.

This oxymoron describes us, too. God made us like himself in every way, only we differ from him in qualitative and quantitative degrees, but not in components. We have them all as expressed throughout the Bible's inductive revelation of them as we go from page to page. This is not to suggest "the evolution of God" as some so foolishly claim, but the progressive revelation of his attributes. Note the three descriptions given above—we are in the "image of God," in the "likeness of God," and "living souls." No physical body is mentioned, yet man is given a glorious machine, designed for and adjusted to this transitory life. It is a good machine, for God has made it. Still, we are spirits, so we must not mistake this machine for an integral part of our natural eminence. Man was created a god in flesh, not a psychosomatic creature. We live as men—God's future companions in his ineffable kingdom—and yet we soon will see that Red has the freedom, this willpower, to raise the body to bad eminence, and the folly of listening to voices other than God's. Paul warns us of the consequence of this deadly fusion: "To be carnally minded is death."

THE VERY GOOD CREATION

As the Creation Hymn comes to its close, the inspired Word of God makes a bold conclusion about the billions of years of endless toil that he has completed. He wants us to know how he feels about what and whom he has made. He says before he observes the world's first Sabbath Day, "Very good!" After studying the Bible for more than 50 years, I could not recall this pair of words used elsewhere in Scripture. We read that God is good, but never that he is "very good." After all, saying God is very good is really bad news, for "very good" is a comparative term arguing for the existence of something even better. It is like those chilling words, "I love you very much." This we must never say. Love doesn't admit degree, not unless you mean something like "I love carmel-coated popcorn," in which case you don't really mean love at all, but "like." Never speak to spouses and children about loving them "very much." I did find three other times "very good" occurred in Scripture, but I quickly dismissed all of them as relatively unimportant. They occurred in minor secular contexts in the Old Testament, not even remotely suggestive of parallel comparison. Nevertheless, this is the only time God says, "Very good!"

Yet "very good" argues as much for "better" as "better" does for "best." It also implies that God fully intends to make his creation even better— yes, even best. This very good creation is not a summary we are likely to make at the end of the day we are about to consider, the eighth day of creation. Nor could we conclude such at the end of any chapter in the sweaty, dirty, painful, bloody history that is to follow over the ensuing six millennia.

Still, God says, at that point in time at least, "Very good!" Scientists and poets agree with this, as do we all at times when our cup runneth over, when we also conclude with David that we have never seen the righteous going hungry, or their offspring begging for bread. I am sure some will rear back at this, citing anecdotal exceptions to this. Yet I must insist that this testimony is right in my microcosm. However controversial this problem may be, there is a far more troubling one that I must share with you. How can the creation—the whole of it, including man—be "very good," and yet Red and Jean skip (if not run) with such bravado, such cavalier abandonment, to condemn the human race to a worse existence than ever came out of Pandora's box? To put it another way, could man be considered a very good creation if he is marginally potentiated, then poised on the brink of disaster? Are we indeed no better than frenzied horses that rush back into a burning barn?

From my earliest Christian experience until a short time ago, I had never been satisfied with what theologians and biblical scholars tell us about what happened to Red and Jean. They speak of "Adamic nature," "original sin," "total depravity" and the like in such a way as to imply that our primal progenitor was created on the threshold of evil, in which case one act could trigger a process that would poison the genetic history of mankind. In a way, this is rather like what the proponents of natural selection believe. Darwin and his followers have been peering into cells of living creatures in search of proof for the notion that the environment enters into the cell's genetic message, thereby changing it. Since the middle of the 19th century, they have sought, but not found, this proof. Now theologians are saying pretty much the same thing about Red and Jean. Some see this Adamic nature as a disease that not only can be ameliorated by the grace of God, but even eradicated. Some see Adamic nature as an evil tree that Christ chops down, whose stump can be totally removed by the infilling of the Holy Ghost.

But what happened six millennia ago in the Garden of Eden? Recall that we are in the eighth day of creation. God had already created mankind.

We do not know how he did it, or how many people were alive as the eighth day arrives. We do not need to know how many lived east of Eden in the land of Nod, where Cain apparently got his wife. In his infinite wisdom, God has not included that information in the Garden Narrative. Nor do we know of other planets in our universe comparable to our own, where life may or may not exist. Still, God does want us to know he intends a second creation, this time of a sanctified family who will express his will to the world, preserve that will in a written document, pursuant to a personal visit he himself intends to make. The goal of that sanctified family is companionship with God in the Eternal Kingdom.

The number 8is the symbol for a new beginning in Hebrew numerology, a novel way ancient peoples had for supplementing their emerging languages. This phenomenon is not used today, yet is important to us because it is significantly present in the Holy Bible. It would be impossible, in fact, to interpret the Apocalypse of John without knowledge of numerology. We have no time to develop this fascinating study here, but suffice it to say that throughout the entire Bible, when the number 8 is used symbolically, it always means a new beginning. Man was created on the sixth day of creation, 6 being a bad number, but the Holy Family started on the eighth day. On this day is born the concept of sanctification, God setting aside certain individuals for a holy purpose and a holy destiny. It follows without dispute that those who do not believe they are in this family come to despise those who claim to be. This explains the murder of Abel, the fierce hatred of Joseph by his brothers, the martyrdom of saints throughout all history, climaxing with the decapitation of John the Baptist and the crucifixion of our beloved Lord Jesus Christ. The eighth day reaches its greatest degree of poignancy on the Day of Pentecost, the day after the last of seven weeks since Passover.

The only meaning of the eighth day of creation that satisfied my understanding of the rest of Scripture is that it's not over yet. Indeed, God intended to add more to Red and Jean than he had to people in his other creation, but what he wanted to give them would take time for them to receive. Their sin was that they were content to have the creation end sooner than God intended. If we must use the term "original sin," it must surely mean that they were the first persons to make this choice, and men have been living beneath their privileges ever since.

Seeing the eighth day of creation as incomplete, we do not have to pursue any further a Darwinian search for some anatomical or physiological explanation for the transmission of some environmental factor to our natures. We do not need to subtract from, but to add to, our natures. Seeing Red and Jean as incomplete gives us further insight into God's proclamation that his creation was very good indeed. Yes, at the end of the sixth day, it was indeed very good, but the story was not over yet. God intended much more.

We see the interdicted tree put into the Garden. This is very good. Man has to have sin available for virtue to become possible. Freedom is meaningless unless it is expressed by self-limitations without the need of a fence. Let us not forget that man is a social creature—not the Marxist concept of being created by society, but the individual needing to give and to receive from others while living in society. Red needs Jean, and she him. Hereby man is directed toward others and away from self, or in the paradoxical term used by Jesus, he saves his life by losing it. Even a greater vision is intended—wide enough to see each other and to perceive beyond what the eye sees. Conscience is an added dimension of their freedom, the quality of behavior added to the direction of behavior. Indeed, God continued his creation until his peers-in-the-making exercised their own willpower, and then he called an abrupt halt to it. Let us see how this all happens by looking more closely at the events of that unending day, the day in which God puts down the sustaining pedal from which the reverberations still resonate in our lives today.

TREES AND RIVERS

Let us leave our balcony for a moment and get a closer look at the Garden. As we draw near the two mysterious trees in the center, we must pass by many a fruit-laden bough, inviting us to see, smell, and eat our fill of the vast variety of taste and texture. What more could we ask for? We are moving over the mossy ground and amidst branches festooned with fabulous blooms nodding in the perfumed zephyrs of this holy place. This is the ideal home for man, fabricated by his Maker. Who would know better than he how to proclaim his love? We from history's balcony know so many things not revealed to our primal parents, things that even add to the sensuous ecstasy of our passage toward the center of the Garden. We saunter along, thinking of the 14 billion years or so during which all this was in the making, but Red and Jean had no way of knowing that. How long had these newcomers been in the Garden, anyway? Only one day is mentioned, so we assume it is now in the afternoon of that day. One scholar thinks they lasted in the Garden only six hours, paralleling the six hours Christ Jesus was on the cross.

In the Garden's exact center we see these two trees. Red was told of only one, and he saw only one as far as we know. We also know their names—Tree of Life and Tree of Knowledge of Good and Evil—something else God did not tell our first parents. Still, God wants us to consider why he did not name the trees for Red and Jean. As I have already said, what God doesn't include is just as important as what he does, and that the sound of silence urges us to conclude something better known if generated from within, instead of being spelled out by Scripture.

On the other hand, when God wants us to obey a specific law, he writes not only so he will be understood by us, but so that he cannot be misunderstood. Recently, I saw Commandment VII on a billboard, "Thou shalt not commit adultery." Then just beneath this was this question: "Exactly which of these words do you not understand?"

There are passages of Scripture that leave out details about which our logic and imagination spontaneously generate questions. This is our participation, our "work" in recreating the Garden Narrative. It seems to me that naming the tree "Knowledge of Good and Evil" for the benefit of Red and Jean would be meaningless. They did not know what "good" and "evil" meant, or "die," for that matter. Satan was aware of this when he made his commentary on God's warning. He might as well have said, "Your eyes will be opened and you will be as gods, knowing strawberries and ice cream." The moment God said this tree was interdicted, we may rightly suppose that Red's response was like a child's response to Mother's interdicted cookie jar. Red thought at once, "Why?" About ten seconds later, "Why?" became "Why not?" He may well have continued, "Why put the tree in the Garden if we are not to eat of it? Why didn't God at least put a fence around it? Maybe this fruit is something God doesn't want us to have, something we may benefit from eating. Something that may raise us up to his level! On the other hand, maybe he really wants us to eat of the tree and wants us to make our own choices about things. What's more, why is it there in the exact middle of the Garden, where we see it every day once or maybe twice?"

There is nothing wrong with asking these questions. God says through Isaiah, "Come now and let us reason together." Note the nature of the transgression. The tree is not poison. The fruit is not poison. Red, as you will note, lived 930 years after he ate it. If he were created at, say, a 40-year-old level of maturity, he would have lived longer than Methuselah! The sin was in Red's decision to disobey God, to eat of the forbidden fruit because it was forbidden. But let's not rush for an ice pick to give him a prefrontal lobotomy. Rather, under the right circumstances, he instead ought to receive a Nobel Prize. Many individuals have been told they couldn't do something, and they then became like the lad in his physics class whose professor told him he couldn't polarize the asbestos crystal—he went home to his basement lab and did it, thereby making Polaroid photography possible.

We will return to Red and Jean stealing a fruit from their Divine Neighbor's yard, but first let's look at the name God gives the tree. He wants us to know it: Knowledge of Good and Evil. When I first read the Garden Narrative as a teenager, I understood it as Knowledge of Good from Evil. A simple mistake—at least an inconspicuous one. I suppose I meant something like "a burnt child fears the fire." I went on to reason that there were three ways to learn. First, there is learning from precept—someone explains a principle to us and we accept it. This kind of learning goes on all the time in our classrooms. Second, we can learn by example—accepting or rejecting actions or beliefs by how they affect people who do accept them. Red and Jean had no such knowledge available to them because they were the only people in the Garden. Third, we learn from experience—like the aforementioned burnt child. William Blake held this view, represented by the titles of his twin volumes of poetry, *Songs of Innocence* and *Songs of Experience.*

The argument goes something like this. Red and Jean refused to learn from God's commandment, or learning by precept, and chose to experiment for themselves. They chose experience as their philosophy. This is a well-known view of reality accepted by many religions, and is the darling of philosophers and scientists without number. It is called empiricism. Hence, man has this philosophy mysteriously transmitted from Red and Jean. I called it a crippled epistemology, the expensive and long-lived process of ranking life's values by experiencing the pain of bad behavior, and by seeing such pain in the lives of others.

All this is good, but there are two things wrong with it. First, it is no more than a reiteration of the universal lament of thinkers from the beginning of recorded history until this very hour. It beats the dead mule. The Road of Life must give us more than this. Our Book is the Revealed Word of God. There is a crucifixion out there waiting for Emmanuel. We must not answer it with an echo of mere human opinion. Second, it is not what the Bible says. It calls the tree Knowledge of Good <u>and</u> Evil. Apparently, many Bible scholars are still failing to see what the Bible really says. The translators of *The New Jerusalem Bible* give us "good from evil" as their rendition of Gen 3:22, presumably to clarify their impression that Moses means empiricism. However, they do this without any justification at all. The Hebrew text is quite clearly "good and evil." These two opposites are presented as coordinates—no causal relationship is indicated. The fact that God tells us up here on the balcony of another tree must also enter the argument.

Let me explain what I mean by including the Tree of Life in our quest for an understanding of Adamic nature. It is the first of the two trees mentioned in the Garden Narrative. This fact alone argues for its full consideration. We all know the legal principle of two kinds of law as regards the matter of volition—mandates and interdicts. These are, respectively, laws that require us to take certain actions, and laws that prevent us from acting. Paying taxes is in the realm of mandates; interdicts prevent us from trespassing on private property. Milton was the first to call Knowledge of Good and Evil the "interdicted tree." I wish the limitation of our subject would allow a fascinating and even edifying exploit into a discussion of these two kinds of laws, examples of which are found throughout Scripture. Suffice it to say that interdicts are much easier to keep than mandates.

Now pretend you are a stranger in Paradise. I tell you there are two trees there, one called The Interdicted Tree. Then I ask you to guess the name of the other tree. What would you say? Of course, you would call it The Mandated Tree, and you would be exactly right. If we want to obey God, what would be our response to the interdicted tree? Nothing at all! We are to avoid it at all cost. What of the mandated tree? We must eat of it as often as God tells us to do so, and to keep eating of it until he tells us to stop. If God tells us that we must eat of it daily, as the Hebrews ate manna in the wilderness, that is what we will have to do. The feast would be a diurnal reality, like eating bread. To have life, we must eat of the Tree of Life—we have absolutely no option in this matter. This ongoing travesty caused by incomplete men, this coexistence of good and evil, this overwhelming dominance of evil over good drives us (a few of us, anyway) to the Tree of Life, where we daily feast. God-Among-Us, Emmanuel, has said, "My flesh really is meat and my blood really is drink." We will return to this daring metaphor of Jesus again very soon.

A river flows through the Garden. It is without a name, though some modern translators have presumed to give it one. Its presence suggests the unbroken cycle of life. The river waters the Tree of Life, which gives life to us. We need not take the geography of Antediluvia seriously. Moses did not really know the lay of the land before the Great Deluge, but it certainly must have changed dramatically after the fall of so much rain. Judging the meaning of the directions given, I think Moses wanted us to believe it is God's plan that the whole world be watered from the four distributaries of this river as it flows out of the Garden. Indeed, the whole world is God's parish; Jesus predicted every nation would hear of his Gospel, and all men would have the opportunity to be drawn to him. In light of the present communication renaissance and the sunset of the sixth millennium since the creation of Red and Jean, we all must agree that this prophecy is fast coming to fulfillment.

The unnamed river that flowed through the Garden was similar to the Jordan in the days of Abraham and Lot. Like other rivers that descend from alpine heights to desert plains rather than to the sea, it forked out into distributaries that nourished the land, in much the same way the Nile River does its delta in the land of Goshen, and as the Jordan once did onto the Plains of Sodom (Gen. 13).

We meet this river again in Ps. 46:4-5, and in the strangest of places— on a mountaintop, precisely where rivers do not flow.

> There is a river, the streams whereof shall make glad the city of God, the holy place of the tabernacles of the Most High. God is in the midst of her; she shall not be moved . . . .

Not only do we meet this unnamed river performing its Edenic function on top of Mt. Zion, but we learn its identity in verse 5: "God is in the midst of her." Note something else strange: "tabernacles" is in the plural, whereas the Law of Moses says there is only one. Indeed, we are the tabernacles, "temples of the Holy Ghost," as Paul calls us. Other references to God as being a river are found also in Ez. 47:1 and Zech.

14:8. Jesus speaks of our being the Garden through which the Holy Ghost as a river flows in John 7:37-38. Moses' names for these four rivers suggest the spiritual power invading Jerusalem on the Day of Pentecost in 28 AD: "to gush," "to spread," "to break forth," and "to be rapid." Finally, the river that began six millennia ago, witnessed to by David in the Psalms and later in the prophets, prophesied by Jesus and explicitly described in John's Apocalypse, comes to its end as the unseen river flowing among us today.

RED GETS A WIFE

To this point in the Garden Narrative, we have learned more about man's first abode than about the man himself. We are told he is a spiritual being, like God. Now we learn, strangely enough, that the creation is not over yet, that the eighth day of creation is just beginning. God, who did not choose someone from the land of Nod to head his sanctified family, now seeks "a helper who is his equal." She is also not from the land of Nod, or even formed from the ground as Red himself was, but taken from his own body. First, God wants us to know what in other generations might seem needless detail, but today needs clear emphasis. God wants us to know the width and depth of the chasm that exists between man and animals. Some, like Charles Darwin, have built intellectual bridges over this grand canyon; some would even like to indulge themselves in the convenience of regarding members of their ilk as animals, and justify treating them as such. Some even worship them. Moses, you will note, seems to present God as using a "let's see" approach on Red. He says to our grandsire, "Let us see if we can find a companion for you. Maybe we ought to see whether some animal will do." Whenever we communicate the activity of Almighty God to each other, we become all thumbs. Reader and writer alike must concede the transcendence from Eternity to time as we approach the task. We can expect our speech to be highly contrived, wholly inadequate to the task. Under such circumstances, we best make a realistic appraisal of our subject matter and the tools we have to use. We must be humble and enter this phase of the Kingdom of God like the little children we indeed are.

So the first thing God wants Red to do is to join him in a quest for an adequate helper. He invites Red to get some practice using the greatest tool of his divine peerage and as ruler of the creatures of this planet. I speak of the conceptual use of language. He intends to convince Red that his helper will not be found in the animal kingdom. As the animals pass by, he notes their use of language is confined to monosyllabic sounds that carry no meaning. The animals use language as signs, not symbols. There is not a communicator among them. This is a fact Red apparently did not share with Jean, who had not been created yet. So when the snake spoke to this newcomer in Paradise, she probably supposed all animals used language as we do.

Red conceptualizes when he uses language. He creates sounds that cluster around images of objects. He stores these in his memory. Later, when he utters these sounds, the images from his memory spring into his own mind and into the minds of those who hear him. Language makes him a toolmaker—he is Lord of the planet, and able to communicate with God. Could he know modern science, he would agree with one who recently said there is more difference between man and ape than between ape and amoeba. What's more, he surely would have been puzzled to know that James Watson, who first saw the DNA as a double helix, had been going around university campuses giving a lecture entitled, "We are Apes."

We cannot help but imagine why God created a wife for Red from one of his ribs rather than from the ground, just as he created Red. Perhaps the resulting genetic identity, even that of identical twins, emphasized their moral equality. This needs special emphasis because man is appointed as head of the family. If a family unit were made up of three persons, a majority vote would always settle matters of dispute. But this is not so— someone has to be the head. Paul says that Red was made first, which means God wanted him to be the head. This is further indicated by the fact that Jean was deceived, thus putting her in a lesser place. Yet one must not suppose that Jean was morally inferior to Red, for both are of the same flesh. Had Satan tempted Red, we have every reason to believe he would have yielded just as readily as Jean did. Why so? Because they were genetically identical! So we must conclude that, even though Jean was physically weaker than Red, both were equal in the more important category—the spiritual.

Red awakes from his sleep to behold the Mother of all creation—Jean, his wife. It is here that our narrative enters into a didactic aside, the grand proclamation so noble in its profundity that it takes its place in most wedding ceremonies. Yet we cannot for a moment imagine that Red's comment is the typical response of a man on first seeing his blushing bride. These two are not meant to be portrayed as a typical or ideal couple. We are to know of them exactly what God intends, nothing else. Perhaps

Moses excludes more detail to give what is said a greater visibility. There is no greeting between Red and Jean. In fact, there never is any dialogue recorded between them. Notice that Red's exultation is about himself: ". . . bone of my bone, flesh of my flesh . . . ." He is egocentric, almost narcissistic, as the psychologists would say. Although we might wish for a less self-serving reaction from Red, yet implicit in it is a responsibility toward Jean tantamount to his self-interest. Paul reminds us that "no man ever yet hated his own flesh."

SATAN ARRIVES

I believe Satan exists. He is my constant opponent, as the name "Satan" implies. He is also a slanderer, as the name "Devil" proclaims. The Apocalypse of John gives him yet another name, "Apollyon," which means destroyer. I have to this very hour experienced his power in all three of his infernal functions. You will note that Moses does not name him among the personae of the Garden Narrative. Red and Jean know nothing about him at all. Only in the New Testament do we have spelled out his appropriation of the snake. I will follow the biblical precedent and say about him as little as possible, preferring rather to exalt the Person of God's Beloved Son, our Lord and Savior Jesus Christ, who came to destroy the works of Satan.

For the present let us return to our balcony and see him camouflaged in the body of a snake, gyrating in air, this Prince of Air, resembling a bed spring, coiling and uncoiling, swiftly and silently moving toward Jean, the Mother of us all. The infinite wisdom of our Divine Lover has allowed him into the Garden. Listen as the Slanderer, Opponent and Destroyer speaks: "God didn't tell you that you couldn't eat of every tree in the Garden, did he?"

Satan wants Jean to say "yes" to him. He is a super salesman and, as such, knows you must always keep the prospective customer saying "yes" to every question you ask. The "yes" to this question implies a negative about God. Satan does not start with, "My! What a beautiful place this is! Who gave you such a garden to live in? He must love you very much." No, definitely nothing like this. He ignores what God did, concentrating on the negative—always the negative.

Where is Red? We are not told. Moses says he is present later—and silent, too—as Jean arrives at the tree, examines the fruit and eats it. Why does Satan tempt Jean instead of Red? We are allowed to imagine that she is the easier target, being less oriented to the place, quite unaware that animals do not use language as she and Red do, or that snakes do not even have the power of speech. It really makes no difference which of the two Satan approaches. We have no reason to doubt Red's total willingness to disobey God. The Garden Narrative in its entirety makes this abundantly clear.

From our balcony seat, we look down on the scene, cluck our tongues, and shake our heads. How we would want to whisper to this Lady Macbeth to be as wise as we are, to resist, to tell the arch enemy to take a hike! Of course, this is a drama, and we are expected to react that way. After the curtain falls, we have a garden of our own waiting for us. However, we give Mother Jean our rapt attention as she parrots what her husband had told her, with the curious addition, "neither shall ye touch it." This is probably added as a reminder that we seldom repeat a quote without some variation. God did not say this to Red, though he might have added it when he warned Jean about the tree. Or maybe it is just her quaint embellishment. This may seem such a minor item, but little things grow. It is the little foxes that spoil the vines. What further ornamentation, might you imagine, will Jean add to this exchange with Satan when she narrates her version of it to her husband moments later? But we have something more important than this speculation to consider. It is something of critical importance, something Jean will not discuss with Red because she will never see it.

It is the Tree of Life. It is also in the middle of the Garden, probably right next to the interdicted tree. Maybe earlier in the day, she and Red had strolled to the middle of the Garden for a look-see at this amazing, extremely important interdicted tree, the only one in the entire Garden that could cause death (whatever that word meant!) from eating its fruit. They did not see the second tree then, nor would they when they returned for the second look. We must not let this important fact slip by us, that there are two things in the Garden that our primal parents did not see, and they are exact opposites—the Tree of Life and Satan, who isn't even named in the Narrative. We are left wondering whether these two blind spots are related. In addition, here is the world's greatest example of selective vision! We see what we want to see, even in the presence of overwhelming evidence to the contrary. Her selective vision had excluded the most important object in the world, the Tree of Life, whose very name proclaims us spiritually dead if we do not eat of it. You say that she was ignorant? True, but man's neglect ever since betrays her blindness as culpable ignorance.

Satan calls God a liar without fear of contradiction: "You will not really die." We have a semantic problem here—rather, Mother Jean has one—one which we must take into account. Psychologists rightly tell us that we cannot understand the meaning of a word unless we can associate it with things we already know. Did Father Red and Mother Jean know what death is? How could this be possible? Then what follows is just as incomprehensible to her, and might as well have entered her thinking like this: "God knows that your eyes will be opened, and you shall be as gods, knowing strawberries and ice cream!"

Just when the conversation peaks, Satan disappears from the scene, leaving the snake flat on its belly. We are allowed to believe that Jean now searches out her husband and gives him her version of the dialogue with Satan, which quite possibly didn't vary much from what had been dancing around in her head ever since Red first warned her about the tree.

Satan is like that. He gets dressed up in red underwear, wearing cute little horns, a stylish beard, holding a harmless-looking pitchfork, and starts his anti-gospel by telling us exactly what we want to hear.

They work themselves up into such a lather that they just have to give this tree another look. They hasten together, full of purpose. They go together in spite of how John Milton presents his narrative. Did Red say to Jean, "Forget about this tree, at least for now, dear wife. Something seems suspicious here. I've never heard an animal speak. Let us explore the whole garden more completely. We have plenty of time"? No, he does not. It seemed to them that what the snake said is what they had supposed all along. Maybe God is unreasonable. Maybe God is being subtle, actually wanting us to eat of the tree, after all. Maybe God and we both generated spontaneously, so we are equals, and he is just trying to keep the upper hand.

In no time at all they were probably running toward the tree. When they arrive at the middle of the Garden, Moses wants us to see events through the eyes of Mother Jean. We discern the three classical categories of sin. First, she "saw," i.e., concluded, that the fruit was good to eat—the lust of the flesh, or somatogenic sin; second, it looked good—lust of the eye, or psychosomatic sin; third, the pride of life—wanting to eat the fruit to be as wise as God Himself. She reaches forth her hand with Red right at her side. He does nothing to stop her. He is sympathetic toward her actions, for she was made from one of his ribs, we remind ourselves. She eats, and he watches to see whether God will strike her dead. Could it possibly be that he was more curious about God's threat than about his wife's safety? Surely not! In any case, she does not drop dead, and when she offers Red the fruit, they indeed are one and the same flesh.

Immediately after, "their eyes were opened." This is an idiomatic expression common to all languages. It means they saw something that was there, but they had not seen before. One feature of human thinking is that it is discursive, ortholinear, in the shape of a line; this is coupled with the limitation of monofixation, the mind's inability to fixate on more than one thing at a time. One disadvantage of this design is what we call absent-mindedness. We become so enthusiastic about something that we forget everything else until the enthusiasm begins to abate. Red and Jean were so drawn by curiosity or so driven by desire that they forgot all about the outcome of what they were involved in until it was too late to do anything about it. But the climax came, and a surprising conclusion descended upon them—in other words, they experienced delayed cognition. In short, our first parents got acquainted with conscience. In the language of Moses, they ate of the tree called Knowledge of Good and Evil, the good of discovery coupled with the evil of disobedience.

Perhaps in the light of all that has been said about "Adamic nature," you may think I understate the meaning of this event, one of the most conspicuous in the history of human thought. Thinking more about the matter, you must conclude that nothing more poignant could possibly be said, nothing more freighted with possibility, good and bad. Isn't it the degree of conscience in human breasts that opens the gates of our prisons and, on the other hand, founds great charitable organizations? Without a conscience, one not only is so exceptional that he is immune to the probings of the polygraph, but he becomes a sociopath within whose reach is every crime conceivable to human depravity, and without feeling a thing! Without a conscience, one could even come to believe Satan would open the eyes of a blind man.

It is St. Paul who portrays for us how delayed cognition relates to sin in an electrifying passage in Rom. 7. It is a passage worthy of our most sober analysis. Scripture gives us several examples of sins easily understood in this light. Consider David in several months of spiritual turmoil during the first pregnancy of Bathsheba. David's eventual awakening brought him forgiveness, but not so as regards Bathsheba's grandfather, Ahitophel, and Jesus' disciple, Judas. Both betrayers ended up as suicides after delayed cognition brought them to the desperate straits of no longer being able to justify themselves to themselves.

Consider Jesus' First Word of his Passion, "Father, forgive them, for they do not know what they are doing." Note that I translate the Greek present tense as the present imperfect, I change "do" into "are doing." This is correct, for the actual impalement is taking place as he speaks. He does not ask his Father to forgive them for what they <u>did</u> or <u>will do</u>, but for what they <u>are doing</u>. Later, Paul reminds Corinthian Christians that "had the princes of the world known, they would not have crucified the Lord of Glory." The crucifixion of Christ and the Garden Narrative are parallel in many ways. Just outside the eastern gate into Jerusalem is a garden, too. It is cluttered about with human bones and is a bit smaller, but in it God has raised the Tree of Life. Men call it Skull Place. At the moment Jesus speaks, the aristocracy of Jerusalem, the "Three P's," as I call them—the politicians, professors and preachers—are in pursuit of preserving the righteousness of God by putting a carpenter from Nazareth to death because he blasphemed true religion.

But will delayed cognition take place? This is a question only God can answer. It came to Paul the day after he instigated the stoning of Stephen. God did for Paul as he did for Job—gave him a personal interview. This we all know. Yet will delayed cognition come to all prior to the Great Judgment

Day? God knows; he is the one in the saving business. Still, there is one question we can answer, one that is of importance to us all, especially in this context. How about the other inhabitants of Antediluvia? Did God give them a conscience, too? Well, we might suppose it came to them as it does to us today, via experiences, negative and positive, bringing us past our callow years into the full age of accountability. If so, why do we need this episode of Red and Jean? Couldn't they have gone through the usual growing up process like the rest of us? This would be possible if we excluded the love of God from our considerations. You see, Red and Jean are something special to God—they are the founders of the Holy Family. He is going to take personal charge of their acculturation to the future home he has prepared for them. A trial-and-error method on the streets of Nod will not be good enough to suit him. Indeed, the Sanctified Family has a Jealous Lover, one who fully intended to slay all competitors for little Israel's affection. Mark you, my companions on the balcony, even now he is preparing to drown all but eight of their descendants! Later, he would cut away the foreskin of their hearts, and still later demand they bear crosses on their backs whenever and as long as necessary to get them exactly where he wants them.

He will write his will down in a Book so clear in its meaning, so persuasive in its rhetoric, so inspiring in its moral excellence that it will magnify the acculturation of the consciences of men way beyond the natural extent possible on the streets of Nod or, for that matter, every other subsequent culture. We up here in history's balcony 6,000 years later must take the matter to heart. If we become part of little Israel, we must figure Skull Place into our Lover's equation. Having not spared his own Son for our sake, it is hard telling how far God may yet go to destroy every idol in our hearts!

THE CURSE

When I first because acquainted with the Creation Hymn and the Garden Narrative, I thought sex was the forbidden fruit prudently clothed in symbolic language. Of course, my youth could be blamed for this, plus the tendency endemic to the human race of regarding this sensible world more real than the eternal one. This home will be ours as soon as we can learn to overcome this world, relegating the whole of it to its subordinate place. Our Beloved Lord emphasized this before Pilate, "If my kingdom were of this world, then would my disciples fight." To the very last he maintained a clear dichotomy about the two worlds, and subordinated the present to the future one. I finally realized that God would never in a million years make sex the forbidden fruit, even temporarily. The more I thought about this foolish notion, the more ridiculous it became. Indeed, why would God create us of two different sexes, place our primal parents naked together, and then forbid sex between them? Yes, even making it the most consequential act of sin the world was ever to know—this, when sex is the mode whereby God gives us children and invites us to join him amidst the confirming ecstasy of the event in creating, *in perpetuum*, the universe he himself willed into existence?

No, it is not a sexual sin or a sexual act interpreted as a sin that Red and Jean committed in Paradise. It was something far worse than that. As we have just seen, sin has three possible sources—the body, the body plus the mind, and the mind only. The first two of these are dependent on our having physical bodies; without bodies, we could not commit a single one of these sins. The third, however, the attitudinal sins, are the most serious. It is ironic, though, that sins involving the body usually get most of the attention. People often suppose they are sinless because they are like the rich young ruler, who declared that he had kept all the Commandments from his youth onward. The truth is that this youth had too narrow a definition of sin. Our primal parents sinned outside any physical craving whatsoever. Red and Jean sinned by wanting what was forbidden <u>because it was forbidden</u>, and thereby have cast a net upon their descendants with a mesh fine enough to catch us all.

Ask yourself—how many fruit trees did Red and Jean have to pass to reach the middle of the Garden? Would I shock you to stop reading this instant and to throw this book into the circular file if I told you that their sin was as bad as David's? Of course, I'm referring to the David who committed adultery with his neighbor's wife, then murdered him and married the woman to keep concealed the pregnancy that resulted from that act of adultery. How many women did he have to pass to reach Bathsheba? You see, we must not confuse quality with quantity when we sit beside God on the judge's bench. God looks not on the outward appearances but on the heart. Another question—which is worse, the murder of Uriah or Abel? If I had to judge (which I do not) and if on comparative motivation (which I am too ignorant to do), I would have to say Cain's murder of Abel was the worse. I am saying it is not easy for us to choose—nor is it necessary.

The sin that is attitudinal—wholly psychogenic—is the worst kind. It is a part of our natures, with or without our bodies. For a brief moment let us shift scenes to heaven and imagine ourselves witnessing God bringing his Son into visibility before the heavenly Host. There he stands, full of the godhead bodily, the express image of the Father. He has the dews of his youth, the beauty of holiness, truly the Vision Beatific. Then God tells the angels his plan to create an adopted family by a plan we know as the Gospel. Then he turns to the Son and asks if he will accept this task of love. The Son replies, "Lo, in the volume of the Book it is written of me. I go, O God, to do thy will." Then that Voice that would soon roar across infinite chaos, "Be light!" now says, "Let all the angels of God worship him!" And they do—but not all. Lucifer, Chief Archangel, refuses and is cast into hell along with angels who for reasons unknown (and probably unknowable to us) follow him instead of God. Now I ask—what was Satan's sin? How did his sin differ from that of Red and Jean?

Let's return to Paradise. The eighth day of creation is coming to its sunset. It is the cool of the evening and Red and Jean have just finished their meal. After a few grunts and belches, they "come to themselves," like the Prodigal Son in Jesus' parable. They see themselves as never before—naked—and they ought not to be. Being disappointed with their behavior, they seek some way to improve their self-image. Perhaps they vainly hope to cover their transgression by making themselves less visible. They may even anticipate clothes as a mutual courtesy, and the cultural enhancement it would soon become. It is also altogether possible that they act merely out of human instinct.

Clothes have never lost their symbolic power. Of course, they are totally worthless to God, who is Omniscient. We are—all of us—as naked before him as we were at birth. Yet men everywhere, urged by the inclemency of weather, the imperfection of the body, and innate expression of individualism, wear clothes. As children move toward adulthood, they instinctively cover those parts of their bodies that differentiate themselves from each other. Nakedness, on the other hand, is a symbol of hopelessness and shame. The Apocalypse of John is full of descriptions of clothing. In chapter 19, he speaks of the bride of Christ dressed in clean, white linen, which is the righteousness of the saints. Jesus is seen in one of its last visions (Rev. 16:15), speaking about clothes:

> Look! I come as a thief. Blessings upon the watching ones keeping their garments [close by] so that they may not walk naked and their shame be seen.

Jesus seems to be saying here that we wear clothes instinctively, and we are—or should be—ashamed to be seen naked.

St. Paul, the tent-maker, envisions himself before the Judgment Seat clothed no longer with the earthly tatters of his worn-out tent, but with something made by God (II. Cor. 5:1-5):

> For we know that, if the earthly house of ours, the tent, be loosened, we have a dwelling of God, not made with hands, eternal in the heavens. For in this [present house] we groan, longing to be clothed with our dwelling from heaven, if indeed being clothed, we will not be found naked. For though being in the tent we groan, being burdened, we do not want to be unclothed, but clothed upon, so that what pertains to death may be swallowed up in life. But he having prepared us for this is God who has given us the guarantee of his Spirit.

Also, recall that just before our shameful parents were "driven out" of Paradise, God made suitable clothing for them of animal skins.

The cursing of Father Red and Mother Jean is well known to us all, and we pass by now with just a few remarks. Ironically, the most important of these is what is conspicuously absent. I ask you, where is Moses' description of the "Adamic nature" that the theologians spend so much time writing about? Frankly, I see no change at all in their personalities. Oh, they are faulty, but that is not the point. We are looking for some indication of a nervous breakdown, some goodness foregone, some evil assumed. We are looking for some effect generated from some assumed nefariousness. Rather, we see Mother Jean spontaneously generating a fanciful world in which God is absent—her mind bowing down before her own reasoning power. Her self-expression was her supreme consideration, and her husband was silently complicit in all she did. Yet all this happened <u>before</u> they ate the interdicted fruit, not after. What changed was not Red and Jean, but the whole wide world about them. It was changed forever, and even included their own bodies. Yes, God changed the universe into a competitive place, a painful place with birth pangs to punctuate the sanctification of the Holy Family, and weeks to fill the garden of the slothful. The starry-eyed dream of a cooperative world now changes into the vigorous, raw-boned competition of the struggle for existence. Our angry, jealous Lover, always committed to bludgeoning to death every idol we might raise, is now furious with Red and Jean. They had been but one day in the Paradise his 14-billion-year-long preparation had laid out for them, and they had erected the deadliest idol of them all, and in the least accessible of places. Self is that idol, and its temple rears up in the middle of the soul. It was self-murder in the first degree. There was no room left "in the inn," as the KJV puts it, or to put it exactly, no shelter from God under the awning at the far end of the sheepcote.

God calls out to our miscreant Primogenitor now hiding with his wife, "Red, where are you?" This is not a substantive question. The Omniscient God cannot ask that kind of question. Rather, it is rhetorical, directing Red to answer the question for himself. It can be a dramatic question as well, merely stating a fact as a question, which is to say, "Red, look at where you are!" We do well to turn all our Joban questions into dramatic ones, like David turning "Why are you cast down, O my soul?" into "Don't be cast down, O my soul."

There is nothing new about shifting the blame, quite clearly evident from the pseudo-answers they whimper out. Nothing need be said, although I am amazed to hear how quickly and categorically Red changes his tune from "Bone of My Bone" to "The Woman Thou Gavest Me." Notice that they are still not talking to each other—not a word.

In God's curse upon the snake, we see a double audience, Red and Jean not included. They were never told that it was, after all, devil—possessed. Knowing Satan was involved would only have intensified their self-justification. The first audience is us upon the balcony observing the events. We are given what would fit the definition of a myth, viz., a popular explanation of a natural phenomenon. We are told why the snake moves on its belly. This will not satisfy the herpetologist, I know, but the Bible is not a book about snakes. It is a biblical fact that our Divine Creator has made snakes travel in the horizontal plain and belly-intimate with the dirt itself as a reminder that Satan is a pure secularist who wants man to slither through life alongside him, and most men do. So here we see the one negative reminder from nature. Otherwise, the heavens, day and night, declare the glory of God. Nature never urges us to embrace atheism, a disease most conspicuous among scientists. It is not nature or education that eggs them on, but their superior intelligence, a gift they have from God. Many scientists accept scientism as their religion because, in that way, they become the high priests. Paul laments, "The better I am to you, the worse you treat me." This irony is also present in secular Greek thought: "The gods shower gifts on those they want to destroy." Sad to say, but men can bear adversity better than they can prosperity.

The second audience is Satan himself, but we are invited to listen in. For the second time now, Christ is seen in the two narratives under consideration, once in the Creation Hymn, and now in God's triumphant proclamation that in the future, though Satan would inflict the coming Son of Red with a blow to the heel (the crucifixion), Satan would receive a blow to the head, a mortal blow.

Reader, recall that you and I are Red and Jean. As the gates to the Garden close, shutting us out of everything but the memory and the dream, God puts his arm around our shoulders and whispers: "I know your sorrows. I will come and save you. I will smite the snake on the head; I will crush his skull. But watch closely, for he will think he destroys me up there on the Tree of Life. Though I am a ceremonial lamb in appearance, I am really the Lion of the Tribe of Judah. And there will be no more curse . . . ." From our balcony, we see our prototypes, Red and Jean, in the words of the not-so-blind John Milton:

> "They hand in hand, with wandering steps and slow,
> Through Eden took their solitary way."

THINGS FOR THE SUITCASE

1. God created the universe; it didn't just happen.
2. God's creation is very good, but it is not complete yet; we must help God finish it, especially in our own lives.
3. Nature is not deceptive; she does not urge us to be atheists.
4. The greatest sin is not eating of the Tree of Life.
5. The worst kind of sinning is psychogenic.
6. Christ is the Tree of Life.
7. God is the River of Life flowing from Eden to the New Jerusalem.
8. Men and women are equal before God in sin and in hope.
9. As a result of Adam's sin, the universe is now a competitive place.

CHAPTER IV:
AFTER EDEN, WHITHER?

Our first parents commit their first sin, then disappear from history forever. They had other sins, of course, and many children during their 930-year tenure on earth. We know the names of three of them, but nothing more. Moses and God wanted us to focus on that one matter—the sin that explains why life is as it is, and not otherwise.

We learn early in the Bible that there are things God cannot do, things that involve his relationship with us. In an instant, he roared across the shoreless void, "Be light!" and there was light. It matters not to him that we measure that instant as 17,000,000,000 years, perhaps even longer. It is but a day with him. Yet when he sets to the task of creating gods like himself, that takes him a considerable amount of time in our world. You see, God needs peers, and he chooses us to work together with him for as long as it takes to get this task done.

What this epic adventure means for us is the subject of the next phase of our journey on the Christian Road toward the millennium sunset. Before we take one step in that direction, we must look at a few more verses in Genesis. We, like Adam and Eve, are not complete yet. We cannot understand what our natures are like, and what they need until a few more questions are answered. How about this knowing good and evil? How far can it go? Which way will it turn? Indeed, how serious is this thing we call "Adamic nature"? Cain waits to tell us—rather show us—the answer. Come, let us take our seats. The curtain is about to rise on Act I, Scene II.

Now that we are comfortably seated in the balcony, let me remind you that we cannot help but bring along our memories of what we know about all intervening events between then and now. Shortly, you may recall Elijah's challenge to the priests of Baal, and God's answer by fire. We cannot—indeed must not—attempt to see this narrative unfold as though we were mere citizens of Antediluvia. God intends that we always bring all we know to bear on the scene, so that we can help piece out the starved detail Moses must use. We are to participate in creating detail. We join the biblical canonist and God in pushing along the stylus that expresses eternal reality in alphabetic letters. It is a joy to celebrate these words that come from our Divine Lover across the millennia, who takes us by the hand and occasionally even whispers in our ear. We remind ourselves that we learn from what is not said—and why it is not said. In addition, our 21st-century knowledge helps us complete the Holy Gospel.

The scene before us is an open plain, not at all like idyllic Eden. It features only two altars of uncut stones in a grassy field. It must be about 50 years later. Cain and Abel are adults. We know only of the first day of their parents' lives, who were without any history at all when they disobeyed God. We do not know what kind of upbringing these men had. They likely knew of their parents' sins. There must have been a time of year when Adam and Eve offered a sacrifice to God, an animal's life as a way of symbolizing the life they forewent by disobedience, and also a way to thank God for their present existence. Then God would always answer by sending fire down from heaven to consume the offering. Their sons had often witnessed this event. Now Cain and Abel are to make their own sacrifices for the very first time.

How do I know this? I don't, but it is my way to satisfy myself about what is not said. It may be that our Grand Ancestor and his wife just intuited the need of making an animal sacrifice. This is what Paul concludes as he ends his masterful plan of salvation to the Roman Christians. He says, "We should present our bodies as a "living sacrifice," then follows it with this being "our reasonable service." Perhaps we ought to say that Abel had a revelation from God that this is what they should do. Why then is there no background information about the animal sacrifice? It seems to me that Moses is saying that it doesn't really make any difference. If the prescription came directly from God or from custom or instinct, it would not have made a difference to Cain. He would still have changed things to suit himself. That is what we must remember—Cain is in charge of his religion, not his parents, and certainly not God. My explanation about the origin of the animal sacrifice satisfies me—it fills a void in my own inquiring mind, and it does not contradict what I know elsewhere in Scripture. You should do the same for yourself, but always remember that such fill-in is no foundation for doctrine, no matter who supplies it.

As I just said, we come now to the second scene of Act I of the human drama. Our first exposure to theology is dynamic, not theoretical. Things acted out are more easily understood than those merely conceptualized, and they can also be narrated. I call this Scene II instead of Act II because the subject is identical in both scenes—the nature of sin—though interestingly enough the word "sin" hasn't even been mentioned yet. We must often be reminded that sin, like Satan (who can transform himself into an angel of light), has two faces—the deceptively beautiful one, and the realistically ugly one. It can appear as a beautiful fruit, blushing-pink, most odoriferous, velvety soft to the touch, full of valuable energy as the eye can plainly see; or it can be the stench of the rotting flesh of a murdered saint, left unburied alongside a bloody limb used to beat him to death—as hideous to describe as to contemplate. Recall Skull Place—human bones scattered all over the place, skeletons on crosses, picked clean by birds of prey. If sin has two faces, we had better see them both as clearly as possible—in our thoughts, in our pulpits, and on any street corner where thoughtless men pass. What Cain left behind him as he wandered off the stage of history is quite different from what Red and Jean left behind them—the remains of interdicted fruit on the mossy ground near the Tree of Knowledge of Good and Evil.

The curtain rises, but my treating theology as a drama is in a bit of trouble. The Sacred Script does not have enough stage directions. You see, Moses has not told us enough, especially about time and place. He says,

"In the process of time, it came to pass," but we do not know whether the offerings of Cain and Abel took place at the same time or in the same place. Indeed, we are not even told whether either knew of the other's offering, or that the animal sacrifice was consumed by fire while the grain offering was totally ignored. We had better not say, as I have heard some claim, that Cain was angry because Abel's offering was accepted and his was not. No, this is not a biblical fact. Why this omission? For that matter, why am I so "picky" about detail? First, because worship is, in the final analysis, personal and does not depend on what others do or do not do. In these days, when the sins of telemongers are as conspicuous as their televised harangues, and even lusty priests get exposed to public reproof, we had better be sure about this. "Let no man take thy crown" is as timely a warning today as it was when Jesus spoke to the Seven Churches of Asia. I am "picky" because I have the utmost respect for God's Holy Word. I read Scripture with the greatest attention and skill at my disposal. He who made the mouth will speak, as the Psalmist says, and he does not stutter or waste words.

We will treat the matters as Moses does—comparatively. We see the Garden Narrative and the Bloody Field Narrative side by side, the idyllic Paradise God wanted us to live in, against the environs of Nod with its wide gate and broad way that leads to hell just off stage left.

Cain is first to offer, and it is an offering—not a sacrifice—for it is of little value, which Moses dismisses with appropriate brevity: "of the fruit of the ground." Considering Cain's upbringing, this is a radical departure indeed! He had always observed the giving of a life for a life, the lamb's life given as a symbolic gift of one's own life, a ritual of parallel symbols, the substitute for the real. But Cain has reasoning power, the same conceptual knowledge his parents exhibited in the Garden. He uses this knowledge and his God-given willpower in worshipping God as he wishes. What he does is to use a symbol for another symbol of reality! He offers the grain as a symbol of the lamb, which is a symbol of his own life. So he is twice removed from eternal reality. In addition, what he offers as a symbol of a sacrifice is of no significant value. He thereby becomes an idolater of sorts, forsaking the prescribed ritual for an invention of his own—he idolizes himself. Martin Luther said that anyone who accepts part of the Bible and rejects the rest is no longer worshipping God, but himself.

But Cain is more than an idolater; he becomes the world's first ritualist. This is most wicked, one of the most popular crimes in public worship today. Its evil is in making a ritual, a wholly virtuous thing in itself, become the reality it is supposed to celebrate. He does not function as a priest does, as a celebrant, but as a ritualist. In other words, Cain is a substitutionist, a nominalist. This heretical role has always been a favorite with men. They fancy God wants to play games with them. The prophet Joel says "rend your hearts and not your garments," to Cain and to the high priest who concluded that the Son of Red was guilty of blasphemy and must be crucified. Men have until now, and will continue to have until the millennium sunset, the practice of submitting symbol for what the symbol stands for, to give God the ritual instead of the reality.

Cain also becomes the father of religion in general—not life, not the Christian Road, but religion such as we see surfacing all over the world as religion in its primitive state. I mean earth religion. He offers "fruit of the ground." Religion begins this way as one would suspect when man relates to the horizontal elements in his environment. Gaia, the earth goddess and Uranus, the sky god, copulate, and she bears Cronus, whose son Zeus murders his father. Whether from the Far East, Near East, Egypt, or elsewhere in Africa and Europe, the story is pretty much the same—earth and sky, sex and violence—the story is everywhere horizontal, hopeless and long-lived. Note how most Western cultures express a fondness for the old pantheons in their naming of things, as seen in the names of the days of the week and months: Tiu, Woton, Thor, Frigga and Saturn become Tuesday, Wednesday, Thursday, Friday and Saturday. Then there are the months: Janus, the two-faced Roman god gives January its name; March is named after Mars, the Roman god of war, even as Thor, the Teutonic god of war, inspires the name of Thursday. Here's a second duplication—Juno, Roman name for the queen of the gods, becomes the name for our month of June, even as the Teutonic queen, Frigga or Frieda, is the origin of Friday. One wonders why the Saxon nations kept these pagan names, whereas the Mediterranean nations choose many Christian names instead. Even the

Pope wears on his crown a name quite pagan in origin, and the holiest day in the Christian calendar (Easter) bears its name from Ishtar, the fertility goddess who was so often denounced in the Old Testament. We really ought to call the day that Christ rose from the dead, Resurrection Sunday.

Let us leave Cain—the idolater, ritualist, founder of religion—staring at his offering, waiting for God to answer with approving fire. Let us imagine a divided stage, which often occurs in modern drama. Abel does what is right. He makes the same offering as God told his parents to make. Remember that Moses, who later includes the Passover sacrifices and many other rituals, is our author and writes about 3,000 years after this Cain/Abel drama occurred. Note the description. Abel offers "of the firstlings," that is, the best of the lambs in the flock. This is in anticipation of the first begotten Son of God, who became God's choice among heaven's flock. Also, "and the fat thereof" is added, which was not only the symbol of prosperity (unlike today), but also a valuable commodity for fuel and food. This fat will add to the combustibility of the fire from above. Righteous Abel believes that, by giving his animal's life for his own life, he may give his life to God. He enters fully into this spiritual event. He and God both contribute to the climax—God's consuming fire.

While this is going on, Cain—whether he knows of God's immediate consumption of Abel's sacrifice or not—waits . . . and waits. No answer! What he had no doubt witnessed before in his parents' sacrifices does not happen. God "had not respect," i.e., he ignored Cain's offering. The radical offering is met with a radical response. Had God even sent a whirlwind to blow away his handful of grain or an earthquake to knock down his altar, Cain would then have had something from God to complain about and to justify whatever else his fancy might wish to try. But nothing happened, and he became angry with God. This must not be missed or interpreted as envying his brother. We need to see evil in its extreme—unmitigated pride. Something was between Cain and God, as it will be with each of us when we stand before the Great White Throne of Eternal Justice. His anger toward God moves him to drop his face and stare in the opposite direction, not uplifting his face, with eyes streaming with tears, brow knitted in empathic quest of some solution for what went wrong—no, nothing like this. Yet God, Love Himself, speaks to Cain. Our Divine Psychiatrist nudges Cain toward the healing course of action:

> Why are you so angry?
> Why are you staring at the ground?
> If you made the right offering, I would have accepted it.
> But if you are not doing the right thing, sin is lying at the door:
> He wants to gain control over you, But you must conquer him.

What is Cain's answer to the questions? No answer. He gives man's most common response. "Is it nothing to you, all ye who pass by?" pleads the dying Christ through the mouth of the prophet Jeremiah. That's right—nothing. But of course, there was nothing Cain could say or do. He simply stared downward. Note that God reminds Cain that he, Almighty God, is good, and thereby all the more intensifying Cain's badness. Then here, seemingly a little late, the word "sin" is spoken. It's Hebrew derivation implies "that which displeases," and later, I will define it as "that which deteriorates." For now sin is personified, as though it were some harmful animal biding its time to sneak in the moment Cain opened the door. Maybe Satan has returned and is coiled on Cain's stoop. We are not told, though he must be close at hand. Then the final warning to Cain, that he must not let this creature into his life. God implies that Cain can successfully bar sin's entrance into his life—and here is a message for all of us. I must choose. Am I to be Cain or Abel? Let us hear none of this nonsense about genetic inadequacies, environmental differences, or the current rage, "being culturally disadvantaged."

> And Cain talked with his brother Abel: and it came to pass, when they were in the field, that Cain rose up against his brother and slew him.

The opening clause of this one compound-complex sentence is painfully general. Though we must not waste time in speculations about what their dialogue contained, we cannot ignore it. Cain was already bitter and smoldering with resentment that was building up pressure within his soul. Given his frustration, he probably told Abel the outrageous way God had treated him. If in response to this frothy narration Abel tells Cain that God had immediately consumed his sacrificial lamb, we can imagine the insane fury that seized Cain. He grabbed a rock or a limb and beat his brother to death. He could not lash out at the message giver, so he silenced forever the message bearer. His response is what our progressive-thinking jurists are fond of calling "temporary insanity." I am sure this is true, but whether it is a justifiable palliative for a lesser sentence than hell is another question entirely.

At this point we must ask ourselves the question, why did Cain murder his brother? Keeping ourselves within the "givens" supplied by Moses, we are left with no other choice than simply to say *because Abel was there*—simply that. We know nothing bad about him, nothing that would cause anger in Cain. The murder of Abel appears to be without any motive whatsoever.

The Bloody Field Narrative parallels the Passion of our Lord Jesus Christ. In John 15, Jesus cautions his disciples for the last time that he is to be crucified. He cedes the illogic of his end by citing a Passion prophecy in two of David's great Messianic psalms—Psalms 40 and 69. "They hated me without a cause." Note that the quote does not say "without a reason," but "without a cause." Then during the mock trial, the High Priest calls for Pilate to execute Jesus. "Why?" What evil has he done?" Answer: "Crucify him! Crucify him!" which is no answer at all, just a repetition of Cain's response to God's rejection of his handful of wheat. Moses here gives us one of many foreshadowings of Christ in all his writings in Genesis, the Book of Beginnings, and in the detailed symbols of the rituals and ceremonies in his later books. In his final appearance (Luke 24), 40 days after his resurrection, Jesus identifies the location of most of the Old Testament prophesies about himself. They are the "law of Moses, the prophets and the psalms."

As we conclude our exposition, I remind you that The Garden Narrative and The Bloody Field Narrative are interfaced because they are the two faces of sin. One final point of comparison these two polarized faces of evil present is the tripartite categories of sin—the lust of the flesh, the lust of the eye and the pride of life. Indeed, we see the pride of life first, whereas it is last in the deceptively beautiful face in the Garden. It is Cain's logical choice of grain instead of God's revealed formula, a sacrifice of the best lamb of the flock. We see the lust of the eye in the empathic down casting of his face, when his anger of soul overleaps the threshold into the flesh, in much the same way the arousal of the fleshly desire often enters through the eye gate. Lastly, the lust of the flesh climaxes in the murder of his brother, the proxy of Christ, who claimed righteous Abel and us Christians as his eternal relatives.

After wrestling with this problem intermittently for many months, and given only what Scripture itself says, I have come to the conclusion that Cain's murder of Abel is the worst sin in the entire Bible. The law—Moses' Law included—makes distinction as regards degree of badness, usually determined by the complicity of the will and degree of cognition. This is to say that premeditated murder is worse than negligible homicide and manslaughter. How aware was the guilty party? Were there mitigating circumstances that make the crime less serious, or special circumstances that make the crime even more serious?

There is something else to consider. When Paul says he is chief among sinners, he does not mean that he is the sole occupant of the pinnacle of badness; there is "plenty good room" there for me and for everybody, as he says. So when I say Cain's sin is the worst in the Bible, I do not mean there is no room for any other sinner alongside him. There are Judases walking our streets. Dante is wrong by giving him a special place in hell. There are many Cains as well. Prisons are full of them, though most I suspect haven't been caught yet.

Consider for a moment those most responsible for the death of Christ. Paul says that, had they known what they were doing, they would not have crucified the Lord of Glory. It may well be that they, due to culpable ignorance, crucified a total stranger. During his trial, they could have asked him where he was born and did not, being content to identify him with the town in Galilee, which had the worst reputation in all Palestine. Indeed, could any good thing come out of Nazareth? While he was being nailed to the cross, Jesus called upon God to forgive these ignorant ones because they didn't realize what they were doing. I am sure Paul and the Roman Jews believed they were doing the will of God when they stoned Stephen. How rich indeed the blood of the first Christian martyr. From it sprang the most talented theologian in the entire Canon, and sent men back to Rome who, like Paul, would never forget the glory on Stephen's dying face as he beheld the Vision Beatific of his risen Lord. What's more, a number of those who stoned him were likely from the Synagogue of the Libertines in Rome, who were probably among the founders of the Church there.

In the most significant way possible (i.e., spiritually), Cain murdered God. In nearly all cases, our courts cannot judge *ante facto*, though it is possible. A man discovered his wife's secret lover and had a friend make two silver bullets, one engraved with the name of his wife and the other with the name of her secret lover. Quite by accident his wife discovered these bullets. Her husband was arrested, and sent to prison for a crime he obviously intended to commit—a rare case, indeed. However, Omniscient God, "whose eyelids try the hearts of men," can make *ante facto* judgment with total accuracy, just as he judged Cain. There is also proxy judgment, as when Christ said that how we treat his children is the way we treat him. Finally, Christ teaches that hatred is murder, so spiritually speaking, Cain murdered God. He committed first-degree murder in his own world, his own private microcosm.

In the *de facto* world, Cain murdered his brother because he could not do so to God. But let me ask the question, what if it became possible? What if God would come close enough for the likes of Cain to reach him? What would happen? The question is answered four millennia later.

Like a meteor that loses much of its substance as it approaches earth, so Emmanuel comes, plummeting out of his spiritual glory into flesh, then into the womb of a virgin. Phalanxes of angels in battle gear stretch clear across the starry midnight, singing good news of a second chance for the failed progeny of Red and Jean. He walks among us in the beauty of holiness, sparkling with the dews of his eternal youth. We endured his blinding love as best we could as long as we could while angels leaned over the banisters of heaven to hear him sing the Song of Songs. And the miracles—we almost forgot the miracles. Most men do. Where were his benefactors when he needed them most? "Cain" comes to the fore after Jesus' 42-month ministry. Strange, but Christ's virtue threatens their wealth and prestige. "Ah, ha! We baited him and he fell into our trap, as well he should, this carpenter from Nazareth, this Son of Red. Crucify him! Crucify him!"

From Adam to Cain, from stealing a fruit to God slaughter in one generation. Surely such juxtaposition of extremes stirs our sensibility to lament our own lot, to tremble at our potential and to fall prone before our Maker to beg his forgiveness for our sins, whatever they be.

TOWARD THE DELUGE

Now that we have seen the sin of Adam juxtaposed to that of Cain, we are ready to entertain a whole set of questions rising from the neutral statement that doesn't seem to go anywhere: "Knowledge of good and evil—that is the curse." It is a curse, indeed. It is as though God rearranged man's brain, so that one lobe was good and the other evil. The curse is man's inability to coordinate, and then to subordinate, in order for each to learn from the other. This is what happens if you become a stranger in Paradise, a half-made god in a world made for a complete god. As such, you will change the perfect world, or you must be driven out of it.

After Cain, the answers come so clearly and quickly. No humanistic efforts will make us new millennialists with a new reality, a new morality, a "bridge to the 21st century," as a recent American president put it. No, Cain is still our contemporary. We do not (as some have supposed) learn to identify good from seeing evil. We do not learn to do good from experiencing the painful results of evil. We do not learn it in our own experience or by seeing it work itself out in others. Cain convinces us at the outset what our knowledge of the subsequent 6,000 years on earth etches in granite and fills the etching with lead, as Job did—that man accepts without reservation whatever is this knowledge by description, this empiricism, this causal chain, this scientism, but refuses with equal fervor to let the cause proceed from one lobe of his brain to affect the other lobe. Cause and effect, but never the twain shall meet. This is moral schizophrenia, truly a crippled epistemology, a short-circuiting somewhere between the ego and superego. Listen to how Solomon describes this moral disease:

> Because sentence against an evil work is not executed
> speedily, therefore the heart of the sons of men is fully set
> in them to do evil. Eccles. 8:11

One more question: If we do not learn how to do good by seeing the results of doing evil, could our natures trick themselves into doing evil by seeing virtue as bad? Listen! The theological expert from Jerusalem has just finished his examination of the miracle performed by the "blasphemer from Galilee, Son of Red from Nazareth, who profaned the sacred and holy Sabbath." Listen—he speaks: "You were very fortunate in calling for me to look into this matter, for you are on the verge of being rained on with fire and brimstone for blasphemy, like the curse that fell on Sodom! Do you know that? Yes, yes, I admit this man was deaf and blind, and probably possessed by a devil, and that now he is fully healed. But we must remember that the Law is more important than mere people. This so-called Son of Red, coming from that God-forsaken Roman caravan stop, Nazareth, dares to rise up and break the Sabbath? How dare he? He has committed blasphemy. He is devil-possessed! That is why he healed on the Sabbath. In fact, because it is a triple healing, it is three times as bad as a single healing. I must conclude that he works his miracles by the power of a devil—no, worse than that—by Beelzebub himself, the prince of the devils! Moses says he must be stoned! Better yet, turn him over to the Romans and let those devils crucify him. Stoning is too good for him!"

In such a way Jesus became the enemy because of doing good. So the answer to the question is yes; men can talk themselves into believing good is evil, evil is good, black is white and white black. When they have colluded with Satan to this degree, Jesus says they have committed the unpardonable sin. They have perverted that part of their godliness that reaches the pardoner, their power of conceptual thought that knows how to rank values. They are now incapable of asking for pardon.

Let us look at our final passage in Genesis before we take up thematic approaches to those more positive concerns we will examine on our safari toward the sunset of the sixth millennium. I refer to the didactic piece of history in chapters 4 and 5. They take the form mostly of a genealogical table, like the ones that begin Matthew and Luke's Gospels.

We see at once that the forbidden tree of Eden is still with us. Abel and Cain were the good and evil; now the families of Seth and Cain bring us onward toward the world's first rainfall, the Great Deluge.

THE HOUSE OF CAIN	THE HOUSE OF SETH
Cain (architect, builder)	Seth
Enoch	Enos (men begin to pray)
Irad	Cainan
Mehujael	Mahalaleel
Methusael	Jared
Lamech	**Enoch** (translated)
Jabal, rancher/Jubal, musician/	Methuselah
Tubal-Cain, metalsmith	**Lamech** (father of Noah)

In the family trees, we notice two men in each with the exact same names, Enoch and Lamech. This makes us a bit uncomfortable because we know contrasting things about two of them, and we might confuse them. Enoch ben Cain appears as a name only, but Enoch in the Holy Family is of the highest order of saints, so holy that he was translated after 365 years of pilgrimage, seemingly a year for each day in the year. Incidentally, one of the non-canonical books associated with the New Testament bears his name, to which the natural brother of Jesus, Jude, seems to make reference in his brief epistle. We are certain, though, about its distinction of making history's first accurate statement of the length of our year. Notice that in the days of Enos men began to call upon the name of the Lord.

We should take special care also to keep the two Lamechs separate. They both finish their family line, and one is expressly notorious for his chest-thumping boast before admiring wives for taking control of his own destiny, and expanding the sevenfold vengeance God guaranteed Cain into seventy-and-sevenfold. He murdered a much younger man for attacking him and enjoyed doing so. He wanted everybody to beware of his prowess. However, he never got a chance to be as bloody a person as he wanted to be; he was the last of Cain's descendants and died in the Great Flood. He does serve his purpose of letting us know that humanity is getting worse. Jesus must have had this ditty of Lamech in mind when he used similar math—seventy times seven—on Peter, though with the opposite intent.

However, Lamech ben Methuselah, the father of Noah, ends his life and the antediluvian segment of the line of Seth with some sevens of his own. He was the son of the oldest of the patriarchs, whose grandfather outlived both of them, for Enoch never died but was translated. Lamech died at the age of 777. The numerological message is most conspicuous. Seven is the number of totality or infinity, so Lamech died after a completely fulfilled life. The last three members of the antediluvian segment of the Holy Family all have exceptionally long lives.

I am sure we will look askance at these conspicuous numbers and be tempted to think something might be wrong. Too much coincidence is evident, or so it seems. Scholars whose faith falters have suspected some kind of propaganda is used by Moses to make a point. They hold a theory I call "historical accommodation," such as is used in communist propaganda literature. Others choose "providential coincidence"; that is, they believe God told Moses to speak thus to make a point, even though the original numbers were not exactly that way. In the first view Moses lied, and in the second God lied! Yet faith feels quite comfortable with two Lamechs, one in Nod and one in the environs of Eden, one snorting revenge 77 times worse than the offence given, and the other living 777 years. It is the Book of Faith that we read. God is in charge of history. He does not need some after-the-fact alteration to get his message across.

I think here is the place to say a word about the fantastic ages of the antediluvian patriarchs. Several theories have been advanced, all of which reduce their ages to modern expectations. The only exceptional theory not only explains how these people lived so long, but also provides a rationale for the Great Deluge of Noah's day. The Canopy Theory, held by several reputable scholars of present as well as former times, states that the earth was once surrounded by a cloud of water vapor. Genesis 1 speaks of the sun and moon as "greater and lesser lights," and of the day as "evening and morning," thereby suggesting a refraction of sunlight by this canopy. Hence, there would never be total daylight or darkness. There was also no rainfall. When the flood descended, the rainbow appeared, seasons were appointed, day and night are first spoken of, fermentation of wine became possible, meat was made a part of man's diet, and the age of man was radically reduced. All these things indicate the presence of this ancient canopy of water vapor. In Antediluvia, the canopy kept out the harmful ultraviolet rays that later joined the animals and weeds in the ongoing struggle of life. Also worthy of note is what happened to these later patriarchs just before the flood. A little arithmetic will answer this problem. Lamech, the father of Noah, died five years before the Flood, and his distinguished father, Methuselah, outlives him by five years, placing his death in the same year as the Great Flood.

Two other comparisons can be made regarding these two separate branches of Adam's family—the evil branch of Cain, which will soon be destroyed in the Deluge in Noah's day, and the branch of Seth, which will continue on through Noah and his son Shem. Notice that only ages of the ben Seth patriarchs are given. Long life is a biblical symbol of God's blessing. It is not the only symbol, nor is it always present, though a possible measure. Christ continues the use of longevity as blessing through suggesting the fullness, or abundance, of life. John in the Apocalypse symbolizes this abundance by speaking of life as 1,000 years, exceeding Methuselah's life by 31 years. Of course, ages for the ben Cain patriarchs are not given because their line was ended with the Great Flood.

A second comparison involves historical asides—seeking a relationship with God through prayers, and the translation of Enoch in the Seth branch; the beginning of ranching, architecture, arts and sciences in the branch of Cain. Here is an interesting point for those who hold the notion popular among some Victorian thinkers that there is a relationship between art and morality. It is true that some great artists were devout Christians, but not enough of them to establish a pattern. Indeed, it would be easy to cite many poignant exceptions.

We also begin to see the place of the "world" in our lives by this seeming boon given to the descendants of Cain. We will look more closely at what we mean by the "world" in our next chapter, but we are prepared amply at this point to see the full dimension of the divinity to which we must aspire, and the depravity we must escape if we are to become compatible enough to live with our Holy Father throughout all Eternity.

We see that humanity worsens quickly. There is not a decent act or thought in Nod, or Enoch Town, or anywhere else in all Antediluvia, except in that one family where three sons are helping their father build the world's first ocean liner.

TWO KINDS OF KNOWLEDGE

I wish to pause to remind you of my intention to include only those essentials I will need for my trip into the millennium sunset. Hopefully, my judgment is representative enough to concern you as much as it does me. I have no time or talent to present a *magnum opus* of Christian theology or a cover-to-cover exposition of God's Holy Word. So with this limitation in mind and God's help at my elbow, I will share only my critical concerns with you. As I leave Eden, then see the events that indicate the degeneration of patriarchs all about me, I also see gradually emerging two kinds of knowledge.

I refer to the age-old division, usually called knowledge about or knowledge by description, and knowledge of or knowledge by acquaintance. I used to introduce this matter to my students like this. If I say, "The center on our basketball team is seven feet tall," I am using knowledge by description. Measure that colossal physique, and you will determine how accurate my statement is. Since we all agree on how many inches are in a foot, nobody could possibly disagree about the conclusion. However, if I say, "The center on our basketball team is the most thoughtful gentleman

I have ever met," you immediately see we have before us a whole new "ball game." Gone is our method of inquiry! Gone is any common standard by which we can measure the accuracy of what I have just said!

Here is another comparison: "God is called a shepherd in Psalm 23," and "God is a good shepherd." Here again are two kinds of knowledge. Existentialists call these two *discursive* and *presentational*, by which they mean that the shape is different, like a straight line (discursive) and like a sunburst (presentational). Sometimes, as you probably have seen in print, the pairs *I-it* and *I-thou* are used, respectively. Existentialists say mere things come to us in a straight line. However, when we meet a person, the mind jumps all over the place with a sunburst effect, something like the eye movement when one beholds a great painting. Imagine that your thought process looks like a string of Christmas-tree lights laid out on a table. What we think about during our workaday world is like the electric wire, and people are the lights. Professor John Baillie used to say, "Others are the real world, and all of life is meeting," others being the lights and our daily toil the wires that connect them. I like to compare these two kinds of thinking to walking and dancing. Studying theology is like walking; a personal meeting with Christ in prayer is not at all that tame. It is a dance of the soul, not at all unlike a sunburst.

Knowledge by description is the only tool of scientists, but they call it by another name—*empiricism,* or sometimes *universal determinism* or *the scientific method.* All these terms mean a belief that everything in the spatial- temporal continuum (including the very bodies we inhabit) is governed by cause and effect. For every effect there is an antecedent cause.

Some scientists become so comfortable living with this very simple formula that they became convinced that all life can be explained by their method and—now get this; it's a jump from science to religion—if it can't be measured and demonstrated by the scientific method, it doesn't exist! This religion is what many Christians call *scientism*, but its advocates enfold it in the high-sounding words, *logical positivism.* Like Cain of old, these ungodly users of knowledge by description have decided to take charge of reality. Their views are so prevalent among fellow scientists that one might say logical positivism is their occupational hazard. A personal friend who is a philosophy professor told me that the entire philosophy department of one of America's Big Ten universities is comprised entirely of logical positivists! This doesn't seem what a university (a unified study of diversity) ought to be, and there is nothing positive at all about this religion, for one of its main tenets is that all ethical standards are only relative. I'll let you guess how they feel about the Ten Commandments!

Scientism holds the behaviorist view of man, which is to say that man is the sum total of internal and external stimuli. William James expands the definition using a bit of tongue-in-cheek. He says it is difficult to imagine how the liver percolating its bile will determine whether I will be a Protestant or a Catholic. Some behaviorists believe consciousness is no more than a powerless observer watching the body carry out its functions. Some conclude nobody in the world exists except the one telling such nonsense to his imaginary audience.

Much of the inspiration for this nigh universal denial on our college campuses comes from Darwin and Freud, but it really got its rationale from a late Renaissance philosopher named Descartes, who proved to philosophers in general that the human mind is logically incapable of proving more than one thing logically: *cogito egro sum*—"I think, therefore I exist." Of course, Descartes would not agree with modern followers of scientism. If anything, his discovery should humble us, but it has had the opposite effect on these godless scientists. They trust all the more avidly in the conclusions their limited minds make, which really are nothing other than leaps of faith. They scorn the medieval academics/schoolmen for basing their conclusion that God exists on a major premise which cannot be proved, then turn around and do exactly the same thing!

Indeed, when Descartes is rightly interpreted, he leads us not to the slippery slopes of ethical relativism, but to the echoing of another Renaissance scholar of an entirely different ilk—Martin Luther. He summarized the conclusions of human logic as "that whore, reason." He alludes, of course, to the John's Apocalypse, chapter 17. The woman is clothed in scarlet and purple, and is seated on a seven-headed dragon, also scarlet in color. She is drunk, holding a gold flagon in her hand, filled with martyrs' blood that she has been drinking.

Christians must oppose this religion based on cause and effect. It is true that there is an undeniable sense of achievement in conducting highly sophisticated experiments in the laboratory, and predicting the results with precise accuracy—every time. We also like to hear the expected drum beat in a marching band or the rhyme at the end of a line of poetry. It's nice to expect something and then to get it. There is, however, so much of life that we cannot measure, like what will happen tomorrow, or how effective a teacher have I been? Then there are the games, more of them now than have ever existed at any one time in human culture. Games are like lab experiments, wholly prescribed, wholly predictable. How children— some in their 30s and counting—love ballgames, computer games, game shows on television! A professional football player seeking counsel as he sought to wiggle out of his third marriage said to me as we rose from prayer, "Wouldn't it be great if life were as simple as a football game?" Novel-reading and dramatic performances are, like ballgames, controlled abstracts of life. They do help us relieve stress, sometimes even inspire us to try harder. How encouraging these "heroes" are as they strut across the stage, always righting the world's wrongs. What's more, look at what we are willing to pay for the games we watch them play, and the games they help us play! Even kings' fools are paid as much, I suppose.

But religion is not a game, and scientism isn't the only religion snarled by this "logic-gone-wild." Consider a heresy hot from television called "prosperity theology." I heard one of its most popular sheep-fleecers say recently to his television audience that if they would send him $5 today, God would reward them by sending them $100 before the week was up. When I think of them, I am reminded of the Pardoner in the *Canterbury Tales*, or even the friends of Job. They taught that if we pushed the right buttons, God would act in a predictable way. This is nothing short of trying to control God—and he is not impressed.

Now we turn to knowledge by acquaintance. It introduces us to the world of persons, to vertical relationships, like those in the family of Enos, who began to call upon the Lord. Perhaps John Wesley best illustrates what we are now looking at. He had spent many years studying for the ministry but felt something was missing in his life. One day he had an experience with God Himself, and his heart was "strangely warmed," as he put it. It was as though he had moved from the house of Cain to the house of Seth, and this made all the difference in the world to him. "Man shall not live by bread alone," and man shall not live by knowledge by description only.

Freud believed the development of the libido moved upward through four stages: narcissistic, parental, heroic (homosexual) and heterosexual. Any person who stopped short of the last stage is described as, at best, sub—normal. But the Christian view teaches yet a higher stage, about which Freud had nothing to say—the agape stage—where God is, for "God is love." Might we not then consider anyone who has not risen above the fourth level as one of God's abnormals or spiritual inverts, as it were? What else can we conclude since we are made for God, and God is love? He is Divine Love. Indeed, to be in full possession of our nature and having eaten of the Interdicted Tree, we must now eat of the Mandated Tree.

Jesus said, "Devour my flesh! Drink my blood." This most daring of all metaphors is not a call to cannibalism, but one to experience Him who is the personification of all we are hoping for. He is light, bread, water, life, guidance. He is I AM, leaving your need to finish his name. I learn from Christ Himself that I must love God with all the ingenuity of my mind, the determination of my will, the affection of my heart and the strength of my body, and then—yes, in addition—to love my neighbor as myself. Do I? No, I do not. Paul says I must bring every thought into obedience to Christ. Do I? No, I do not—but I am trying; I will never stop trying. I cry out, "Judge me, O God, according to the integrity of my heart," as David, another sinner, said. I take great comfort from that man!

Now a question looms up before us—how long will it take me to go as far as I can to gain these ideal plateaus? Well, it took Abraham 175 years, Isaac 185, Moses 120, Methuselah 969, yet the Penitent Malefactor and St. Stephen hardly any time at all. You and God will work that one out. Work out your own salvation with fear and trembling. It takes a lifetime to break some bad habits, and as long to establish good ones. We pray daily for God's will to be done, knowing it will be done, whether we pray so or not. We do want his will to be done in our lives, we want to see it happening, and we want to help make it happen. We want to experience the bending of our wills to his divine will. We want to experience the ranking of our values according to the "plan given on the Mount." We must stop seeing men as trees walking, stop despising the day of small things. We want our acts of virtue to be so spontaneous that we will be bewildered at the Great Judgment when he ascribes virtuous acts to us we had long since forgotten.

How long will it take? A lifetime—God cannot do it in less time. The Omnipotent cannot because we are so limited, slow and reluctant to do our mandatory part. We are so minimally endowed that we will have to seek his aid every day in every way. Why? That is a Joban question I cannot answer, but I think it is because he loves us so much that he doesn't want a day to pass without our asking him to help us. Since we are to live forever with him and his saints, we must learn to bless the bars of our protective custody, to bear under the load and, as the Australian, trudging along the outback under all his earthly belongings, sings songs to his load, calling it "Matilda," so we must learn our own verses of the Song of Songs, and learn to dance the *Mahanaim*, "Between the Rows." Fellow marchers to Zion, we are still in the eighth day of creation, the day that started six millennia ago but is soon to end. It is the longest love story ever written. I am happy beyond words to be a major player in the plot.

We should be aware, though, of what is exasperating about vertical knowledge. It's not transferable, as knowledge by description is. Indeed, you may memorize all the names of the keys on the typewriter, but that doesn't mean you will then know how to type; you may learn how to read music in hardly any time at all, but after you do, you cannot sit down at the piano and play. Conceptual motor skills, like typing and piano-playing, require more than knowledge by description. Even so, knowledge by acquaintance is not transferable from father to son, from friend to friend.

More books have been written about Jesus Christ than about any other person. Yet reading all of them is not equal to knowing Christ Himself. In fact, the two things are not even in the same category. A person isn't even necessarily drawn closer to knowing him by reading all those books. Indeed, the opposite could be true. The more the high priest knew about Jesus, even from Jesus' own mouth, the further he was driven from him. There is no transfer merit from knowledge by description to knowledge by acquaintance. Neither can virtue be passed from father to son any more than you can buy a dime's worth of enthusiasm at the candy counter.

For this very reason there is no such thing as progress in history. We experience cultural accumulation and technical proliferation, but no true progress. People are not better persons in 2,000 AD than they were in 2,000 BC. Progress exists only at the personal level—progress is self-transcendence. Say I decide to walk from Chicago to San Francisco, each day walking 20 miles. At the end of a month, have I made progress? Not at all. But if I increase my speed and mileage each day, that would be progress. We must never imagine that the communication renaissance we are experiencing this very day will help us write better or improve the quality of our thinking. Indeed, the opposite is proving true. Television and computer games are doing their best to reduce us, as Fred Allen once said, to creatures with eyes as large as cantaloupes and brains the size of a split pea.

Knowledge by description is continuously accumulating, but knowledge by acquaintance always begins at zero. I have often called it vertical knowledge because above us is where it begins. We are the creation, and God is our Pattern Maker. One of the first trade secrets a carpenter learns is that one must cut a set of studs to a single template. Our Template is not far from any one of us. Recall that Adam and Eve, with their minimal experience, recognized immediately the voice of God, so unlike our modern-day, antiseptic, smock-clad, tri-focaled scientists who say, "I think it thundered!" I, too, have heard him speak. Each day, his voice is louder, clearer, always echoed by the message on the Sacred Page.

It is easy to share knowledge <u>about</u> with those who are willing to listen. I say, "God is Omnipotent," and that is knowledge by description. The scientist, though he may be an atheist, knows as clearly as Elijah or Paul about what that sentence means. But strange to say that when I say, "God is love," it is experienced as knowledge by description, except by the ones who know God personally. This commonly shared knowledge by acquaintance becomes what Scripture calls a "mystery." This is, after all, what knowledge by experience really is. It is mystery because it is remote, conditional knowledge. Man's will cannot generate it. The oldest song in our hymnal, by Bernard of Clairvaux, ""Jesus, the Very Thought of Thee," has in it this line that says exactly what I mean, "The love of Jesus, what it is/ none but his loved ones know."

So we were designed by God to hear his voice, and the quality of our acquaintance with him is the very best. If we start with Him, no man can take our crown, no matter how disappointed we may be about his behavior. Telemongers selling cheap religion and priests too weak to be examples for their flocks have nothing to do with my relationship with God. Imperfect patterns do no more than make the perfection of the Pattern Maker the more glorious. The arm of flesh will fail us, but underneath are the everlasting arms. We expect the highest quality in our relationship with God. As St. Anselm says, "He is that Being than whom none could be conceivably greater." The existentialists speak of the presentational experience with persons as being like a sunburst. Scripture calls the light that glowed on the face of Moses, the "glory" of the Lord, and we do not hear enough about this glory, this beauty we behold in the face of Christ, which Stephen saw as he was dying beneath a hail of stones. In sculptures we see shafts extending out from holy faces to suggest rays of holy light, as there are haloes in paintings. In Scripture—especially in Psalms, Isaiah and the Apocalypse of John—we find teachings about God's glory.

There is one strong point of aesthetic theory I would like to end with. It relates directly to the beauty of God and Christ. I refer to "signification in art," which is to say, a work of art is beautiful because it reminds us of some moral perfection. So what reminds us of virtue is beautiful! For me, beauty has always been a matter of balance. There is beauty in the four cardinal virtues of the Greeks: prudence, temperance, justice, fortitude. What do they all have in common? Balance. I have seen the beauty of the Almighty. I have seen Christ, as the Psalmist did in his stupendous 110th offering, "in the beauty of holiness." Paul saw him on the Road to Damascus, and later when he was caught up into the third heaven, and there beheld visions beyond the laws that govern grammar, syntax, semantics and logic. Yet what captivates me is the daily portion of this glory that awaits me in my private place after I have shut the door. And the glory grows. Best of all, I have the promise of seeing him soon in his unmitigated glory.

CONCLUSION

In Chapter III, the Genesis writings of Moses introduced two innate attributes needed to bring us at last to the peerage of Almighty God, our Divine Lover—conceptual thought and willpower. These two qualitatively relate to the omniscience and omnipotence of God. We are like him, so we have his attributes.

In Chapter IV, beyond the confines of Eden, another attribute is introduced which has the unique feature of needing to be developed by us with God's help. Such development takes time and effort from us both. This attribute is knowledge by acquaintance (knowledge obtained by subjective experience). In the Christian sense, this subjective knowledge expands our awareness and concern for others, beginning with God and reaching out to others among our eternal peerage. It is seen in the desire of Abel to connect with God by using the method described by God. Then in the line of Seth, men began to pray to God, while Cain's descendants built towns, forged metals and designed musical instruments. Enoch "walked with God" so perfectly that he was translated. He had perfected knowledge by acquaintance. Noah, Moses tells us, had the same reputation.

In Chapter V, we will focus our attention on the curse of God upon the race of mankind. For now, we leave the narrative in Genesis and turn to Solomon's inspired essay, Ecclesiastes, to examine the tool God uses on us as we work with him in developing the final attribute. We must change the world by finishing the work of Jesus Christ. We must be creators.

FOR THE SUITCASE

1. I can be Cain or Abel; it's my choice.
2. It is possible for man to believe good is evil, and evil is good.
3. Man's curse is a willingness to live with good and evil.
4. Never let ritual become the reality it celebrates.
5. Man's logic is extremely limited.
6. Scientism is a religion that denies the validity of religion.

7. Some use religion in an attempt to control God.
8. It takes a lifetime to get ready for Eternity.
9. Progress is self-transcendence.
10. Knowing about God is never the same as knowing him personally.

Chapter V:
The Road Home

When our first parents disobeyed God, the universe about them changed into an unfriendly, competitive place, and that change generated a change in them. God also changes, though he is immutable. When we speak of things beyond our comprehension, we should not think it strange that we must contradict ourselves by lapsing into oxymoron. Remember, the Scripture says several times that the Immutable and Eternal God repented. But what this means is that men changed toward God, and that change drew upon a different aspect of his nature. That is to say, he functionally changes, not intrinsically.

Even so, Adam and Eve tampered with Divine Will, and then God needed to repair the damage by altering the relationship he had with them. He "changed his mind" about where they were to live, forcing them into a place where half-right Mr. Darwin says we have to struggle to stay alive, and only the fit survive. So they, like God, changed functionally, though not intrinsically.

Why haven't men improved our lot over the intervening six millennia? Some will rush forth and claim we have improved. The first thing they cite is education. For example, they point out that 94% of Americans read. Yet still, after six thousand years, 80% of the world's population is illiterate, and half the world goes to bed hungry each night. I must add, what has education and the highest standard of living the world has ever known to do with getting rid of evil? When I first began studying German, I went to a German restaurant. After translating the menu and ordering dinner, I noticed an inscription on one of the exposed rafters above me. I struggled through to the message: "Liquor, money and education have never made a fool of any man; but each, in turn, has given the natural born fool a larger stage and a bigger audience."

I am sure a German wrote that bit of folk wisdom. Yet where were the educated and powerful in Hitler's Germany when they were critically needed? In one of the world's most talented nations, all the cultural talent in and about them meant nothing. Education, talent and power have nothing to do with getting rid of evil. In fact, they almost always do the opposite. Who is more capable of harm, an ignorant or an educated evil person? I used to tell my freshmen each fall that they must not expect their professors to give them truth and virtue. We give them facts, and truth is the pattern each presses upon those facts. It's their responsibility to develop that pattern. Our task is to enlighten and inspire; they and their God will have to develop the truth and virtue.

But which truth? This was asked by a frowning Pilate. This was only a dramatic question, of course, no more than a statement anticipating an unsatisfactory response. He essentially said to his Holy Listener, "What? You, too? Everybody claims to know what truth is, and nobody agrees. I'm not the least bit interested in what anyone says about the subject!" As he turns away from the silent Christ, we Christians shake our heads in sorrow. Who hath believed our report? To whom has the Arm of the Lord been revealed? These words from Isaiah go through our minds. We know the answer to his question. Truth is a Person walking among us today, just as he did when he pitched his tent among the ancient Jews. He told us God is Love, then he showed us how Love lived so perfectly that he was Love Personified. He fulfilled the prophecy in the Holy Books. Then he tricked us by proving what we didn't want to know, exactly how far Love would go. He uninhibited the likes of us to the degree that we responded just as Cain would have done, by killing him in the most despicable way possible. So now we know about Love.

Well, Pilate, that is the Truth—and he called himself Truth, too. He was Truth in action. Accepting him as our Glorious King would change this world back into the Paradise God made for Adam. He would do it overnight. But men do not believe Jesus was God-among-us. They are not interested in Divine Love. They keep as far away from it as they can. They are satisfied with their own way of life.

I would like to push the "refresh" button for a moment. We need to look again at what I spoke of in the last chapter, moral schizophrenia (the Greek word meaning "split mind"—exactly what relates to the Interdicted Tree, Knowledge of Good and Evil). Man has been trying and failing for the past 6,000 years to learn good *from* evil and it hasn't happened yet. I did not say that men have failed to define evils and virtues, but that they have not turned our negative knowledge of evil into good behavior. One reason for this (introduced in the last chapter) is that the virtue generating from our experience with God does not pass from father to son, from friend to friend. Each person begins at zero. Since such moral improvement is so rare, it seldom has moved the general public upward; even when it does occur, it is for a decidedly short duration.

In addition to this inborn limitation on moral progress, there are other problems taller than the Twin Towers of the World Trade Center in New York City that directly contributed to their destruction. Everybody admits there is good and bad in the world, but some have managed to strike a balance, leaning back and doing nothing about this lamentable status quo. In fact, they have become accustomed to conforming their minds to it. Like the high priest of Jerusalem, they would destroy anyone who might upset it. "Am I my brother's keeper?" they say. Others may agree about a certain evil, proposing ways to overcome it. Then along come opponents and say that the evil is not so bad, maybe even good, or that its good outweighs its evil, *ad nauseam.* Then some come along, victims of the time-laps deception Solomon spoke of, viz., "Because sentence against an evil work is not executed speedily, therefore, the hearts of the sons of men are fully set in them to do evil" (Ec. 8:11). These litigious fellows ask you to prove that gambling and free love debilitates society. Show them a piece of salacious writing, and they say, "This is not pornography! This is art!" Others join in, "Haven't you heard about our sacred freedom of speech guaranteed by the First Amendment?"

Finally, there is a growing group of souls lost in a world of game—playing and hero-worshipping, distancing them from reality so thoroughly that they feel overconfident about life, and are thereby made the more vulnerable to its temptations, and more certain to fall into its disasters. If they are not victimized by bad art, then they are sucked in by simplistic telemongers who present Christ as one who came to make life easier rather than better.

Why go on? Men do not get the message. No more than a few ever will. Jesus tells us why: "Go in through the narrow gate. For wide is the gate and broad the road that leads to destruction, and many there are who go that way, because narrow is the gate and difficult the road that leads to life, and few there be who find it." Note that Jesus has nothing to say about the nature of the broad road. Proverbs 14:12 gives us a clue as to why. "There is a way that seems right to a man, but the end of it leads to death." There are many characteristics of that road—one's own road that seems right and as unique as it is different, but it has one thing in common with all other roads, the same destination—death. The nigh infinite variety that is in man comes to a common destiny. This, of course, does not sit well with men. They can't stand God being categorical with them. Do people believe their religious philosophies, life styles, systems of priorities—whatever word one chooses—these roads they walk are destroying themselves and lead to damnation? Not on your life!

Of the other road, Jesus states two characteristics. The road to eternal life is *restrictive* and *difficult*. The KJV says, "strait and narrow," a poor combination, for both mean the same thing in modern English. "Narrow and difficult," I believe, is precisely what Jesus means. Men will have to admit they are 100% wrong about life, and that the road to eternal life will be difficult to follow. One difficulty is immediately obvious. Those who walk the road to life will be in an overwhelmed minority. They are devoted to loving God and their neighbor. But men don't want love. It obligates their conscience. They will dislike you if you love them. If they can't escape being around you, they will show you their displeasure. The closer your love comes to perfection, the closer you will be to crucifixion. I say this on good authority.

To this point we have seen all but one characteristic of our divinity. As I have said, we have all the attributes of God—all of them, though in a lesser degree. Theologians have listed up to a dozen or so. There is some disagreement about the matter, and some theologians offer the possibility that God has others that we cannot yet know anything about. We will concern ourselves only with the two kinds we do have clear knowledge of, the transcendent and the immanent. The transcendent include, among several others, the spirituality and immutability of God. We have never experienced either of these because we have always had physical bodies, and change is the essence of living in such bodies. There are immanent attributes we burgeoning gods must have, expressed in the four characteristics Moses has presented so far: 1) conceptual thought and 2) willpower, which were demonstrated in the Garden Narrative; then 3) acquaintance, the subject of our last chapter, and now 4) creativity. We see it in the first sentence of the Bible, "In the beginning God created . . . ."

So, with God and "by the sweat of our faces," each of us must create the synergistic miracle of a new self. Life never stops with a new birth; that's but the beginning. Moreover, we must also help Christ finish his ministry. We must never forget that man interrupted God in the Garden of Eden by choosing the wrong tree, and then during Christ's ministry, man interrupted God again in the Garden of Gethsemane. He pitched his tent among us and lasted only three and one-half years, 42 months, 1,260 days. It is the task of each of us to enter into the project of finishing his work and bringing his advent to a seven-year fullness, parallel to the seven millennia in God's great plan.

Let us take an overview of the road ahead, fading into the lengthening shadows of the millennium sunset. It is coming toward us steadily, ever reminding us of the gathering glory just beyond our knowable horizon.

WE GET A NEW OLD TESTAMENT

For those Christians who are able to escape the demands of life long enough to dig a little more deeply into Scripture, there comes a time when we see conflict in versions of the Old Testament. Remember that those who wrote the New Testament had only the Old Testament to preach from. They preached from Isaiah, Psalms and examples from the great narrative passages of Moses and other historians in the Sacred Canon. Strange to say, the texts they quoted were not their own translation from Hebrew into New Testament Greek. Rather, they quoted from the Septuagint, the name given the translation made by 72 Hebrew scholars at the request of Ptolemy, the general Alexander appointed to rule Egypt after his death. This translation was popular among Empire Jews, whose native tongue was Greek. During New Testament times, the Septuagint (Greek for "seventy") was even used in Palestine. Since Gentiles were knowledgeable of Greek, the New Testament canonists used this Bible exclusively. Indeed, all the verses they quoted from the Old Testament were taken from the LX X, the customary abbreviation for the Septuagint.

I have included this bit of textual history to explain why some of my quotations differ from the KJV, even why some of the verses it uses in the New Testament differ from its own translation of the Old Testament! For example, have you noticed the spelling of names, like "Noe" instead of Noah? Also, in Jesus' interview with the rich young ruler, note that his citation of the Ten Commandments expresses the puzzling inversion of commandments VI and VII. "Thou shalt not commit adultery" occurs before "Thou shalt not murder." Nobody knows why the 72 Septuagint scholars made this change. Some think they had a manuscript available to them that now is lost.

I hasten to add that, even though we find unexplainable differences between the Hebrew and Greek Old Testaments, there is no theological inconsistency or, worse yet, contradiction. The situation between these two versions of the Old Testament is the same as confronts us in a comparative study of the Synoptic Gospels (Matthew, Mark and Luke) in that though there are substantive differences, there are no theological inconsistencies whatsoever!

As I said at the beginning of our spiritual inventory, I want to make as fresh an approach to our study as possible, avoiding biblical cliché as much as possible. One thing I intend to use to accomplish this objective is to draw upon textual references from often neglected sources. This will become increasingly apparent as we examine more closely the nature of the road we sons and daughters of Red and Jean have been on, and will continue to endure at times as Jesus warns us. It is narrow and difficult. Still, when we see it is our own fault that the road ahead has to be this way, we will sing the more loudly as the shadows across it give way to the glory that is before us.

Have you ever wondered why Jesus gave us those wonderful laws of the marketplace in Luke 16, and even shocked us with the worldly advice of "making friends with the mammon of unrighteousness?" Then he even condemned the man to whom he entrusted one gold bar because he didn't invest it! To show you how consistent Jesus is here with the Old Testament, I want you to look with me at a passage from Ecclesiastes. It was written by Solomon, that famous natural ancestor of Christ, who authored this brief essay on philosophy. It anticipates approaches made by ancient Greek philosophers and many others up to this present day. Those views that he doesn't denounce summarily, he dismisses as inadequate for the abundant life. By the way, there is a great deal of difference in translation between the LX X and the modern Hebrew text, most of which is due to the primitive language this genius needed to use to speak of philosophy, the most abstract of subjects. Be amazed as you read the metaphysical statement he has to make about our spiritual makeup.

ADAM GETS A GUEST

> I have seen the difficulty God has given the sons of men
> to be exercised by it. He has made everything beautiful at
> his time, yet he has set the world in their heart so that no
> man can find out what God does from the beginning to
> the end. (Ec. 3:10-11, LX X)

This terse observation anticipates the famous statement of William James about metaphysics, our investigation of the identity and nature of what exists. As a pragmatist, he concludes such is a worthless study because every avenue of intellectual inquiry ends up in a cul-de-sac, like deciding on which came first—the chicken or the egg—or how many angels can stand on the head of a pin. He says that metaphysics is a lion's den into which all footsteps lead and from which none return! Nice commentary on Solomon's essay, isn't it?

But before we relate this quote to the Christian Road, we must settle on two definitions which determine its meaning. They are, as you might suspect, *world* and *heart*. The word "world" presents a minor problem because Solomon's emphasis is different from that of the New Testament. In his day, nearly every man and surely all slaves, indentured servants and hourly laborers worked 12 hours a day, six days a week. Only about one percent, if that many, worked less than that. People who could read were so rare that the average person lived all his life never having seen a book or someone actually read one. Most people were buried within a few miles of where they were born. The world meant one thing to them—hard labor.

The New Testament was written at a time when people could at least see, if not enjoy, the pleasures of the world. In some instances people could even come to love the world. So the average understanding of *world* in Solomon's day meant the workaday world, but in New Testament times it meant the world's pleasures. Jesus on one occasion blended them, which is especially applicable today when a workaholic may be married to a full-blown hedonist. He said in his Parable of the Soils that the thorny soil represented people who were overwhelmed by the cares of the world ("age" in Greek) or by the deceitfulness of riches. So the world involves the pain of living (which we cannot avoid) or its deceitful pleasures (which we cannot ignore).

We have another problem—one of translation; a problem of blowing definition way out of proportion. I refer to C. I. Scofield, whose work I would quietly pass by, except that he has presumed to take up the quasi—sacrilegious practice of putting disputed information via footnotes in Holy Scripture, thereby leading many astray. Not only did Dr. Scofield make a difference between "Kingdom of Heaven" and "Kingdom of God," but also between the words *kosmos* and *eon,* the former meaning "world" and the latter "age." When Jesus spoke of those who backslide because of being preoccupied with the "cares of the age," does he mean his age only? Of course not. He means every age. It is best, then, to use a word inclusive enough to apply to all the readers. The word "world" meets that need. The same applies to the Great Commission at the end of Matthew's Gospel, ". . . and lo, I am with you always, until the end of the world." Dr. Scofield takes exception to the KJV translation, preferring the Greek in its most literal sense, ". . . until the end of the age." Now we ask, which age is Jesus speaking of? Certainly not only the age the apostles are living in. The Greeks have no word for eternity. Instead, they use the term *age of ages*. No root word for "eternity" ever emerged from their language. The meaning is clearly that age which is more important than other ages, like saying Christ is King of Kings. In what way does this age Jesus speaks of rise in status above the others? In the only way possible, in the one thing we know about them, viz., the duration of time. So the phrase "age of ages" means "the timeless age," or "forever." Greek and Hebrew use some terms more "loosely" than scholars who yield to the temptation to exaggerate just to create something new. We should concern ourselves with today, the realities that begin and never end, leaving the worries and calendar of future events to our Lord. I note that the word "eternity" occurs only once in the entire Bible.

In truth, the Hebrew word in question could be translated "eternity" as well as "world." It means "ongoing reality." But the KJV translators chose "world," as did the LXX translators. Still others, no doubt troubled by the New Testament prohibition about the world, insist on "eternity." There is no doubt eternity is "in our hearts," but such a substitution has no meaning when one attempts to relate it to the remainder of the sentence. How would the desire for eternal life serve to limit our perception of reality? One would suppose the exact opposite. However, the world, i.e., the workaday world, not the carnival world, becomes so close to us that we cannot argue back to the beginnings nor onward to the endings of things. The "sweat of our faces" has blinded us.

In the category we call the world, we must also include our bodies, the beautiful planet on which we live, and the universe out there that stretches out to such incomprehensible size that our minds cloy from exhaustion and leave us staring blankly into nothingness, like an empty-headed idiot. Solomon says elsewhere in Ecclesiastes that such contemplation makes our faces flush with awe, and that to be unimpressed is to earn the world's hatred (LX X). We must look again more thoroughly at our bodies, which have a philosophy of their own, and also "Mother" nature.

The word "heart" scarcely needs a definition, yet our understanding is too limited if we stop with making the heart a matter of affection or emotion only. Men knew even before the late Renaissance physician Harvey discovered its true function that, when it stops, we die. Since the heart is in the center of our bodies and so conspicuously associated with life, we can easily see how it is a symbol of the whole being.

In this vein, I cannot help but think of that fascinating word *holism,* which is a belief that the whole is greater than the sum of its parts. My first teacher of composition said something I will never forget. It was on the very first day of the twelve years I would spend as a college student. He said, "When you write one sentence, that's a matter for science, the science of grammar; but when you write two sentences, you have three things, the third being the artistic relationship between the sentences." I was destined to return to this deep, deep saying many times and in varying contexts later in life. We read often in Scripture of serving God with "whole heart and whole soul," which actually means "heart" with a synonym added for emphasis.

So we see that Adam gets a "guest," even though it takes a bit of imagination to see the workaday world as a guest. It is more like the cow bird that lays its eggs in other birds' nests. A victim of this supplanter seems quite content to raise another bird's chick as her own, being none the wiser. Abraham Lincoln was caught with a book propped between the handles of his plow so he could read while working. His uncle who hired him for an honest day's work said, "Didn't your father teach you to love work?" to which the 17-year-old sage replied, "Well, my father did teach me to work, but he never taught me to love it." So this "guest" is such by where he is, in the heart, but he is often anything but loved.

Why did God do this to us, especially when one considers the results involved? God put so much work in our hearts to exercise us, and though everything is beautiful in its time, we cannot know when that time arrives because we have to know the beginning and end to know how well it fits in. Timeliness and its beauty are denied. What God causes or allows to happen has its place in our lives, and that place and even the time when it comes has a beauty of its own.

Perhaps Solomon sees the world as Jesus saw it, as a distractor from and distorter of reality. This sweat, we ponder, is not what life is all about, is it? A good night's sleep is not all I get from wielding an axe all day long, is it? Or in a New Testament context, is a hangover my reward for a night of chambering and wantonness? Indeed, God has withheld these answers to the disquietude rising from our uninvited guest. Why? So we will be so exercised by our disappointment that we will turn to him for our answers. Our jealous Lover wants to be the only channel through which we receive any and all things beautiful and sublime.

The question for us is not whether we will be "worldly," but how worldly? Which kind of worldliness will it be? Is it possible for us to call our guest by some euphemistic name, like Matilda, and then write a song about her funny side?

A VISIT TO OUR PSYCHIATRIST

Just before we get into this most important matter of the nature of the work before us Christians, we must be absolutely sure we are fully equipped for the toil and the trip yet before us. Isaiah cautions us that not everybody will be able to get on the highway of the Lord. Nothing that defiles, nothing unclean, no ravenous beast shall travel on it. Indeed, are you weak enough for the trip? Paul tells us of himself that when he is weak, then he is strong. Are you ignorant enough to seek advice? The way is difficult, we are told, and there are many carnival barkers along the road to tempt us into Bypass Meadow, or the Slough of Despondency, or to spend the night in Doubting Castle. There are also other weaknesses that will drive us to our Omnipotent Lover for strength.

William James in his great classic on religious experiences said there are two kinds of religions, the religion of the healthy soul, and the religion of the sick soul. He tells us what I already know, though my ego at times smarts when I think of it—that Christianity, the Road of Life, is for the sick soul. But of course! My own memory condemns me. I wasn't 18 years of age before I realized my life was headed toward suicide, inadvertent or deliberate. I think one of America's self-made billionaires was dead right when he said that Christianity is a religion for losers. I agree. That is precisely why I came to Christ. I was lost. I was the Prodigal Son. We Christians should never hesitate to admit this. If you are still iffy about the matter, it will not be long until you learn that you owe everything you have and are to the salvation of Jesus Christ, and to him only. What is salvation, anyway, but being saved from what would destroy you?

So let us go to our Psychiatrist for an internal inventory. Our trip on the Christian Road should often give us need to consult him, for he is our designer, sustainer and destiny, as well as one who will give us an accurate diagnosis and effective therapy for all our problems, psychological and otherwise, and without price. How foolish we are at times, forgetting who Jesus Christ was and is! Even if we don't forget, at least we act as though we do. God came to earth and told us how to live. Then he demonstrated what he taught. Shouldn't our lives involve significant effort in Bible-reading? I will have much to say later about the daily contact—prayer—that fits hand-in-glove with the written contact.

I wish to direct your attention to the personality configuration common to all of us "sick" souls, who because of Christ Jesus' ministry among us, are sustained as the most healthy-minded people on earth, and will remain so as long as we derive our strength, our *raison d'etre,* from him!

I refer to The Beatitudes in the Sermon on the Mount, which I call "The Gestalt of the Redeemed." I once contemplated writing a book about the Sermon on the Mount. I talked about doing so with a publisher who is a personal friend, but he dissuaded me. He said, "They don't sell well." Why? I have asked myself this so many times. It has to be that the subject, called by one the "Propaganda of the Great King," was either not adequately presented, or people in general are not adequately prepared to study the matter. Perhaps people are just forgetting who is speaking, which alone should make this sermon the most important speech ever given. Yet I almost forgot—the world is upside down. If men can believe the Devil can open the eyes of the blind, they themselves are too blind to recognize God speaking from his Omniscient lips.

I call the Beatitudes, which are defined as conditional blessings, The Gestalt of the Redeemed. Gestalt psychology, named after the psychiatrist who first advanced its practice, is based on holism, the belief that the whole is greater than the sum of its parts. It means that we must avoid isolating features of the mind to interpret them. We must consider all of them together, thereby discerning features that we could not otherwise see. Jesus gives us eight characteristics that make up the personalities of people who will come to him. In true Gestalt fashion, we must insist that the Christian have all of these, or he has none of them. They constitute an integrated whole. I list them parallel to the Gestalt of the ungodly person.

GESTALT OF THE REDEEMED

The Elect	*The Ungodly*
1. humility	1. pride
2. regret	2. optimism
3. meekness	3. aggressiveness
4. desperation	4. self-satisfaction
5. mercy	5. revenge
6. sincerity	6. expediency
7. peacefulness	7. indifference
8. determination	8. determination

Quite painfully, I must restrict myself to a few remarks about this gestalt. It deserves a book—several books—but such elaboration, edifying though it would be, is not here possible. I assure you that this is my list based on the words of Jesus as recorded in Matthew's Gospel. Though I have thought long about this matter, still I am not wholly satisfied with my terms. Then there is the second list. I do not mean by "ungodly" that the unregenerate souls in the world are in hot pursuit of doing evil, as the term in pedestrian usage might suggest. I have to call those who have not yet discovered Emmanuel something, so I use the biblical term to designate them. The term is quite adequate, for most men live as atheists, without any input into their thinking and living from God. Note that I list one thing common to both the elect and the ungodly—determination. It follows that, if men respond to you for being humble, regretful, meek and desperate for finding and doing what is right, merciful, sincere and peaceful by insult, slander and even inflicting bodily harm on you, they match your determination to serve Christ, no matter what the cost.

As you look at my list, you will soon see that it is in two parts, just like the Ten Commandments. The first four relate to our personal experience with God, just as the first four of the Ten Commandments do. The second four involve our relationship with our fellow men, as do the remaining six of the Ten Commandments. One might form the first list into a set of questions: Who am I? How do I feel about myself? How am I supposed to relate to God? How do I spend of my life? And the answers are as short as the questions: I am a total failure, especially when I compare myself to my Lord Jesus Christ. This makes me perpetually dissatisfied with myself. I am silent before my Maker, willing to do whatever he tells me to do. I will seek whatever means possible to discover what is right and then to do it.

Let us go quickly through the list, with a word or two about only those items that might be misunderstood. The rest I leave for you and me to work out for ourselves. I have memorized them, recite them at least once a week in my closet. But my task here is to explain. The exhortation lies within us personally. God will see to it that we are adequately reminded, convicted and chastised. The synergistic miracle of our rebirth is ongoing. God holds the mirror to our faces. I have but a bit of polish to apply.

The first beatitude is the antithesis of that sin that flung Satan, erstwhile called Lucifer, from the ramparts of Glory. It is the pride of life, the choosing of one's own universe, one's own ranking of values. We are dressed, we ragamuffins are, in the filthy tatters of personal failure. We look to that life than which none could be conceivably more virtuous, and are silent. Perhaps our greatest desire is a desperate need to be needed. Yes, we must help each other wear the weeds of our common despair with the greatest dignity possible. Our "hungering and thirsting after righteousness" means attending church (not listening to the harangue of some telemonger), Bible-reading and prayer. Note that the Greek uses participles, "hungering" and "thirsting," an ongoing experience, like another shortcoming of the KJV, found toward the end of the Sermon on the Mount, which speaks especially of prayer, ". . . for the *asking* receive, the *seeking* find, and to the *knocking* it shall be opened." Jesus makes special emphasis on being merciful toward others, listing it here, in the Lord's Prayer, and as a comment following that prayer. Indeed, what is more symptomatic of pride than retaliation, treating others exactly as they treat you—or even worse, like Lamech ben Cain, 77 times worse?

The expression "pure in heart" does not mean sinless, as one might suppose at first reading. As enviable as that objective would be, Jesus does not ask the impossible of us. Nor does it mean "perfect in intention," which gives our rationalization too much latitude. Rather, it simply means "sincere." Perhaps Jesus meant the opposite of "opportunistic," using other people, manipulating them for one's own purpose—in effect, cannibalism, as it is often called in the Old Testament and flagrantly practiced on a daily basis by those who sell illegal drugs. Notice that being sincere occurs between two other beatitudes which involve temptations to be opportunistic, viz., in handling others' abuse of oneself and in peacemaking, or helping a second and third party to reconcile differences.

Finally, consider meekness for a moment, the most misunderstood beatitude of all, which because of its location and its attending promise, seems all the more unrealistic. It comes just before Jesus' exhortation for us to be aggressive, to hunger and thirst—or as the Greek has it, the "hungering and thirsting after what is right." Then if we are meek, we inherit the earth? Well, indeed, this seems logically contrary to reality. If you are meek toward the earth, you are likely to starve by giving your fields to the weeds. If you are meek in the workplace, your competitor will stomp you into the ground. If you are meek toward the malefactor, lawlessness will overwhelm society. If you are meek toward your children, you are crippling them for life in a world that isn't at all like you. However, if you are meek toward God, you will inherit the earth. There's the solution. Meekness is located in the first grouping of beatitudes, which relates to your private life. Become God's little lamb, and he will turn you into a tiger in the marketplace. Count on it.

Then we are to be meek only toward God? Not really. Men get ahead in the world if they keep the chain of command clearly in mind. Confucius suggests the whole of life is made up of relationships. He established the world's only major religion that is wholly without any supernatural element, so by no means does my endorsement of his fivefold relationship among men take on equal standing with what is commanded in Scripture. Still there is wisdom of a salutary sort in our studying to conform to the limitations implied in the relationships between man and government, boss and worker, father and son, husband and wife, friend and friend. Also recall Emerson's belief that every man was his superior in some way, and he was every man's superior in some way. I am as meek before my medical doctor as I always expected my students to be before me. There is also the promise that meek people will inherit the earth. Understanding that meekness applies here to a man-to-God relationship, this is true as it stands. However, if one still is in doubt, he could well interpret this as a hyperbole, for Jesus did indeed use such: "gouge out your eye and throw it away" and "cut off your right hand and throw it away" leave no doubt about it.

After this brief trip to our Psychiatrist, do you have any doubt that Scripture teaches that Red and Jean left the Garden as incomplete persons? That you too are incomplete? Our diminished capacity does no less than to invite the greatness of God to assume control. He is like Michelangelo in his studio. You are the chisel in his left hand, Christ the mallet in his right hand, chipping away at the amorphous marble, turning out something of such quality that it deserves to live forever. The Sweet Singer of Israel expresses it another way, "Out of the mouth of babes and sucklings hast thou ordained strength."

BY THE SWEAT OF OUR FACES

It is plain that we must change the world into a spiritual Eden, where we feast on the Tree of Life every day. It is also plain that God will use the world to help us make that change. This is taken for granted by our Gestalt of the Redeemed; such an incomplete life as it displays is not a viable one. The world will also do its part. Solomon assures us that our contrary intimate guest, compared to the ethereal soul that is its host, will jar and grate within us, exercising us always by its presence. Yes, we must experience a lifetime the opposite of what God intended to give man, so man being taught through the pain of its nearness, would turn to God for amelioration and ultimate redemption. This is not to say that the mind must close to experimentation, but relegate it to the world of things. "No pain, no gain," the muscle-builder reminds his pain-ridden body. So we see in this labor before us, especially the raw-boned, bread—and-butter things of life, a rationale for the coexistence of good and evil—yes, even the dominance of evil over good, the visualization of character-building, life by policy and not expediency, reaching toward our Lord, who is the Personification, the I-AM of all virtue.

In the Sermon on the Mount, Christ tells us we are to be salt of the earth and the light of the world. How generous will be the sprinkling? How brightly will the light shine? We have nothing to measure these by, so we will have to take our value and growth by faith. Yet we had better not hold our breath waiting for the world to see us in these functions. Jesus is interested in a one-to-one kind of change, one that turns the other cheek to offences, that gives the underwear with the outerwear to the claimant in a court of law, and carries the Roman soldier's armor another mile under the merciless Judean sun. We are to pray for our enemies until insight shrinks them into nothingness, or else teaches us to see the goodness in them that others see. We are to check the movement of hand and eye, thereby limiting the world's allurement. Even tomorrow must be changed. God Himself must take the place of worry. Above all, we must treat others the way we expect God to treat us, or at least the way we want them to treat us. The Sermon on the Mount expects each of us to create a sanctified microcosm, a new Eden with the Tree of Life restored, from which we bountifully eat our daily bread.

If we have this uninvited guest as a lifelong occupant in the intimate part of our lives, the *sanctum sanctorum*—as we are told, we don't know where he started from or where he is going, and since he is two-faced, a sweaty slave and then a carnival barker—since all this is so, we do have a problem, both critical and ongoing. Our hearts are as full as that sheepcote was so long ago, with no room at the far end under the awning where shepherds sleep on thatches of straw. So Mary gave birth to Jesus out in the corral part, where sheep give birth at that very time of year. Yet we, over 2,000 years later, have seen the King in brighter light and are positive that changes must continue to be made, so he will occupy progressively as much room as he wants.

In short, we must do something about the world. We must not love the world, like full-blown hedonists who make the world their oyster. On the other hand, we earn our living from the world. Jesus implies we must not hate it either, but make friends of the "mammon of unrighteousness." Paul says the work in the world is there for us to use to gain a livelihood. He warns us that we must work. He worked as a tentmaker when he had no financial support for his ministry, which was so successful that, had it continued to grow after his death as rapidly as it did during his life, according to one estimate by 300 AD the entire continent of Europe would have been evangelized. Yet the writings of this genius and his ministry often had to wait upon his worldly occupation. He warned one church that "if a man does not work, neither should he eat."

The problem actually gets bigger. What are we to do with this world, especially since we are heaven-bound? Aren't we "paid up, prayed up and ready to go up," as the hill country preachers often claimed? My fellow adopted children of Almighty God—heaven's royalty—we do indeed see scrubbing floors, changing diapers, digging coal and plowing corn in an entirely different light! What the Bible tells us about this uninvited transplant is that we are to overcome him. Like Jacob, we may have to wrestle all night—yes, the rest of our lives with the world, but we must overcome it. We must do so daily, for the barkers never cease their harangue, and the employer will never be satisfied except by one more dollar. In addition, part of the world is nature, still faintly reflective of its Edenic perfection, and our gently handled bodies—so soon to be dust, weakening ever—are yet temples of the Holy Spirit. These also are part of this problem, by which God has chosen to exercise us.

It is interesting to note that over 90% of our knowledge comes through our sense organs, about the same percentage of DNA we have in common with the apes. This means only a mere 5% comes from our logic, memory, imagination, intuition and judgment—all taught by the grace of God. With such a thin buffer zone involved, which Job calls "the skin of my teeth," it is little wonder that one of the chief functions of the world is to deceive us. Not that the world is as much to blame as we ourselves are, often yielding to the temptation of seeing the world as we wish it were, even so strongly that fiction becomes fact. So it is our monumental task, not of loving the world, not of hating the world, but of overcoming the world.

Overcoming the world is one of the most conspicuous doctrines in the New Testament. Jesus assures us that he overcame the world. Elsewhere we are told to overcome evil, the wicked one, false prophets, the Devil and many other spin-offs of our fallen world. The key word from John's Apocalypse is surely "overcome." It occurs at the end of each of the Seven Letters to the Churches of Asia. Jesus, speaking through John, offers victory to him who overcomes the world. Paul sees part of the Christian's victory as being over death and the grave. Indeed, O grave, where is thy victory? When Jesus and Paul speak of "victory," are they not implying warfare? Both words, "overcome" and "victory" relate to the battlefield.

If God has made the world a place where we are to be exercised, it must have its good aspects, too. We are to overcome the bad things in the world so that we may, as it were, inherit the earth. We are to become alchemists of a sort, those who change base lead into gold. Let us look at a few ways this miracle becomes possible.

The world acts as a catalyst on our spirituality. The catalyst, a quickening power in biblical language, is also an office of the Holy Ghost. So we have two sources of inducement toward greater spirituality. The world, strangely enough, does it by denying us time to be spiritual. We are all aware that one of the most difficult problems on the Christian Road is finding enough time to do the walking! To begin with, two-thirds of our lives is already used up during the workday and sleep, and the contenders for the remaining third are many, indeed. If you fall on your knees just before bedtime and find yourself too tired to pray, why not overcome the world by going to bed an hour earlier, and then reserve an hour for God when you awaken refreshed and at a greater distance from the world by a full eight hours of sleep? This is just one way you can change your environment as part of your working with God to make a new you. You will find other ways to fend off the intrusions of the world—God will see to it.

Then there is the power of transfer merit. This phenomenon is well known in higher education. Teachers are aware that learning one subject can help a student learn another better. Learning to write makes a person a better public speaker; exercising oneself in the brutal and unforgiving discipline of mathematics can help improve one's piano playing, as musicians have often claimed.

This can happen also in the interchange between the spiritual and secular worlds. As a student in seminary, I went to work at a secular job to help make ends meet. The boss asked me to perform a certain task, which I did in such a way that I gave him more than he asked for. I saw this as acting like God, for he always extends me "unmerited favor." There is always a chance for carry-through of Christian virtues into the marketplace. Your frequent and intense self-analysis in prayer will also increase your discernment of others. If you despise not the day of small things in your spiritual life, you will find it easier to pay closer attention to the details in secular employment as well. Get in the habit of denouncing the negative factors in your own ego, and the negative actions toward you from other egos will decrease as well.

In the book of Proverbs, you will find much overlap between the secular and spiritual worlds, each a mirror of the other. In his introductions to Romans and I Corinthians, Paul speaks of comforting members of these churches with the same comfort wherewith he himself has been comforted, and that he expects an interchange of blessings between himself and them. It happens. Look for ways this miracle interlacing of worlds manifests itself. Did you ever consider how living in a spiritual dictatorship argues forcefully for living in a temporal democracy? Or how one's hunger and thirst for right living helps us seize and devour the mammon of unrighteousness? Or that God makes us fierce aggressors toward the competitive world because we are meek toward him?

Then there is the matter of competition, the very soul of capitalism, the blood pressure of the marketplace. Some people thrive on the challenge of competition, while others are reconciled to live with it and make all the necessary adjustments. Then there are the socialists. These people tamper with human nature and prefer believing—or at least want everyone else to believe—that cooperation is the far better way. Among other tamperings with human society, they hold the view of "legislated brotherhood," which one serious thinker of our time calls the deadliest deception of modern man. Still, most of us at least learn to live with competition and count it a blessing, if only a blessing in disguise.

One doesn't have to be a Christian to see the benefits of competition and, indeed, the evils in not having the freedom it needs to thrive. Interestingly enough is the prominent notion of modern existentialism that the only thing we cannot give up is our freedom. This refers to freedom in its purest sense, the power of volition. Still, it is quite plain that kinds of freedom can be curtailed—political freedom, economic freedom and physical aspects of freedom. That we have as much of these as possible should be the hope and prayer of every Christian.

One way we can be exercised by the competition freedom provides is to emulate virtuous behavior in others. Paul says we should not measure ourselves by ourselves, i.e., congregations should not become ingrown, but look at what other groups of Christians are doing for God. This also applies to individuals. We can also be inspired by the efforts of others in pursuit of secular crowns as we pursue our own gilded crown with a glory that never passes away. Some concert pianists, for example, admit to practicing eight hours a day. I know of a novelist whose average time at his writing is at least twelve hours a day, usually including Saturdays.

There are other ways of competing. We can compete against our former selves, always being reminded that progress is self-transcendence. Then there are the effects our environment or circumstances have on us. Do you imagine the great poetry of Paradise was written by someone in Samoa or Bali? Rather, it comes from England, parts of which have fog 300 days a year. This is also true for the music of Paradise. In addition to enduring the rigors of the northern climate of Germany, Bach was so distressed by arthritis in his hands that, during the composition of his *Mass in B Minor*, the publisher often had to call for clarification of his hand-written manuscript. Bach was not of the same disposition as a soprano of my acquaintance who absolutely would not perform unless she "felt one hundred percent!"

We must not yield to arthritis, bad weather or any other challenge the environment may throw at us. Double your fist and slam it down on the writing table and say, "It will not be so! I will not let it be stronger than I!" Such determination often works. It will certainly take you further than the aforementioned soprano would go. In such competitive environments, the world has not only been overcome, but saddled and spurred into carrying us to our goal. I submit that there was a profound relationship between Beethoven's deafness and the composition of his final quartets, between Milton's blindness and his vision of Paradise. How many of our tears have fallen upon the sonnet he wrote about his blindness? Who cannot help but be inspired by Helen Keller's determination to triumph over multiple physical challenges?

Yet surely there must be some Christian optimism about the innocent pleasures of the flesh, the arts and ventures forth into the unvarnished beauties of nature? Indeed, but we need no more than a paragraph here. For nearly all of us, restraint is more called for than exhortation. We do need psychic relief and aesthetic distance from creative employment; even David saw this in his great psalm of repentance (51:18), when he looked forward to pause from more difficult matters to help "build up the walls of Jerusalem." This Moses did, too, when he sanctified work and saw it as a synonym of beauty in the concluding verses to his single contribution to the Hymn Book of the Hebrews, Ps. 90.

Of course there are dangers. Some become workaholics. They are busy laying up for their old age, they work to escape a sour disposition at home, or in an attempt to make up for some sin of the past. Such people make as inappropriate a use of the world as the hedonists do. Still, whether they lean toward too much work, too much pleasure or both, such people come to what moral critics are calling the sin of this age—secularism. Jesus denounced this sin when he warned his listeners of the coming judgment. He cites Antediluvia and Sodom as examples to avoid. Note also what is often overlooked in this heyday of the homosexual, that the sin for which Sodom is eternally infamous is not even mentioned by Jesus. He says just before the fire fell that the citizens of Sodom were eating, drinking, buying, selling, building, planting—and that was all. That not a single item on his list was intrinsically sinful is often overlooked as well. Jesus implies that any life without including him is sinful and headed for destruction.

There is also the matter of nature. Some in Rome, Paul said, worshipped nature, the creature instead of the Creator. On the other hand, others must be disabused of the false notion that we are about "conquering nature," which is impossible. The best we can do is to cooperate with nature. Nor can we break nature's laws—gravity, for example. We can be broken by it, but we can never break it. Nor does nature, being neutral, urge us toward atheism. Faith plus nature loudly declare the glory of God. Yet without faith, nature remains sort of an analog computer. God's creation does not deceive us into embracing atheism.

Finally, this long-time resident of toil grows old with us, leaving us with no more than a feeling of frustration along with louder bodily murmurs. Yet even this disquietude has its blessing, because frustration stimulates hope. My feet have been bloodied walking on shards down that Avenue of Broken Dreams, which was, after all, my fault. Too often I listened to the carnival barker. So now I conclude that the workaday world has done God's work by making me do its work. It is the old trick God plays on man, using us to condemn ourselves, and at the same time to convince us that, if he would allow us to crucify his Only Begotten Son, he will give us another chance. By us and for us he restored the Tree of Life in Eden, where we daily feast.

By this we are comforted, yes, but still frustrated. Whoever said life ends like sailing off into a quiet sunset? Maybe that was Tennyson's message—maybe not—but the poem comes across that way. Rather, I prefer Dylan Thomas' "Do not go gentle into that good night." Never have I been more frustrated than now, yet never has hope been more sharply defined. He stands before me with open arms, this Fabulous Lover, this Personification of everything I have ever hoped for! It is frustration that has "quickened" me, making my closet visits more intense and, hence, more intensely enjoyed. The world's arthritis, tinnitus and other distractors of the flesh, never more insistent than now, do no more than to enrich my hopes. Then there are my dreams out there on the horizon, where they can be tinted with eternal colors until dreams and hopes coalesce into the countenance of Jesus Christ. This vision is out there tugging at me. It is like the sun and moon that tug at our oceans, washing the human filth from our shores. I see it more clearly as I eat my bread by the sweat of my face—maybe even because of the sweat on my face. As Solomon says, I cannot see the beginning and ending of things, so I cannot see their beautiful pattern, but I do know the Patternmaker.

FOR THE SUITCASE

1. We were made imperfect so we can participate with God in finishing his work in us.
2. God wills that the world live in our hearts as a negative stimulus to our ongoing spiritual creation.
3. We are not to love or hate the world, but to use it.
4. The world has two faces, work and pleasure.
5. We do not know the full significance of whatever happens to us.
6. The Christian's road is restrictive and difficult.
7. The Beatitudes are the Gestalt of the Redeemed.

CHAPTER VI:
THE LAUGHTER OF GOD

Road Maps: Genesis 15, 18, 22; Psalm 2

Whenever I think about predestination in the context of today's needs, two words always come immediately to mind—limitation and laughter. This is strange, I know, yet if I had space to add another adjective to the mix, it would be "strange" itself. Maybe the biblical term "mysterious" would be better, or best of all "transcendent," though it is not a biblical word. When Solomon said, "Boast not thyself of the morrow, for you know not what a day may bring forth," he meant the future is transcendent. Jesus said it even better when he told his disciples not to worry about tomorrow.

Our communication renaissance has made popular religion more widespread than ever, and its appeal is based largely on the notion that God can do everything just for the asking if you are a simple-minded Christian, or just for the taking if you are a simple-minded Muslim. There are things God absolutely cannot do, and they usually are the very things men most want him to do. While television brings "prosperity theology" and "only-believe" religion into every room in the house, it also gives equal time to heresy and disbelief. At times, I must confess, it seems that the overwhelming majority of unbelievers will win out against the orthodox faith of God and his Beloved Son. But faith never settles on "seems." There are seven thousand men who have not bowed their knees to Baal. When I sit down and review how God has won every battle to this very hour with his nigh invisible minority, I want to have a good laugh. God has made history my laughing place. I see the wisdom in Dante's calling his poem, *The Divine Comedy.*

As we begin our very limited approach to one of theology's most voluminous subjects, note that predestination occupies very little space in biblical exposition. In fact, the doctrine is named only twice by St. Paul. The rest of the time, biblical canonists take predestation for granted. It is so inescapably implied by God's attributes that the writers take it for granted that he is, in fact, quite in charge of things. Indeed, how can we believe in the eternity of God without also believing in his foreknowledge? This implies his active or permissive will has to be involved in all that happens.

Since so many Christians believe in predestination, what is the controversy all about? It involves how much control. Who holds at least 51% of the willpower—man or God? That question we will come to directly, but first let us look at how the Old Testament introduces the subject to us. Genesis shows us that God directs the lives of those who are his willing agents. None is a better example of this than Abraham, the founder of the Jewish spiritual nation, and also of Christians during the past two millennia. There are millions today with the blood of Abraham flowing in their veins, and millions with his spirit guiding their lives. Truly do Jews and Christians own him as father. Let us see why, since the leaves do not fall far from the tree. What happened to Father Abraham will happen to us in one form or another. We are invited to share his faith and his laughter as well.

THE FATHER OF ALL ISRAEL

God comes to Abraham when he is 75, promising him two things: 1) to make Abraham the founder of so great a nation that the whole world would be blessed because of it, and 2) that he himself would also be a blessing to that world. All Abraham has to do is to obey God. He is already a prosperous person, but has no heir, so he obeys God in hopes of becoming the father of a great nation. God leads him, his wife Sarah, nephew Lot and their herds and servants into the land of Canaan.

God comes to Abraham first as a voice, then in a dream. One night, he visits Abraham with the remarkable forecast of the Egyptian sojourn of his family and their return to the land of Canaan after 400 years. The dream ends with a promise of land from the Nile to the Euphrates. What we should remember especially from this visit is Gen. 15:6, one of the epic verses of the Bible.

> And Abraham had faith in God, and he judged it to him
> as righteousness.

So great is this text that it is quoted three times in the New Testament: Rom. 4, Gal, 3, and Jas. 2. Several other New Testament books make reference to the passage. However, the old adage, "to be great is to be misunderstood," applies to this one verse. Its translation is inadequate, and its promise is exaggerated beyond intent. As I have said before, we must never translate the verb for "faith" as 'believe." The Greek verb for "counted," often rendered "reckoned" elsewhere, is too weak in modern English. For example, what do I mean when I say, "I reckon so"? The Elizabethan usage means to add up to a total. We speak of the Judgment Day as the Day of Reckoning. We will have to use these two words—*faith* and *judged*—to get the doctrine expressed as correctly as possible.

Another point of clarification is called for. In common parlance, "righteousness" equals "holiness," though on the moral scale, holiness is a much higher-ranking word. Righteousness means "right living," or doing the right thing given a certain set of circumstances. The verse says that Abraham had faith in God, and God said he did the right thing. We even do the right thing about the wrong thing when we confess a sin and repent of it.

Unfortunately, some suggest this epic statement means a divorce of faith from ethics. This is to say that God accepts belief in him as a substitute for right living, as though Abraham had opted for a second-class ticket to heaven, and God took pity on him and moved him into first-class accommodations! Here is a view many "only-believe" Christians use as their foundation. It is quite similar to the God-of-the-gaps attitude toward faith held by some scientific people. It fills God into the gaps of yet undiscovered knowledge about our universe until some new scientific discovery fills the gap, at which point God is no longer needed. We end up with a shrinking God. Furthermore, should we interpret this verse as faith instead of good works? Not so! Knowing sin first-hand as I do, I see such an interpretation as no cure, but rather an inducement to sin all the more.

It is impossible to please God without faith. Indeed, by having faith we concede life is transcendent; there are things in life that are unknowable. Also, faith is not a substitute for obedience. This final paraphrasing from St. Paul's Roman Epistle: Since Abraham was justified by faith 400 years before the Law was given by Moses, one does not need the works or rituals of the law to live the right life for God.

So Abraham, in spite of all the disappointments, the unfulfilled promises, the dangers, the dominance of evil over good in the world, and in spite of all that was yet ahead for him, was determined to live by faith. Are you? If you are, get ready for a roller coaster ride, for a sauna bath. Such things were ahead for Abraham, as they are for us all.

Now comes the long wait. Two years have passed since God gave him the promise, and he will be 100 before Isaac is born. Imagine what went through Abraham's mind during the long days, months, years, and all the time his old biological clock was ticking away, moving a fulfillment of the promise into the realm of the impossible. Let's imagine that faithful Abraham spent a modest five minutes of his daily prayers talking about his problems in this matter, gently reminding God of his promise, perhaps probing everywhere in the process of self-examination for reasons why God might have been delaying. Twenty-five years of this prayer regimen would yield approximately 45,655 minutes or 761 hours of prayer—not of total prayer, but just the portion focusing on God's promises to him.

Abraham and Sarah wait about 10 years and finally decide on a compromise—having a son by Sarah's Egyptian maid. Maybe, he thinks, this is what God has intended all along. So Ishmael is born. This son is included in those five-minute petitions, but God is silent about Ishmael, and thirteen more years pass. Abraham turns 99.

God calls to Abraham. Perhaps Father-of-Us-All feels God comes to announce Ishmael as the one anointed for the conduit of God's promise— not so. God adds more detail to the promise during each visit. Even so, now he gives them new names and gives the coming child the name of Yitzak, or Laughter, and orders the circumcision of all the males in Abraham's household. Then God departs and Abraham obeys. I suppose by this time he has even given up thinking in impossible dimensions, let alone hoping. But God is far from finished with this man of universal importance. He must yet become qualified to be the father of us all.

A short time later, Abraham is sitting in the opening of his tent when three men arrive seemingly out of nowhere, but he is not fooled for one minute. These men come from heaven. He persuades them to stay for dinner, and a royal feast is cooked by Sarah and served. She then goes into the tent and eavesdrops on their discussion. The promise first given 25 years before is given again, but with this stinging, bitter addition heard for the first time by Sarah. She is named as the 90-year-old mother of the coming heir. She laughs a bitter, quivering laugh, the laugh of unbelief, not of ridicule or defiance, but of one whose disappointment had cheated her out of all joyful laughter over the long, long years of sterility—a disappointment to herself, her husband and even now the object of ridicule by her Egyptian maid. We join God in forgiving her for lying about her laughter to the three guests.

Notice how many chapters in Genesis anticipate the birth of Isaac, and only one brief paragraph describes it. Remember also the woman who had a bleeding disorder for twelve years, and had spent her very last cent before she was prepared to be healed. In the fullness of time, Paul says, God sent his Son into the world—a promise much longer in fulfillment than the 25 years Abraham and Sarah waited for the birth of Isaac.

God acts only when he can. He is limited by the very limitations he puts on Abraham. Still, the time is near, and nine months from this last meeting with God, Sarah will give birth to a son. But Abraham will be 100, and Sarah will be 90 or 91, depending on whether she would have a birthday within the next nine months. What of that? We are dealing with the high and lofty one who inhabits Eternity. It was Abraham's spiritual development that limited God, not such a minor matter as being 100 years of age.

The child is born, and Little Laughter brings great joy to his mother. She laughs, but not the bitter outburst of nine months ago. This is the kind of laughter than transcends its natural context, a laughter that belongs to eternity and never dies. Her laughter will be heard as long as God's Word endures, will go where it goes, challenging us to endure the uncertainties of God's transcendent governance, and learning to laugh at the dominance of evil over good. Job puts it like this: "Blessed be God my maker, he who gives songs in the night."

Yet there is just one little fault with Sarah's laughter—it came after the fulfillment, not at the time when the promise was given. We can hardly blame her for this, and besides—we are not in the blaming business. God is Sarah's judge, reckoning when and whether her days of trial are over, how far short she falls of the mark he has set for her. We in the eternal audience know she and Abraham still have some spiritual stretching ahead of them. Death is out there, of course, but what God has in store is far worse than mere death, which Christ has reduced into a metaphor of sleep. I laugh at it, and so should we all. Kierkegaard said, "There is no Christian but who welcomes death." Do you hear Paul laugh as he writes? I do. "Oh death, where is thy sting? Grave where is thy victory?"

The climactic event for Abraham, the defining hour, the epic milestone is The Moriah Test. One of the worst mistakes of the KJV is found in Gen. 22:1: "And God did tempt Abraham." James, the natural brother of Christ, said that God tempts no man, and he is right. The Hebrew word quite plainly means *test*. In this regard, some of our only-believe Christians find trouble with the last petition of the Paternoster, "And lead us not into temptation . . . ." Here Jesus uses a literary device known as a negative affirmation, stating something negatively as a reminder of what will not happen. Jesus wants us to pray in such a way that we remind ourselves what God will never do. There is no need to retranslate the petition to read, "And do not put us to the test . . ." as some do. What would life be without testing from time to time?

God comes to Abraham for the eighth time. The number eight signals a new beginning, and if anything is new, it is The Moriah Test. There is nothing like it in Scripture before or after Abraham. He is quite anxious to see God, for it is time for him to start seeking out a wife (or several wives, for that matter) for Isaac. He has reached puberty and should get started as soon as possible on this famous family he is to sire. Again, Abraham is wrong, wrong, wrong! He is so amazed that he is totally speechless. What happened during the long night that follows the command to make a human sacrifice of his son? We will never know, but we can safely imagine that there was no sleep for this 114-year-old Father-of-Us-All that night. There is something else we can be relatively sure of. Abraham would never have stopped searching for the motive for God's seemingly contrary behavior, and we are told in Heb. 11 that he found an answer he could live with.

In trying to imagine Abraham's thinking, we must be sure that we do not go beyond the givens. One theory about The Moriah Test is that Abraham was told by one of the three mysterious strangers who visited him that this test would come, but that he shouldn't worry about it, for at the last minute God would give him a substitute for Isaac; he was told about the ram caught in the brush in advance. This theory is no more than playing games. Abraham makes an A on the exam because he gets the answers in advance. Life doesn't go this way, and we know it. We dismiss this shallow thinking without further comment. It is not justified by Scripture and ought not to be considered. It is not one of the givens.

What is given are as follows: God loves Abraham. God cannot break his promises. It was really God who asked Abraham to make a human sacrifice of Isaac, a practice of the worshippers of Molech in Abraham's day, but opposed by his Loving Heavenly Father. One Russian novelist has a character calling God cruel for treating Abraham this way. God, he says, was acting like a nobleman who sicks his hounds on a peasant lad, tearing him to death. Abraham knew, moreover, that it was through Isaac that this great race was to come. How can this be if he is to make a sacrifice of Isaac? He was caught on the horns of a dilemma. On the one hand, if he kept Isaac alive, he would preserve the means for fulfilling the Covenant, yet break the Covenant by his disobedience. On the other hand, if he made a human sacrifice of Isaac, he would destroy the means for perpetuating the Covenant, though keeping the Covenant valid.

The leaden hours of the night slowly passed for this aged Patriarch. Here is where the action really was—not atop Moriah, but in the prayer closet, atop his invisible Gethsemane, where he and Jesus both wrestled with reality and win the victory. He thought, "Has the past 39 years of faith and obedience come to naught? Does the immutable God change his mind? Is he a cruel God and lies about what he intends to do? Is he naïve and driven like a politician to change his mind to suit new circumstances? Does he take pleasure is taking away what he gives? Now he wants me to bind my son like an animal, plunge a dagger into his heart and burn his body to ashes with the smoke ascending up into his nostrils, giving him delight!" Then the answer came, and when it came, he became a blessing to all the peoples of the earth: "God, this Loving God, whom I also love, to keep his promise to me absolutely has to raise Isaac from the ashes of fire! He has to do it!"

This is the same conclusion all Christians arrive at as we stare into the open door of an empty tomb, just like Father Abraham. It seems to me that, at this very moment in the wee hours of that first night after The Moriah Test began, a heavenly peace came over Abraham. This same peace came over Hannah, as you recall, when she "prayed through" her having a son. She had faith in God, and God judged it for right behavior, the right response. She and Abraham had faith in advance!

The party of four makes their way north from Beer-sheba to Mount *Moriah*, which means "seen of the Lord." Today we know it by another name—*Zion*—a word for "conspicuous" or "indication" or "marking." Later, Abraham is to give it a third name, *Jehovah-jireh*, which means "The Lord who provides." Indeed, this will be a most notable mountain, as all three names imply. Three temples will stand on this site. It is on the eastern slope of Moriah where Jesus Christ was to be crucified. He prophesied to Nicodemus and us all that if he is lifted up (by the cross—and by us as well), he will draw all men unto him. Finally, in the Apocalypse of John it gets its final name—*Har Megiddo*—the "Mount of Rendezvous," where all the world of men will be judged.

It is here at the foot of history's highest mountain that I must pause for a moment to feed into our discussion comments from the New Testament that come to bear upon the events that make it so famous. In Gal. 3:16, Paul draws our attention to the fact that the "seed of Abraham" in Gen. 12-24 never occurs in the plural, which we Christians are directed to apply directly to Christ, though in modern English usage "seed" could be understood in the plural number. Paul is not using our language, but ancient Hebrew. He has the advantage of being closer to it than anyone alive today, and judges the singular as prophetic. It may be that Paul refers only to a particular passage like Gen. 13, in which "seed" occurs three times, using the singular pronoun even when the plural would seem better. In these chapters, "seed" occurs 17 times in 13 separate locations. Of this total, I find 8 refer to the offspring of Isaac, and the remaining 5 use "seed" as singular.

Paul's interpretation becomes more convincing when we discover Jesus' commentary about Abraham. In John 8:56, he says, "Abraham, your father, rejoiced to see my day. He saw it and was glad." I wonder if Paul ever knew Jesus said this to the Jews. We often forget that Paul was dead before any of the Gospels was written, or at least formed into a complete document. All this aside, Jesus makes the point most clear that Paul was correct in saying Abraham came to know the symbolic significance of The Moriah Test. When did this enlightenment take place? We can be more sure about when it did not take place, i.e., never prior to the test itself. It had to be in retrospect. We are given no clues as to exactly when.

Now that Jesus and Paul tell us The Moriah Test is more than meets the eye (as is always the case when God is involved in our lives), and already knowing that Abraham is the Father of us all, let us take our place behind him as he and Isaac climb up the mountain together. He climbs, this 114-year-old Patriarch, slowly and deliberately, a knife in one hand and a torch in the other. Isaac follows close behind with a bundle of faggots on his back. Of course, we have an advantage since we know what is to follow. We see Isaac beneath his burden, and we cannot help but see someone else going along that same trail with a cross upon his back. Jesus turns and says to us, "Do you want to come after me? Then you must deny yourself. This means you must take up your own cross and you must follow me."

Getting out of the world of time and space, we take up a mallet in our right hand and three iron spikes in the other. We know we must do it for ourselves, for Romans are no longer involved. We remind ourselves that our own past has denied us any other action than to crucify the person we could yet become, our future selves. We must impale our hands and feet to the purposes of God.

Abraham props his torch and removes the bundle from Isaac's back. Then with the supernatural power God gives his ancient hands, he seizes the youth and binds him, trussing him up as he had done so many other times when he butchered animals for a sacrifice. He is deaf to the child's screams. As he quickly he raises his dagger on high, God speaks! Abraham has passed The Moriah Test! As the Holy Voice is soon to tell him, it was himself that he sacrificed, not Isaac.

Abraham never moved faster in his life. The knife he had honed to make Isaac's death as painless as possible quickly cuts the lad free and together they slay the ram caught in the thicket. He is full of joy, which soon turns to laughter. Isn't that what happens when one rejoices? He renames *Moriah* as *Jehovah-jireh*, or "The Lord who provides."

About an hour later, the voice of God speaks a second time, repeating the same message Abraham first heard 25 years before (Gen. 22:15ff.). But notice God's refusal to use the plural pronoun, even when good style would call for it. One person is his focus, though he again speaks of the offspring as beyond number. He proclaims Abraham his hero of the day, then departs.

It must have been in the days to follow, after his return to Beer-sheba, that Abraham intuits the significance of The Moriah Test. It is my feeling that the point that set him on the right track is that God, for the second time, had given him information in advance. First, God told Abraham 25 years in advance that he would have a son. Second, he orders him to make a human sacrifice three days before the actual event could take place. He asks himself, "Why did this Loving Heavenly Father of mine cause me to wander sightless and hopeless in the bowels of hell for three long days, then just at the exact last possible second, he stays my hand?" Then he did what each of us would do; he compared this strange behavior with his logical conclusion that God would have to raise Isaac from the dead, and with the double promise of his fathering a great nation and being a personal blessing to all peoples.

It was exactly then that these comparisons crystalized, and he saw the existence of two worlds, one paralleling the other. In the spiritual world, God had a son, too, an only begotten, who was to come to earth, teach us how to live, and become the sacrifice for our sins. Then Abraham saw his own part as having faith in the anointed Son, thereby passing The Moriah Test, thereby assuring men everywhere that the righteous life is possible. He then saw clearly that only by the enduring of such poignant specifics and extreme anguish was he able to arrive at this prophetic truth. God had to intensify the parallelism to such an extreme that Abraham's far-seeing eye of faith could penetrate the Good News of two full millennia hence. Then came the backrush of such glorious knowledge. Abraham had become the one and only archetype of Almighty God Himself, as Isaac was of God's Beloved Son.

Now we come to the final paragraph of our little trip into biographical theology, Gen. 22:20-24. It is one of those suspicious segments of Moses' writing that we have met before. We ask ourselves, why is this especially here? It does nothing to advance the plot, and it seems so disjunctive that it could occur just about anywhere in the entire narrative. It is exactly here for a blessing to Abraham and us all. Let's examine its contents against what has just happened, viz., Abraham seeing the day of the Son of God revealed to him as the result of a series of most remarkable circumstances.

What exactly does this passage say? You will recall that Abraham had two brothers who never left their home town of Ur. Haran was the one who fathered Lot, who went with Abraham, but of Nahor we and Abraham know no more than the name of his wife. Now, 25 years after he last saw Nahor, news arrives that this brother has had eight sons and four more sons by concubines. Had this information reached him at any time prior to The Moriah Test, it would have been just more salt in a grievous wound. How heavy his heart would have been. However, now that he has passed the test of faith, the news has the opposite effect. Not only will he father a nation, but he has become the world's example of righteousness, the prophet of the coming Messiah, and the Archetype of God Himself. Now the news about Nahor arrives. "He has had eight sons by Milcah? Well, good for him!" he must have thought. "Yet I, with only one son will become the Father of a great nation and all the world will be blessed because of me." I think he began to laugh—he rejoiced! He shouted hallelujahs to his Almighty Lover! Perhaps Sarah caught the contagion and joined him. There they stood dancing and laughing and singing, she at 127 and he 136. How sweet they were, these songs in the night.

Sarah dies a short time later, but Abraham lives on 40 years longer. Yet as eventful as these years must have been, Moses compresses them into eight verses. No doubt he continues to have challenges to his faith, but all would be anticlimactic compared to the monumental Moriah Test, which the annals of human culture yet to be written give due place. The loyalty and inspiration of Abraham continue to bless those on the Christian Road to this very day, and will do so to the end of time.

We see that Abraham's faith continues to be challenged by contrary effect, i.e., God's action seems to be the exact opposite of what Abraham and we would expect. We are quite taken aback by God's delay in calling for a wife for Isaac. We can be sure that Abraham must have asked God at least weekly, if not more often, to allow him to choose a wife—or wives— for his son. Yet God delays until Isaac is 40. Why? We do not know, nor do we need to know. It may be a challenge to Abraham's faith, but it does not fit among the coordinate details of the narrative. Again, it is now Rebekah who is without child for a long, indefinite period. It could have been from 15 to 20 years, and still fit into the time frame of specified dates. In addition, sometime prior to Isaac's marriage, Abraham takes another wife who bears him six sons. This means that Abraham sired a total of eight sons—or is it more than eight? We cannot be sure. Gen. 25:6 speaks of "sons by concubines." Were these the sons born to his wife or additional ones? As his last recorded act, he sends them all away "eastward, to the east country." Moses says it twice for emphasis, and adds "away from Isaac."

I can see Abraham sitting in the door of his tent, watching the caravan of at least six camels fading against the horizon. They are the sons of his second wife, Keturah. They are going back to Ur of the Caldees. Surely, the 175-year-old Father-of-Us-All must have recalled the news about his brother Nahor's eight sons and four born to concubines. Now he, too, has eight sons and maybe four born to concubines. Maybe Isaac is now standing by his side. Maybe Abraham chuckles a bit, or laughs outright at how things worked out perfectly, just as God had said they would. True, he now has left in his tent only one future heir, a grandson, Jacob, not yet 20 years of age. Then he laughs again and sees a pattern to God's contrary effect. Oh, the blessed irony of it all!

As we join Father Abraham and Isaac, watching the caravan disappear, we remind ourselves that we know more than even he knew. Jacob, too, would have the same number of sons, eight by his two wives, Leah and Rachel, and four others by their handmaids. We see the pattern of God in history, and we wonder how some pattern may be working out in our lives.

At some time between The Moriah Test and his death, Abraham formulates another doctrine from his experiences in the life of faith, the right kind of life—righteousness—as the Bible calls it. We don't know exactly when or under what circumstances it occurred, but we know it happened, and happened by necessity. Abraham's life can be summed up as a life of reduction, whereas God promised him the exact opposite. Maybe in one of his prayers, he said something like this, "O God, you know that I do not want to seem impatient with your care of my life, but at the rate things are happening and given my advanced age, for your Covenant to be fulfilled in my lifetime, I would have to live . . . well, forever." Then there is silence, and in that silence the answer rises to his trembling lips. "And that is exactly what the message is! I must never calibrate my life by human measurements. Life overflows logic, and life overflows time as well." Yes, Father Abraham, you absolutely must live forever, though earthly time is running out. The innumerable nation will yet "dwell in the gates of their enemies, and all the world will come to bless your name."

FROM EXAMPLES TO PRECEPTS

Thus concludes this lesson on predestination by biblical example, and it seems as though we were not studying theology, but being entertained with an astonishingly beautiful narrative beside some flickering campfire in the dark of night. What has happened is that God has brought us to the entrance of his gold mine, and now we must start digging. The gold will then be ours, bought with our effort, though under God's direction.

We are given a biographical narrative—didactic history, as we called it in a previous chapter. In fact, we are learning theology as we learn life by observation and experience. Classroom study is force-feeding that must wait for some future time for its application. Of course, learning theology via narrative was a helpful memory aid in biblical days when writing materials were expensive and literacy was quite rare. Yet the main lesson from learning doctrine this way is that it parallels our own experience. Like Abraham, God makes us participate in the solution to our problems.

Sometimes God even expects participatory answers to our prayers—putting legs to our prayers, as the old saying goes. You will notice that so many of the miracles of Jesus were performed for people who took the initiative by coming to Jesus. We must move Christian doctrine out of the nursery of theoretical incubation and into the living room of persons. Jesus said, "I am the truth." The way of Abraham is our way of making Jesus-the-Truth into Jesus-the-Road. You do not own a Christian doctrine until it walks in your shoes.

There are times when we create problems for ourselves. To put it another way, we bear crosses that do not have our names on them. I do not mean that we fall into heresy or hypocrisy, but simply wrong thinking. Job was such a person. Please do not suppose I intend to focus on his calamity, his loss of all his wealth, the lives of his ten children, and then come down with smallpox, all within one single day. No, this was not his problem. Job could even endure these, this heroic champion of faith who said, "The Lord gives and the Lord takes away. Blessed be the name of the Lord." His problem was that he felt he would be content if God would only tell him why all this happened. Then God came on the scene and, strange to say, he began flinging questions at Job left and right. So rapid did they come that he forgot to ask his question. He did eventually pause to ask himself what God was driving at by asking him all these questions that God Himself knew he could not answer. Why was God acting like this, like a fiendish teacher who wanted every student in the class to fail his exam? Why? Then it hit him like a boomerang—precisely then, when God could draw the answer out of Job's own mind, a teaching technique God had used on Abraham. God was treating Job exactly the way Job had been treating him. Job had been asking a question of God that God Himself indeed could not answer! Of course, God's inability is not due to his own intellectual limitations, but to Job's. Job could not understand the answer. Job failed to recognize that life is transcendent, so God is limited in dealing with our limitations.

Job, like Abraham and all of us, had to experience such contextual impellents toward the truth that it spontaneously became a part of his thinking. The hand of God sometimes wears the surgeon's glove; sometimes his feet walk in our shoes and his voice vibrates our vocal cords. It is then that I-am-the-Truth becomes I-am-the-Road.

Sometimes God has to use the Iron Rule when we are too stubborn to learn from the Golden Rule. The Iron Rule is, "As you treat other people, they in turn will treat you." Both the Iron Rule and the Golden Rule are in the Sermon on the Mount, as you recall. We all remember times when we have not had the "ears to hear what the Spirit was saying to the churches," when we have proved to be stubborn asses like Saul of Tarsus, and have kicked against the goads. What then does God do? On one occasion he even used the vocal cords of a jackass to stay the madness of a prophet.

I used to ask my philosophy students, "What is the highest mountain in the world?" My point was that we had to determine what we mean by the terms used before we could intelligently answer the question. What I suggested to them was that we had to define what we meant by "highest." Then I told them that Mt. Everest is the highest above sea level, Mt. McKinley is the highest in panorama, Mona Loa is the highest from point of origin, and Mt. Chimborazo is highest in distance from the center of the elliptical spheroid on which we live, and also closest to the sun. Indeed, if you want to be as close as possible, stand atop Chimborazo on either March 15 or September 15, and you will be there. You would be over 200 miles closer to the sun than if you stood on Mt. Everest any day of the year. Indeed, it is quite important to define your terms before you answer such a question. Sometimes even the dictionary you use will vary your answer.

However, what if we make cultural or historical impact the criteria? In this case, one of the highest I would choose is *Moriah/Zion/ Jehovah-jireh/ Har Megiddo*—all names of the most important mountain to Judaism, Christianity and Islam. Yet the highest of all not only includes the events on Mount Moriah, but involves all religions from the beginning of time until now. It involves a matter for human logic, reaching so high, like the Tower of Babel, that it becomes religious in nature, and it seems almost sacrilegious to set a foot upon it. It is also without a name, though I will call it Mt. Providence. Its purpose is, as John Milton puts it, "to justify the ways of God to men." Anyone who reaches its yet unconquered summit will have balanced the Absolute Power of God with the Necessary Freedom of Man. We will all die with unanswered questions about where one leaves off and the other begins in a world overwhelmed with evil, yet controlled by a Holy and Omnipotent God.

The Bible does not attempt to prove the doctrine of predestination.

Paul introduces it with one of its synonyms in Romans 8: "For whom he did foreknow, he also did predestinate to be conformed into the image of his Son." Perhaps you are familiar with its other names besides providence, viz., the sovereignty of God, election, foreknowledge, and by the name of its most celebrated defender, Calvinism.

It all boils down to this—predestination is so obvious a biblical doctrine that we cannot avoid studying it, though all attempts to solve its mysteries are still inadequate. How can God exert enough control of the world and our lives to guarantee us success in our pilgrimage to his bosom, and yet also guarantee us enough freedom to make our choices meaningful enough to be truly free? This is a big problem, especially since we are only marginally endowed, "scarcely saved" as Peter puts it, or "saved by the skin of our teeth" as Job spoke of it. God's control and our initiative seem to be always on a collision course. It is obvious that we are not prepared or able to surrender faith in predestination or free will, especially since the Bible endorses both. I must have freedom to create and to cultivate a capacity to receive people into my life, and God must have control enough to make sure this is developed.

It may be that predestination is a non-forensic doctrine. By this I mean that it is not suited for debate. This could be so because God wants us to put it among other such doctrines, such as his own Trinity, the virgin birth of Christ, and his resurrection from the dead. Faith (conviction without proof) has to be the end of argument for our limited minds as regards these critical doctrines of the Christian Road. On empirical grounds, we must conclude that free will is possible, for we are conscious of making choices, and can demonstrate that ability any time we choose. Yet on logical grounds, we must conclude Providence is in total control. Since God is Omnipotent, he has the power to do anything he chooses; since he is Omniscient, he has the skill to do so; and since he is omnipresent, he has the occasion to do so. As I have said elsewhere, God is <u>absolute</u> in quality, <u>infinite</u> in degree, hence <u>ultimate</u> in value. In the language of the jurist, God is accessory before the fact, to the fact, and after the fact to all that happens. All things happen either because of his active will, or allowed by his permissive will. So when we pray, "Come your kingdom!

Be done your will! as in heaven, so on earth," we are not actually praying a petition, but acknowledging that God's will <u>will</u> be done, and we want to be included in the doing of it. How are we going to reconcile absolute power with necessary free will?

For me the answer comes in two words—limitation and synergism. Since God is Omnipotent, he also has the power to limit himself. Can he not invade our lives to effect his will by aiding us in doing what he wants us to do? Even by inspiring in us a willingness, a compelling desire to do his will? This working together with God we call synergism, a combination of two Greek word parts: *syn* + *energy*. Paul uses the idea often. We are "workers together with God." When God and I want the same thing, his help is an inspiration; it is not a mandate that turns me into a robot. God is working with me, not taking charge of me.

The world has to live with many unanswered questions, and so must we. Which is more influential, heredity or environment? The warfare over this question is perennial. Which is more important, wisdom or beauty? The Greeks started it, Homer recorded it, but the behavior of men ever since has left the question decidedly moot. Idealism or realism—which is the best way to discover what life is all about? Plato and Aristotle started the warfare, but the battle is far from over. I spare you the many questions about the mysteries of our bodies and so many other areas. If I fail to get to the top of Mt. Providence, I will not worry too much about it. The fact that I tried is what concerns me. I first came to a clue about a solution to this problem when humanity entered the atomic age. Max Plank and others discovered that the closer we draw to the world of atoms, the greater degree of lawless behavior occurs in atomic particles. The point that is significant to us is that this lawless behavior doesn't seem to have any influence on us. Some of these lawless ones are like aspen leaves—they shake all day long but never go anywhere. While some theologians took a Chicken Little view of this new discovery, saying we now live in a lawless universe and maybe God doesn't exist after all, I was peering into the possibility of some grand and glorious way to understand, if not to solve, this seeming conflict between Absolute Power and Necessary Freedom, to find the place where human initiative leaves off and divine control begins.

INTO THE STRAITS

There is no such thing as absolute freedom. God is Omnipotent, yet he limits himself. God is also Ultimate Value, which means he is most valuable—but to whom? Let us imagine the time when God made his first creation, the archangels. They are inferior to him, of course, so in dealing with them, this Ultimate Value must limit himself to their level. He is like the Southern slaveholders in that they had to think like slaves in order to keep control of them. We then see that the limitation of God is a self-limitation.

God then created even lower creatures. Our argument follows that the lower the creatures are, the greater God's limitation has to be while dealing with them. But suppose that God created animate creatures who have no rational understanding. Is his omnipotence now free? No, God is still significantly held in check—or better said, holds himself in check—even though he doesn't need to communicate with such low life. The animated denizens of our planet, from the 100-ton blue sperm whale to the smallest known virus of only 50 millimicrons in length, do not have the power of conceptual thought. Again, God is limited in dealing with them by his own being. Why is he Ultimate Value? Because he wears the heavy chains we call *summum bonum*, a term meaning the highest good for God and his universe. Since God is Good and God is Love, he is limited by who he is. One thing God cannot do is to escape himself. So we see two reasons why God is limited—he is limited by the limitations of his thinking creatures, and by who he is.

There is more. We must see God's laws and his promises as limiters of being, too. What's more, they work both ways in that they limit both him and us. So we limited creatures must enter into the ongoing process of creation by limiting ourselves, or by "denying ourselves," as Jesus puts it. If there are 5,000 promises in the Bible by which God is limited, you can be sure there are at least 5,000 conditions that limit our benefiting from them. One example comes at once to mind. Jesus said, "Come unto me and I will give you rest," and with the very next breath he says, "Take my yoke upon you." Did you note that the promise is conditional? It is offered only to those who "labor and are heavy laden."

While on this subject, let us examine another biblical reference to burden-bearing in Paul's letter to the churches in Galatia, chapter 6. In verse 2, he exhorts us to bear one another's burdens, which is good discipline for those who are trying to love their neighbors. Yet then in verse 5 he seems to contradict himself by cautioning us that everyone must bear his own burden. Even if we accept this less-than-adequate KJV translation, we can see how salutary this advice is. When we help our neighbors with their burdens, we become immediately disillusioned if they sit down on the job. However, the Greek text is clearer than the KJV. Paul uses a different noun in each of these verses for "burden." In verse 2, "burden" is precisely the meaning, but in verse 5, we must use "load," or "cargo." Being a "carter," or "porter," in biblical times was a common occupation. Every member of a household, you can be sure, had a yoke available for toting things around. Many people made their living carrying things for others. The meaning of both verses blended together means something like this: "We must help one another in times of need, but every one of us has the responsibility of earning a living for himself." If we ask him, our Beloved Carpenter from Nazareth will fashion the best yokes possible for us. It is a promise, you see, that puts his expertise at our disposal just for the asking; he limits himself by making this promise. Yet we must make no mistake about it; a yoke is a yoke. He promises to fit the best yoke possible to your neck and shoulders and to make your load light, but not to carry it for you.

In these days when the telemongers are busy spewing out simplistic half-truths about the promises of God, we do well always to search out the conditions placed on these promises and to become as acquainted with the requirements of salvation as we are with its blessings. However, for a refreshing moment, let us look at the breadth and scope of what I believe are the two grandest promises in the entire Bible. They are, if rightly understood, without any modification found anywhere in the Bible, categorical in their sweep and infinite in their depth. Gold doubloons they are flung upon the narrow and difficult path ahead by our Divine Lover, who joins the cloud of witnesses up yonder, urging us with songs of triumph to pick up these coins and press the journey on!

I trumpet forth these two treasures with a blast from St. Peter. In II Pet. 1:4 comes this fanfare, ". . . great and precious promises by which we are partakers of the divine nature . . . ." What is this? It is nothing short of a miraculous interlace of being, interstitial occupancy, an atomic blend of God and each of us! Have I not said that we are gods? If we had a custom among us of wearing phylacteries, little pouches containing Bible verses, I would wear one on each temple. The first is Romans 8:28, "And we know that, for those loving God, all things work together for good." This verse summarizes the whole of predestination. It is a benchmark decision spoken by Almighty God and signed in the blood of Jesus Christ. Here, it seems to my feeble mind, is the greatest possible limitation God could ever assume.

In Rom. 8:28 we see the Golden Text clearly implied. We love him because he first loved us. Notice how my translation differs from the KJV, with which I have no quarrel. "Those who love God" is the same in meaning as "Those who are loving God," as they are both in the present tense. However, I point out that my translation has it closer to the Greek. The promise is limited to those who are loving God. "All things"—what could involve more? The present, the future, the past recollected. The present trials that make the future victory all the greater; the present pains that catapult to future ecstasy; the limitation in one area that generates compensating greatness in another area; the lead that is in the process of becoming gold in the hands of our Divine Alchemist; the space-saving minerals that, after intense heat and pressure, crystallize into diamonds, rubies, sapphires; the grit in oyster shells enameled into pearls of greatest price. I tell you that the dream of the medieval chemists is realized daily in our lives. But you have to be walking on the narrow, difficult Christian Road to pick up each golden promise—yes, even to recognize it for what it is.

It may even be that at times we are such strangers to ourselves that we cannot see the gold, and that is why Jesus wants us to include the second petition of the Paternoster in our daily prayers, "Come your kingdom! Be done your will as in heaven, so on earth!" Not my will, but thine be done. I have learned from experience that tears from such self-denial often wash the vision clear enough to see the gold.

The second great promise, the one that is for the other phylactery, is a negative one, a guarantee of what God promises not to do. I Cor. 10:13 reads, "No temptation has ever taken you but what is common to mankind. But faithful is God, who will not allow you to be tempted beyond your power, but he will make also with the temptation a way of escape that you may be able to bear it." Here is a reflection of the last petition of the Paternoster, and it seems to me that it is also the chain that limits Satan "for 1,000 years," as John symbolically expresses the abundant life promised by Christ. This is to say that the Christian lives a fuller life than even Methuselah did during his 969 years. Implicit in this promise are two cautions we do well to consider. First, having Satan limited does not mean he is impuissant. He is still a lion, but on a chain of certain length. If you get inside the circle of his influence, his limitation no longer exists. This power over Satan is given as the dynamics of the Holy Spirit within our lives.

The second caution is that sin is laid directly at our door, as God said it was at Cain's door. I become my worst enemy. Satan would be powerless except for my cooperation, my affinity with the world's allurement, of which he is the Prince. The identity of the "way" of escape should leave no doubt. Christ says, "I am the Way." Practicing the presence of our Lord is the old story, daily made new for us by a constantly changing life. Prayer, meditation, Bible-reading, public worship, witnessing—these make up the way of life and the way of escape from sin.

These two verses are the most comprehensive of all the promises in Scripture, and their fulfillment generates a spontaneous limitation on God equally comprehensive. Since God cannot break his word, by putting a chain on Satan he actually also puts one on himself. So we must rise to Love's occasion with chains equally as binding.

ABSOLUTE POWER AND NECESSARY FREEDOM

What I am about to share with you is not the Bible, but it does not contradict anything that is in the Bible. Schemes attempting to explain such matters as the Trinity of God and Divine Providence (or predestination) can be helpful explanations of biblical truth. Indeed, they are like the parables of Jesus—fiction that makes infallible truths more easily understood. They are metaphors of reality, not reality itself. You might liken my scheme to the scientific model I saw above the fireplace of a friend who teaches biology. It is a three-foot long conglomeration of about 100 ping pong balls of varying colors, all connected with dowel pins. They comprise a model of one protein molecule. It may well be that such a molecule and the atoms that comprise it do not look like this model at all, for nobody has yet seen an atom or even a protein molecule; however, nothing we currently know about the molecule is incompatible with this model. So until we know more, this is a good enough window into the atomic structure of the primary building block of all flesh, one protein molecule.

I would like to explain my model of how Absolute Power and Necessary Freedom work together in this world. It is my model—it works for me, and I hope that it will give you insight into what will work for you.

Before I present my scheme, I would like to prove to you that I do indeed have free will. I stand on the shore of a smooth pond. I have the choice to throw a stone into the water or not. I decide to do so and start hunting. How heavy a stone will I throw? How far do I want to throw it? What shape should it be? I answer these questions for myself. I am in charge, you see. I finally find the ideal rock, a flat one of about two— pounds weight. I choose to skip it across the lake.

Am I really free? Yes, but only within a given context, like a convict walking around in his cell or a lion endlessly pacing his cage from corner to corner. Mine is, at best, a limited freedom. In a way, I am not free at all. Then I get into my wind-up, without which I cannot reach the pond. I am not free to forego the wind-up. I heave the stone toward its destination. Yet the moment I do—the very moment the stone leaves my fingertips—God takes over. His laws of aerodynamics are in control. From this moment on, everything is predestined to its end. The stone hits the pond, sending out concentric ripples that hit the shore and return with diminished force back to the place where the stone first hit the pond. Theoretically, the motion I have created never ends. Newton's laws of motion, universal causation and inertia take over. I am no more than an observer. I willed the cause and God predestines the effect. The kings of the earth plotting against God forget that there is no freedom beyond context. Yes, we have freedom to act, but not freedom to design or control the effect generated from that act.

I see this world as having an immense, invisible Neutral Zone that operates like the membrane in our lungs, a two-way passage for the gases that go in and out of our blood, making respiration possible. Maybe Jesus expressed something like this to his disciples in that grand literary conceit of the Good Shepherd. He sees his sheep going in and out, and finding pasture. All events go into the door of entry and before they make their exit are either modified by fire, or die like the waves in the pond caused by the rock I threw. So slight is each effect that it loses independent identity. These ripples become like *pi,* presently calculated to the 10-millionth decimal place, yet its precise value is not known. They come at last to causal dissipation and go into what I will call the C-dump. I suppose they are like the aberrant atoms Max Plank worked into his new mathematics. The Bible speaks of this dissipation in a popular way, too. Remember Job? He said, "I know you hate me, God. No more! Let me die! My life is vain!" This is also what Solomon said as he reached the cul-de-sac at the end of every avenue of philosophy he followed. "Vanity of vanity, all is vanity and a striving after wind." He said it several times, as you will recall. How petulant the human mind is if it cannot find a scheme of things closer to the heart's desire!

Into this Neutral Zone come a continuous flow of humanity, and as we are led to expect on every page of Scripture, they are of two kinds—the lost and the saved, the ungodly and the Family of God. God, of course, is in total control in this invisible place. He exerts direct force on all events as they exit out into the battlefield of life exactly as his active or permissive will dictates. Nobody knows what his determinate will is, but his will <u>will</u> be done, whether good or bad or sometimes configured into things impossible to identify, beyond either good or bad. He uses the fire to separate gold from dross, and to even change lead to gold, as the occasion calls for. So a coin is put in a fish's mouth in the Lake of Galilee, or a cosmic cloud begins its journey to earth in time for Good Friday, 28 AD—both are within the parameters of the will of God.

Still, be it known to all men everywhere that they are always free to effect their own destiny. They may go the world's way, or the way into the City of God. God does exert control over them, but it is control by design only. This is to say that a man cannot design the particulars of either destiny, the world or the City of God, but he is always free to choose which of the destinies is to be his. He chooses which fork in the road he will take, but he does not determine where they occur, how many there will be, or where their ends lead.

There are also two exits. The world's is as continuous as is the entrance to the Neutral Zone. The world's exit provides fodder for the daily news media, until the end of the Sixth Millennial Day when Christ returns. Then, as Peter says, "the elements shall melt with fervent heat, and the world and every work in it will be burned up." As regards individuals, each in his dangerous or glorious freedom is moving at this very hour toward his exit, where he will "go to his own place," whichever his life has elected.

One of the most conspicuous controls God exerts in this Neutral Zone is to convert evil to good. Of course, we see this only *post facto* by an examination of historical events. Paul speaks out boldly, "Even Pharaoh was a servant of God." Yes, that is the way everything worked out, though the Jews involved in the Exodus from Egypt, I am sure, didn't think of him in such a role. Notice the subtle way that Moses speaks of him in the Exodus narrative, chapters 4-14. Nine times he says God hardened Pharaoh's heart, twice he says Pharaoh hardened his own heart, and four times the neutral passive voice is used, implying either or both causes: ". . . and Pharaoh's heart was hardened." It seems that Pharaoh and God wanted the same thing! However, the effect proved to be the exact opposite of what Pharaoh had intended.

There are many examples in Scripture of evil causes being transformed into good effects, among which are the evil roles of Joseph's brothers, King Saul's relentless pursuit of David, and David's great sin becoming a necessary link in bringing Solomon to the throne of Israel to reign during the height of its glory, and to produce three uniquely valuable books for the Canon of Sacred Scripture. What seems sublime is the martyrdom of Stephen, resulting in the conversion of Paul and possibly other early converts from Rome. It is thought that the death of Stephen had as much of an effect on those who stoned him (some of whom were likely members of the Synagogue of the Libertines in Rome) as it did on Paul, who abetted the crime.

Yet some have lives so amenable to God's plan that they seem to pass through the Neutral Zone without any modification at all. Enoch walked with God and was not, for God took him. Noah enjoyed such a reputation as well. Paul describes his own life in Phil. 3:12ff. He sees himself as running a long-distance race, forgetting everything behind him, and stretching forward to everything before him, running with all his might, his hand reaching out to grab the laurel crown in the hand of the referee up ahead. He tells us that the referee, Jesus Christ, has exactly the same attitude as he has—both with equal ardor want Paul to win the race! This mutual effort of the saved and the Savior is indeed a blessed contemplation. It is equaled only by that scene in heaven of the Pre-incarnate Christ contemplating his descent to earth in Ps. 40:6-8.

Paul speaks of the ideal, of course. How many things in our lives will end up in the C-dump? How much incinerated in the fiery trial? What bad things yet in our lives will, via the mysterious will of God, make it through the world's exit gate and shame us in tomorrow's newspaper? In a positive vein, how much are we laying in stow to enhance the persons we are yet to be, even now waiting to be added upon us as a wedding garb? Paul cautions that we are building even now, and that the fire—not that reserved for the wicked at the end of time—will burn away all wood, hay and stubble.

We will never know how the conversion or dissipation of forces contrary to God's will take place any more than we know WHY he allows certain forces obviously contrary to his ultimate will to pass through the Neutral Zone unscathed, approved for passage by his passive will, if not his active will! Neither do we know how the world of atoms is often aberrant to the same laws that make possible for 20-ton pterodactyls to soar skyward on aluminum wings and carry us easily to our destination beyond the speed of sound. Stranger yet, those same laws tell us a bumblebee could never fly—but it does.

This brings us to the larger question about Divine Providence: Why would a Good God, limited by the *summum bonum*, allow the coexistence of good and evil? A quick answer would be because we tolerate the coexistence of good and evil in our own lives. Before getting deeper into the subject, I want to pause a moment and speak about this puzzling expression, "coexistence of good and evil." It brings to mind what a critic of American culture once said about the stock market. He claimed that if he could be right 51% of the time, he could be a millionaire in no time at all. Given certain limitations, I suppose this would be true. But how about the notion that "marriage is a 50:50 proposition"? Such an arrangement would be doomed from the very start. It suggests a contest, a balancing act, a precarious balance between disastrous alternatives. It takes 100% investment from both parties to make a marriage work.

If we look at predestination vs. free will like this, we get into the same kind of trouble. The Good News is that God gives 100% because love goes as far as it can. It demands total commitment from those who would follow Jesus to his heavenly home. He says this so many times in the Gospels. Speaking about the coexistence of good and evil is a great deal like speaking about the separation of church and state. Both ideas are true if you keep your definitions precise. However, in the latter instance, one rarely keeps legal institutions separate from personal values when talking about the matter. Government should not make laws regarding church organizations. What has that to do with praying at school functions and acknowledging God in our salute to the flag?

Even so, when we speak of "coexistence of good and evil," immediately we think of 50:50, which is not true at all. As it stands, it suggests that God is like Zeus, as he is pictured in the *Iliad*, sitting up on Mount Olympus with a pair of scales lifted up in his right hand, Achilles in one pan and Hector in the other. Not so! Rather, the Bible presents us with the dominance of evil over good. We see Gideon's minority with a 1:1000 ratio, or Samson against a whole nation. We see God generating strength from "babes and sucklings" because of the enemy. Their hands are open to receive the hand and arm of the mighty God of Jacob. All this because of the size of the enemy and, of course, the infant size of the reaching hand.

It is easy to see why men would rather think of the coexistence of good and evil as well as the desirability of divesting government of all forms of the Christian witness. A 50:50 moral status quo suggests a divisiveness in God's care of the universe, and even that he is trying to obscure the distinction between good and evil via equal representation. This is probably why the ancients used to speak of Zeus as "The Deceiver." Also, when a person dulls the difference between good and evil—indeed, even denies the possibility of the existence of such categories as good and evil—he takes comfort in imagining the existence of gods with judgment as foggy as his own.

Yet when we see evil as dominant, it is not God, but the failure of man to improve himself that quite visibly is recognized as the source of the problem. Amid this gargantuan failure of man comes the ongoing victory of God working like yeast, invisible to most, and to others a city of transparent gold superimposed on the human race.

No matter what we may say about God's reason for allowing the dominance of evil over good, men still are blinded by Satan, as Paul tells us.

They want to be their own gods so badly that they must deny the existence of our Loving Heavenly Father, because any god they could imagine would destroy evil. However, some theists reject Christianity because of another doctrine clearly evident in Scripture, viz., limited atonement. Rather, they see eternal life positioned on a sort of grand staircase, with each occupant on a step of his own. They envision no "great gulf" between heaven and hell, as Jesus teaches in his parable about the rich man and Lazarus.

In II Pet. 3:9, the apostle says God is ". . . not wanting anyone to perish, but that all turn to repentance." Note that the KJV uses the word, "willing," instead of "wanting." Their choice, however, is too strong, for it suggests deliberate action, rather than strong desire as the verb chosen means. In contrast to this, Jesus concludes his Sermon on the Mount by warning us with the prophecy that, "because narrow is the gate and difficult the way," few will ever be saved. A blend of these two statements implies that men choose not to be saved, contrary to what God wants them to do. God has made all men with necessary design and opportunity to be saved. Heredity and environment have nothing to do with it. No one had greater advantage than Judas, yet he elected not to follow Christ. No one had less advantage than the Penitent Malefactor, and yet he sought salvation from his dying Savior.

Certainly the invitation rings out in the marketplace, "Whosoever will." Never did Christ turn anyone away, but some say there are limitations implied. For example, Jesus did not require, as does the police force of London, that all who come must be at least six feet tall. There are no financial, educational, environmental limitations, nothing to suggest Christians had to be from some elitist group. On one occasion, he said only sick people need a physician. Only the weary from labor and bowed down under heavy loads are invited to wear his yoke and to carry his load. In the Sermon on the Mount, he prophesies that only those who have all the characteristics of the gestalt of the redeemed will ever come to him: They must be humble, dissatisfied with themselves, meek before God, searching, merciful, sincere, peaceful, determined—all of these. Otherwise, they are not invited.

It is evident that Jesus requires of his followers only what is already accessible to everyone! Nothing exotic, nothing costly. Enoch "walked with God." There are no laws against doing that, are there? No specific equipment required? Jesus said great powers await those who follow him, and the only requirement is that we give ourselves to much prayer and fasting. I am a great admirer of Martin Luther, and the more I delve into his biography, the greater my admiration. John Wesley is another. These men were indefatigable, to say the least. All I have to do to be like them is to do as they did. Luther prayed two hours every day, and Wesley preached some of the best sermons of the eighteenth century, and often preached nearly every day of the week for an exceptionally long ministry. Why do people not come to Christ? Why do I fall so far short of the cloud of witnesses gone before me? We ourselves are the ones at fault. Let us not say, "God didn't make me religious," or some other nonsense like that.

In short, only those who cannot make it on their own are invited. Only the sick, physically and mentally limited, culturally disadvantaged, poverty-stricken, drunkards, prostitutes, cripples, the blind, deaf, maimed and crippled need apply. Paul describes what kind of people will follow Christ in the opening chapters of I Corinthians. It is in this way that the invitation is restricted and salvation limited. Christ did not die for all men, just for those who need him. God loves the world so much that he gave his Only Begotten Son as a sacrifice for their sins, but only those who have faith in him will be saved.

Each of us is free, and we cannot give up that freedom. We are defenseless before a merciful God for not using it to choose to honor his son. It is true that we did not design ourselves; that God did. We cannot see our own faces or touch our right elbows with our right hands, nor can we fly with the angels, nor can we go to an afterlife of our own design. But we are free to tighten the parallel lines between heaven and earth with the help of the Holy Spirit, our companion who guarantees God's presence.

Man is free, ironically enough, to "limit the Holy One of Israel," as the Psalmist says. Mr. Henley was right on the mark in his poem, "Invictus" when he said he was the captain of his soul, the master of his fate. Mr. Henley is with his Divine Judge, as we all will be at the end of this last millennial day.

A LOOK FORE AND AFT

After all our Bible study, our theological adventures, our sound and justifiable logical disputes, we are still not fully satisfied. We come at last to see that predestination starts with our creation and the One who created us. He was just as involved in the wombs of our mothers as in the womb of the Virgin Mary. David saw this in his stupendous Psalm 139. Even our genetic messages were inscribed in God's book before the foundations of the earth were laid. We were so formed, so potentiated, so environed in time and space by our Almighty Maker that we join all things made due to the counsel of his own will.

Still, it so happens in this world of ours that nobody is exactly satisfied with what God has done. I have never met anyone who would not have wished he had this man's personality, that man's talent, this woman's face, that woman's grace; oh, yes—I almost forgot to mention the other fellow's money. Always able to see those who (we suppose) are better off than we are, we wish God had done a better job in our behalf. On the other side of the creation issue, we see paupers as well as princes, imbeciles as well as geniuses, the ugly and the beautiful, the average and the gifted. We may swing to the other extreme and wonder why God treated some people so unfairly.

Paul saw that predestination came to rest on this issue. He hears the complaints of men, "Why did you make me this way, God?" His reply does not satisfy us at all: "Shall the pot say to the potter, why did you make me thus?" Answer? This is no answer at all! What Paul does is to put us on the access road of faith, onto the narrow and difficult one that leads home. We have here a Joban question. His problem is ours. We are too intelligent to keep from asking questions, the answers to which we are too stupid to understand.

So we are dissatisfied—good! That is exactly what God wants us to be. He wants us to be hungering and thirsting after right living. We must remember that we are gods en route to our ultimate potential. We are working synergistically with God to create another self "designed in heaven," as Paul says in II Cor. 5. We are creators, and our task is to build new selves by helping others build their new selves. We must keep as much of our potential out of the fire and the C-dump, i.e., to keep wood, hay and stubble out of our lives, and reduce vanity to a minimum.

What plays a major part in our building new selves is to remember the things God cannot do for us, most of which we must do for ourselves. Remember that as we near the City of God, angels will be leaning over the ramparts asking one another, "Who is this coming up out of the wilderness leaning on her beloved?" Notice that we are leaning—not going it alone, and decidedly not being carried.

I supposed we all learned in Sunday School that God cannot make a square circle or a stone so big that he cannot lift it. We know intuitively that God cannot lie, (nor can he make nature lie, either), and he cannot break a promise or the laws he gave men to live by. Thus, he could not break the law of gravity and jump from the temple, and then have men accept him by faith.

I am sure you can come up with an item or two to add to the list, as I did the other day. I realized God could not do something we find quite easy to do. God cannot ask a substantive question, i.e., one that generates from ignorance in quest of an answer. He cannot because he is Omniscient. He can ask rhetorical or dramatic questions, but not substantive ones.

The final item I have for this list is that God could not—absolutely could not—tell Job, the wisest of men the significance of the great calamity that happened to him. Let's listen in on the dialogue:

"God, please tell me why all this calamity came upon me. Why did you take away all my wealth, cause the death of my ten children and then smite me with smallpox all within one single day? All I ask is that you tell me why, and that will satisfy me."

God replies, "Job, you have no guarantee whatever that the answer will satisfy you! You are that ignorant of yourself. In fact, I know in advance that you would not be satisfied at all. So why should I give you an answer that will do no more than make you more miserable than you already are?

"Moreover, Job, your mind is too limited to understand the language I would have to use, and your life is too short to wait for so long an answer, which must start before the foundation of the world was laid—you would die of old age before I finished. Your memory, Job, could never retain the beginning of the answer by the time I reached the end of it.

"Job, if you wish, I will appoint Gabriel to instruct you for the next 20 years to speak the language we use up here in heaven. This will take four hours a day, every day. The vocabulary will take another 20 years, and by that time your head would be the size of a watermelon. Given how you already look with all those smallpox boils I gave you (for your own good, of course), this would make you awfully grotesque. Are you sure you want to go through all this? And remember, I told you that you would not be satisfied with the answer."

Job replies, sobbing, "Oh, Lord, forgive me! I have uttered things too wonderful for me to understand. Now I see that you love me, and that is good enough for me. I am perfectly content to wait until I get to heaven to ask the question—that is, if I don't forget to ask it."

Returning now to the present, let us add a few questions to the mix—even bigger questions like the Waco tragedy, the Oklahoma City bombing, and the demolition of the World Trade Center in New York, where nearly 3,000 innocent people were killed in the name of religion. What about such matters? Some are saying, "God had nothing to do with it," I am astounded that people can believe in the omnipotence and omniscience of God and then say that. It suggests to me that they are afraid to admit God allowed these events to occur because conscience may make a personal demand on them. Involving God in the matter would be like asking a Jew if Hitler was a servant of God, just as Pharaoh was during the Exodus. On the other hand, we have clergy going to their pulpits with a litany of sins that caused God to bring these tragedies upon us.

Both attitudes are wrong. These events did not occur beyond the scope of God's involvement, and the motive for his allowing them to happen is a Joban question, beyond our investigative powers. Jesus tells us what our reaction ought to be. He speaks of the falling of a tower in Jerusalem that crushed 18 men to death. He asks, "Do you suppose these were sinners above all others in Jerusalem?" Then he tells us to repent.

"But we have already repented," say some. Repentance, like so many other spiritual realities, is an ongoing attitude toward life, not some milestone located decades ago, when we forsook our egocentric universe for God's theocentric one. As long as we pray the Lord's Prayer, we need to repent, for we are to repent not only of the incidents of sins, but also of the proximate and even remote causes of our sins.

You might ask, "Is that all? Just repent? Isn't there any message for the United States as a whole?" Yes, there is, but I am not the person to give it. I am not qualified to respond to this matter. I will leave it to the experts. It is obvious to us all that there is nothing religious at all in the matter of the WTC massacre. What we do have is a gang of Middle Eastern dictators trying to conquer the world using religion as their motivating factor. They tried it once in the eighth century and nearly succeeded, and now they are trying it again in the 21st century. Let us pray for the leaders of our country that God will use them in making his response to militant Islam, if indeed that is the appropriate name for this gang of international terrorists.

Against the backdrop of the limitations of God, there is also the laughter. When we go with Gideon or Samson facing overwhelming odds, our laughter will be all the greater. Part of its *sforzando* will be in response to the belly-laughing against God and his Messiah going on in our very own American culture. When the Warren Court reached its decision about religion and public education, Satan hijacked the aircraft named First Amendment and plowed it into the American destiny with everyone on the Christian Road aboard. The Court claimed to be defenders of the First Amendment, i.e., free speech and so-called "separation of church and state," and that is exactly what it attacked by its decision. The Court entered the realm of religion, which was forbidden it by the First Amendment and, in effect, made laws against religion, which is tantamount to making laws establishing it. In addition, what of decisions legalizing the abortion of unborn infants, and the implications on religious convictions?

As the ungodly press forward in other areas, nibbling away at morality, the home, the traditional values by which man is named as a god en route, the perpetrators in their back rooms are having a good belly-laugh. They are, as they suppose, dragging America kicking and screaming into the 21st century, or building bridges to the future, as one of their leading advocates recently said.

The laughter is loudest in our entertainment industry, which is perhaps the most influential industry in America from the standpoint of media exposure for a large audience. I have heard of art exhibits and dramatic performances in our larger cities, whose degenerate pornographic specificities, frequently poking fun at orthodox Christianity, defy description, so filthy they are. Certain quarters, you see, are having a good laugh. Do I believe Jesus Christ is a superstar? Indeed I do, but my definition is not that bandied about Times Square. Secular Jews may fondly chuckle about God being a fiddler on the roof, but he was much closer to Moses than that, and his work among us is not best epitomized as fiddling. They have put Joseph before the limelight as a mere dreamer, just as his brothers did. Who wouldn't laugh at a recent depiction of Noah as a high-level moron at best, and a movie of Jesus as having a serious moral flaw?

Yet the laughter reaches its highest point—no, not with a portrait of the Virgin Mary smeared with elephant dung—but with a dramatic performance which deigns to give God a nickname, a French word for knee-high rubber boots that farmers wear to slop the hogs. God is the main character in the play, too, only he never comes on stage—that's the point, you see. God refuses to come to the aid of men. The play plainly tells us the "bush" of Moses and the "tree" on which Christ died are not quite enough. The play, *Waiting for Godot*, won a national prize for best play of the year. This must surely mean there is a lot of laughter going on.

Psychologists tell us that irony is one of the most popular causes of humor. We see it in behavior on stage that is contrary to reality, and we chuckle, for we join the author in laughing at the incongruous behavior. We see such irony in Psalm 2, which is a clearer message to repent than anything unexpected in our daily lives, the twin towers of the World Trade Center notwithstanding. It is the inspired message of God to us.

The Omniscient One knows how to capture the attention of men. The scene opens with rulers of the kingdoms of the world conspiring against Almighty God and his Messiah. See these rulers sitting on their thrones? But what is really the case? God has them in chains, but the thoughtless crowds do not see the chains. Some of them think God is up on the roof playing "The Flight of the Bumblebee." The kings, however, feel the chains, and they plan to rid themselves of these manacles, the God who cuffed them, and his King of Glory whose throne we in the audience see clearly—there Christ sits at the right hand of God.

It is now that we hear the laughter of God. The Hebrew word is more akin to the English "guffaw" than just laughter. And why not? What other response would one suspect when mere men are opposing Almighty God? How ironic. The fact that most of them have talked themselves into atheism makes God laugh all the louder. "Yet have I set my King upon my holy hill of Zion," saith the Almighty.

We, his children, will also laugh after we grow into spiritual maturity and become ready to be clothed with that edifice which is from above, after the valleys of deadly shadows, after the ascent up Har Megiddo, after we are able to see the whole picture. It is then that the irony of it all will overwhelm us. Do the ungodly believe me? Of course not. Yet the irony of their denial adds all the more to its spontaneous laughter. Who wouldn't laugh when our *Summum Bonum* comes from behind the veil of ambiguity that faith requires Him to wear now, and we shall see him face to face?

CHAPTER VII:
AMEN TO LAUGHTER

Road Maps: Isaiah 53; Philippians 2; Romans 8;
Psalms 22-24, 40, 110

The holy joy of Almighty God first entered literature in the theophany of Job, which is probably the oldest book in the Bible. God asks him, "Where were you when the morning stars sang together and all the sons of God shouted for joy?" God refers to the holy borne toward which our narrow and difficult path leads, before God spoke this immense universe into existence. It was a time of perpetual joy and laughter, when all speech seemed more akin to grand opera than to prosaic speech. Job's contemporaries—Abraham, Sarah and their son Isaac (Laughter)—learned to echo this inexpressible joy that goes on in our eternal home.

As we have seen, David spoke quite boldly of God's laughter in Psalm 2, guaranteed to be heard by all, especially those who presume to boast against the Almighty. Another of several other examples is Psalm 126, one to be sung by pilgrims making their effortful way from Jericho, up 15 miles of rugged footpath with a gain of over 3,000 feet in elevation by the time they reached Jerusalem. So difficult the trip was, especially for the aged in hot weather, that it frequently took two days to ascend. But as we read, we see they were expected to forget the difficult ascent, and rather to remember how happy they were when they returned to their home after the Babylonian Captivity. Listen to them:

> When the Lord brought back those that returned to Zion,
> We were like those that dream.
> Then was our mouth filled with laughter
> And our tongue with singing.

There are many other moments of laughter found in the Old Testament. Anyone reading in succession Psalms 22, 23 and 24 will experience the full gamut of human emotion, from the unfathomed sorrow of Skull Place to the ecstasy of bringing the Ark of the Covenant back to Jerusalem. In Psalm 22, David as prophet foretells of the Passion of the Lord Messiah 1,000 years before the event, followed by the joy of the resurrection and the birth of a new spiritual nation—the Church—which he calls "the great congregation." Then in Psalm 23, we are sheep following our shepherd with quiet confidence, though we are walking through the valley of deadly shadows. In Psalm 24, the scene changes to the return of the Ark to the Tabernacle in Jerusalem, with David leading the parade. Overcome with joy, he casts aside his brocade robe of state and dances before the Ark in his linen undercoat as it moves slowly up Moriah to its holy resting place in the Tabernacle. Then in Isaiah, there are moments of bliss as he, too, contemplates the "great congregation," and bids us to burst into joy as we see the Gentiles adding ecumenical dimensions to the worship of God.

The canonists of Holy Books are always jumping ahead of their contemporary scene—that's expected. We all do that. We laugh as though we were already home. Our anachronistic joy is used by God in his plans of evangelism. Yet our mountain-top experiences are rare, as they should be. We must come back down into the valley to eat and sleep and to participate in God's creation of the future, part of which is to join two other voices in confirming the laughter of the Father—Jesus, his Son and the *Paraclete*, the Adviser/Comforter, the Holy Ghost. God as a Holy Trinity sings and laughs in his polyphonic glory during this Sixth Millennial Day. We must hear these amens, and amplify their laughter to our uttermost!

To start with the advent of the Beloved Son, Messiah of prophecy, we must visit heaven again. It is David, the poet, prophet, warrior, king, lover of God, and son of Jesse, who is given the solo part to sing. Of all who foresaw events in the short ministry of Christ—Job, Abraham, Moses, Isaiah, to name a few—David more than all others is the prophet of the Passion. No one in the Old Testament more clearly and bountifully forecasted the Lamb of God who takes the world's sin away. Out of the necessary sufferings David endured as a result of his own great sin, he experienced such specific parallels to Christ's passion that he also saw Jesus' Day even more clearly than Abraham, and rejoiced. Indeed, who more than David could pierce through the veil to see the Universal Atonement? Who would need it more? After reading David's great Psalm of repentance (Ps. 51), one biblical scholar said that David was a Christian born 1,000 years too soon.

David also saw, more than anyone else in the Old Testament, the Pre-incarnate Glory of the coming Messiah. Twice he visits heaven before the foundation of the world was laid to see Christ enthroned beside the Father, finally victorious over future enemies. Referring to Psalm 110, Christ told the Jews this psalm was indeed about himself, and that he was David's Lord, not his son. He also removes all doubt about the nature of the psalm, and about David's role in writing it. David was not, as some suggest, writing about circumstances happening to himself that we could later apply to Christ, i.e., by "Providential coincidence." He was instead a conscious prophet of the coming Messiah—Jesus says so. David saw Christ's day just as clearly as Abraham did, and he rejoiced so intensely that he took up the prophet's pen and wrote down his visions of his coming Lord.

David begins Psalm 110 by quoting God telling his Son that he will be victorious over his enemies because of his strength. What is that strength? It is "the beauty of holiness," making him similar to Melchizedek, whose name means "King of Righteousness." Notice the "dews of his youth," which he will have forever. He is like Melchizedek, not only in expressing holiness and righteousness, but also in lineage. Note that the Scripture does not speak of his birth, death or ancestry. This, the Epistle to the Hebrews says, is Moses' way of expressing his eternal existence. See also that "his willing people" will include the Gentiles, here translated as "heathen." His advent will create two kinds of people—living worshippers in his kingdom, and dead bodies strewn over his battlefield. In verse 7 is a subtle reference to Christ's baptism and anointing of the Holy Spirit. Of interest to all devotees of the arts is the world's oldest statement of "aesthetic depth," or "signification." This is the theory that an object is beautiful because it reminds us of virtue, exemplary behavior. Surely this is similar to what John meant by calling Jesus *Logos*, the ideal man.

David's second visit is in Psalm 40, where he is quoting the coming Messiah himself. He is in heaven, in his Pre-incarnate Glory. Though the entire psalm is about the earthly ministry of the Messiah, we must confine ourselves only to the third stanza, verses 6-8. He is standing before his Father, apparently with a scroll in his hands. He has been reading the law of Moses. Yet remember that all this occurs before the fact, even before the foundation of the world was laid. Speaking to God he says, "You do not want a sacrifice or offering—my ears have you opened—burnt offering and sin offering you have not required." Here is subtlety and compression, a feature of the style used often by David. Also, we can derive two possible meanings from the verb, for it means "pierced" as well as "opened." The first meaning relates to Hebrew law. If a man sold into indentured servitude by his father comes to the end of his term of service, but does not want to leave his master, his ear is pierced with an awl as a sign that he now belongs permanently to the household of his master. Indeed, Christ would gladly submit to such a ceremony, for as Paul says, Christ will take on the role of a slave. So the verb chosen by the KJV translators stands as correct.

But what does the expression mean? I think the next line gives us a clue, "Then I said, Lo, I am come; in the scroll of the book it is written of me: I delight to do thy will, O my God." The expression "lo" is part of an idiomatic phrase common to most languages. It usually occurs in English as "lo and behold" and probably is a version of "look," as if to want to emphasize an important discovery by compounding the verb. We see another example of such a device in Lam. 1:12, as Christ speaks from the cross through the prophet Jeremiah: "Nothing to you, all ye who pass by? *Behold and see* if there be any sorrow like my sorrow . . . ." We are exhorted to look closely and analytically at the sorrow of Christ. What is that sorrow? The scourging that has gouged channels in his back and belly? The crown whose fierce acanthus needles pierce his brow? The spikes in hands and feet? No—none of these! They are a bargain for our Divine Lover to pay to show us his love. It is the indifference of men who would rather live with a devil's brew of good and evil and profoundly wish he were a god of hate to match and justify their own hate—this is what gives him sorrow.

Back to David, we read, "Lo, I am come," not in the future tense, but the present, what we in the eternal bleachers must see as God's extension of eternity into time. As Lord *Logos* utters these words, he seems to be standing on the outer rim of heaven looking toward humanity below, speaking to them instead of to God. I seem to hear him: "People, O Great Congregation of the Eternal City of God, I am coming! I am on the way even now. I know your sorrows and am coming even now to help you. See? Read the Book! It promises my coming. The sacrifices and burnt offerings prescribed by my servant Moses were only a temporary measure. They were never intended to be more than a school master to prepare you for my advent. I will atone for your sins. I come! I come!" Then, as a final good-bye to the Father, he turns and says to Him, "I delight to do your will, O my God. Yes, your law is in my heart." He then plunges downward, invading human history, diminishing his holy being into comprehendible dimensions, a slave he is, seeking the womb of a virgin girl, who like her Lord, delights to do God's will. Let us make no mistake about this passage. It is to be interpreted as a scene in heaven centering on the Pre-incarnate One, the Hope of Nations, the Messiah of the Great Congregation.

Turning to the New Testament, we discover two passages dealing with the Pre-incarnate *Logos,* who tented among us as Jesus of Nazareth. First is one of the most remarkable passages in the Bible, the Prologue of John's Gospel, the contents of which are so profound that it would take a long chapter just to list the bibliography of material in print about it. I will draw our attention only to the verses that speak of the Pre-incarnate *Logos* in our quest for seeing how God limits his omnipotence in our world, and then invites us to share in the laughter over the inevitable victory he shares with his entire Sanctified Kingdom.

John gives the Pre-incarnate Son of God the name of *Logos*, or narrowly expressed in English as "Word." In the Greek it means much more, indeed. As all biblical scholars are aware, the ancient history of this word would fill many pages of fine print, but I will give you only their summary as best I can—it means the Ideal Man who, in the thought of Plato and other Greek philosophers, dwelt in the spiritual and eternal world. These lovers of wisdom believed in two worlds—the real and the ideal—the real being but a spatial-temporal extension of the ideal. All things in the eternal world are perfect, or ideal. The perfect man went by the name of *Logos*.

You will see then that the philosophical meaning of the word has nothing to do with "word" as the primary unit of thought, speech and writing. Rather, we see John's meaning expressed in the names of collegiate disciplines such as psychology and sociology. Such usage takes *logos* as meaning "essential nature," and the essential nature of man is the Lord Jesus Christ. One might even think of John's Gospel as a run-on definition of *logos*. Emmanuel wastes no time in telling us about himself. Our Mighty Wordsmith takes his sledge in hand, puts his spiritual anatomy upon the anvil and strikes so loudly that the echo has gone round the world, through cultural barriers of all sorts, iron curtains, bamboo curtains and the like. Through centuries he makes our hearts his echo chambers, 108 angels as his orchestra, an infinitude of saints his choir, drowning out the din of war to this very hour. Until the end of time he proclaims: "I am the water of life, I am the bread of life, I am the light of the world, I am the good shepherd, I am the door, I am the road, I am the truth, I am the life, I am the resurrection, I am the morning star—before Abraham was, I myself am." After that last claim, they picked up stones to stone him. In the Garden of Gethsemane, God took over his lungs, larynx, cheeks and tongue and roared, "I MYSELF AM!" so that those who came to take him went tumbling backwards, like dead leaves before the autumn's blast!

John says that in heaven God and the *Logos* are an inseparable duality of One, and this doctrine is straight from heaven, viz., that Christ is the instrument of divine action by whom the universe was made. Then John says the life in him is the light of men. Here John joins two worlds, making himself and mankind inhabit both worlds. The Prototype of man becomes the template by which we measure our present selves (much to our disappointment), and participate with God in creating our future selves (to the increase of our hope). As light is to our natural selves, so is he to our souls.

It is here that we must leave the rest of the Prologue, as *Logos* becomes flesh and pitches his tent among us. However, we must not leave heaven just yet. Paul, who was once caught up into the third heaven and beheld unutterable things, perhaps describes such to the Philippians (Phil. 2:5ff.). He wants to voice his echo of our Old Testament citations and most of what John had to say. He repeats that Christ is equal with God in his pre-incarnate state. He becomes the lowest of men and dies for our sins after leading a perfect life. Paul then makes the grand sweep from Pre-incarnate Glory to the Great Judgment as he foresees a time when every knee will bow and every tongue will confess that Christ is Lord to the glory of God. This in general terms is what the Bible says about the glory of Christ. One observation Paul shares, though, is unique and of extreme importance to theologians as well as us. It is the verb "emptied." The Divine *Logos* reduced himself to human form. This reduction of Lord *Logos* to human form relates to our theme of limitation.

Before the foundation of the world was laid, all the works of God were planned (Heb. 4:3), and this includes the Kingdom of God, which we will inherit (Mt. 25:34). Indeed, we were then chosen to be saved citizens in the Kingdom (Eph.1:4). Our names were then known, the hairs on our heads were numbered and all our members were written down in God's book (anthropogenic metaphor for the omniscience of God) before we were created (see Ps. 139:13-18). In his great high-priestly prayer in Gethsemane, Jesus told the Father that he was aware that he loved the Son before the foundation of the world was laid (John 17:24), and both Peter and John echo David in Ps. 40 by saying the crucifixion of Christ was also predestined (I Pet. 1:20, Rev. 13:8). In the Apocalypse, John says the names of the ungodly were excluded from the Book of Life at that time (Rev. 17:8). So we were designed, predestined to inherit the Kingdom prepared by the Christ, who was to be crucified for us, and also would have been for those who refused to accept his universal atonement, and whose names were blotted out from the Book of Life all before the foundation of the world was laid. What can I then conclude? If God be for us, who can be against us?

So Lord *Logos* leans over the edge of heaven just over 4,000 years ago, and says to all of us in the eternal audience of desperate souls, to us prisoners of hope, "Lo, I am coming, just as the scroll of the Book says I will." Then he straightens up and turns to the 108 of angels tiered upon the ramparts, smiles at the Eternal Father of us all, and shouts "I delight to do exactly what you want, O my God! Yea, I delight to do thy will! Thy law is within my heart," and plunges earthward! As he leaves our future home, he loses the eternal extension of that glory too intense to share with us. Yet what he brings even now glows on our faces, and on the pages of our version of the superlative life of Lord *Logos* having become Jesus of Nazareth, the Savior of the world.

And what is it that we see? Is he as tall as Saul of Kish? As muscular as Samson? As fair as Joseph? David? No, he wears none of these distracting disguises. He is as common as an annual weed or a root protruding from the ground. He has no beauty of physique or face. He has come *in* flesh and not *for* flesh. The Lord *Logos* has pitched his tent among us. His name must also be common, the Hebrew word for "Salvation of the Lord," *Yashua* (or Jesus to us Westerners), son of Joseph the carpenter from the Gentile town of Nazareth in Galilee, on the outer limits of civilization where Roman merchants outfit camels for trips to Damascus to buy silks and spices from Cathay.

His arrival will be unspectacular, too. He will be born to a peasant girl in that sheep station just south of Jerusalem, Bethlehem. She will bring forth on the bare ground one winter's day in a stone quadrangle, a sheep pen, among ewes that also give birth this time of year. There is no room for her at the far end of the pen under the awning where shepherds sleep on soft, clean straw, sheltered from the dews and rain, maybe even snow. This area is called the *kataluma*, charmingly translated "inn." The porter, who owns the stone enclosure and rents space nightly to shepherds and their sheep, has opened a collapsible feeding trough where she may lay the infant.

We must pass by this awesome beginning which, for the first 400 years of the Christian Era, was virtually ignored by early Church Fathers, who were preoccupied with his greater glory that would outshine the sun. Our narrative begins on the bank of the Jordan River, where it empties into the Dead Sea. In one biblical language it is "The Floor of Heaven," and in another "The Roof of Hell." It is the lowest place on earth. Jesus, coming toward the waters of baptism, is confronted by one of the holiest men who ever lived, whose lips are immediately seized by the Holy Spirit, and they cry out for all to hear, "Behold the Lamb of God, who takes away the sins of the world."

Who is it on whom the Spirit of God descends as he rises from the baptismal waters? We can never fully know, of course, not even as much as we know each other. Certainly, we will not attempt a psychiatric study of Jesus, as Albert Sweitzer did as he set forth on his quest for "the historical Jesus." Our best approach is more in keeping with an adaptation of St. Alselm's definition of God.

Recently, Harvard Medical School announced it had just admitted its youngest medical student at 12 years of age. He had already graduated from college and was admitted with an IQ beyond the upper limit of any known intelligence test. Let us imagine Jesus as having that much reasoning power, memory, and even more. In the words of Alselm, he has the logic and memory than which none could have conceivably more. This is true also of his intuition, imagination and judgment, and whatever other categories satisfy human definition. He is that human than whom none could possibly be greater, plus the infusion of the Holy Spirit. So endowed, he sets forth to speak, as we would expect, as no man had ever spoken, to live as no man had ever lived, to do what no man has ever yet been able to do. He called himself Ben Adam—Son of Red in translation, as we have previously noted. This is probably the closest he could come to what John means by *Logos*. This name is probably the most written—about common noun in any of the world's languages. Lord *Logos* has been reduced to a being than whom none could be conceivably greater, "full of grace and truth," as John says.

To say that Jesus Christ is the totally endowed human being is also to say two other important things of a negative nature. First, he was not a spirit disguised as a man. He was a real flesh-and-blood person, wearing our clothes, needing our food, experiencing our temptations, yet without sin. He would prove by his teaching and living that we humans can overcome carnal dependence, become citizens of his spiritual kingdom, and in the process be forgiven for our willful mistakes—our sins. Second, he had no help not available to all men of faith who receive the Holy Spirit into their lives. This is why he said that we could even do greater works than he did. For us to believe this, we must see that Christ had no X-factor in his makeup, or supernatural help not readily available to us all.

Only when we see Jesus without an X-factor do we see his life as an open-ended challenge to us to keep trying to be more like him. Only then are we kept humble as we see the attainable yet unattained. Only then does the living Christ pitch his tent next door to us. We must avoid at all cost this erroneous X-factor notion that crept into the early Church.

Since Christ differs from us in degree, even as we differ from each other in degree, we must assume he had the same kind of compensations at work in his life that we have. His intuitive power enabled him to see potential virtue in people with unerring accuracy. That same power meant equal discernment of potential evil in enemies determined to destroy him. He was able to intuit what people thought, whether good or bad. He also knew how to motivate people, how to bring into play the means of uninhibiting their potential for good or evil, and anticipate their responses to what he said, be they virtuous or violent actions. His unwavering priorities evinced from others varying degrees of challenge, both positive and negative. As regards aesthetic judgment, compensation was most evident in making the cheap and sensational the more painful to experience, and the class of the best the more blissful to enjoy. There are other categories and convincing citations for them all, but I must do no more here than to exhort us all to continue our search for ourselves, which, after all, is the best way of knowing.

Nothing we have yet said about Christology explains Jesus' frequent expressions of prescience, or knowledge not available to human experience. Recall how he shocked Nathaniel by saying he saw him earlier in the day under a fig tree. Apparently, Nathaniel was convinced nobody but God could possibly have known he was under that tree. Jesus also told the Samaritan woman of her marital history, and sent Peter to find a coin in a fish's mouth—a matter that stretches the ratio of probability beyond the limits of our present numbering system. He knew of Lazarus' death, though he was many miles from Bethany at the time. He told his disciples where to find an ass for him to ride on Palm Sunday, and how to locate the house where they were to eat the Passover. During that supper, he spoke of the disciples' desertion and Judas' betrayal, ending with the prediction that Peter would deny him three times before the cock would crow twice. If Christ had no X-factor, no outside help, how are these things possible?

Jesus tells us that God takes total control of him at such times. On one occasion, Philip asks Christ to make the Father visible to them and they will be wholly satisfied. Jesus tells him that his question is irrelevant because he and the Father are one and the same person. That is, if God were to take human form, he would appear exactly as whom they beheld in his person. Then he tells them, "Do you not have faith that I am in the Father and the Father is in me? The words which I speak to you, I do not speak from myself, but the Father dwelling in me does the works." Notice that Jesus includes what he says and does as being the work of the Father. We have then Christ's explanation of how he is prescient and performs the mighty acts of God, and he tells us all that we can move mountains, too.

In searching for Christ's amen to the limitation of God's power—or rather, the accommodation of God's power to our limitation—and the laughter of God's triumph, we must turn to the Passion of Christ, roughly contained within the last two weeks of his earthly ministry, especially being led by John's Gospel, which spends virtually 50% of its volume on that subject. We must never think of Christ's Passion as expressive of Christ's weakness and God's withdrawal from the scene, both of which have been implied or expressed by some theologians. Nothing could be further from the truth. It is in the nature of things that opposites become more visible when brought together in extreme circumstances. We speak correctly when seeing the agony and ecstasy conjoined in the creative process of great artists. Love and hate are not antonyms at all—each is but one side of the same coin. To the degree that you love, to that same degree you hate what would destroy whom you love. It is apathy that is the antonym of love. As passivity in one invites activity in another, so weakness opens the door to strength. "For when I am weak, then am I strong," Paul tells the Corinthian Christians. Pain and laughter can be as intimate as the twins, Jacob and Esau, though they are as opposite in looks as in behavior. Just ask Mother Sarah if this is not so. Her pain made her laugh as the angel told her that she at 90 would give birth to a son.

It is in Jesus' Passion far more than in anything else in his three-and-one-half-year ministry that brings him to laugh at Atlas with the earth on his shoulders. After all, it weighs but a mere 1017 tons. Rather, without doing a thing, by *being* and nothing more, he will uninhibit the Satanic forces in human nature for all to see. By just *being* he will force their hands to strip him naked, and thereby generate a cosmic cloud to cover that nakedness. In that midnight at high noon, his enemies become naked, too, and see God and themselves as no one has ever been able to before or since. They see Jesus, his flesh scored by the Roman flagellum, hands and feet impaled, brow crowned with acanthus, him wearing the tattoo of their depravity and the love God has for them.

He wins! The long-awaited one came and did what he said he would, and he used their hands to do it. Of course, they did not know what they were doing. Still, they lifted him up, and he continues to draw all men unto himself. On that day, his light outshined the sun, and yet in the truest sense he didn't do anything at all—he was just *being*.

It is in John's Apocalypse we get the best summary of what happened on Good Friday, and it is almost as amazing as the Christ who did nothing. He summarizes the Passion in a two-word paradox we call an oxymoron. In chapter 5, John gives us a vision of God seated on his throne in heaven. He holds a large scroll made up of an axle on which seven important messages are stacked. Nobody is found worthy to open the scroll, over which John weeps until he is told that "The Lion of the Tribe of Judah" will open it. Yet when the vision presents this Lion, he appears as a Lamb, whose breast in imbrued due to having its throat slit in preparation for sacrifice. It also has surrealistic features—"seven eyes and seven horns, which are the seven Spirits of God gone forth into all the earth." The message is that the slain

Lamb is also omnipotent, omniscient and omnipresent, using Hebrew numerology. John is promised a Lion and gets a Lamb! This is the Lion-Lamb oxymoron.

I will never forget the time I asked my students to solve this oxymoron as part of their final examination. Those who chose this question did miserably. Essentially, they said that sometimes Christ acted as a Lion and sometimes as a Lamb. This will never do—we must never see two things, but one only, viz., the Lamb. The Lamb must present the Lion as more leonine than were the Lion considered singly. Since we are dealing with metaphors, we must abstract only one feature of each—the power of the Lion and the meekness or passivity of the Lamb. Our task is to understand how the power of God becomes more forceful when it is passive than when it attacks directly, as lions are wont to do.

Of course, we think immediately of Aesop's famous fable of the wind and the sun. Both claimed to be the stronger of the two, so they had a contest. Each attempted to make a passerby take off his coat. The wind blew, but the harder his effort, the more tightly the man held his coat in place. Yet in no time at all, the sun raised the temperature so high that the man gladly took his coat off.

Even so, the power of God, the Lion of Judah, reveals himself to man via the passivity of the Lamb to man's violence. The Lion also reveals God to man via the passivity of the Lamb to his Heavenly Father. That revelation is Love. So we see how closely akin love and hate are. The love of God endures the hate of men with such intensity that love must reveal the hate that most desires to conceal itself. The Lion and Lamb as seen in the Apocalypse are fused into one. How God hates what makes men hate! How he loves the hating ones, who have so disguised their hatred that they imagine a love for God that compels them to cry for the crucifixion, and their hatred of him is no more than a projection of what they hate in themselves.

If our meekness makes us inherit the earth, even so can the staggering little Lamb with a bloody bib splattered on his white breast become the Lion of the tribe of Judah! Oh, the omnipotence of God, passivity at its highest limit, like a black hole in outer space, a less-than-nothing drawing all things into itself. So the passivity of Jesus of Nazareth draws that six-inch iron spike into the palm of his outstretched hand while he says, "Father, forgive them, for they do not know what they are doing."

Indeed, what are they doing? They are acting without a cause! Such inability to supply causes for their action lays bare their reasons, which the crucified Son of God demands that we supply for ourselves. This discovery about human nature, like all other discoveries, once entering history never loses its presence. Such is the power of the Lion-Lamb.

GOTTES LIEBESTOD

As you see, I begin our thematic study of Emmanuel's Passion by borrowing one of Wagner's greatest titles, just as John robbed Plato and Heraclitus of one of their favorite terms. There is no harm done when we sanctify the secular—God alone knows how often the ungodly have profaned the holy! Besides, I am in constant quest of new ways to sing the Old Story, so that the newness might catch the attention of the ungodly and turn them from the cant of cliché to hear anew the trumpet of the approaching day.

According to John, the Liebestod aria, the Song of all Songs, or the Beloved's Dance of the *Mahanaim*, begins a fortnight before his own. This day that started with weeping, and with Jesus weeping, ended with laughter, delirious joy, unchained ecstasy that lasted at least a week. People came and went—family, friends, saucer-eyed curiosity seekers and dignified clergy—some of whom had actually attended the funeral services, all wanting to see for themselves a miracle greater than Elijah's raising of the widow's son. Indeed, Jesus had not only restored the spark of life, but reversed the process of deterioration as well. This they all knew, and many went away believing that Jesus was the Messiah.

This did not sit well with the top clergy. At first, they said Jesus must die; then they saw their damage control must also include Lazarus. Surely, they believed, the two of them somehow had faked Lazarus' death and postponed this little "miracle" of theirs until such a time as only God could possibly perform it. Caiaphas reminded his inner circle that he had prophesied that Jesus would die for the people to unite them and to bring back God's people from the nations of the world. It may be that Caiaphas thought of Jesus as an Elijah being used by God to prepare the way for the military Messiah that would bring little Israel into world prominence. Whatever he thought, John mentions this prophecy to indicate their "spiritual" justification for plotting murder.

I trust we all see quite clearly the parallel between the ascent up Moriah for these 12 disciples and that of Abraham. Jesus told them in advance the unbelievable news that he was going to the home of his friend, Lazarus, and raise him from the dead several days after he had died. Were they happy about this? Not at all. Yet they would be loyal, these "Little Faiths," as Jesus was fond of calling them, and go with him to their certain deaths. Peter, James and John had been eyewitnesses to the raising of Jairus' daughter. Maybe at first they thought Jesus might raise Lazarus—if he hurried, that is. Yet the one-day's trip of less than 20 miles was not to be.

We ought not to stray from our study of Christ's amen to the limitations and laughter of our Heavenly Father, yet we must pause to compare the events in John's Gospel with those of the Synoptic Gospels if we are to understand how Jesus' retinue would take four days to make a one-day's trip. Luke tells us they went through Jericho, where two well-known events took place—the healing of blind Bartimaeus, and the dinner at the home of the tax collector, Zacchaeus. Of course, we see Jesus thronged by crowds in both instances. It may be that he spent the night, and perhaps even the next day in Jericho. He was delaying, you see! He was in touch with all events in God's timetable, and he was pacing them. During this delay, we see the disciples, like Abraham, being told in advance so their faith would grow during the delay. Still, they also become like Jairus, almost ready to collapse with anxiety as Jesus is deterred by fingers in the crowd desperately stretching toward the hem of his garment. The time element seems so crucial to Jairus as well as to the disciples. As they follow Jesus up the narrow and difficult way up Moriah, what are their thoughts? They know what Jesus said he was going to do, no doubt about that. Did any yield to a whisper from the Holy Spirit, "Could not one whom you just saw open the eyes of Bartimaeus also raise the dead?"

"Yes, but after four days . . . ?" he would have thought . . . and so might I.

Four days ago? Martha hastens to remind her Lord about the condition of Lazarus' body, thinking Jesus intended to "pay his last respects" to the departed. We all know the rest of the narrative. How could we ever forget it, having read it even once? Still, we go back to this show of omnipotence, mainly because we need it ourselves. We read, ponder, and rejoice as our own "comma" is placed on our final page in history. I hear him roar with trumpets, "Lazarus . . . John . . . Mary, come forth!"

Before the celebration begins, there is one somber note; someone is running to the High Priest with this amazing news. John speaks of this messenger as being unhappy at what he has just witnessed, but that is to be expected. It will be that way when we all rise from the dead—some will hate most what is most loved by others.

We see evil men in pursuit of their own goals, and that God is using them (without asking their permission) for purposes other than those they would approve. God's invisible hand is still at work, tricking the tricksters—and why not? What could be a better teaching device? John Stuart Mill sees this invisible hand controlling the marketplace. We see its raw power on the athletic field. What really wins the game with two opponents having equal prowess and skill? Out-tricking the opponent!

We Christians must look at history and our own lives in this way. God not only makes available to all both heaven and hell, but also a heaven so expressive of man's profoundest hope that seeing it and not having it would be hell, indeed!

On our way to the Garden of Gethsemane, we pause a moment to note (as Jesus said we would) an act of kindness paid him that would never be forgotten. As was the custom among the well-to-do in those days, Mary had purchased an alabaster box full of pure musk, sealed with beeswax. It was to be used to anoint her own body for its funeral. She anoints Jesus with this musk at one of those meals celebrating Lazarus' returning from the grave. Which meal? Whether it happened on the Saturday night before Palm Sunday, as John says, or on Tuesday of Holy Week as the other Gospels say, what really matters is that its fragrance was present in all the scenes of Christ's Passion. Visitors at Windsor Castle are invited to smell the drapes along the grand stairway. They still faintly exude the odor of the musk Queen Victoria was fond of wearing. So it is certain that all witnesses of the Passion will smell it on Christ's person. Some will be in awe—he acts like a king, and he smells like one, too. Others will be in paroxysms of anger, like Judas, who is, at that very moment, strangely moved by the heavenly odor by the invisible hand of God. Mary's act of love has uninhibited the Satanic force within. The Lion of Judah is working through the Lamb of God, and will again. Keep this in mind as we move along. Ask yourself what effect it worked on those sour priests, Pilate, the soldiers, the Penitent Malefactor, the Centurion. Did God waft some holy fragrance, drench the air with some sacred effect to accompany Christ's "Amen Chorus" to his Divine Will? Some say Dante's one line is the most beautiful in all poetry, *E'n la sua volontade e nostra pace*—"In his will is our peace." The excellency of Christ may be so great that you may have transfer associations among your senses, like the Shulamite; "Thy name (to the ear) is like ointment poured forth (to the nostrils), and therefore do the virgins (all the senses) love thee" (Song of Sol. 1:3).

We arrive at the "Upper Room," or "guest chamber" as the KJV translators call the *kataluma,* the same word used for the shepherds' shelter at the end of the sheep pen where Jesus was born. Now it is but a makeshift tent raised on the roof of a stone house. I mention it only to show the difficulty translators have in translating Empire Greek as spoken two thousand years ago into modern English.

As you experienced readers are quite aware, the differences between John's Gospel and the other three increase as we near the end of Christ's 42-month ministry. We will leave feet-washing, his surprising omission of any reference to Communion, and his great sermon on The True Vine for another time and occasion, but two matters in this *kataluma* bear directly on our theme—the two references to Judas and Jesus' claiming victory in his prayer. He tells the disciples that one of them will betray him, then at an inconspicuous moment, he makes Judas fulfill the Divine Will of having Christ crucified *during* rather than *after* Passover. The most the priests had hoped for was to destroy Christ after everyone went home, especially those Galileans who were more wholly convinced that one of their own was God's Messiah. Now that Judas knows for sure where the disciples and Jesus will go after the Passover meal, he is equipped to move toward his destiny—God's version, not his. So our Lord, always in control, always with escape at his elbow, never being surprised by some unpredictable turn of events, joining the Father who wishes him to die during Passover, with simple words opens the door for Judas to escape out into the midnight darkness.

Let us pause a moment to correct an error in the popular version of our thinking. This is not Maundy Thursday; that's according to earthly calendars. Passover began at sunset, so it is Good Friday. The Passover Meal, the betrayal, capture, trial, execution, death and burial of Jesus all take place on the same day, within the same diurnal passage of time according to the biblical definition of the day. Because creation begins at "evening," as we read in Genesis, so does the New Creation two thousand years ago.

At six hours into the sixth day of this week, Judas rushes eagerly to the high priest, gets his coins and thinks about the favor he has done his master. He has cleared the way for Jesus to become King! He will perform a miracle and overthrow the Romans. God has used him to make all this possible, and his purse a lot heavier, too! "Isn't it great how God works things out?" he must have joined Caiaphas in thinking.

Back under the *kataluma*, we hear Jesus giving his final words to his disciples, the final message of his 42-month ministry. He notes (John 16) how close pain and pleasure often exist, joy coming after the pain and dangers of birth pangs. I am reminded of the birth of Rachel's last child, a breach birth, which causes her death, but not until she names her son Benoni, "son of my birth pangs." Jacob soon changed the name to Benjamin, "Son of my Right Hand." This reflects our Lion-Lamb theme in that Jacob chose a name for his last son that is better than he ever would have chosen had the birth been average in nature. What's more, Benjamin became, as some scholars have felt, the prototype of us Gentile members of the Sanctified Race.

Before the little company sings a hymn and goes out to Gethsemane, Jesus prays his High Priestly Prayer (John 17), a formal prayer, not one that expresses closet intimacy, but for all to hear like the one uttered by a minister during public worship. From its ocean of thought, we take but two drops. First, note his bold proclamation of power in verse 2, his victory over the physical world, "power over all flesh." He speaks of himself in the third person, in contrast to what we see in verse 5, a request in the first person, "glorify me with your own self, with the glory I had with you before the world was." A blend of the first with the third person, the past with the future through the present, proclaims victory over the two entities that summarize this evanescent existence of ours, this space-time disorientation with eternal reality fits an understanding of what living spiritually means: When the recollection of past events and the anticipation of future events modifies present behavior, then we are living spiritually. This, and absolutely nothing less, will qualify our Lord to endure what he must a short time hence.

Secondly, note a limitation on his entire life, a major requirement of his slender ministry among us—the demand given by Moses, David and all the other prophets in specific prophecies of his ministry. In verse 12, he specifies his fulfillment of the foretelling of Judas' perfidy. Two things our natures demand: that he fulfill prophecy and live the life he preached. There must be a Gospel *about* him and a Gospel *by* him. We are made to tremble, fellow Christians, as the Negro spiritual says, knowing that what Love gives, it also demands. Still, let us brush the tears aside for a few more moments—he will yet make them jewels of joy upon our cheeks.

IN THE LOCKER ROOM

In our study of the Lion-Lamb effect of our Lord, have we nothing to say of his standing before Herod? No, because before him Christ does and says nothing at all. This brother of the Herod who decapitated John the Baptist flings a royal robe around Jesus' shoulders as a personal message to Pilate. Before Pilate, on the other hand, Jesus admits he is a king, and then takes away any excuse Pilate would have to condemn him as an enemy of the state by saying his kingdom is not of this world. Then he repeats the most obvious dictum of historiography—that all our earthly power comes from God. We leave this now to note something that is not quite so obvious about history, but just as true, viz., that men, in their attempts to "help" by means of compromise, usually end up making things worse. We need to have this clearly in mind as we enter the locker room. Mr. Pilate would have Jesus scourged and then let him go. After the scourging (the odor of musk, as exciting to his tormentors as to Judas), the thorn crown that shadows his face and the purple robe hide his bleeding body. So Pilate cries out, *"Ecce homo!"* and all that the Jews see are the robe and the thorn crown—they are oblivious to his bleeding body and his countenance "marred more than any man's," in the words of Isaiah. They eye him, and as Isaiah says, there is no beauty that they should desire him. They cry out for his crucifixion. Their king is the Blessed One above, who has nothing to do with this thorn-crowned son of a carpenter. So Pilate's compromise makes things worse than using the direct approach of condemning Jesus outright. His attempt to convince himself that he has been a fair judge and rid himself of a sticky problem at the same time has failed. A symbolic washing of his hands deceives nobody but himself.

We needn't stop here any longer amidst this show of human weakness. We must go off stage left since we wish to see the Lion-Lamb at work. The slain "lamb" of our aging bodies needs to feel the Lion of Judah surging in us as whichever millennium sunset comes next, the personal or the universal.

While they are taking off Jesus clothes and preparing the whipping post and the flagellum, I pause to note something from the *Poetics* of Aristotle. Poetry is quite appropriate here, what we define as "crystalized thought expressed in eloquent language." That is exactly what is about to happen. Aristotle said we can have a drama without a plot, but not without character analysis. No place here to argue the point, but the truth is evident that the scourging of a criminal in this locker room, which must have happened almost daily for decades prior to this day and will occur again countless times henceforth, is not as important as to whom it will happen on this day. The person always transcends the event.

Who is it who is about to experience this seemingly compassionate gesture of Pilate? None of the rules of language make a definition possible for me at this moment! John in his Apocalypse tells us of silence in heaven by the space of half an hour. We join them at that more comfortable distance in silent wonder as the King of Glory begins his suit of love. I will let his naked body and the flagellum of Rome speak directly to our souls.

One leading Bible scholar made famous for his paraphrases of biblical passages spoke of this first wound of Jesus as needing a modern word, one we today can more readily understand. He recommended we change our English word "scourging" to "flogging." This seems overstated to me. Flogging is what happens when a cat-o'-nine-tails is used. We are speaking of using the ancient Roman flagellum. We also must forget all about the 40 stripes per punishment. Five strokes of this device was all a man in the prime of his life could endure. So damaging was this device that it is never used on animals, lest they be damaged so badly that their usefulness was diminished. The Roman flagellum was for human beings only! The Romans were quite accustomed to stooping as low as needed to keep their empire under control, and when you treat people as less than human, you become as low as you make them. In Ps. 22, we read of Jesus' tormentors, "Dogs have beset me round . . . I am become a worm and no man." The power of man lowers the flagellum; the power of God rises to meet it with silence. Hear the roar of the Lion-Lamb?

The flagellum consisted of three layers of leather, wide as a barber's razor strap and much longer. To the inner layer were attached flat lead weights, and protruding from the outer layers were iron barbs bent toward the handle. The malefactor's bound wrists were attached to a waist-high iron ring in a wall or a stone post. Then two soldiers would pull at his hips until his torso was parallel to the ground. When the flagellum fell, its weight would force the end to curl under the body and embed the barbs into his flesh. With a powerful jerk, the flagellum was drawn away. Sometimes eyeballs were torn from their sockets, a cheek was ripped away from the bone, a gut was torn from the viscera, ribs were exposed, and blood flowed freely. You can understand the relief of Paul when he once escaped being "examined by scourging," by proclaiming his Roman citizenship. So damaging was the flagellum that it could be used on citizens of Rome only after they had been convicted of a crime. Paul had, however, endured the traditional "flogging" five times at the hands of the Jews. He received, according to custom, 39 stripes on each occasion.

They are now lashing Christ's wrists together. They are limiting the Holy One of Israel, as the Psalmist laments. What is about to happen offers no surprises to Jesus. He and his Father had already discussed this impromptu compromise of Pilate. They had agreed that the Lion-Lamb must show his greatest power, so men henceforth would stand forever in awe of him.

As they were trussing him up, he must have recalled the words of Isaiah, reminding him that God is using Pilate, using the powerful youth now taking the heavy flagellum off the wall, using the royal scent of the musk, and will use Christ's own response to the hideous claw of the flagellum—his silence—to work all things according to the counsel of his own will. Scripture says Christ will be silent, so he must do God's will.

The first lash falls—the wounds of our Lord's Passion have begun! I seem to hear angels chanting, "He gave his back to the smiters, and his cheek to them that plucketh off the hair." Indeed, the first lash caught his cheek, and now indeed his "countenance is marred more than any man's." Maybe he thought, too, of the promises of Rom. 8:28 and I Cor. 10:13, that all things worked for his own good, and that no temptation would be more than he could endure. Believing then what Paul would someday write reminds the silent, bleeding Lord of Glory that the worse they did to him, the more clearly his Lion will roar through the silence of the Lamb.

His tormentors wait for his scream of agony, but his silence and that royal odor from the musk, though admirable in themselves, serve now to anger his tormentors. So he will not say a mumbling word? The master of the flagellum will lay-to with greater force. Again the flagellum arcs into the air and falls across his shoulders, tearing into those muscles of the upper arms and shoulders. He will not be able to carry his cross across town and out the Beautiful Gate to Skull Place. Christ hears again the almost joyous voices from the Great Congregation of 20 Christian centuries, "Surely, surely, he hath borne our griefs and carried our sorrows! All we like sheep have gone astray. We have turned everyone to his own way, and the Lord laid on him the iniquity of us all."

The flagellum falls again! He hears, "And with his stripes we are healed." Then perhaps the vision of the Shulamite comes into view. She sees through other eyes as though from Eternity. She describes his torn flesh: "His body is of ivory, veined with sapphires." This is what I, too, see.

Once more the devil's claw tears at his flesh in the lower region of his viscera, the soft underbelly of his body. Who knows what is torn? What pain rushes out of his bleeding flesh? Yet the Christ who rose to victory in the Garden now exhibits it here. His shattered flesh and his silence in the world's locker room join to high heaven where we hear that the Lord, "who put him to grief," is now satisfied! He who sees the travail of his soul, being wholly innocent, enduring punishment for no cause whatever, now lays the reasons bare. The inner Christ, suffering and soon to die without wife or issue, will turn his suffering into birth pangs for the whole of humanity, turning Skull Place into his own maternity ward. Hear God Himself speaking through the lips of the far-seeing Isaiah, "When thou shalt make his soul an offering for sin, then shall he see his seed, he shall prolong his days and the pleasure of the Lord will prosper in his hand."

Good News in the locker room? Indeed so. At times—this time especially—our laughter is too deep for the grunts, grimaces, jigging, thrashing the air with our arms and spasms of the diaphragm. It is more like the restrained laughter we feel at funerals of saints being trumpeted into the throne room of the Eternal Father, disguised with respectful tears.

But we have not yet left the locker room. The ingenuity of depraved humanity has not fully spent itself. The soldiers no doubt feel a bit cheated by the royal silence, and still edgy about that persistent musk so distinct as they drew near to put his clothes back on him. They need closure; they need to be paid for their effort. Are you aware that the thorn crown is the only wound of Emmanuel not found in prophecy? Did you see the leaves of the acanthus plant are fashioned in stone atop the Corinthian column, and its thorns are for the Lord of Glory? Maybe the omission is to suggest that this wound is so bad that God did not want David, Moses, Isaiah and others to even think about it. The soldiers mock him, slap him, bow down before and cry out, as we all will someday. But their "sport" is short-lived. Pilate wants the Jews to see this bleeding, pathetic lump of humanity, but there is no sympathy even possible, for his countenance is obscured by the crown he wears, and the purple robe covers his bloody flesh. Pilate has failed in his "do-good" attempt. As "luck" would have it, Jesus must now experience double jeopardy for a crime he didn't even commit. Pilate rationalizes to himself, "So they cry for Barabbas? Well, why not? This Jesus is a worm and no man. I agree with Herod; he's too insignificant even to comment about. I wash my hands of the whole affair."

By some means or other, the cross is secured to Jesus' back. Two other evildoers are brought into line behind him, likewise trussed up. So the *auto de fe* proceeds slowly down *Via Dolorosa* toward the exit from the city, called The Golden Gate, to Skull Place, a knoll next to the road most often traveled.

ON THE *VIA DOLOROSA*

With the weight of the cross upon his torn and bleeding shoulders, Jesus begins his last mile toward God's ultimate show of divine power to the gods he has created. True it is that this Jesus does not resemble the Pre-incarnate *Logos,* nor this cross the throne of his glory, but all we behold is part of the disguise whereby God shows man his perfidious dimensions, and tricks the trickster himself. For had the kings of this world known what was really happening, they would not have crucified the Lord of Glory, nor would Satan, Prince of Air, have been so totally complicit in the event!

Jesus is staggering along this last leg of his 42-month journey that in God's dimensions began before the foundation of the world was laid. He is about one mile and seven hours from the gate to Paradise, clearly and precisely ahead. I ask you, how could his life be otherwise than having more strength than before, and therefore be more on the threshold of unmitigated joy? Yes, he is a strange mixture of extremes, this wonderful Lord of ours. His eye pierces the narrow canyon ahead. He sees the mile as Jesse Owens saw it—a matter of self-determination, not of muscle power. It's as it always has been: the significance of carrying a cross is determined by who is carrying it. We must lay aside our stopwatches and yardsticks—Jesus of Nazareth is passing by, and in his wake emerges a new universe.

Jesus knew who he was and what he was doing, and that it was exactly what God wanted him to do. No one could take from him the joy that comes from such knowledge. As Dante said: "In his will is our peace." Jesus also said it: "He who seeks to find his life will lose it, and he who loses his life for my sake will find it." Now he is going the way of Abraham to Moriah, though now it is called Skull Place. The eternal future is radiant on the horizon, and he is about to take on the glory he had before the world was created, just as he said in his final prayer with his disciples a short time before. The recollection of past events and the anticipation of future events are transforming the present into the Garden of Paradise, and he will by his divine show of power bring the Tree of Life into equal visibility alongside the Tree of the Knowledge of Good and Evil, and say at last to all the people of the world from his throne, "Come and dine!"

Perhaps he also considers his own limitations generated from the many promises he made to those who followed him. If they were to take up their crosses and follow him outside the city, he must do so quite willingly. If they will find their lives by losing them, then he will do the same. He is going from grace to greater grace, from peace to a peace that passes understanding, from joy to joy unspeakable, and from strength to strength, from ebbing of the natural to increase of the spiritual. This valley of deadly shadows he now goes through will become like the dawning of light that shines more and more unto high noon. God must make for him the outgoing of this very morning and evening a time to rejoice. It is a categorical imperative—the limitations implicit in his promises to us demand that it be so.

The company slowly makes its way down this narrow street with a large crowd following. As *Via Dolorosa* is today, scarcely eight feet wide in most places, so it must have been then, quite characteristic of ancient cities of the Near East. It may be that this street is not the route taken, but as the procession nears the city gate, we may assume it widens enough for spectators to stand alongside those dragging their crosses to Skull Place. It seems as the procession draws near the gate, Jesus either falls beneath his cross, or is not going fast enough to suit his Roman executioners. God, too, intends a short work on the earth, as he did at the first Passover. There is a cosmic cloud on its way. It will arrive at noon, bringing total darkness to the day. The public temple service will end at 3:00 pm, and God wants to end the ministry of Christ at that time exactly. His body must also be in the grave by sunset, at which time the Sabbath begins.

Two events occur in rapid succession, or so it seems. The officer in charge sees a man entering the city, coming up "out of the country." They commandeer him to bear Jesus' cross. He will prove to be a faithful follower of Christ in years to come, as will his sons, Alexander and Rufus. He is Simon, an Empire Jew from the North African city of Cyrene. No doubt he had come to celebrate Passover, but he enters history as the first Christian to begin fulfilling his own portion of Jesus' half-of-seven-years ministry. Blessed forever is Simon of Cyrene, who experienced the satisfaction of easing the suffering of our Lord.

We get another message, too—our part in finishing the incomplete ministry of Christ among men. It is not that God needs us to do his work for him. It is that we need to lose ourselves in that which is greater than ourselves. No, there will not be an angel to raise the cross from Christ's bleeding shoulders. You and I must do it and thereby enter into divine-human synergism. We become like Simon—workers together with God.

Jesus now stands erect and can look directly at people standing on the sidelines. We may correctly assume that the procession is just outside the Golden Gate, and has only a short distance to go. Places of execution were always located near the main entrance into cities of the Roman Empire. This particular one, called *Golgatha* in Hebrew, *Calvary* in Latin, *Chronos Topas* in Greek, and "Skull Place" in English, was named, no doubt, for the abundance of skeletal parts scattered about. The Romans didn't bother removing bodies from the crosses, as they were good advertising—a strong inducement for obedience to Rome. The area was always so near the road that travelers could hear the dying screams of pain, the cry for water, and smell the effluvium of rotting flesh—anything to make it clear to people exactly who was in charge.

But what is this loud lament coming from a group of "daughters of Jerusalem"? Jesus stops the parade—God sees to it that it is indeed stopped. Something needs Jesus' attention. A "popular theology" is afoot that needs to be corrected. These women are probably imitating the sounds of the professional mourners used at funerals. There is a word they chanted repeatedly in sad tones, "A-la-la-la-la-la-la-zo!"

Jesus always answered what people were thinking, not what they said. What were these superficial observers of a common execution thinking about? Isaiah gives us a clue. "A-la-la-la-la-zo! A-la-la-la-la-zo! There he goes, poor Jesus! First our handsome young King Josiah, and now him! Such a pathetic figure, all bowed and bloodied, wearing that ridiculous mock crown. He's so common-looking, nothing like a king at all. More like a fragile weed or a tree root. Oh, such a pitiful figure! And he thought we would accept him as our Messiah. Honestly, we squint our eyes and turn our faces away from him. He is downright pitiful. So young, and not even married. He doesn't have any children, does he? Poor Jesus! He didn't get a fair trial, we are told, and those crooked politicians of ours wouldn't be satisfied to just give him a jail sentence. No, poor Jesus is headed for Skull Place! A-la-la-la-la-zo! He's not from Jerusalem, so it's off to a common plot unless some corrupt rich man will give him a grave. A-la-la-la-la-la-zo!"

I don't think I miss it by much, and it is strangely redolent of the attitude of some people today. These daughters of Jerusalem, appearing just after Simon the cross-bearer, represent all forms of superficial religion, especially that which is based on emotion. They forego the grain and settle for the chaff, the beeswax instead of the honey, the frothy spindrift and ignore the vast ocean beneath.

Jesus tells the daughters of Jerusalem that their pity is misplaced. Indeed, in light of the coming fall of Jerusalem, they should pity themselves. It is a universal fact that Titus laid siege to Jerusalem on Passover 68 AD. This is exactly 40 years to the day from the time Jesus was crucified. Josephus gives us an eyewitness account of the city's siege that lasted for two full years. With this frightening future before them, will they repent? More importantly, do we still hear their "A-la-la-zos" shrieking pity for poor Jesus as he assumes the increasing dimensions of the omnipotence he had with the Father before the foundation of the world was laid? This Carpenter from Nazareth is extending the upright of his throne to where north meets south, and the arms thereof to where east meets west. Let us push these ladies into a closet quickly and watch him show us who exactly is in control!

SKULL PLACE

The party arrives at Skull Place, where Abraham sacrificed his love for Isaac, or at least very near it. Yet this location is hardly newsworthy, for such executions happened often, perhaps daily. There are other crosses there, too, in varying stages of "advertising" for Rome. Temporarily, the birds of prey fly to the city walls where they wait to return to their feast. *Moriah* means "seen of the Lord," which Abraham renames *Jehovah-jireh*, "the Lord will provide." However, since God is omniscient, he need not look, and being omnipresent, he need not go anywhere to provide. He wants us to see and analyze carefully what he provides. "Look unto him, all ye ends of the earth and be saved," he is still roaring across the intervening centuries and continents. Recently, I read a three-volume work on the Passion of Christ, coming to well over 1,000 pages. Its author conceded his work was incomplete, and so it will be to the end of time. Now we will look at only a very few syllables of the eternal story, a look at the wonderment of the Lion-Lamb as he takes away the sins of the world.

Christ is offered the customary cup of vinegar laced with the syrup of opium, the customary show of mercy by Rome. It would help dull the pain, temporarily reduce the awareness of the sufferer, and garble his speech. So by this merciful cup, Rome becomes quite Machiavellian by silencing vocal opposition and making a show of mercy at the same time.

Christ knew he must not take the cup, for he had yet many vital messages to give a waiting world. Yet he must taste it; men needed to know that he knew what he was rejecting. See his mighty power, you who are digging your graves with your teeth, you who soften reality with drugs, or depress it with alcohol, or mesmerize it with a plethora of escape mechanisms offered by our modern technology! Jesus is nearer to his future than are his lips to the comfort of the cup. He wants us to join him in the extension of life, rather than to the diminution of it.

These experts make short work of the task before them, having done it many times before. They strip Jesus naked, lay him on his side. Two hold him tight while a third positions one ankle upon another, and the fourth drives a spike through his two talus bones. Then they lay him on the cross and drive a nail through each palm, then raise the cross erect. The advertisement that never ends now begins. While this is happening, Jesus says to all, "Father, forgive them, for they do not know what they are doing." The KJV has it in the present, viz., "what they do." Both tenses, the present and the present imperfect, are correct. The present imperfect, "what they are doing," makes the activity and the commentary as intimate as possible; they are both going on at the same time.

Haven't men made this intimacy also contemporaneous? In truth, Christ is no longer here, but they can crucify the crucifixion. Some dangle the cross from their ear lobes and wrists, or have it bounce against their bellies as they go mincing along. Or they decorate it with flowers, sunbursts, diamonds or tattoos. Some wear it or carry it as a good-luck charm to discourage violence against one's person or keep the car from accidents. Others are rewriting it out of history or passing laws against it.

Little wonder such opposition. For in the most meaningful contexts possible, made possible only by our Lion-Lamb, Christ offers the world *universal salvation.* Man rises in his badness to the point of impaling the Mighty One of God to a cross, whose mighty power allows them to do it, and while they are doing it, he forgives them. Only when the greatness of the crime and the greatness of the forgiveness rise up together does forgiveness become possible. Man must be convinced that the forgiving one knows whom he forgives. So the Psalmist sings, "Mercy and truth are met together, righteousness and peace have kissed each other." This happens now, in the ongoing present. While we are enemies, Christ dies for the ungodly, as Paul says.

But listen! A stranger just now happening on the scene might think Jesus was a stand-up comedian the way the laughter now reaches abroad. See otherwise dignified priests do a jig in front of the cross, wagging their heads and insulting him. Here comes the soldier with the narcotic cup Jesus refused to drink, dancing before him with the cup in hand, offering him a second chance at its contents. The "three P's" were there—the priests, professors and politicians, and even the two malefactors are mocking. What is it that they are saying? They are asking him to do what they think he can't do, or wouldn't do even if he could—to come down from the cross so they could have faith in him. My, how little people seem to change; today they are just as sloppy in their thinking, for one cannot have proof and faith at the same time. Faith is conviction without proof. They confuse belief with faith—they are not synonyms! Jesus could not save himself and others too when his death is the means whereby he saves them.

One point we must make in passing is that one of the malefactors changes his mind. Why? We will never know for sure, but we notice that between his "joining in on the fun" and his cry for mercy, "Lord, remember me when you come into your kingdom," one event occurs—Pilate's sign arrives and is tacked above Jesus' head. Jesus hears his enemies read it aloud, hears their resentment and sees some run to tell Caiaphas about it. Perhaps the malefactor is impressed in ways we know not of—maybe a slight breeze wafts the royal odor of the musk still radiating from Christ's feverish body, and this urges him onward to his desperate conclusion. I know not how such a quick conversion would open the Gate of Paradise for him, yet I am happy because of him, even encouraged by him when my way gets difficult. In fact, I wish everyone would accept the universal atonement and be saved, and so does God! As Paul says, "It is not his will that any perish, but that all come to salvation."

After Jesus' Words II and III, which we regretfully pass, there is nothing but silence, or perhaps a little more abuse from the "three P's" and their likeminded crowd of spectators. "And sitting down, they watched him there." During Christ's six hours on the cross on this the sixth day of the week, there is a great deal more of silence than one might suspect. I clocked myself recently saying aloud Christ's known words from the cross. I said them slowly and thoughtfully in his own language. It took me less than one minute. So much silence is there that we might regard it as one of his last words. There is a sound of silence. What might that sound convey to us? For me, it is a message that Divine Power is waiting and still in control. It matters not, of course, what men think. Our sense organs are blinded by the white radiance of Eternity. I hark back to that electrifying scene in the Garden of Gethsemane when they answered Jesus question: "We seek Jesus of Nazareth," they said. And he answered with "I AM." It is not "I am *he*," as the KJV has it, though their addition is grammatically correct as an option. In this case, it is the answer God gave to Moses' question about his name. And what happened? They all tumbled backward and fell to the ground, Judas included. My point is, Jesus could have, even impaled there, sent them tumbling backward with the power of his voice, or called for legions of angels to attend him. No, he is not silent because there is nothing he can do and there is nothing more to say. He is silent, waiting for the time of the next power play, so surely on its way as was the Bethlehem Star that announced his birth. As the Judge Deborah said, "Even the stars in their courses fought against Sisera."

Where and when the great cosmic cloud that passed through our solar system started we do not know. That's really not important, but who sent it is. It arrives at high noon on that Good Friday, 28 AD. In 2,000 AD, a science-oriented periodical came out with a lengthy article on possible ways the world could come to its end. One of them was a dense cosmic cloud drifting across our sun and staying there.

This cloud, however, covered the sun only three hours. Some hold the view that the darkness was caused by an eclipse of the sun. Such a belief is wrong, for Passover always occurs at or very near full moon. Eclipses can occur only when the moon and sun are on the same side of the heavens, the opposite of where it always is at Passover, and where it would have to be a new moon.

Another error about Christ's Passion involves the meaning of Word IV. You are aware, I am sure, that the Seven Last Words of Christ are sequenced by an analytical blend of the four Gospels. Over the nearly two millennia of studying the New Testament, scholars have come to almost unanimous agreement about their order. You may also be aware that we are forced to conclude that each of the Gospels is incomplete, though never contradictory to the others, as to what it includes of the Passion Narrative. Given the Seven Last Words as they stand, we see that three are unique to Luke (Words I, II and VII), three are unique to John (Words III, V and VI), and Word IV is unique in three ways. It is the central Word, it is the only Word involving three languages (similar to the sign above Jesus' head), and the only word repeated in more than one Gospel—Matthew and Mark. It rises even higher in our consideration when we compare it with Day Four of the Creation Hymn and Day Four of Holy Week. Recall that the Hebrew day begins at sunset, not sunrise, being consistent with the language of the Creation Hymn. Word IV is said at high noon, just after the day had turned to darkness, and this is the day in the Hymn when the sun and moon are designated for seasons. (Notice the reference to "night season" in Ps. 22:2.) Day Four of Holy Week includes the Anointing of Jesus as Messiah King, Mary doing with musk what David does in immortal poetry, followed by the collusion of Judas with the chief clergy of the nation to betray and kill Jesus. "My God, my God, why are they doing this?" we cannot help but cry out in utter amazement. Such contrasts and such parallels obviate all supposition of coincidence, and intensify our attention on what Jesus is doing by saying Word IV in the midnight-noon of Good Friday.

Thinking about the coming millennium a few years ago, our previous President spoke of building a bridge to the 21st century. It has already been built! In Eternity and before the foundation of the world was laid, Christ planned for all the events of this day. Then 1,000 years before he said the words of Ps. 22:1, he inspired David to write them down. Yet more than that, all 12 stanzas of the psalm contain the richest quantity of prophetic specificities found anywhere in the whole of recorded literature. In Word IV, Christ gives us the object of our faith in Scripture. He is saying, "I MYSELF AM THE BEING! I am in control! I am fulfilling Scripture." He is telling us he is, has been and will yet be in control of all events, beginning from Eternity, throughout his 42-month ministry, and henceforth. The cosmic cloud has arrived and even the three sidereal crosses are exactly right in the darkened sky above. Never has Scripture been so highly extolled, and never could we be pressed to pursue its meaning more forcefully. Truly we see the white radiance of Eternity piercing the midnight.

See also how ignorant the clergy are. Had Jesus quoted the verse in Hebrew, we would expect these experts to recognize the quotation. Instead, he quotes the Aramaic version, which should have been even easier for them to understand. But no—they mockingly say, "He calls for Elijah. Let us see whether Elijah will come and save him." In fact, "My God" and "Elijah" are very similarly articulated in Aramaic and Hebrew. Yet I suspect the case was with them as it is with most fierce auditors listening to their enemies—they hear what they want to hear.

What exactly did Jesus mean by Word IV? There are those who entertain the notion that God is playing games with us, making Jesus become a scapegoat of sorts on whom he loads all our sins, then cringes away from him while Jesus gives the pound of flesh that justice requires. Such a view is not only dangerous in its implications, but also unscriptural. In John 8:25-29, Jesus speaks specifically of his crucifixion, and assures us that God will be with him when this happens because he always does the things that please God. Again in John 16:32, Jesus tells the disciples that they will forsake him, but that he will not be alone because God will be with him.

Examine closely also Isaiah 53. As often occurs, you will see a shift in speakers indicated by pronouns. The prophet will be speaking, then God. Even the audience occasionally changes. However, in this dialogue the speaker changes from the prophet Isaiah to God Himself twice in the middle of a couplet. In verse 8, Isaiah asks a question, then God answers it. In verse 11, Isaiah tells the people that God will be satisfied with Christ's accomplishment, then God assures us that Isaiah is exactly right and continues until the end of the chapter listing the achievements of his glorious Son. These haploid couplets are a device used in Hebrew poetry to suggest intimacy between two speakers. Psalm 22 also abounds with this device. God is right there, actively involved. These verses and several others, as well as sound logic, persuade us that something deeper is intended than a first reading might indicate.

Isolated from context, Word IV is questioning Divine Providence. Notice how fragmentary the Hebrew is, as though the speaker is sobbing, or is short of breath and can hardly finish the clauses. The stresses used in Hebrew are also in boldface: "God of **me**! **God** of me! Why have you forsaken me . . . far from helping me . . . the words of my roaring?" Since his baptism, if not before, Christ knew his earthly destiny. He understood he was the sacrificial Lamb of God. How out of place, then, to imagine that Christ is asking God why he is suffering! Then in Ps. 22:2 we are astounded by the prophecy focusing on the two halves of Christ's time on the cross. The "night season" is used only one other time in Scripture, in Job 30:17. It means part of a night, perhaps one watch, which is a period of three hours. Christ is asking this question for us. Like our Grand Sire Adam, we are reluctant to ask the right questions. Jesus is doing more than striking a parallel between David and us, as proper as it indeed is. He is pleading with us to read Psalm 22! It is there that we fully understand the power and glory of the events at Skull Place. Beginning with verse 22 to the end of the psalm, we go even beyond the Roman killing ground into the Pentecostal birth of the Church of God and a city of transparent gold, a cube 1,200 miles per side, descending upon the Mediterranean world. Indeed, we cross the Millennial Bridge, 1,000 years wide (from the time of David to that of Jesus), of a single span—and that span is a person, The Person who is the Road, the Truth and the Life. "Go read Psalm 22!" he says.

Nearly three hours of darkness pass. We know nothing of them. The people probably grow quiet, contemplating why the "eclipse" is lasting so long. The public Passover service in the temple is packed from wall to wall with people totally oblivious to what is going on just outside the Golden Gate. Christ is waiting to stir everybody up from their private thoughts. The Messiah has yet one task to accomplish—a bit of unfinished business. In quick succession he will utter Word V "I thirst," then Word VI "Father, into your hands I commit my spirit," but only at the right time. We must turn to Ps. 69:21. The first half of its prophecy was fulfilled nearly six hours before: "They gave me gall for my meat." He must fulfill the second half to complete his task: "and in my thirst they gave me vinegar to drink." John is careful to make sure we understand why he asks for drink, "So that the Scripture might be fulfilled." In John 19:28, notice carefully the change in tense and mood between the two uses of the same verb. First John uses the past tense, "Jesus, seeing that all already *was fulfilled,* so that the Scripture *might be fulfilled*, says, I thirst!" Since everything Jesus had intended to do and to experience at the hand of others was completed, so he turns to his last act of completing what is not yet in reality. Verse 30 shows Jesus receiving the vinegar and saying Word VII, "It is finished." The record could not be clearer; Jesus said Word V for one purpose, to complete the prophecy in Psalm 69.

No doubt, the body of our Lord was screaming out for even a drop of water, like the rich man in Jesus' parable of Lazarus the beggar. But we must never forget who is up there on the cross inviting a universe to be drawn unto himself! Would he, so near heaven and so spiritually powerful, give a second's notice to the needs of his physical body? Would he be so naïve as to mistakenly imagine that his tormentors would give him even one drop of water? No, he practices what he promises to the Samaritan woman—"never to thirst again."

He is but a few breaths away from Eternity now. The Mighty *Logos* within transcends the average body that human cruelty has brought so close to death, and with a puff of air activates an unnamed soldier into action with "Tsam!" Under other circumstances, the "tsam" would surely have been ignored. No comfort is to be given anyone dying of crucifixion. Doing so would intercommune the person who gave comfort to a dying enemy of Rome. But this is God's Friday, so "tsam" moves a soldier to dip a sponge into a jar of bloody vinegar used to clean the instruments of their profession. He squeezes the vinegar on a branch of hyssop from a convenient bush nearby and raises it to Jesus' lips.

After Word VII, Jesus' bedtime prayer as recorded in Luke's Gospel—a quotation of Psalm 31:5—we go back to Matthew and Mark for a final word from the Lord. It, too, is a word from the cross. Since we are not told what Jesus says, we erroneously suppose it is not worthy to rise to its proper place as Word VIII. It certainly is not the bedtime prayer given in Luke, but resembles in tone a prophecy in I Th.4:16 that describes Christ's great shout with the voice of an archangel as he returns to earth at the end of time. Let us not suppose some scream of pain, some snarl of revenge. In the light of all I know about and have experienced personally of Jesus, I hear nothing but the shout of victory.

Or could it be laughter? In his Sermon on the Mount, Jesus told us to respond to insult, slander, and even persecution with rejoicing and exceeding gladness. I ask you, how close is exceeding gladness to laughter? You may hesitate to go that far, but just maybe we are forgetting (as we often do) who is up there drawing all men unto himself! As Uncle Laban disappeared on the eastern horizon, Jacob gave a huge sigh of relief and then turned around. What did he see? The panoply of heaven, tiered up in glittering ranks of angels in battle gear, swords drawn, ready to do battle in Jacob's defense. Did Jesus see less at Skull Place? Methinks he heard hallelujah choruses and *Kom, Herr Jesu* to tunes that would move even Bach to envy, sung to the accompaniment of "10,000 harpers harping upon their harps." Yes, it was more akin to laughter than any other emotion I can think of. Its context allows me no other conclusion.

THE ONGOING LAUGHTER

When God came among us, it is only logical to assume that the supreme uniqueness of the event should have a new name, even a new literary genre to describe it to men, and this is exactly what happened. In English we call it the "Gospel," but in Greek it is "Good News," based on the same root word from which we get the word "angel," or "messenger." A new genre of literature appeared as well—a persuasive biography—the first ever, and the last because it will never be needed again! In biblical studies, we are fond of calling the men who wrote the four Gospels the "Evangelists." This Good News is exactly what the angels themselves announced to the shepherds in Bethlehem when Jesus was born. What, indeed, could be better news than Almighty God paying us a visit?

Yet we are in for a surprise because most men are absolutely horrified at the notion that God Himself would take on flesh and come to show us how badly we need to be saved, how we can be saved, how we can solve the worlds horrendous problems, and then die for us to prove that he loves us. Why is the Good News bad news? It obligates them. True, we all will take a free gift with no strings attached, but when omnipotence and omniscience are involved, that is something else. Man thinks like this: "One who can do whatever he chooses and then singles me out—well, there will be strings attached! One who knows all things has absolutely no naiveté or ignorance involved in what he does. He knows me 100%, and still he dies for me? No, I will have none of that, for there are indeed strings attached. One who is omnipresent chooses to interrupt his governance of the inconceivably wide and deep universe to zero in on me? Yes, he has strings attached. He knows what he is doing, he knows how to do it, and he wants to get me involved. Frankly, I like things just as they are!"

So the Good News becomes bad news. What further proof do we need that man is the avowed enemy of God? This soliloquy I have suggested represents man being honest with himself. However, most of the time he disguises the fact that he wants to be his own god so badly that the only thing he can do is to run the other way. The most conspicuous symptom that this is so is laughter. Like Br'er Rabbit, he also has his laughing place. One claims the Bible is his joke book. Another says there is no God and Mary is his mother. The ways of making light of God are as varied as the people who use this tactic to deflect the obligation they (and we all) have to him for what he has given freely to all—forgiveness and true freedom through Jesus Christ. I wonder . . . when such as these have their appointment with the Lord of Glory, how much laughing will there be then?

FOR THE SUITCASE

1. Isaiah is the Messianic prophet, but David is the prophet of the Passion and Pre-incarnate Glory of Christ.
2. Jesus takes his name from that given the Old Testament leader, Joshua. The name means, "Salvation of the Lord."
3. When John calls Jesus "Word," or "*Logos*," he means "The Ideal of Man."
4. Christ was not a "pure spirit" made to appear as a man, nor did he have an X-factor, or any help available to him not also available to any man.
5. Christ's perfect nature did not exempt him from the temptations and limitations experienced by all men.

6. Pilate proves that in dealing with inspired truth, compromise always makes matters worse.

7. Christ twice quotes from Scripture while on the cross.

8. Christ as Lion-Lamb means that the ultimate expression of omnipotence is love.

9. The ultimate badness of man and the ultimate expression of the love of God met at Skull Place.

CHAPTER VIII:
A VISA FOR THE TRIP

Road Maps: Psalm 130; John 3; Philippians 3;
II Timothy 4; I Corinthians 13

When I say love is the visa we need for the trip of all trips, I use a figure of speech called a metaphor. When I say God is a rock, I use an amazing metaphor, for God is a spirit, which seems the exact opposite of what we think a rock would symbolize. Yet in several ways God is indeed a rock. He is immutable, eternal and omnipotent, all qualities easily suggested by a rock. When Jesus gave his chief of the apostles, Simon Ben Jonah, the name "Rock," or "Peter" in English, he had in his thinking the future power this frail giant would have after the Holy Ghost came upon him. When I use Lion-Lamb, I use a very special metaphor for The Very Special Person. It is a metaphor in the form of a two-word paradox called an oxymoron.

Experienced readers of the Holy Library are well aware of its abundance of metaphors. Isaiah saw the coming Messiah as being "the shadow of a mighty rock within a weary land." A favorite metaphor of God's omnipresence is seeing him with the wings of a bird, or even as a mother hen (Ps. 91). Seeing God as judge of the world, the poet warns deceptive people that "his eyelids try the children of men."

Everywhere we turn in Scripture, we meet metaphors that liken its truths to something in the inanimate world, the animal kingdom, and especially in man and his society. It is true that they often give us "windows" into reality that are more vivid than using language in a logical way. More than that, we cannot live without metaphors because we are pure spirits captured in "time machines," an expression I use as a metaphor for our physical bodies. Perhaps we should speak of them as "coffins," a metaphor not attractive to young people, I know. They would prefer something like "life is a beach" or "time is a river I go fishing in." Yet for those of us who must soon bid good-bye to our time machines, our bodies quite accurately resemble coffins. II Cor. 5 (see also Chapter IX), for example, is one of the "roadmaps" for the next "leg" of our "journey" to the "Celestial City"—all metaphors! Paul certainly wanted to escape his "coffin," his "tent" that was on the verge of collapsing.

Modern science has thrust us into a new dimension of existence denied those who lived before the 20th century—the quantum world. This entrance into the world of the infinitely small, as well as the world of outer space, has forced us into a greater need of metaphor. For most of us the "window of opportunity" and "motherboard" are clear enough. However, the other day I read about the size of a hydrogen atom. The author first expressed its dimensions and weight in numbers, which meant absolutely nothing to me. Then the writer said the distance between the proton and electron of one hydrogen atom is comparable to the distance between the sun and the planet Mars. Then he said man is halfway in size between an atom and a galaxy. These two metaphors enabled me to understand immediately.

When we speak of metaphor as it relates to the Bible, we must define the word in broader terms than we use today. In fact, all biblical literary devices involving metaphor come under the Greek word *parabole.* I am sure you have noticed how loosely "parable" is used in the KJV. Sometimes the text announces a parable, and what follows is a proverb or some other literary figure! What has happened is over the centuries is that this word in English has taken on a meaning not intended by its biblical writers. It comes from two word parts—*para,* meaning "alongside" as in "paramedic," and *ballo,* "to throw." Parable meant a "comparison," nothing more. Most of these comparisons in the Synoptics are what we presently mean by "parable," but we do not find any at all in John's Gospel. Instead, John uses multiple metaphors which we call "literary conceits." A metaphor abstracts only one feature of a familiar object to make a point, such as in the old Scottish reference to a person of good character as being "all wool and a yard wide." When an object is used to make several points of comparison, the metaphor becomes a literary conceit. The most famous literary conceit in the Bible is Psalm 23, where the role of a good shepherd caring for his sheep is like God caring for us. David shows us several ways in which this is so. Jesus uses the same conceit when he calls himself The Good Shepherd.

One point of caution is to define biblical terms as they relate to biblical times. Another more serious matter is to be sure we recognize "comparisons" for what they are, figures of speech. They must never be taken literally. Some modern Jews see their coming Messiah as a military leader because they make literal interpretations of many of the Messianic passages in the prophets, which *prima facie* indicate a military role for the Long Awaited One. However, Jesus tells Pilate (and us all) that his kingdom is not of this world. Paul also reminds us that our weapons are spiritual.

The warfare spoken of by Isaiah and other prophets means a battle of the soul against the world, not an Islamic *jihad* or Christian crusade to take up the sword against a material foe. It is God who will lead Christians with battle gear more powerful than the Muslim scimitar or an atomic bomb. Then the benefits of God's conquests will bring a paradise to the soul, which our prosperity theologians interpret literally. Christ comes, they seem to say, to fight our battles for us, and tops it all off with a thousand years of Paradise right here on the earth. These millennialists, like the Jews I refer to, interpret prophetic visions literally rather than symbolically, and thereby "chain" us (and not Satan) to the limitations of physical objects. God wants us to see through objects, not to be dazzled by them. Without justification, they give a literal interpretation to what is clearly metaphor.

One of the main thrusts of John's Gospel and Apocalypse is to rescue people from this kind of carnal interpretation of prophetic writings. His thematic organization of events in Jesus' life stresses this point. In chapter 2, John shows Jesus cleansing the temple. The Jews ask Jesus for a sign of his Messiahship. He speaks of his body as a temple, but they take his metaphor literally. In chapter 3, Jesus speaks of salvation as a second birth, but Nicodemus makes a literal application of this metaphor. In chapter 4, the Samaritan woman imagines Jesus is referring to the kind of water she came to draw at the well. Then in chapter 6, this human failure reaches its climax on the day following his feeding thousands on bread baked in heaven. The people are so desirous of eating more of this free bread that they walk many miles around the lake to get it, probably walking all night. Jesus then tells them that he himself is the bread for their next free meal. "Eat my flesh, drink my blood." They insist on more literal bread as a second show of his Messiahship. Finally, he changes his verb, "*Devour* my flesh, drink my blood." Then by the droves they slowly depart, thinking he had become deranged. Only his twelve disciples remain.

Our Holy Library is about two worlds—one is the space-time continuum, the other eternal life. It is impossible to speak of the life beyond space and time without a metaphorical use of objects in space and time. If someone asks about when my process of salvation began, how can I answer? It began in Eternity before the foundation of the world was laid. When will the process end? At the moment I leave this coffin, this cocoon, this worn-out time machine, this collapsing tent. Hence, the question one might ask me, viz., "When were you saved?" is asking for a material answer to a spiritual question. When using the language of the space-time continuum to speak of things eternal, how can I avoid metaphor or other forms of comparison that the Bible calls *parabole?* We must live with this awkwardness in this valley of deadly shadows until the daybreak when the shadows flee away. When Jesus says from the cross, "My God, my God, why hast thou forsaken me?" he is not to be taken literally, as though he is asking God to tell him why there is no supernatural aid to save him from dying on the cross. He is actually telling those witnessing his crucifixion, "Go read Psalm 22."

Love is our visa for the trip. A passport tells the authorities who we are, but the visa determines where we may go. Since I ascribe to love as the power of a visa, I mean that love is the universal virtue that is accepted everywhere. Paul says rulers do not pass laws against love—it is welcomed by all. Like faith, it is a cardinal virtue of Christian life. Commandment I of the Decalogue requires that we love God with all our intellect, affection, will and strength, to which Jesus adds loving our neighbor as ourselves. On these two commandments hang all the law and the prophets. Though we read that God is love, and without faith it is impossible to please him, yet neither virtue is defined in the Bible.

It is true that Scripture is full of examples of how love behaves, but it does not supply us with a conceptual definition of love. At times, biblical writers describe love. Indeed, the very life of Christ is an exposition on love; it is the very breath of God. Theologians and philosophers from the most ancient times until now have spoken about this matter. Yet no inspired thinker has given us a definition that spontaneously rises above all others with such force and clarity that it becomes in writing what it is in experience to the love-hungry soul. Why can we not define love? I think the trouble is that love is too big for language. It is so strong that it cannot be directly seen, like the sun—visible only as reflected upon the moon. No attempt has thus far satisfied us. We read definitions, and we give our approval, yet love is also more than that. So it is with faith. These two words are not given conceptual definitions in the Bible because we lack adequate language to do so. Then what do we do? We make comparisons by using *parabole*.

The Greeks attempted to define love by partition, using three different words with three different shades of meaning—*eros, philos* and *agape. Eros,* from which our word "erotic" comes, refers to sexual love. *Philos* is loosely applied to friendship, though sometimes in Scripture it is interchanged with *agape*—divine love, unmotivated love. The Greeks reasoned that *eros* and *philos* were dependent loves—reserved for expression toward the opposite sex, or toward people of like affinities. Therefore, they were inferior to *agape*, which is a love of people because they are people.

This kind of love is at once less and more than most people suppose. It is more than the other kinds because it admits no exceptions, and it is less because it does not necessarily involve emotions. Essentially, it is what the angels proclaimed on the hillside of Bethlehem when Jesus was born—goodwill—all of this, but not more than this.

When Jesus was born of Mary in that small village, the least significant town in all Judea in the year 5 BC, all but three of the world's dominant religions had already been established. They spoke of divinities that dwelt in the spirit world, the creation of our universe, how man ought to live in this world so that he would be happy after he died, and many other things. These religions were founded by honest men who left us advice that, if it did not make us better people, it would at least give us enough control to make life better in society. None of these men claimed to be more than honest searchers after truth—none but Moses. He claimed that the universe was made by one omnipotent God, who had met with him and given him a message for mankind. God called himself "I AM" because there was no word in human language that could adequately describe him. This had never happened before! With Moses, the concept of revelation for the first time entered the history of religion.

The nation Moses was directed to give God's message to could not long abide by the commandments God gave them. They tried, they struggled, they admired Moses and other leaders that God spoke through. They experienced miracles that confirmed the glorious fact that God had sanctified them, but their nature required something more. To gain victory over their carnal lives, they needed an infusion of divinity, nothing less. This alone could enable them to rise to the standards God had demanded when he spoke man-to-man with Moses atop the fiery Mount Sinai. God agreed, and told his prophets that he himself would come and show them how they were to live. He would found the world's last and final religion because it alone would be established on Ultimate Value, and that value is Love Personified.

That happened 2,000 years ago, and the promise, fulfilled in Jesus Christ, proved true. God—absolute in quality, infinite in degree, hence ultimate in value—I AM, pitched his tent among us. That is why there have been no new religions established since the ministry of Jesus Christ. This is not to say that there have not been attempts, of course, but the two dominant religions I previously mentioned are not original religions at all. I speak of the two reactionary, syncretistic religions—Islam of the seventh century and Sikhism of the 16th century. Mohammad borrowed extensively from Judaism and Christianity, even the concept of revelation itself, and Nanak borrowed from Islam and Hinduism in founding Sikhism. Neither of these religions has added even one positive, creative thought to world religions; everything they say has been said before. However, both of these have done good; most certainly both have joined all other religions, including organized Christianity itself, in being supplanted by the violence of hell throughout their bloody history. Jesus told the religious leaders of the Jews that they were of the devil, and the history of religion, including Christians, Muslims and Sikhs, has shown that organized religion has proved to be a coveted dwelling place of Satan!

Yes, the Devil has gained entrance into churches in the past. Yet what is more frightening is that he is presently gaining inroads into all churches, and is constantly invigorated by his remarkable successes. When the Son of Red returns, will he find faith on the earth? However we answer Jesus' frightening question, we must remember that organized churches are not the true Church, as St. Augustine said so long ago. We must never lose heart, but remember God's triumphant words to Elijah, "I have 7,000 men who have not bowed the knee to Baal."

Even after we look at the blood-splattered pages of church history, and then out at the alarming condition of our present world, we must still insist that the foundation of our Road of Life is paved with love. We can be satisfied with nothing less than the exchange of love among ourselves, our neighbors and our God. We must never confuse individuals with institutions. As we have seen, love cannot be defined with language, yet we must speak of it using *parabole* as well as live by it.

We are also called upon to conquer the time element. The Scripture says, "We love him [today] because he first [two millennia ago] loved us." To the Philippian Church, Paul speaks of running a race, one of his favorite metaphors. He tells us that Christ has in hand a "righteousness crown" to give him and all who love his appearing at his Second Coming. He gives all his effort to winning that race, always keeping this in mind: forgetting those things that are behind, and stretching forth to those things that are ahead—with his eye on the finish, he dashes forward! Notice that Paul does not say "having forgotten," but "forgetting," as a daily, ongoing reality. Regret, we have all found, is so poignant that it frequently rouses up unwanted memories, like Paul's abetting the martyrdom of Stephen. Whether such memories are from our guilt or weakness, or from God Himself so that he may flex his mighty muscles in flinging them away again and again, it matters not. Maybe they are even allowed to surface to keep us "poor in spirit." Daily we must keep forgetting. When Christ first speaks to John in the Apocalypse, he is introduced as the one "who is, who was, and who is coming." Whether we realize it or not, we Christians are often in a most fantastic time machine, one that spans two millennia, from the Advent to the Parousia, or Second Coming of Christ. We are required as part of our spiritual training to convert our yesterdays into the forecasts of the eternal tomorrow.

In this amazing time machine that goes forward and backward at the same time, we are quite like Father Jacob. You will remember his escape from Uncle Laban. Surely, Laban would have liked nothing better than to kill Jacob on the spot, then take his daughters, their children and all the wealth of Jacob back to his native land. However, God sees to it that Laban does no such thing. We see Father Jacob standing there, watching Uncle Laban and his makeshift army retreat back to the east. Finally, he exhales a huge sigh of relief and turns around to go back to camp, when he sees a sight comparable to what the shepherds of Bethlehem beheld when Christ was born—a panoply of the heavenly host in battle gear ready to come to his aid should Uncle Laban attempt to take his life. Jacob named the place where he stood *Mahanaim*, a dual form of a noun meaning "between two armies," the army of Laban and that of heavenly angels.

Yet another trial, even more severe in consequence, was about to occur in Jacob's life. His own brother Esau was coming toward him with a company of young men, and those bad memories returned. Surely his thinking must have gone something like this: Is Esau coming to kill us all? Does he think I have returned to claim my two-thirds of our father's estate? If Uncle Laban would have killed me and taken his daughters, children and my possessions for himself, what will Esau do? Kill us all and keep my wealth and inheritance for himself?

Jacob was between two armies a second time. There was the army of heaven against that of Laban, and now that same heavenly army against the army of Esau. These two men, an uncle and a brother, represent the past and the future. This is why I call him Father Jacob! Like Father Abraham, he goes before us as a spiritual progenitor. By the time of Solomon, it seems these two events in the life of Father Jacob were celebrated by a dance. In Solomon's allegory of the Song of Songs, we see Christ happy to see our rejoicing because of his protection of our lives. The chorus sings, "What will you see in the Shulamite? [then answer their own question] as it were between the rows of dancers" (i.e., the *Mahanaim*). He sees her skipping joyfully toward him between the two rows of dancers and says, "How beautiful are thy feet with shoes, O prince's daughter," which refers to dancing shoes, of course. So we Christians must get into our time machine, use all the literary devices available to us, sing the Song of Songs, dance the *Mahanaim*, skipping joyfully between the rows of dancers, the armies of Laban and Esau, which become the harmony and rhythm of our Song of Songs. We must seize the past and the future, mix them with a plea for mercy, and bless the fiery trials that spark our heels and daily burn away the wood, hay and stubble of our yet imperfect lives.

We have a God too great to have a name. We are cultivating a faith and love too glorious for verbal expression. So we lapse into metaphor as we attempt to reach one another, and maybe even love some neighbor into God's everlasting arms. Let us re-examine our visa for a little while as we see it stamped on the passports of Jesus and saints of the Sacred Canon.

LOVE'S GREAT PARADOX

It is evident from a comparative study of the four Gospels that Jesus often needed to repeat himself. Given the brevity of his ministry, we can see why this would be so. One of his teachings occurs no fewer than six times in the Gospels, leaving us to imagine the many other times he included it in his preaching as he moved from town to town to declare the Gospel. Here it is in two slightly different versions, both found in Matthew:

He finding his life will lose it, and he losing his life for my
sake will find it. Matt. 10:39

For whosoever will save his life shall lose it, but whosoever
will lose his life for my sake shall find it. Matt. 16:25

Here is Love's Great Paradox. In these two versions, Jesus partitions
all humanity into one of three categories: 1) those who think they have
found their lives, 2) those who are still looking for it, and 3) those who have
dedicated their lives to the service of Christ Himself. These in the third
category, he says, are the only ones who have really found life. John's one
version goes like this: "He who is loving his life will lose it, and he hating
his life will keep it." This expresses my description of the Adamic curse in a
previous chapter. I call it a willingness to live with good and evil in one's life,
being quite cozy with this devil's brew, even to the point of denying it exists.
Luke and Mark record this teaching as identical to Matthew's version, but
John's indicates our hatred for tolerating good and evil in our lives.

Note something often overlooked in this famous paradox. Jesus has
nothing to say against wanting self-realization. I have often heard preachers
imply that we are to love our neighbor *instead of* ourselves. Not so! It is
difficult enough to fulfill the command as it stands; let us not make it
say more than that. What Christ quarrels with is how we achieve self-
realization. He tells us that it is expressed, strange to say, by means of a
paradox: We achieve self-realization in the process of self-denial. We are
to be saved by helping Christ save others, but we must do it in such a way
as to bring glory to God and not to ourselves.

Bearing testimony of Christ is a great deal like writing, which is itself
a mode for bearing testimony. Psychologists have found that grade-school
children write only simple sentences in their little essays; that is, they never
use subordination, placing minor ideas in dependent clauses. However, as
they grow up, they discover life is not all Goldilocks and the Three Bears.
Like painters, they begin to see life in more than primary colors—they
discern secondary colors, then shades, hues, tints and pastels. Professional
writers tell us that mature style has half its volume in subordinate clauses.

This is an ideal something like what we Christians strive for. We write and speak our gospels to our neighbors. Some of us claim to be presenting a biography of Christ, to be as Paul says, "epistles known and read of men," but end up presenting autobiographies instead. They actually do speak of Christ and his work, but put both in dependent clauses, while putting themselves up front in the main clauses. A case in point is the physical appearance of those involved in some of the "Ma and Pa" religious programs on television. Their mouths are full of the praises of Christ, but the way they speak and the way they dress draw attention to themselves, not to mention the Plexiglas pulpits they stand behind. There are subtle ways some Christians use Christ and his work to bring glory to themselves.

For a positive example of how we ought to witness, read Psalm 130. It is one of the greatest poems about repentance ever written. It has the popular name of "De Profundus," because of its haunting first line, "Out of the depths have I cried unto thee, O God." It is a lyric poem, i.e., it tells the reader how the poet feels about his subject. The temptation is there for David to put himself on parade, but does he? In its brief eight verses, David uses seven pronouns that refer to himself, but he uses eight pronouns and eight nouns that refer to God. One of the most despicable sins among men today is opportunism, though we hear precious little about it from our pulpits. Using people, and especially Christ, for our own carnal advantage is spiritual cannibalism. Moses was 120 years old when he used God's power to draw attention to himself when he performed a miracle in his own name, and for that God denied him entrance into the Holy Land.

Our fulfillment of Love's Grand Paradox goes far beyond our methods and styles in conducting public worship. It involves the whole of life—life in search of life. Scripture tells us that anyone who is in Christ Jesus is a new creature, and that all things become new. This radical change does not take place in the things themselves, but in our attitude toward them. Things are new because they are newly seen. We are like the medieval scientists who believed in a geocentric solar system. Then we read that Copernicus went out and looked again at the heavens above him, and they become new because they were newly seen. In like manner, we gradually leave behind the narcissism of our infancy as we grow into maturity.

Then there comes to our minds the realization that we do not live in an egocentric universe, that God is our center. I submit that it will take a lifetime of skillful adjustment to reach the ideal Jesus expressed in his Paradox of Love.

Since we are on a quest for the meaning of love through *parabole*, let us determine exactly why Jesus presents this great commandment as a paradox. It is a figure of speech, like the oxymoron, that uses contradictory words to slow our thinking down, so we will spend some intellectual effort to understand it, and appreciate more fully what is being said. Again, God is seeing to it that we spend time with this central command of his Son. That is why it occurs so often in the Gospels and is presented as a paradox. It is interesting to know that just about every relationship between ideas can be expressed in paradox. Take, for example, the common statement, "You can't win for losing." This is a colorful restatement of the law of compensation.

Why are we destined to spend our entire lives struggling to conform to this ethical paradox? I think the main reason is to help us avoid what I call The Great Deception. One of Jesus' shortest parables explains this weakness far better than an attempt to give a dictionary definition. I call It The Parable of the Bigger Barns. He speaks of a farmer who was not satisfied with the size of his barns, so he decides to build bigger ones. He was deceived by things, thinking his particular formula for happiness was comprised of things. Apparently, he was convinced that he had a fulfilled life. He did not realize that appetite grows by what it feeds on, and that his selfish pursuit shrinks him as his appetite increases. In spite of all this toil for a secular future, he dies unfulfilled. Jesus says in the paradox that he loses his life. He was 100% wrong about how to achieve self-realization. The longer he lived, the poorer he became because he was not rich toward persons, and chiefly the Person of God, his Maker.

The Great Deception is endemic to the human race. Americans are accused all over the world for their materialism. This is true, of course, but it does not mean that our accusers are any less materialistic. This matter is a great deal like the "deception of riches," a term used by Jesus. Who is more likely to be deceived by riches, the rich or the poor? The poor, of course, likely because they are wishing for something with which they have had no experience. Even so, those who accuse us are materialistic, too, and probably guilty of envy as well.

When Jesus speaks of the impossibility of serving two masters, God or Mammon, we tend to forget the truth he implies, that we will end up serving one of them. God made us that way. How many, do you suppose, are caught in The Great Deception? They are drowning in a Sargasso Sea of things. That is why Paul tells us the love of money is a root of all kinds of evil. Some argue that the reason covetousness is denounced as the last of the Ten Commandments is that it is the summary sin, versatile enough to be involved directly in all the other nine. Paul also notes that the love of money is a form of idolatry, and so dominant is its god that men gave him the name of Mammon long before the time of Christ. Jesus uses a powerful metaphor for The Great Deception, that of darkness. He says, "If the light in you be darkness, how great is that darkness."

Remember what Solomon said about the world being in our heart. We cannot escape handling things, working to accumulate wealth, establishing as secure a future for our families as possible. In fact, if we do not work toward these ends, we are found at fault—poor stewards, irresponsible husbandmen. Jesus implies that it's a matter of attitude. Since the choice is God or Mammon, we rightly conclude that we are either using people to get things, or using things to win people. The cloth of our lives has Christ and his proxies as the warp and the world of things as the woof. This intimacy of opposites, this polarization, becomes the activity of character-building and creativity. These two qualities of divinity were not given our Progenitors in the Garden of Eden because such are developed—not endowed, as willpower and conceptual thought are. God is the Creator, and he demands that our godhead be full and complete; we must create. Life then is like sitting at a loom and weaving, but either God or Mammon chooses our design.

Yet people are not convinced about all this. They do not see either God or Mammon in charge. Since they are satisfied with a blend of good and evil in their own lives, they are, quite predictably, of the foolish notion that they themselves determine the end product. Given their penchant for subjective judgment, imagination and memory play tricks on them. Recall those of Jeremiah's day who refused to stop worshipping the Queen of Heaven because their daisy-picking of memories betrayed them into believing the preposterous notion that serving Ishtar (after whom Easter is named!) brought them prosperity in the past, whereas serving God brought them nothing but trouble. Like so many political pundits of today, they want certain things to happen so badly that they actually present them as fact! They get carried away. Nirvana, Utopia, Xanadu and Walhalla do not exist! Sailing toward them, one loses his life. "He that seeks to save his life will lose it," says Emmanuel. He knows—he created us that way.

So if we are to save our lives, we have to lose them for the sake of Christ. We must grant him top priority amidst a universe of competitive things. How are you doing? Are you loving God with all your mind, will, affection, strength, and your neighbor—every one of your neighbors, enemies included—as yourself? I admit that I have a long way to go, but I am working at it, and I do see progress. Sometimes I wonder why God makes such categorical demands on us. He requires what seems impossible! Yet I suppose had he demanded less than all, we would end up giving him nothing at all! Yes, 100% demands 100%—love is like that.

This brings me to one big, troubling question: Why did God, who obviously loves us, create us so close to disaster? I don't know about you, but that's my personal assessment, and yet I am promised a bountiful eternal life. Why was Peter scarcely saved? Why was Job escaping the skeptic's plunge to hell by the skin of his teeth? Why was Paul still chief of sinners at the very end of his earthly life? Why were we created so far from God, and so prone to making the wrong choices about life that we need to stop seeking our self-realization to finally get it? I have an answer that satisfies me, and I want to share it with you. Our marginal existence is due to God's intense love for us! He has made us so obviously limited so that we would have to get him involved in everything that happens to us. "Be careful for nothing . . . casting all your cares upon him." As our infants are totally dependent on us, so we are on God. He really wants to be relied on because he loves us, and this dependence continues our entire lives. The race is not over until we get the checkered flag. The stack of silver dollars cannot be evaluated until we count the last coin. The battle is not over until we slay the last enemy.

Once we understand that we are gods, and that being gods is like God Himself, who is Creator and the Universal Lover, it is then that we see we cannot belong to ourselves as devils do, but belong to God as he belongs to us. "My Beloved is mine and I am his," this is the Song of Songs. So we find ourselves by denying ourselves.

Do we actually find our lives? Henry Ward Beecher, one of the rarest talents ever to grace the English-speaking pulpit, told his congregation toward the end of his ministry that as he thought back over life, his happiest recollections were of things he did for other people. Dr. Beecher exhibited true wealth in this statement. We were made to own people and to be owned by them. Adam, as you recall, was incomplete in the Garden of things, including four-legged things. True happiness comes to us as suggested by the famous law of motion—for every action there is an equal and opposite reaction. The act of kindness is twice blest. It blesses him who gives as well as him who receives. We all know that we cannot throw mud without getting our own hands dirty. Yet don't forget that we cannot rub precious musk on the body of Jesus without getting it on our own hands.

I always make a great deal of participating in public worship, which begins for me at 5:00 a.m. each Sunday morning in my prayer closet. I pray especially for the minister. I do believe in intercessory prayer, though I do not believe "prayer changes things," as the homespun saying purports. Prayer changes me toward things, but not the things themselves. I leave the things to God's care. I want his will to be done. Why, then, do I pray for my pastor? I find that I expect more from his message, or rather the interlinear message of the Holy Ghost guiding me through the message, and so I get more from the sermon. I am changed toward the minister as well. I may even have something to say to him of a constructive nature that would not have occurred to me had I not prayed. During my intercessory prayer, I may discover ways of helping him, and thereby help myself. I grow in grace. Finally, my optimism becomes contagious—by loving, I inspire others to love me. That's the Iron Rule, as valid and as valuable as the Golden Rule; as we treat others is the way they are likely to treat us.

I have found that heaven visits earth when the Golden Rule activates the Iron Rule in Christian fellowship.

CROSS-BEARING

I am sure you have noticed that Love's Great Paradox is accompanied by another paradox of even greater severity. It is about cross-bearing, which is most certainly a metaphor. In no way did Jesus mean anything like the practice of well-intentioned Latin Americans carrying life-sized crosses through the streets of their cities on Good Friday, some even nailed to crosses for the six hours that match Christ's time on the cross. No, nothing that easy! When thinking about it, have you ever felt (as I have) like praying, "Well, there you go again, Beloved Christ, telling us to do the impossible"? Then I imagine that he whispers back to me, "If I asked anything less, then you would end up giving me nothing at all! Your goal should always exceed your reach, or what else is heaven for?"

Still, is Jesus' command that we bear crosses a paradox? I know that at first it does not seem to be. It lacks the parallelism and contrast we expect, like, "If you find, you lose; and if you lose, you find." Nevertheless, it does have one essential ingredient of a paradox, and that is irony, like "He was in the world, and the world was made by him, yet the world knew him not; he came to his own, and his own received him not." This occurs in the opening chapter to John's Gospel, and is the greatest irony of them all.

The irony of cross-bearing is that if we want to follow Christ to heaven, we must go there via Skull Place. Stated another way, the abundant life goes down the *Via Dolorosa*.

Before we attempt to apply cross-bearing to our lives, let us put it into its historical context. Truly, being told this must have shocked Jesus' hearers. They were quite aware of this Roman method of executing political criminals. Their Latin conquerors had created killing fields outside all major cities in the Empire. The one near the main gate of Jerusalem even had a nickname, Skull Place, or *Kronos Topos* in Greek, *Golgotha* in Hebrew, and *Calvary* in Latin. They had learned to expect such barbaric acts from these Gentiles. Did these heathen not include as part of their public entertainment the fiendish pleasure of watching wild animals devour people, and gladiators fight to the death? How like gods these ladies and gentlemen of Rome must have felt when they signaled thumbs-up, the traditional sign for the victor to give the vanquished his death blow! They enjoyed pretending they had the power over life and death.

Now this Preacher of Love tells them not only that he himself would be crucified, but that those who followed him would also end up on crosses. Strange, indeed, this version of abundant life he promised for following God! From our vantage point in the bleachers of history, we see this daring metaphor in clearer light. We know that we cannot live by Love's Great Paradox of finding our lives by losing them without being willing to carry a cross outside our own cities. We also know that Jesus is not talking about going to church on Sunday, but about life—the whole of it.

Jesus says, "If anyone wants to come after me, he must deny himself, he must even take up his own cross, and he must follow me." Notice that I use the adverb "must" three times. This is so because the Greek uses the imperative mood. We have it in English, but only in the second person. Jesus here uses the third person, so to translate what Jesus says into English, we have to add the word "must," which is not needed in Greek. Make no mistake about it—Jesus is leaving no wiggle room for us. Also notice that he is not requiring self-abnegation or self-repudiation. He appeals to our self-interest by promising us future life in his eternal home. There is no death to desire in this command, and included is a specific cross—not your neighbor's cross or Christ's cross, but your own.

We also see the twofold nature of our salvation. We are totally saved from the punishment of sin by Christ's dying for us, and we are progressively saved from the commission of sin by the lifetime service of self-denial. In effect, these two companion paradoxes focus on one thing— bringing us under the control of God. Here is the very foundation of living in a free society, as well as getting ready for heaven. We cannot have civil freedom unless we have personal control. I think one of our founding fathers had it right when he said, "Be ruled by God, or by God you will be ruled." Let us make no mistake about it, there is an inverse relationship between external freedom and internal control. Our forefathers were able to throw off the yoke of Mother England only because they were willing to assume internal control of their own personal lives. Today, the financial dependency on government by some is slowly bringing all of us under the control of government. Jesus implies that the choice is up to us. Who knows? Perhaps we will yet be able to shake off the heavy, velvet-covered chains of economic slavery that we wear, according to latest estimates, a full six months of each year.

So cross-bearing relates to the kind of government we will have—a free state or a slave state—but also to the Christian's role in history. We are all familiar with the famous statement that those who do not learn from the mistakes of history are destined to repeat them. This requires that we must keep the memory of the past alive. We must never forget why the Roman Empire fell, lest we likewise fall; how Adolf Hitler came to power, lest we fall victim to the nostrums of some worse political sycophant; who caused the Twin Towers Massacre, lest we come to believe that we must behave like devils to please God; why the likes of us could endure the effulgent glory of the Son of God for so short a while, then deliver him to so ignominious a death; lest we come to call vice virtue and burn righteousness at the stake. It is our task to answer Jesus' half-week ministry by finishing that week with our witness. Jesus calls us to keep history alive, to recapitulate his Passion in our own lives, to keep Skull Place squarely before men's eyes as the highest mount in human culture.

The way to do this is to experience the events of Christ's Passion in our own lives. Listen to these electrifying words of Paul: "That I may know him and the power of his resurrection, and the fellowship of his suffering, being conformed to his death." Do you see in these gracious words Paul's own trip down the *Via Dolorosa*? Right enough, Paul sees his task, not only as declaring the Gospel, but also as nourishing that declaration by experiencing the events in Christ's life. Our knowledge comes to us in two ways, by precept and by experience. That is to say, we learn from accepting what others tell us and from life itself. It is quite easy to see which is more fruitful and more forceful. It is experience that enriches our witness; it gives us insight into what we believe. Paul says he learns more from experiencing the sufferings of Christ Himself than from only talking about his Passion.

This gracious quotation from Paul is anticipated by Psalm 19, a poem praising the starry heavens and Law of Moses. About the heavens David says something quite important, but lamentably obscured by a faulty translation of the KJV. In verse 1, the second line says the same thing as the first, a technique used often in Hebrew poetry. It is used for emphasis, clarification and as a memory aid. I translate them thus: "The heavens are declaring the glory of God; even the wide dome above is showing his handiwork." Verse 2 is of the same structure. Notice that these four lines have four verbs associated with speech. Now come some italicized words. You will recall that italicized words in the KJV Bible are what we need in English to understand words not needed in the Greek and Hebrew. Those in verse 3a, "There is," are correct, but "where" in 3b changes the intended meaning, or at least obscures it. David is telling us that the message of the heavens is loud and clear everywhere on earth, and yet the heavens have no means for audible speech, no tongue or vocal chords at all. So the heavens speak through their actions. In effect, David says, "actions speak more loudly than words." Likewise, Paul has two messages—one preached and written about, and one lived.

In our last chapter, we looked at one amazing fact about the Passion of Christ as recorded in Isaiah 53; the far-seeing eye of the prophet discerns God in total control of all events on Good Friday: "Yet it pleased the Lord to bruise him; he hath put him to grief" (Isa. 53:10). But look at the remainder of that verse. What exactly is the prophet saying? Exactly what John says in his Gospel when he introduces the metaphor "born again" as describing our conversion experience. Notice earlier in the chapter the lament that the Messiah will die young, without any children. Here in verse 10 is the response to that lament. "When thou shalt make his soul an offering for sin, he shall see his seed, he shall prolong his days, and the pleasure of the Lord shall prosper in his hand." He will begin an eternal dynasty at Skull Place, that plot of ground outside the main gate of Jerusalem now covered by nearly 20 ft. of soil deposit and topped by a Muslim cemetery. Most surely does Christ's birthplace deserve a new name. It will be *Har Megiddo*, the "Mount of Rendezvous" for the whole of mankind.

We are born again into the ongoing family of Christ, the eternal family. He begins the Christian segment of this family right after the first Christian has entered it—we call him the Penitent Malefactor. Jesus says, "Woman, behold thy son; son, behold thy mother." Yet where are Mary's sons—James, Joses, Simon and Jude? God could have had them present, but Jesus proclaims from the cross that the heavenly family transcends the natural. Mary and John were to enter into that higher relationship, and so do we—Love's Paradox says so. We are saved by participating in the salvation of others. We are elevated far above the accumulation of things into the service of the God of gods. Let us never forget that we are gods who serve the God of gods (see Ps. 136).

When Jesus demands that we take up our crosses and follow him, he is saying that we must keep his saving work foremost in our segment of contemporary culture. It is said of painters that they need occasionally to lay aside their work in subtle shades and hues, and refresh the retinas of their eyes by looking at a color chart. This is what we must do, too. But how? By hearing sermons, studying Bibles, and participating in public sacraments? By all means. Yet to the man on the street these are somewhat like the shades and hues of the artists' brushes. They hear no more the roar of the heavens above that continuously, universally proclaim the glory of God. David invites us to consider the written Word of God, and still the eye of man is bedazzled by the neon, daytime midnight of Las Vegas. It matters not to men that the Written Word proclaims Christ as the Living Word. How are we to do the same in our own lives? The answer is that each of us must become a Living Word; we must recapitulate the Passion of Christ. He joins our experience, and that is why he requires that each of us cultivate total complicity, so we can experience life in his context. This is what men need, and they need it from us.

As the Book of Genesis comes to its end, we see its third type of Christ. First is Adam, then Isaac, finally Joseph; all three are specifically cited as types of Christ by New Testament scholars. As you recall, Joseph forces upon his ten brothers a recapitulation of their treatment of him. Only then are they forced into self-analysis and a view of themselves in their wretched circumstances. Even so, the Passion Narrative exhibits before us parallels in our own lives. As we have seen in ourselves the weaknesses of Christ's tormentors, we are now required to join Jesus in making a contemporary revitalization of his Passion. God's willingness to share man's mortality helps man to transcend that mortality. The mode is our historical recapitulation of Christ's Passion within individual contexts, which makes Christ's gift of love visible to man, and makes each of us, in the words of the street preacher, a confrontational evangelist. We also must pitch his tent among them. This is the end purpose of these two great paradoxes—Love and Cross-Bearing—we have just studied.

OUR THREE-DIMENSIONAL CROSSES

We do well to exhort ourselves and our fellow pilgrims to be aware of the trick some play on themselves of assuming someone else's cross as a way of avoiding their own. Some call this the martyr complex; others call it sloppy agape. I call it "water-spigot" religion. Of course, this bearing others' crosses is always easier than bearing our own, much easier—in fact, it is no cross-bearing at all. Since every human being is infinitely complex, none can bear any cross but his own. We deceive ourselves when we avoid spiritual problems in our own lives by busying ourselves with those of others. I have known people who have even created imaginary crosses that have no foundation in reality whatever, like the men who carry crosses of wood in a Good Friday parade. Some even see cross-bearing as a group effort. I have found one thing all false efforts have in common—they all are within the control of the bearer. With the slightest provocation, these crosses are cast aside. That is why I call such efforts "water-spigot" religion. Real crosses, like the one Jesus bore and the one he asks—rather, demands—that you bear are not easily borne and cannot be laid aside.

I define cross-bearing as patiently enduring the consequences of living like Christ. When you bear yours, and to the extent that you do, the world, the flesh and the devil become your avowed enemies; God becomes your intimate companion; your conscience becomes a constant accuser. This is not a bad thing. God wants you to be poor in spirit, wants you to mourn and be meek in his presence, wants you to feel constantly the pain of hunger and thirst, so that he may be your constant supply. On one occasion Christ offered men better yokes to wear together with a promise that he would see to it that their burdens would be lighter than they were before.

As is the case with all physical objects, your particular cross has three dimensions. You may not be aware of more than one at a time, but they are there, and you are promised that, like Jesus, you will bear your cross successfully. Of course, the cross of self-denial is clearly named and the cross of persecution is implied, but there is a third we must also consider.

It is often overlooked, yet strange to say, it is of longest duration and also the most conspicuous. You will have it until the day you die.

The cross of the status quo. If you are uncomfortable with the Latin expression, you might call it "The Cross of Inequality." This is so because the status quo presents each of us as unique, hence unavoidably unequal, in every single way but one; we are all equal before God's law. By this, I mean that we all have the guarantee of being objects of his *summum bonum* (Rom. 8:28). We also hope for such equality before our human courts—our ancestors shed their blood that we might have it. However, that is where the equality ends; there is no other equality, not even before God. Recall Paul's most mysterious and highly provocative quotation, "Jacob have I loved, and Esau have I hated." In addition, there is no doubt that Peter, James and John had a higher relationship with Christ than the other disciples, and that John was even a little bit higher than the other two. He was, as you recall, "the disciple whom Jesus loved."

No, there is precious little equality in the world. Any attempt to legislate it, say economically, has ended in bloody disaster. We have heard enough of this nonsense, "From each according to his ability to each according to his need." It is plain as your DNA that we are not made equal. In fact, I have never deluded myself into thinking it is a good thing to be equal. I do not want to be equal. I have always wanted to be superior. I also want the very best of everything, and I am out to get it! Immediately, someone will say to me, "Aren't you now agreeing with the proponents of the latest modern heresy, the prosperity theology?" Not at all. I use God's dictionary to define my terms. I say, "Give me neither poverty nor riches . . . . Feed me with the food that is needful for me" (Proverbs 30:8).

Here is a far better prayer than the Prayer of Jabez! What wealth could be better than exactly what God wants me to have? He and I, working together, will see to it.

Equality before the law in a free society is what Abraham Lincoln meant when he said, "We are all equal at the starting line." The good news in this is the fairness implied, but the bad news is that there is where the equality ends. I am not competing in a race alongside Jesse Owens. Our big toes both touch the same white line, but the moment the pistol fires, the equality ends. Paul reminds us that in races on the athletic field, only one will win, but he says that we ought to run as though we could win. Indeed, as I tell my freshmen students in their writing course, they are not competing against one another, but against an ideal in my mind. So it is with God; we are competing with an ideal in his mind, which was expressed by the life of his own Son, who was and is the Road, and the Truth, even the Life. It is possible with God that all can win the race.

However, there is a price to pay. Consider one of the final encounters with God in the life of Father Jacob. It was a long way from buying Esau's birthright with a mess of pottage to spending a night wrestling with Christ to get a spiritual blessing. Toward dawn he achieved success in receiving the blessing. He went away from the contest with a new nature—and a limp that he would have for the rest of his life. It became part of his spiritual inventory, his status quo. So it is with all of us. It is my belief that we all have wounds, visible or invisible, like Jacob. I don't really know this for a fact because I haven't asked that many people if they limp. The truth of the matter is that I am as reluctant to speak of my limp as I am to ask others about theirs. I rarely ask because it is such an intensely personal matter. I know anyone would be put on the spot, and I hesitate for fear an affirmative answer would invite me to ask or even to contemplate what it could possibly be. Yet I do ask it indirectly, like this, "Do you suppose everybody needs a crutch, visible or invisible?" The answer has always been "yes."

I am reasonably certain that everyone has some kind of an impediment. It might be called a thorn in the flesh, which Paul admitted having, though nobody knows exactly what it was. Others may have impediments they cannot hide, like some kind of physical infirmity, mental limitation, tragic personal losses, or being afflicted with one of the many psychopathic personalities. Others are burdened with social problems they cannot escape. With some, the burden is delayed until midlife or even later, like financial reversals or the limitations that come with aging—the variety is endless.

As I have said before, we are created with these needs so we will seek satisfaction from God Himself. The first step is to accept our status quo, take it as our own Joban question, and seek divine help to bear what must be borne. Yet some rear up against God. I know of a very successful clergyman whose only son was killed in World War II. He turned to bitterness, quit the ministry and lost his faith. What of those inflicted with homosexuality? Here is a supreme challenge to one's faith, given our modern emphasis on sex. Why would God allow this abnormality? Why without one's consent? Why especially this person and not someone else? So it seems that God is unfair, but isn't that what faith is all about? Trusting God for what we cannot understand? If people with such afflictions attempt to legislate change in others' attitudes toward them, or trick themselves into believing Scripture does not condemn overt expression of this weakness, they worsen their condition. They cannot legislate respectability. God sets them on a most challenging quest. He wants them to turn their affliction into a positive experience. This they must do— but how? That is part of their own salvation, which must be worked out "with fear and trembling," just like everyone who seeks to transcend this world and spend eternity with God. Think of the lonely man in the outback of Australia. All he sees ahead are endless miles of dry land. His relatives, if he has any at all, are half a world away. All he owns is in that heavy backpack. So what does he do? To begin with, he gives his pack a name, a woman's name. Then he calls the endless trek ahead "waltzing," and so he goes, waltzing Matilda. That's a beginning—his beginning.

If we look about us, it will not be long until we see someone with a more challenging status quo than we have. If they are following Christ, they encourage us to try harder. That is an excellent reason for us to cultivate friendships with fellow pilgrims, and attending church is the best place to find such friends; above all, Christ Himself is the most excellent of friends. We must make no mistake about his position on this matter. He tells us that heaven and earth will pass away, but his word lives forever. What does his Eternal Word say? Deny yourself ! Take up your cross! Follow me! He promises us that he will beautify the meek with salvation. He will save us from ourselves. We must not try to conform ourselves to the world or attempt to change the world to our liking, but rather to transform ourselves, a task impossible without his leadership. The first step is to let him change our environment. Abraham was told to leave the town of Ur, and Lot to leave the town of Sodom. I am sure there are many saints in heaven who were homosexual, but they left Sodom or sailed away from the Isle of Lesbos. Christ called himself the Road of Life. He means that everyone of us must walk away from our version of the City of Destruction toward eternal life.

The cross of persecution. In the fullness of time, God sent his Son among us to give the final statement of his message, to demonstrate before us how to live, and to express the power that comes from that living. As the Epistle to the Hebrews puts it, Christ was the effulgent glory and essential character of Almighty God. In a little more than three years, Jesus, the Living Word of God, exposed his Omnipotent Love to the race of people who would be most likely to receive him, and they saw to it that he was put to death in the most ignominious way possible. Men are 100% wrong about reality, and Jesus Himself said that the closer his followers lived to him, the more likely their lives would end like his. History has proved him right to this very day. Christians can expect to suffer insult, slander and persecution.

As I slowly turn the pages of church history, I almost feel guilty that I have not suffered for Christ as did my spiritual ancestors. I am comforted only by a hope that I would prove faithful should I be called to endure what they experienced. I recall the words of one of the field preachers of Scotland, who died as one of the last of the English martyrs, "There are no more Christians than there are martyrs in resolution and affection." However, it may be that worse times will come upon us, even sooner than we imagine, and sometimes persecution comes from church people. We all are imperfect and have no right to imagine perfection anywhere in society, be it in government, churches or even families. All those who live godly lives in Christ Jesus will suffer for it.

The cross of self-denial. If I must lose my life to find it, as Love's Great Paradox says, then I am to experience a surrender of my being at the most fundamental level. This involves the third item in that ancient three-part category of sin, the pride of living. Remember the command to Abraham as regards the sacrifice of Isaac. God asked him to do what was absolutely opposite of what he would expect of God. If he obeyed God's command, it would seem to suggest God was no different from the local bloodthirsty gods of the culture he had left behind, and also that God breaks his promises. Of course, Abraham was wrong because he could not see the whole picture. He had to trust God when trusting contradicted his own logic and experience—and so must we.

This kind of choice happened only once in Abraham's life, and nothing comparable is likely to happen again. Yet there is something quite similar to it that presents potential difficulty to us all. When I was a young Christian, I remember hearing a sermon about the "risk of faith." I had faith, and I did not feel I had risked anything at all. But as I grew in grace, I began to see the differences between the good, the better and the best, and that they would sometimes compete with each other. I must confess that I did not always give precedence to the best, and here I saw is where the risk of faith came in. In his famous chapter on the resurrection from the dead, Paul confesses that his choices would be different if the dead do not rise. So I must deny myself even the good or the better when they compete with what is best. It is good to spend an hour listening to Bach or Mozart; it is even better to spend it studying the Bible; but it may be best to go next door to help my neighbor hang his Christmas lights, or to take home a hopper full of soiled diapers to wash because his wife is in bed with the flu. This is what the minister meant by the "risk of faith."

CONCLUSION

In our next chapter, we will enjoy a foretaste of our heavenly home and what we will be like when we get there. One thing that climaxes then is in process even now. At the Great Judgment, all will have become sheep or goats. These two metaphors of Jesus tell us that we will have either completed a regenerated self based on the love of persons, or will have degenerated into a lover of things. To end up as sheep depends on our conforming to the two paradoxes we have been studying. Notice that these paradoxes are not commandments. Of a truth, they are invitations sent to us over 20 centuries of time. We will end the lives we are living, even now moving toward being sheep or goats, the worshippers of God or Mammon, the god of wealth.

Most people will be goats, according to Jesus. The narrow and difficult road will not appeal to them. They will be tricked by their own pride into the Great Deception that a person's life consists in the abundance of possessions, as Jesus taught in the Parable of the Bigger Barns. It is true that things can give pleasure, especially beauties of nature and works of art. However, as things they are passive, static and incommunicable. Therefore, overexposure cloys the mind, and the resulting boredom leads to a restless pursuit of even more things. As time passes, these things imperceptibly change. Appetite grows by what it feeds on. Things cannot help but migrate into a self-centered world, mummy-wrapped by an endless gauze of things. God made people to relate to persons, not things, so these worshippers of Mammon experience islands of loneliness. And what comes next? They begin to treat things as people, and people as things. Philosophers call this unhealthy deception the "pathetic fallacy."

Of course, these goats do not believe a word I have written about them. They have heard about the earthly visit of the Effulgent Glory of God, and they flatly reject him. The longer their self-centered lives continue, the more certain they become about their own righteousness. Yet Christ insists only two kinds of people will stand in the Great Judgment; those who choose to deny themselves that they may find themselves in Christ are the sheep, and those enthralled by The Great Deception—materialism—are the goats. Jesus is telling us by sound inference that only animals are in pursuit of things because only they are oblivious to persons. Only devils turn persons into things, and only they practice this kind of cannibalism. At Skull Place, dear friend, it is easy to see how those who seek to find their lives will lose them. Self-realization cannot be based on a self-determined system of values, which always leads to an acquisition of things. Persons in pursuit of things as an end-in-themselves are dying animals, gods in eclipse, waning luminaries, devils in process. What else could they be called?

Those of us who recognize Christ as Emmanuel accept the person— approach to life. People are not passive, but active peers—unpredictable, often problematic, but also sublime and a renewable source of pleasure. It is a life of touching lives, not a hall of mirrors and echo chambers. It is a narrow and difficult way, but it is heaven in process at times, and at my age a joy unspeakable and full of glory. We have been to Skull Place and seen man totally uninhibited (as Cain was) meet Omnipotent Love. Such a meeting had never been before, nor need it ever be again. We see enough to know that God so loved the world that he gave his Son, his Only Begotten, that whosoever is having faith in him will not perish. We see the one time when man could not be conceivably worse toward God, and Christ could not be conceivably more expressive of Love.

I am told there is one spot on the Bright Angel Trail in Grand Canyon National Park where it is possible to see all five visible geological ages without taking a single step—the Archeozoic rocks through which the Colorado River rushes, the Cenozoic hills of the Painted Desert just over the rim of the Canyon, and the three remaining ages in between—all quite visible. This much cannot be seen at any other single spot on the face of the earth. Yet this pales in importance, achievement and notability by what can be seen at *Moriah, Zion, Jehovah-jireh,* Skull Place. Like Abraham, God felt it deserved a new name, one suited for the Great Judgment. He calls it *Har Megiddo,* "Mount Rendezvous." Indeed, we will all be there from Adam to the last person born at the end of this final day of the Millennial Week.

I go there often, at least once a day. I see again Christ wearing my tattoo. The thorn crown of my vanity and self-deception. The fist of my violence and the claw of my greed fixed there with nails. The belly of my lust and gluttony pierced. The persistence of my sins along with their great number and their shameful duration scourged—repeatedly—upon his holy body. My foot that wandered and my foot that would not walk, both impaled. Why do I see me there, his stigmata as mine? Because if he forgave the Romans even while they were in the very act of committing their worst offence against him, then surely I am forgiven, too.

The Jews were the most privileged nation on earth. God bore them on eagles' wings and brought them to their sanctified land. Over the centuries, they were carefully instructed on how to recognize the Messiah when he came. Of all the nations on earth, they would be the most likely to recognize him. Still, they did not. Persuaded by their leaders, they called for his execution, and while he was being nailed to the cross, he forgave them. These participants in the Passion, by being the most prepared to recognize Christ and to benefit most from receiving him, make us their proxies, motivated by the same greed, envy, fear and pride in our lives. Even so Christ, by forgiving their worst of crimes, forgives ours as well, and makes all men henceforth his proxies to us. How we treat all in need of the same salvation we have freely received is tantamount to how we treat Christ Himself. Ignoring them is ignoring Christ; slamming the door against their importuning is refusing to open to the Christ who knocks at the same door.

There are other strata of truths to be seen, different layers of meaning. I see the Father's love as being most conspicuous, for he conjoined his Son in setting his tormenters free to do exactly what their envy, fear, greed and pride urged upon them. Then another layer became apparent later in life, after I had been coming for many years to Skull Place, after my feet were bloody treading on the shards of my broken dreams, dreams I myself had broken. I saw that the crucifixion is contemporaneous, i.e., always contemporary. Now in the afternoon of my life, I begin to see in the midnight noon of my ignorance that there upon the cross was the historic me. Yes, clear as noonday, I saw how I had crucified the man I might have been by preventing God's use of my lips, hands, feet—the whole of me. How I had sullied my reputation with the dust of vanity and the scars of rebellion. I had hedged his thought out with a thorn crown of wasted energy of mind, the glooms of paranoiac guilt, the vanity of now-forgotten pleasures.

There is more. I see the contemporaneity of his Passion reaching into the future. Will I even crucify the self I could yet become? As long as there is sin in my life, that is exactly what I will be doing. Could I but anticipate tomorrow, perhaps I could fend off at least some of my sins. Yet I have on good advice not to think about tomorrow. Whenever I do not allow the Holy One of Israel to use my lips, hands, feet, mind—any part of me—I limit him and me as well. Still, God knows my future, and I know he does, for my times are in his hands. Sins may surprise us, but they never surprise him. When he called me unto himself 60 years ago, he knew the tally of them all. It is of no small comfort to know that he called me anyway. This frailty of mine guarantees my poverty of spirit, that I will continue to mourn, to be meek in his presence, to hunger and thirst ever for right living.

Finally, in the midday darkness, I come to the deepest layer of meaning. I see God as loving himself. If I am to love my neighbor as myself, then it is all right for me to love myself. He created me to love myself, and he is good. So I reason that God so loved himself that he gave his Only Begotten Son to win me unto himself. God chose me in him before the foundation of the world because loving me is a way of loving himself. I am in ecstasy as I think and think about what this means. The eternal reality that lasts beyond the cross is heaven's visa, the Love of God.

FOR THE SUITCASE

1. There are key biblical words that defy definition.
2. Christianity is the last major, original religion to be founded. Nothing has been truly new during the last 2,000 years!
3. Agape love does not necessarily involve emotion, but it does include everybody, including our enemies.
4. Self-realization is not wrong, but there are wrong ways to get it.
5. At the Great Judgment, people will be of two kinds only.
6. Civil freedom is based on personal control.
7. The prayer of Proverbs 30:8 is far better than the often touted prayer of Jabez in I Chronicles 4:10.
8. Accepting life as God has dealt it to us is one of the hardest crosses you may have to bear.
9. Strive to get the best for yourself, but let God define what is best for you.
10. You will see more at Calvary than anywhere on earth.
11. God loves himself, and you should love yourself, too.

Chapter IX:
Getting Ready For Al

Road Maps: Romans 7; Ephesians 6; I Corinthians 3;
II Corinthians 5

Aging and death are as much a part of the Christian Road as are finding a mate and having children. For exceptional reasons, some do not marry or start a family, but as regards aging and death, "there is no discharge in that war," as Solomon cautions us. It is true that we tend to make war against the onslaught of age and to resist with all our might the day of death. We do not want to think about it, or listen to others talk about it. When I was a student pastor, I suppose I did preach too often about getting ready for eternity. One Sunday, a dear lady in her 50s, obviously on the verge of giving in to obesity and gray hair, said to me as she left church, "There you go, Pastor, preaching our funerals again!" She was quite upset with me.

The Bible calls on us to treat age and death like everything else in this life, as alchemists. We are not to be conformed to this world, but transformed by the renewing of our minds. We must change lead to gold. To paraphrase Paul, though our outward man perishes, yet the inner man is renewed day by day. So with the ebbing of our body's strength is the renewal of our spiritual strength. Like the pilgrimage trek from Jericho to Jerusalem, we go from strength to strength. Paul triumphed over death and the grave: "O death, where is your sting? O grave, where is your victory?"

He saw death as the door to eternal life, and the older and weaker he grew, the stronger he became. "For when I am weak, then I am strong," he said. This reversal of fortune comes only to those who begin early on the Christian Road dealing with such a matter, like William Cullen Bryant, who wrote his great poem *Thanotopsis*, "a view of death," when he was only 17. As I recall, I was required to memorize it in junior high school, along with Longfellow's "Psalm of Life." I bless the memory of the teacher who made me do it.

We must stop putting so much emphasis on the physical appearance of things. Did you ever notice that the Bible from cover to cover almost totally ignores what people look like? One rightly remarked that we know more about the physical features of Goliath than about the youth who slew him. Why is this? Because all flesh is grass. What did Jesus look like? Isaiah is the only one who ever spoke on the matter. He said few would recognize Jesus as the Messiah because he looked as average as an annual weed ("tender plant" in the KJV) or a tree root sticking out of dry ground. Because of the Bible's silence, each of us can envision a Christ of his own imagination—after all, he belongs to us all. What about heaven? Nothing, or at least nothing specific. It is just as impossible to describe our eternal home as it is to give God a proper name. Let the religions of the world speak of gods, giving each a name. We celebrate the transcendence of the Almighty Father with a simple, common noun, or if we choose, we may take the Hebrew "I THAT I," until the shadows of our valley turn to eternal day, and we know as we are now known. Of him and the home he has prepared for us, there is nothing we can say except what would limit or distract from the glory that awaits us.

The world's most famous poem on aging and dying is found in Ecclesiastes 12, and is addressed to youth, not as one might suppose to the aged. It is a highly sophisticated poem in the form of a literary conceit, likening the process of aging and death to the progressive dilapidation of an old building. The poet slows our thinking down so we will pause and think through each part of the body it symbolizes. In Eccles. 12:2f., the symbols apply to internal parts of the body. Some have speculated that the Hebrew children recited this as a "finger poem," gesturing toward each part of the body as the poet introduced it in symbolic form. For example, when the poem says, "and the almond tree shall blossom," the children would point to their hair to indicate getting white-headed. Then for "or the grasshopper will be a burden," they would lay their hands flat on top of their heads to suggest getting bald. The poem says the more obvious the reality of aging and death becomes, the greater the miracle will be of God's daily care of our lives.

I would like to return to Abraham's Moriah Test one more time. He and Jesus join hands to bring us a very important doctrine that is often neglected. We tend to pay it lip service, but we tiptoe past it quickly, lest some might think us stupid, superstitious, or even a bit crazy. I speak of a doctrine that has absolutely no proof at all, just like so many other doctrines we accept on the authority of Scripture by faith (conviction without proof) because they come to us from him who is the personification of all we hope for, and whose relationship with us proves the existence of the unseen world to come (Heb. 11:1). In an earlier chapter, we saw how The Moriah Test presented Abraham with a set of parallel circumstances that revealed Christ to him. Jesus said, "Abraham saw my day and rejoiced." He saw that God also had a son, who would become the sacrificial lamb to die for the sins of Abraham's descendants.

Jesus tells us that when we speak of Abraham, we speak of a living person. "He *is* the God of Abraham," not of someone dead. Jesus speaks of him most lovingly in his parable about the beggar Lazarus and the rich man. At the raising of the other Lazarus, Jesus says to Mary and Martha, "He that has faith in me *even though he were dead*, yet shall he live; and he who has faith in me and lives will not, never die." (the Greek uses this double negative). The italicized words indicate the use of the subjunctive mood, which suggests that death in exceptional circumstances may occur, such as in the son of the widow of Nain, Jairus' daughter, or Lazarus. These are the exception. This scripture teaches that we depart from this life prior to the body's death. Stephen, our first Christian martyr, experienced the Parousia of Christ before the first stone struck him. Jesus, in Matthew 16, says some of his listeners would experience his Parousia before they would come to natural deaths. Of course, this puzzles us, but remember that we are speaking about the eternal world that has no spatial-temporal limitations. So in that world, it would be possible for Christ's Second Coming to appear to each of us and all of mankind at the same time! I believe that I will never taste of death. I have it by faith in the promise of Christ. "O, death, where is thy sting?"

This departure from the body prior to death is an often neglected truth, clearly pronounced and exemplified in Scripture. There are, however, views held by many that are deceptions—false hopes not at all found in Scripture. The most frequently held is the notion that God will make them into new creatures at the Great Judgment. It is true that there will be a new heaven and a new earth and we will have new bodies, but not new natures. If a man is to become a new creature, it must happen in this life, not the next. People who cling to this false notion are not interested in any change whatever. They are completely satisfied with their lives as they are. They are not poor in spirit, do not mourn, do not hunger and thirst after righteousness. They probably have been baptized and are *bona fide* members of a Christian church. They see the observing of rituals as the ongoing guarantee that they will earn a radical change of being at the Great Judgment. They want God to do the impossible, to recreate them then into what they will not allow him to do now.

Some go from the illogical to the fantastic and imagine a second chance via reincarnation. Others fancy themselves taking a lower status as angels, or being given the option of annihilation instead of hell. Some fancy the notion of being servants of God, like the Prodigal Son. Remember his musings about the love of his father who just might take him back as one of his hired servants. He even rehearsed exactly how he would approach the matter. Yet when the blessed reunion took place, he did not get a chance to offer himself as a servant—that is, even if he remembered to make the offer.

These false ideas are just a few inventions of the carnal nature. We will take up no more space to speak of such things as eternal life being like a vast staircase, each on his own level, life as an unbroken continuum, or more optimistic yet, that everybody will be saved and hell will be no more than a purgatory. Rather, let us look to what we do know from Scripture, and precious little it is. Yet we know God, and God is love, and he is in Paradise.

TRIAL MEMBERSHIP IN THE 100% CLUB

One way to look at the Christian Road is as trial membership in The 100% Club. Maybe it is even the best way. I say "100%" because that is what Love always gives and always demands from the one loved, or else love is not love. I say "trial membership" because I have not yet been able to give 100%. I know God wants me, every scrap of me, the real me—not wood, hay or stubble. He has given me himself—Skull Place says so. Still, I sleep a third of my life and work at secular employment another third to cooperate with God and the world in order to put bread on my table. That final third is choked with the dust of anonymous vanities, distracted by the carnival barkers of evanescent luxuries, and eroded by the ever-increasing complexity of domestic living—precious little time is left. I am still a ragamuffin, and I so often mourn at Skull Place that it seems to be my habitual rendezvous, and has been for the past 60 years. Quite plainly, I am not far enough along with my mourning, my hungering and thirsting, forgiving and being forgiven to take out full membership. It is about all I can do to lend a hand to my neighbor as we help each other wear our rags with dignity. I just cannot love *everybody* as much as, and as well as, I do myself.

Raving thus, I came to the conclusion that just maybe I see my task as larger than it really is. Indeed, God never asked me to love *everybody*. I Remember Henry Ward Beecher's perceptive conclusion about Christian ethics. He said, "A universal philanthropy is a passionless sentiment." Thinking he may be right about this, I asked my Heavenly Father, "Do you mean that I am not to love cats and dogs, elephants and alligators, Eskimos and Hottentots, the aborigines of Australia and the Ainu of Japan?" Then he answered back, "That's exactly right. None of this sloppy agape. Just love your neighbor." That is exactly what Jesus did say. He speaks of neighbors, using linear distance as the sole criterion for identifying our service to mankind! There is genius in that command, for it gives us no room to dispute about who exactly that is. Compare this with Mohammed's command for each follower of Allah to love all the other followers. I asked an Iraqi how his country could go to war with the Iranians. His answer was quite simple: "They are not true Muslims, and being in error they are worse enemies of Allah than you infidels!" You see, he had an out—Allah had left the definition up to him. In contrast, who can argue with who their neighbor is? One day it could be a man lying beside the Jericho Road in a pool of blood, robbed and left for dead. The next day it could be the unsolicited telemarketer calling you at dinner time. In other words, my neighbor is with whomever I come in contact.

We are to love God first because he is "nearer to us than breathing, closer than hands and feet." Next is the spouse, the sole recipient of all three kinds of love—*eros, philos* and *agape.* Then the children, then the next-door neighbor and everyone else, friend and foe, that God brings into our microcosm on any given day. Of course, it is never easy to love an enemy, but you can shrink him by fervent prayer for him, maybe even unmask him and see a friend instead. You may find that you yourself turned him into an enemy because you, for some morbid reason, needed to have an enemy around. Perhaps you needed a whipping boy because you refused to discipline yourself. Or maybe God wants to show you an example of how you can become your own worst enemy, without whose cooperation Satan would be powerless. Yes, pray yourself onto loving ground. That's what Jesus did, and turned a Roman killing field into the Paradise of our hope!

We must never forget the love of God goes as far as his omnipresence allows him—to infinity—100% of the way to the human heart, to sacrificing his Only Begotten Son so six millennia of men could never doubt his gift of universal salvation to whoever has faith in him. So what he gives, he expects in return. Love is like that. Since we are not ready yet to qualify for full membership, let us act like the trial members we are—wholly indebted to him. We owe him, and he has made payment possible by designating the neighbor as his proxy, whether Iraqis or Iranians. Paul says, "Owe no man anything, but to love one another." So we are in debt, and that is why we pray, "forgive us our debts because we have forgiven our debtors."

During the time remaining for us on this Road, we must endure the stinging, mocking silence resulting from those Joban questions which we cannot seem to keep from rising in our minds and escaping from our lips. Our condition is like Job's—we are too intelligent to keep from asking questions, the answers to which we are too ignorant to understand. Do not forget to ask the antecedent question, i.e., the question that not only satisfactorily answers all Joban questions, but even obviates the asking of them. "And what," you ask, "is THAT question?" It is, "God, do you love me?" This question he delights to answer in the affirmative, and to answer it the more emphatically the more frequently you ask it, even though he has already categorically answered it through Jesus, our Ultimate Altruist. Let us cart loads of questions every day outside the city to Skull Place. Indeed, the path is already so well-trodden by so many during these past two millennia that Skull Place should have a God-given name, one appropriate to the universal need of our daily coming. God calls it *Har Megiddo*—"Mount Rendezvous."

My dear fellow pilgrims on the Christian Road, let us rest our weary bodies here beneath the "shadow of a Mighty Rock" while our souls get aboard our time machine and soar higher than our astronauts ever travelled. They landed on the Moon, whereas we journey to the *ouranos,* the third heaven, where Paul received a vision so wonderful that all the laws that govern language could not adequately share it with us. If we look at Scripture with the reverence due it and with the expectations it generates in us, we will see that Paul did, more than any other of the canonists, give us some exciting specifics which, though they might never satisfy us, are not inconsistent with what he saw but could not describe. As far as we know, he is the only canonist who reached the third heaven and was allowed to return to earth to tell us that he had been there. May the Holy Ghost lend us wings as we soar beyond the few years remaining in this sixth millennium of God's Holy Week.

THROUGH THE FIRE

We turn now to the two brief portions of the Corinthian letters, which are, I confess, worthy of a book-length treatment. God's Word is, as David said, a great deep, an ocean without a shore. We could never fathom its depth because it is a growing body of eternal subject matter. It speaks of life, and life means growth, and growth means change. Each time we read it, we bring a changed self to the Eternal Message before us. So we see more of God's ever changing, yet ever the same, Holy Word. This must surely reflect what Christ said about the merchant bringing forth from his store things both old and new—not two things, some old and some new, but the same things with both qualities inherent, the old and the new. The old becomes new because it is newly seen.

We are in the last day of the millennial week and must restrict the fascinating subject before us—the study of the last things often called eschatology. These are the events: Cataclysms, Parousia, Resurrection, Judgment and Eternal Life. Of course, there is controversy; some want to add other divisions, or at least subdivisions. Yet I refuse to be tempted into affirmations or denials of additional matters that are not clearly expressed in Scripture. On the verge of the Eternal Tomorrow, we all surely appreciate most a consideration of the "fire" and "lashes" that serve to get us ready for the Parousia (I Cor. 3), and the glorious nature of our eternal bliss. This we see in contrast to our present state (II Cor. 5), which is the only way we can look at our eternal bliss, for it is so great that eye, ear or imagination cannot make comparisons.

We turn now to I Cor. 3. Paul sees us first as infants—at least some of us. Then we become garden plots, then builders, and finally temples. Many metaphors of the Christian Road strongly suggest hard work. Isaiah even sees us as blacksmiths beating our swords into plowshares and our spears into pruning hooks. He also sees us as civil engineers with bulldozers at our disposal, shoving the mountain tops of our superfluity into the valleys of our wanting and neglect, then carving a straight road into our crooked thinking, and disking our rough natures into smooth, level roads. He also depicts us as wild animals becoming tame, lions eating straw like an ox, the wolf and lamb lying down together, being led by a little child (who symbolizes faith). In his thinking, we become a hospital ward of impotent folk—too blind to read Holy Scripture, too deaf to hear it, too lame to walk to church, too maimed of hand to reach the offering plate or to lay a cool cloth on a neighbor's fevered brow. Then like Paul, he sees a battlefield. David likewise sees God as the "Lord of Hosts," which means God dressed in armor, leading his troops to battle. Paul spoke often of running a race, but in this passage we are presented as builders.

This at first seems almost contrary to the Bible's main theme, and most certainly a main theme of Paul, viz., salvation by faith and not the works of the law. This would be true except for the fact that salvation is not the main theme! It is life, living for God, with a heavenly birth as its beginning.

We see this matter clearly when we distinguish between three kinds of "works." The first is the works of the law, or rituals involving worship, personal and public. A repudiation of these as the means of salvation is stoutly affirmed by Paul in nearly everything he wrote. It is difficult, though, to distinguish between faith and works, as Jesus' natural half-brother, James, writes. His main theme in his one brief submission to the Canon proclaims that faith without works is dead. This is true indeed, and is no contradiction to what Paul says when we see the difference between the works of the law and the second kind of works. Paul himself writes in Titus 3:5, "Not by works of righteousness that we have done, but according to his mercy, he saved us . . . ." Even to this very day, there is confusion among Christians about good works and works of the law, or rituals. I strongly feel than many people think works save them, that rituals become the reality they profess. The history of science shows even trained minds can confuse cause with effect. In Eph. 2:8-9 Paul speaks of both kinds of works, denying saving power to the one and exhorting us to perform the other:

> For by grace have you been saved through faith, and not
> by yourselves; it is the gift of God, not of works, lest any
> man should boast, for we are his workmanship, created
> in Christ Jesus unto good works, which God has before
> ordained that we should walk in them.

The third kind of works is the same as the second kind, but differs in circumstance. I call it spontaneous compassion, or the assistance we show to those in need as needs arise. Jesus speaks of them in his teaching about dividing people into two classes at the Great Judgment, the sheep and the goats. Observing rituals of religion cannot buy salvation, but one's relationship with others via acts of spontaneous compassion does indeed determine the degree of rewards in the afterlife. In Matt. 16:27, Jesus says, "The Son of man shall come in the glory of his Father with the holy angels, and he shall then reward everyone according to his works." So we must conclude that when the Bible says we are saved by faith and not works, and yet that each will be judged by his works, two entirely different kinds of works are meant.

We are to be like the Carpenter from Nazareth—builders. Remember that we enter life with divine abilities—conceptual thought and speech, and willpower. Yet two other abilities also must be ours if we are to spend eternity walking with God and his Holy Son, Jesus. These are sensitivity to people and creativity developed over a lifetime of experience. So what we do is very much like building a house.

Still, things are not quite that simple. Notice that Paul does not hesitate to bring more than one metaphor to bear upon the nature of our cultivating sensitivity to others and our ability to create. As chapter 3 begins we are babes, then we become garden plots, then God's husbandry, then a building, then builders and finally temples for the Holy Spirit. Such a multifarious consideration should cause us to remember that a metaphor has only one application. Notice that the first here—"babes"—has (let us hope) only temporary reality! Regarding the rest of the metaphors, I suppose all apply concurrently.

An interesting question we would surely want to ask Paul is what is the name of the edifice we are building? He names the foundation as Christ Jesus Himself, but nothing more specific is said, and nothing of its function or nature is given here either. It is not God's building, for that is already in existence, and is called the temple of God's Spirit. It is not the church, for it has the apostles as its 12-part foundation, and it has but one builder, Christ Himself. Did he not say, ". . . and on this rock I will build my church"?

What is this building that we must spend our lifetimes building? We are not told in this chapter, but we will identify it in our study of II Cor. 5. Yet we do have the building materials supplied. Nothing else will do but what meets specifications. As Moses said, "See that you build according to the pattern given in the Mount." We have approved for us gold, silver and precious stones—rejected are wood, hay and stubble.

Not only do we not know the nature or name of this structure, but Paul does not define the gold, silver and precious stones, or the wood, hay and stubble. These questions are answered elsewhere in this epistle and several other places in his writings. Both triads are significantly sequenced in descending order of value. It may be that Paul intended to define gold, silver and precious stones later, so he declines to do it here. They are quite visible metaphorically in I Cor. 12-13, in Rom. 12-14 and many other places. In Rom. 1 and in Rev. 2-3 we will also find examples of wood, hay and stubble—all amenable to our enlightened consciences.

I think the main reason for avoiding specificities is Paul's fear of omitting some of the virtues implied by the metaphors, or worse yet, neglecting some vanities, faults and sins in the categories of wood, hay and stubble. Consider also the matter of degree. Paul was sure that such shades of meaning should be determined by each person for himself. As Paul says in Gal. 6, each must bear his own load, and elsewhere that we have to work out our own salvation with fear and trembling. God is always saying to us, "Come and let us reason together. Though your sins be as scarlet, they shall be as white as snow; though they be red like crimson, they shall be as wool." It is plain to us all that the building materials are virtues and the combustibles are secular vanities, faults and sins. Our building must be founded on Christ, and the tools we carpenters use are clearly expressed in Scripture, viz., prayer, Bible-reading, churchgoing, good works, witnessing and fasting; all these with love for God and our neighbor as ourselves will guarantee a successful building experience.

But what if we fail or fall short? Paul's answer is the fire from our jealous Lover, and stripes from his loving hand! But when? A quick answer would seem to be at the Great Judgment. After all, from our earliest exposure to Scripture until this very hour, we have been taught to associate fire with eternal punishment. "The earth and all the works therein shall be burned up," says St. Peter. Jesus speaks, too, of hell as a place where the fire is not quenched. In John's Apocalypse, we behold an end "in the Lake of Fire and Sulfur." From these and many other proof-texts, we can easily see why the climax of all human life would end with fire.

Yet metaphors can symbolize more than one thing. Luke's Gospel gives us more of the message of John the Baptist than the other three Gospels. Using fire as a metaphor for cleansing or purification, he says of Christ, ". . . he shall baptize with the Holy Spirit and with fire, whose fan is in his hand to cleanse the threshing-floor . . . but the chaff he will burn up with unquenchable fire." Later, in the same Gospel, Jesus characterizes his ministry like this: "I am come to send fire on the earth," and in Mark's Gospel, "Everyone shall be salted with fire." At Pentecost we see tongues of fire upon the apostles as the Holy Spirit comes to finish Christ's ministry on earth by working with men to evangelize the world. Finally, Peter tells us to expect our faith, just like gold, to be tried by fire (I Pet. 1:7). In Luke 12, Jesus uses two metaphors to describe the cleansing process of the Holy Spirit. In verse 47, Jesus ends his prophecy about those who have lost faith in his Parousia. They give themselves up to drunkenness and cruelty. He warns them that they will be corrected by stripes, few or many, depending on how knowledgeable they were about his will. Here he anticipates the traffic policeman's frequent retort to the speeding driver: "Ignorance of the law is no excuse." Jesus goes on (verse 49) to say, "I am come to send fire on the earth; and what will I, if it be already kindled?" So fire is also a metaphor of purification as well as punishment.

Turning now to our final paragraph in I Corinthians 3:14ff., we see the foundation of this structure is Jesus Christ, which he himself proclaimed in the conclusion of the Sermon on the Mount, in an anecdote about building a house founded on a rock. So we are to build on this foundation, which is not a doctrine, not an ethical principle, not some esoteric rite, not a postulate of science or a dictum of philosophy, not a social need, but the Person of Jesus Christ. Paul tells us to look out for shifting to some other foundation; he uses the imperative mood, as if to say, "Look out!" By the new fangledness we behold in Christendom at this late hour in the Millennial Week, we are left to wonder whether many churches are not fulfilling the prophecy of Dean Inge, "Any church that marries the spirit of an age will find herself a widow in the next."

Some are seeking other foundations on which to build with wood, hay and stubble, but such inferior material is destined for the fire. It is my humble opinion that Paul is not speaking of some eschatological fire, but an ongoing conflagration, the invisible hand of Almighty God keeping his Church pure and free of heresy in his own inviolable way. Some Christians, I know, have a third option for these few or many stripes—Purgatory—yet not all Christians believe in such a place. Consequently, they see only two choices, and therefore maintain that purification is an ongoing reality.

This passage is about those who follow Christ, including those who follow less successfully than others. They will suffer loss, yet will be saved. Nowhere in Scripture are we told of any suffering required for followers after the General Resurrection. We are told, "For the day shall declare it because it will be revealed by the Holy Spirit." This brings to mind a dictum of the early Congregationalists. They said that we must have a faith that is biblically based and publicly examined.

Note also that the use of the future tense for the verbs in these I Cor. 3 passages might give some the impression that the fire and stripes come in the infinite future at the end of time. "If the purifying fire is ongoing, why is it spoken of in the future tense?" one might ask. Historians would quickly come to my defense here, for they, writing always about the past, are vexed by always having to use the past tense in their writing. At times they use the *historic present* even when speaking of the future. To make their points seem closer to people, writers and preachers often use the *contemporary future.* So when the future tense is used, we must always ask which future is being spoken of. The General Resurrection is, of course, in the infinite future at the end of time. In fact all eschatological events are in the infinite future. However, look at the Beatitudes and see yet another use of the future tense is called for. Beatitudes I and VIII, viz., being mournful and suffering for righteousness' sake, have the blessing part in the present tense. For all others, Jesus used the future tense! By no means is he speaking of the infinite future; rather, he is using what some call the *conditional future.* So, at whatever time in the future, when you hunger and thirst after righteousness, you will be filled. There are other futures, too, but we will leave that matter with the grammarians. The emphasis that concerns us is that we should not always make the future tense mean the infinite future. In most cases, the future is now: "You shall know [in the immediate future] the truth, and the truth shall set you [as soon as you know the truth] free."

In verse 15 is yet a third reason this purification by fire is ongoing. "If any man's work shall be burned, he shall suffer loss, yet he himself shall be saved, yet so as by fire." I do not see this as occurring at the Judgment, for such an interpretation would suggest that a man could live a worthless life, all of it, and then would be saved? No. This is, rather, ongoing, a day-to-day work of the Holy Spirit, adding dynamic blessing to gold, silver and precious stones, and turning to ashes the vanity, crippling faults and sins in our lives.

As we move to our study in II Corinthians 5, keep in mind the ongoing nature of those negative features of our salvation. For the redeemed there is no reducing fire after the Lord's return, only glorious additions, as we shall soon see; no lashes for disobedience then, only embraces and shouts of victory. Let us go to our closets, shut the door and welcome whatever grit and polish God designs for our perfection, so that at the Great Judgment we may indeed have a righteousness that outshines the sun. Let us say, "Lord, send the purgatory fire now! Wield the lash for whatever disobedience remains! Only let me see the scar upon the hand that purges me!"

MANSIONS EVERYWHERE

I have said elsewhere that the Christian Road differs from the world's religions in that it says virtually nothing specific about the nature and activity of our eternal home. It is true that certain Christians have ventured into print with fantastic scenarios, fabulous riches, even sensuous pleasures of such a nature that they likely do more to distort that blessed reality than to clarify it. Heaven just has to be like God our Creator, who tells us our languages, minds and even the physiology of our speech are so inadequate that we cannot even give him a name. As with his name, so with the eternal home he has built for us. All things pertaining to heaven are so great that we will have to wait to know how great. Such greatness argues for our determination to use whatever time remains for us toward getting ourselves ready to receive the largess of our Almighty Lover and his Beloved Son, our Matchless Lord, whom we adore and worship.

Is there nothing specifically promised us besides "ineffable glory"? Immediately, some will rush to John's Apocalypse and remind us of those "10,000 harpers harping upon their harps," "a host no man can number," and "108 of angels and thousands of thousands." We must be careful here— we tend to get carried away from John's time frame. Because the Apocalypse is the last book in the Bible, we automatically think it speaks only of the last things. John might actually be telling us of things as they ought to be or of a reality now, not just in the future. His last vision is of the New Jerusalem, a 1,500-mile cube descending—but when and to where? Most scholars see this city of transparent gold as a symbolic description of the Church as it appeared on the day of Pentecost. We must look carefully at every vision in the Apocalypse and remember that John is using human language, and even though his pen is guided by the Holy Spirit, what you read is limited; we all, including John, are chained to the earth, babbling in a three-dimensional reality of something that is at least of four dimensions. There are a few generalizations given to us, such as the verses we are studying in the Corinthian epistles. Recall, II Corinthians ends with the account of a vision of Paul being caught up to the third heaven. Even though he cautions us that he cannot share this visit with us, what he saw and experienced will have some effect on his writing. We hungry souls seize upon such inferences as we find them, so dear is the matter to us.

This is how things ought to be. After all, we want the best, which God tells us is beyond our descriptive power; the vocabulary, syntax, usage, grammar involved are just not up to the task. We would not have it any other way. So we press on, continuing to send raw material into the heavens, where it is refined (sometimes with fire), and fit into God's mosaic. This we are privileged to examine, guided by the excellent language of Paul and quickened by the Holy Spirit. Heaven is now. The Kingdom of the Heavens is within each of us. The scepter's sway of its King increases in power and in joy until that thing called death is no more than a dirty, old tent, coming apart at the seams, allowing us, at long last, to escape and receive our new selves. I plan to pirouette right through the doorway. It is said that Nijinski, when he danced *The Spectre of the Rose* used to break curtain six feet in the air, and so will I. I will dance the *Mahanaim* every morning, and get in voice with the Song of Songs.

Now, where was I? Oh yes, just ready to plunge into the golden prose of Paul, and discover some grand truths that the KJV scholars didn't seem to see. We will concentrate on the first ten verses of II Cor. 5. I remind you that we will use my translation of verses 1-2. It will not read as smoothly as other translations, but it will deliver the meaning more exactly. As we read the Holy Word, I want us to look as closely as we can, just as we would read the small print in an insurance policy.

> For we know that, though our earthly dwelling, this tent, be collapsed, we have a dwelling of God, a structure not made with hands, eternal in the heavens. For even in this [tent] we are groaning, our mansion, the one from heaven, earnestly desiring to put on . . . .

At the start of our investigation of this portion of Eternity's insurance policy, we see my change of "if" to "though," which is quite allowable, as seen in several places in the New Testament and also in the LX X. For example, Psalm 23 reads: "Yea, *though* I walk . . . ." It is the same word in the Greek text. Since the death of our bodies is a universal reality, let's not be satisfied with "if it were," when "though it be" states that reality exactly. Also, the verb translated "dissolved" is a poor choice. This creates a mixed metaphor, viz., tents do not dissolve. The Greek verb says exactly "according to loosening," which is awkward English, but good Greek. So Paul gives us two metaphors, one for death and one for our bodies, "though this tent be collapsed." You will recall that Paul scolds the Corinthians for not supporting him, not giving him enough money to buy food. So he works at tent-making to get by. Can you not see him sitting cross-legged, lacing the seams with strips of leather? God knew all about his needs, but he wanted Paul to relate tent-making to the human body. He gave Paul the occasion to make this comparison by requiring him to do this work.

We are not halfway through the first sentence when we get a third metaphor for our body, and there will come even a fourth before the passage is completed. Please examine the following lists of Greek words that show the variation in spelling, which the translators expressed with the common words "house" or "building."

MODERN	ENGLISH	BIBLICAL GREEK
house	dwelling	OIKIA
home	tenement	OIKOS
building	mansion	OIKODOME
edifice	residence	OIKETERION
structure	domicile	
habitation	abode	

From these two lists we can discern that there are many more words available in English than in Greek. This is by no means to say that Greek is less sophisticated than English—far from it. In those days illiteracy was high. Hence, a simplified Greek was needed throughout the Roman Empire. It is called Koine Greek. My New Testament dictionary has only 5,600 words. All 12 in the English listing could be expressed by one or more of the words in the Greek column. I think you can see now why translations vary so much, sometimes even radically.

There is something else glaring at us in this list. The Greek words are all based on one root, *oik,* but the English column has several roots, which come from Saxon, Latin, French and Greek. Since England is an island, she has had a constant stream of foreign languages feeding words into everyday use, whereas Greece, like Germany, made up new words out of old word parts. In the few words we are to study, Paul uses three of these four choices, which I have tried to make evident in my translation.

So we expect the tent to tear apart at the seams someday and collapse, but God has prepared for us something more permanent—a dwelling, a structure, a residence. Paul obviously means one of more durable material, probably stone. This dwelling is not handmade, but God-made, and it is eternal in the heavens. This plural is correct even as the singular in the very next sentence is also correct. So we have this house in the heavens (plural), but its design comes from heaven (singular). How many heavens are there? It depends on when you ask the question and to whom. A theologian in first-century Greece would have an answer different from that of a 21st-century astronomer, and both would be right in context.

The ancient Hebrews believed in two heavens; one starts in the air about us and extends to the farthest star, and the other is the place where God lives. The first one, however, was never considered separate from God's control, and that is why the singular form is never found in the Hebrew Bible. The dual form, *shamayim,* is always used.

The Greeks had a more elaborate cosmography with three heavens. The *aer,* where birds fly and weather is created, is the lowest heaven. Once in the New Testament, the Greek text reads "birds of heaven," but the translator makes it "birds of the air." Stars dwell in the second heaven, the *aithmos,* and where God dwells is called the *ouranos.* The first two have made their way into English ("air" and "atmosphere"), but the third did not. It is the name of the first male god of Greek mythology, Uranus, the sky god who sired a son by the female goddess, Gaia. She brought forth Kronos, who sired Zeus. We need not trouble ourselves over the pagan origins of some of our vocabulary, since early Christian literature sanctified several words used by idolatrous people. One Hebrew word for "idol" means "nothing." So be it with the etymology of words made holy by Christian use. I remind our Catholic readers that the title of the Pope, appearing at the base of his crown, is *Pontefex Maximus,* the title given the pagan high priest of Rome, and means "Master Bridge Repairman." Its colorful and quite pagan etymology has nothing to do with the man who now wears it.

Of course, all this is interesting and valuable background information, but how does it come to bear upon II Cor. 5:2? Quite significantly, for we must determine what is meant when the biblical writer uses "heaven" and its plural form "heavens," especially when both forms occur in the same paragraph. Surely, the change in number was intended to designate different places. This happens several times in the New Testament, and almost always the translators ignore the text.

In the Lords' Prayer, the Paternoster, recorded in Matt. 6 and Lk. 11, God is addressed as "Our Father, who is in the *heavens*" and then the Prayer says, "Be done your will, as in *heaven*, so on earth." There two lines are identical in the Greek text of both Gospels, but look at the translations, obviously made by two different translators.

> Matthew: "Thy will be done on earth as it is in heaven."
> Luke: Thy will be done, as in heaven, so on earth."

In the KJV, only Luke keeps heaven first, whereas Matthew's translator inverts the two items, and both Gospels disregard the change in number from "heavens" to "heaven." But what does this plural form mean? It does not mean, as a restrictive modifier would, that you are reminding God that you are aware that you have two fathers, and that he is the one who is in heaven. That would be ridiculous, yet a singular rendering of "heavens" would seem to say as much. When you translate it accurately, you are reminding yourself that God is omnipresent and spiritual. If he is in all three heavens, he is everywhere; and only a spiritual being could be in more than one place at a time. What's more, if God is in the *aer*, he is where we are in the closet, and being in the *aithmos* and *ouranos*, he must be omniscient as well. So you begin your prayer by celebrating the attributes of God, who has the knowledge, skill, occasion and power to answer all our prayers as a Loving and Omnipotent Father.

The word *ouranos* occurs 284 times in the New Testament, 94 of them in the plural. Many of the plurals, however, were passed over by the translators, apparently because they judged there was no difference between "heaven" and "heavens." We appreciate the fact that the translator of II Corinthians took no such liberty. Notice Paul's plural at the end of II Cor. 5:1, then the singular in 5:2. He tells us this old tent with frazzled seams has waiting for it, no longer an *oikia*, but an *oikodome,* a structure of greater importance. It is a spiritual one, since it is in all three of the heavens. This change, this gradation upward, is not over yet. The Kingdom of the heavens is in you and also in all three heavens. Our God is using the gold, silver and precious stones you send outward and upward to him.

In verse 2, Paul waxes even bolder. He will change the "ragged tent" metaphor once again. He starts with a tent, a house, which he changes into a more substantial abode, from *oikia* to *oikodome* (from which come our words "dome" and "domicile"), probably a house envisioned as a stone structure. Now he chooses the most elaborate word in his vocabulary—*oiketerion*. It could be translated as any of these English words—dwelling, tenement, mansion, residence, domicile, abode. I see a pattern here, with Paul moving from tent to house to stone structure—and now what? Of the six, I would choose "mansion." My choice is certainly better than the choice of *monia* as "mansions" in John 14, which is better translated as "rooms."

We learn that the task of sending building materials out and up into the heavens, or "bearing the eternal weight of glory" as Paul puts it, is hard work for old shoulders, and it is getting harder. We groan. We long for a change, especially if Christ is preparing a mansion for us. Notice that the noun is omitted: "for even in this . . . we are groaning . . . ." Paul, like others of us "senior citizens," is so dissatisfied looking at those wrinkles, those liver spots, those sagging and shrinking and misshapen limbs, that he does not even name the tent again.

There is a delightful subtlety Paul uses, which we ought not overlook. He says we are to "put on" a mansion. Right away, the teacher part of me sees a mixed metaphor, for we do not "put on" buildings of any sort. By using this error in logical consistency, he reminds us that, after all, a mansion is but a metaphor. He is telling us that "mansion" is a metaphor of that future part of yourself that will replace the "tent" part, a personal part infused into your eternal person, whereby you will know as you are known, and accomplish things beyond your present reach—even beyond your fondest dreams. That part of me, which God and I are building together on a daily basis made of gold, silver, and precious stones, I give the nickname "Al." So getting ready for Al is one way of saying what this present life is all about.

During our pilgrimage on the Christian Road, I have already referred to one word beginning with "Al"—alchemy, the study of ways to change lead to gold. Another is altruism, the losing of oneself in a cause greater than oneself. Since alchemy summarizes the creative part of my pilgrimage and altruism is the summary of Christian ethics, I choose to name that future part of me "Al." We are to create, to change lead to gold, hate to love, covetousness to generosity, isolation into hospitality, and the list goes on. We also find altruism is the summary of Christian ethics, and leads us to cultivate concern for others, to love God foremost and our neighbor as ourselves—these essential parts of our future selves that we cultivate with God's assistance. Hence, the name "Al." If you wish to use this nickname for your future self, but would prefer something of a feminine gender, Alma will do, which is the Hebrew word for "virgin."

In these first two verses of II Cor. 5, Paul has moved us up from dirty, ragged tents that are even now coming apart at the seams, to palatial mansions. We seasoned Christians and our co-worker God are putting the finishing touches on Al out there, spread abroad in the three heavens. This future self was designed by God before the foundation of the world was laid, up there in heaven—the third and highest of the three, where Paul visited briefly. David, the world's first great poet, speaks to this matter in Psalm139:13-16. Read and rejoice as you heave more gold, silver, and precious stones upward and outward into the heavens.

When will we put on Al or Alma? We certainly do not want to appear before the King of Glory naked, as Paul observes, so the other body (elsewhere called a "temple" or 'glorious body" or "spiritual body") will probably fuse with our spirits as we rise from the dead. So before our final hour, we must keep throwing gold outward to souls who are waiting for our help. They are Christ's proxies; we owe them who are now in Christ's stead. It is our task to heave this gold, this "eternal weight of glory," which keeps the contemporaneous Gospel squarely before mankind.

MOVING DAY

We near the end of our journey, but before we change our dirty, old tent for a mansion, we must be doubly sure we are ready and able to make the leap. We are not talking about a fortnight at the beach, but Eternity in Paradise. Our life-long process is not a matter of conforming ourselves to this world, but of transforming our whole spiritual beings into a radically new universe, from the space-time continuum to a spiritual Eternity. We slowly close the door to the world of our yesterdays—it clicks behind us. We are not coming back, we know. Everything of value has been packed. We promise not to look back, as Lot's wife did. The unthinkable climax is upon us—now is not the time to hesitate, not even for a moment.

We who have lived driven by our past and drawn on by the future are not strangers to transition. God makes the move easier for us by the process called aging. He has also chosen his servant Paul (name in Latin, meaning "small") the tentmaker, who was first named Saul (Hebrew, after a tall king), to be our guide. Meditate on the remaining verses of this little giant's great passage about the end of our journey being like exchanging an old tent for a mansion. In his final contribution to the Canon, II Tim. 4, he returns to a blending together of two of his most popular metaphors, that of a battle and a footrace: "I have fought the good fight, I have finished my course [the prescribed trail for the long-distance runner], I have kept the faith," yet it is here in II Corinthians that he exhorts us to have the right attitude toward what we leave behind. He wants us not to be merely resolved to endure the transformation, the teleportation of our fire-cleansed and fire-shrunk selves into that higher reality we call Eternal Home, but to welcome it with an attitude befitting the occasion.

This attitude has a twofold aspect—our attitude toward where we are going (which we will look at later), and our attitude toward what we are leaving behind, which Paul touches only lightly, viz., the hatred toward all former things, especially toward the fleshly calyx loosening its control over the blooming of our eternal selves. Perhaps this is what Jesus refers to as recorded only in John 12:25: hating ourselves (the very selves that he implied in the Golden Rule we would spontaneously love) that we may be saved from death and hell. Our transport is so close now that we are preparing to leap over the threshold, through the curtain of ambiguity, and into the infinite joy of absolute reality, fusing with Al and joining the holy entourage of saints made perfect.

In II Cor. 5:3-4, see how lightly Paul touches on the negative aspects: "not to be unclothed, not to be naked, but . . . ." is how he puts it. We must overcome the negative aspects of the warfare about us. Look again at the old tent coming apart at the seams, not at its inadequacy (who needs to be reminded of that?), but its place in our personal histories. Who then is our worst enemy? Take a good, honest look into the closest mirror you can find. Or first, read in Romans 7 about the Christian's dilemma.

Carefully note how he takes the middle ground as regards the body, "I know that in . . . my body dwells no good thing"—not evil, but simply "no good thing."

Consider the philosophy of the flesh. It has an autonomic nervous system that operates without your will, so it is a behaviorist. The more bad habits gravitate into that realm, the more behavioristic you become. The body is also a hedonist; it loves pleasure, hates pain. It is, I have found, most uncooperative during prayer. Still, I must endure hardship, as Paul says, like a good soldier. Finally, it is a sensuous immediatist; it knows nothing but what is stimulated by its sensors, and only during the stimulation itself. It knows nothing of tomorrow, or yesterday.

So as a behaviorist, hedonist and sensuous immediatist, the body has an ominous, formidable potential. Yet it is I who has made it my enemy. I blame not this unthinking animal part for my sins. How often I lament on my knees that I have been my worst enemy, that without my compatibility and cooperation, Satan, would be totally impuissant, chained for these thousand years of my potential, abundant, though marginal, living. I truly hate that part of me!

As I prepare to wiggle out of this cocoon, I am reminded of those amazing South Pacific pearl divers who plunge to great depths and go so long without breathing. They save time by carrying heavy stones as they descend. They quickly harvest a cache of oysters, release the stone and zoom upwards to the surface. They are glad to sever the rope that binds them to the stone—indeed, they must. Even so, I am weighted by the flesh into the pit of ever-diminishing options, cut into by the pendulum of intensified consequences. Out of the depths I cry to the Lord, who cuts me free at last so I might buoy upward toward Eternal Day.

As we move toward heaven, we should expect climax, as in any work of art. I think of a great symphony, not like the *Pathetique* of Tchaikovsky that fades away in a quiet gurgle of the double bassoon, but rather like Beethoven's *Ninth Symphony* with the whole orchestra playing loud and fast, with a choir in addition to all the instruments, with grand pauses followed by sustained *sforzandos*! Aging is a process of saying good-bye to so much and so many. The memory begins to fail, the sight and hearing fade, the step is slow and difficult and fearful. We have lost more friends than we now have, and loved ones are gone or, like us, in the process of going. Even our language tempts us to think negatively of death. We say someone is 80 years old, not 80 years toward heaven. Instead of saying, "I am going to die," say, "I'm going to get rid of my weathered tent of mortality so I can take on Al."

In Philippians 2, Paul speaks of Christ surrendering what we hope to assume before long, taking on the form of a slave and then dying as the worst of men so he could assume the highest place of all. Paul tells us to adopt this kind of a mindset toward our passing. We must never insult Almighty God by having the slightest degree of hesitation when he calls. We must repudiate the pessimistic attitude of the European peasantry who often say, "Mourn at a birth and rejoice at a death!" Solomon also says to those who live with God, "Better is the day of one's death than the day of his birth." Yet listen to his father, David: "The path of the righteous is as the dawning of light that shines more and more until high noon" (or "perfect day" in the KJV). David becomes totally inclusive in this gem: "He makes the outgoing of the morning [youth] and evening [age] to rejoice." Paul then summarizes in II Cor. 5:4 with, "mortality might be swallowed up by life." Note that he summarizes this negative subject by casting aside his metaphors. He uses plain speech by calling the body, the old tent, "mortality." This is a rhetorical device called *synecdoche*, likening the whole to one feature of it, so we will see it in its spiritual significance. Our bodies are mortality to be swallowed up—making it the nourishment of life. So the body we now have is to enhance that process. Paul puts the body among other subordinate things—all things imaginable in fact, which are not worthy of being compared to Love Personified, waiting even now with Al, just over there on the Eternal Shore.

How can we be sure this is so? We have a lifetime to confirm the promises of the Holy Bible, plus we have the guarantee of the Holy Spirit. He is guiding me as I write just now, and you as you read. He is the ruler of this age, and is our constant companion, our adviser or *Paraclete,* whose advice always comforts us so unerringly that we are comforted even on that final battlefield, when old mortality itself joins the world and the devil. Recall that mortality is a hedonist, and cringes away from the pain. As a sensuous immediatist, it knows nothing of that Great Day. So we need the confirmation of the Holy Spirit, our only companion for the trip. Greater is he who is in you than he that is in the world.

In II Cor. 5:6-9, Paul reminds us that this sagging, leaking tent of ours bars our entry into Eternity. He pauses in this grand conclusion about life to remind us in a parenthesis that we must for one last time resist a *prima facie* interpretation of life. Being at home in the flesh is a curtain of deception, the veil of ambiguity required by faith that now is faith's finest hour, opposite the message of the eye, ear, and the tactile sensors of mortality itself. Even though 90% of all we know comes through the eye-gate, we have cultivated a fish-eye vision, a 360 degree sweep of the past, present and future parts of life.

THE COMING JUDGMENTS

The Sixth Day of the Millennial Week is coming to its end. It will be ushered in by plagues and cataclysms; their spread will be worldwide and their severity hitherto unknown. Christ's Good News will have been preached in all countries and generally rejected, and all nations will beat their plows into swords and their pruning hooks into spears to make war on the Church from without, while heresy, duplicity and desertion will work to destroy her from within. Christ will appear before all men with clouds of witnesses, shouting with a great voice as he descends to meet those rising from graves and oceans everywhere. The trumpet of heaven will sound his arrival, and a universal voice will proclaim his name and title. All knees will bow and all tongues will confess that he is the Lord of Glory. The quick division among mankind occurs; the followers of Cain, egoists of every stripe, go to hell, and the children of God, the altruists whose lives were lost in works of gratitude to Christ and his proxies, come to the end of the Road to the Heavenly City.

All this is recorded in Scripture, and it is indeed Good News. Yet one thing about Good News we cannot escape is a desire to learn as much detail about it as we can—detail that is precisely not given! Most of our knowledge of eschatology comes from a few words on Jesus' final day of teaching, John's Apocalypse, and a few scant statements of Paul. It is true that just about every New Testament writer speaks of the Second Coming, but only a few say anything specific, especially as regards the calendar of events. Recalling a principle of biblical interpretation may help us in this matter. Remember that the Bible speaks to us also through what it does not say. So what can we discern from this omission? Any explanation that goes beyond a general statement leaves the realm of the *unknown* and enters that of the *unknowable*. Listen to Paul: "The things that eye has not seen, ear has not heard or even entered into the heart of man—these are the things God has prepared for those who love him."

It is plain then that we will have to leave most eschatology to faith. The fact that we are told we cannot now know more about the future life because its greatness transcends our knowledge should make us all ecstatic with anticipation and quite willing to wait. Still, some will venture into uncharted waters and conjure up fancies appealing more to our senses than to good sense. This does no harm, I would suppose, so long as we don't take up too much time with the matter, or start worshipping our own opinions and expect others to believe as we do.

I am reminded of the time during my first year of ministry when I enjoyed the company of a group of ministers who met weekly for lunch and fellowship. One day we discussed eschatology, and they soon discovered that I did not endorse their commonly held belief. Next week, a day before our meeting, one of them called to tell me I was no longer welcome to come to their luncheon. These men were dangerously near worshipping their own opinion. Of course, we are free to upholster the furniture of heaven as we like, so long as we do not contradict Scripture. The point is that the belief that there is to be a literal 1,000-year reign of Christ on earth is a doctrine that must never become a test of Christian discipleship.

Before going on to the few specifics available, I feel I must dismiss briefly what is definitely not biblical. One is the belief that there are more than two categories determined at the Great Judgment. Jesus told us as one of the last teachings he gave that the Great Judgment will end with two kinds, the sheep and the goats. The other gross error is to see the judgment of God as confined to the afterlife. Even the most modest search in a concordance will indicate that God is directly involved in the ongoing affairs of men in this life as well as at the Judgment Seat. He has his oftentimes mysterious ways of keeping the Ten Commandments and the cross of Christ forefront in the affairs of men. At this writing, one of the hottest issues in law is the nature of the Ten Commandments. Are they the opinions of Moses, or the discovery revealed to Moses of the minimum controls needed for living in society? Since they are the latter, they will survive all attempts to bury them. Those who attempt to do so will die with their shovels in their hands and an empty pit staring them in the face. As long as men are men, they will say "amen" to the Decalogue, which is as inalienable to manhood as life, liberty and the pursuit of property. Heaven, hell and the purifying fire of the Holy Spirit begin now and never end.

Let us turn from those perplexed judges attempting to put the Ten Commandments into a closet to consider things of a positive nature. In what order do the events of our eschatology occur? The moment we say "when," we use a word that has no meaning outside this spatial—temporal continuum. I would hope that my pilgrimage is an overlap experience, wherein my groping fingers reach into Eternity, and Eternity gradually reaches back into me. Perhaps the Greek plural, *ouranoi,* refers to the past, present and future as well as to the homes of the birds, of the stars and of God Himself. I want to experience now the conflagration of my wood, hay and stubble, and tier up (or add arms and legs to) that eternal part—Al—while I am yet in this coffin of flesh, this threadbare tent, this earthen vessel, this pit-and-pendulum of spatial-temporal disorientation with reality. Indeed, how can I write now, using ortholinear letters to portray that which is beyond spatial-temporal linkage? Paul has it right; the laws that govern our language now make description "unlawful," to relate things to heaven that are not worthy of being compared (Rom. 8:18), or even contrasted to the glory awaiting us.

However, we time-and-space-oriented gods cannot help asking when; for example, when will we put on that wonderful being waiting even now to clothe us. I ask, will it be a spontaneous rise from the grave as I rise to meet the Lord in the air? Will it be before or after that interview when I shall give account of myself before God? Where and under what circumstances will I receive the reward according to what I have done, whether good or bad? Even as I ponder these matters, I know I cannot answer my own questions, and suspect that even my asking will then be silenced. Like Job, I will forget to ask the question as I stand there open-mouthed and saucer-eyed beholding the wonderment of heaven and of Christ!

Maybe the sequencing of eschatological events is inductively presented, like the doctrine of the Trinity, so we must do a great deal of digging on our own. Or maybe we are meant to think only generally about these final epic events, which demand the utmost of our imagination, cloy our logic and exhaust our intuitive power. Perhaps the best approach is using surrealism, as we find in the Apocalypse of John.

Of this one thing I am dead certain: I have no fear of the Great Judgment. I anticipate no embarrassment or shame—I experience these now. Daily, I tune my instrument, then kneel upon the concrete floor of my study's closet, thereby turning it into a sea of glass mingled with fire (i.e., the opal gem). My shutting that closet door opens another in heaven. The walls about me become transparent gold, and the darkness turns to light from the holy face of him who has loved me from the foundation of the world. I have daily tried to experience as much of tomorrow as I can so that when it is called today, there will be nothing new except the infinite dimensions of what I have always known, the absolute quality and the ultimate value of it. What is categorically beyond my present comprehension will be experienced by a better me, then equipped to receive at last what limitation has hitherto denied me. I will at last know as even I am known.

For a moment, look with me at the end of II Cor. 5:10, which speaks of receiving the consequence of our living in the body, whether good or bad. One might quickly judge Paul of contradicting his "crown jewel of Christian theology," viz., salvation by faith. How then would our end differ from that of all men who rejected Christ as Savior? Where is the "great gulf" between the rich man and Lazarus the beggar? The matter here is not an adding up and subtracting, or balancing and averaging, but of how well we did our part in the synergistic effort. Some were willing to participate with God more completely than others, some more consistently. The "good and evil" in this verse has nothing to do with salvation, for we are saved by faith. It has everything to do with eternal rewards of those already saved. Yet still I fear nothing at all, for I could not then be more disappointed with myself than I am now. I have not loved God with all the ingenuity of my mind, all the affection of my heart, all the determination of my will, nor all the strength of my body; nor have I loved my neighbor as myself. I expect the lowest seat in heaven, the smallest abode there in that holy place. So how could I possibly be disappointed?

It has always been a rule of my life that the more of heaven I can draw into my life now, the better my life will be when I get there. Indeed, my wish is like comparing the gestation time of the human embryo to the newborn infant, as this life is to Eternity. It stands to reason that the more fully developed the prenatal infant becomes by the time of birth, the less severe will be his adjustment to the world outside the womb. Another way to put the matter is expressed in my definition of living spiritually—when the recollection of past events and the anticipation of future events change our life today, precisely then are we living spiritually. This is exactly the point made in I John 4:16-17:

> We have believed and we have had faith in the love that God has for us. God is love, and he living in love lives in God, and God lives in him. Herein this love has been completed in us, so that we may have boldness in the day of judgment, because *as he is, even we are in this world.*

In this amazing passage, John tells us that love, "the bond of perfectness" not only welds us to God, but to the past and future as well. Love is the greatest power in the world; it gives its all, and it demands what it gives. The love of God transcends time and space, for God is eternal and omnipotent; therefore, his love is everywhere and never changes. Since we are the objects of his love, we share love's dynamics of giving and demanding all. The conclusion is inescapable—as he is, so are we in the world; our situation is identical to his. So close are we to him that the coming day of judgment has no dread for us at all. We will be bold! Like Job, we will come before him as a mighty prince, we will be as familiar as was Jacob who dared to wrestle with him at *Mahanaim*.

Living as though the future is now reminds me of a luncheon several of us students at seminary had with Andrew Blackwood, the well-known Professor of Homiletics at Princeton Seminary. During the meal our conversation centered, as one would expect, on preaching. We came to the rather trivial matter of giving titles to sermons. Dr. Blackwood said he had an attractive one, but could never find a text to fit it. It was "Living in the Suburbs." He offered it to us for the taking. That was 50 years ago, and I finally found a suitable subject. Drawing the luxuries of heaven into our lives today is living in the suburbs of heaven. Paul speaks of such "mountain top" experiences when his joy was unspeakable and full of glory. That is surely living "a foretaste of glory divine," living in the suburbs of our eternal home.

The past plays its part, too. For example, there are recollections of past achievements. We will all concede that Job was in great need—penniless and bereaved, sitting on a manure heap, scraping the puss from his boils with a shard of broken pottery, he cries out, "Have not the loins of naked men blessed my name? Have not I made the widow's heart sing for joy and been a father to the orphan boy?" The recollection of these acts of charity gave him confidence. He knew the best way to get an answer to his prayers was to be an answer to the prayers of others. In the Paternoster, we are told to recall the times when we have forgiven others what they owe us, so we may expect God to forgive us wherein we fall short in serving him.

I used to think of salvation as a historical fact, like repentance. I later discovered how wrong I was on both counts. It is obvious from the Paternoster that confession of sin and repentance are ongoing realities. As long as we have sin to confess, we have repentance to make. If we repented of a sin yesterday, perhaps today we should repent of the fault that caused the sin, or the nature from which the fault generated.

Examine a subtle portrayal of the ongoing nature of our growth in grace, our spiritual exercise of drawing on the past and the future for strength today. In Moses' didactic history of Jacob, we see a puzzling use of his new name. After his several-hour wrestling match with the Pre-incarnate Christ, he received a blessing, which was memorialized by a new name. He is quite emphatically told that his new name is to be Israel (contender with God) and no longer Jacob (heel-grabber, or opportunist). To make the reader sure of this change, Moses records a second visit in which God repeats his giving Jacob a new name. I will give a run-on quotation of several fragments from Genesis 32, 35, 45, 48, 49 and 50, all involving naming this beloved patriarch after God had given him a new name. "And God appeared unto Jacob again . . . Thy name is Jacob . . . Thy name shall not be any more called Jacob; but Israel shall be thy name; and he called his name Israel . . . and Jacob set up a pillar . . . and Israel journeyed . . . and Israel dwelt . . . the spirit of Jacob their father revived . . . and Israel said . . . And God spake unto Israel in visions of the night and said, Jacob, Jacob . . . and one told Jacob thy son Joseph is come . . . and Israel strengthened himself . . . and Jacob said . . . and when Jacob made an end . . . he yielded up the ghost . . . and the physicians embalmed Israel." A careful analysis of these passages will show a mixture of the past, present and future. You also have a new name written down in Glory. You are moving closer by the day to that future life most expressive of its meaning. As a friend of mine pointed out, the name "Israel" itself came to mean "Prince of God," for only a peer of God would attempt to restrain him to the point of forcing a blessing from him, or so it seems to our limited minds. I am of the mind that the Omniscient God never changes his mind, and that by the end of that wrestling match, Jacob discovered in retrospect that what he wanted, after all, was exactly what God wanted him to have. Therein lies the glory of the future reaching into our lives today. There is truly no greater freedom or no greater joy than to want uppermost exactly what God wants you to have.

A final example, this time a negative one, is found in John 11. This is one of the most famous in Scripture because omnipotent power reaches into the grave of Lazarus. So riveted are we to the open door of that tomb that we fail to notice that John is using a bit of didactic history to make a point. He brings out the two greatest oppositions to the miraculous that rise in the human mind, and these oppositions are found in a most amazing place—in Martha "Hadaben" and Mary "Willabee," shifting Divine Will to the remote locations of the past and the future—anywhere but the ever-living present. Nowhere in Scripture is the lesson more emphatically impressed upon us that the future begins now.

FOR THE SUITCASE

1. When the recollection of past events and the anticipation of future events modify present behavior, then are we living like God—beyond space and time.
2. There are 50,000 promises in the Bible. Have you found out how many are in the conditional future tense, waiting for you to qualify for their fulfillment?
3. We and God are builders together now, building eternal replacements for the bodies we leave behind.
4. God satisfies all Joban questions when he answers the antecedent question, viz., "Do you love me, God?"
5. Let's ask God for our stripes and the burning of our wood, hay, and stubble now, and for the wisdom to see who sends them.
6. A universal philanthropy is a passionless sentiment; it is enough to concentrate on the neighbor instead.
7. Good works cannot save us, but they can improve life here and hereafter.
8. Living close to Christ in the suburbs will make us bold in the Day of Judgment.
9. Jesus assures us that we will never die.
10. The veil between is only a millimicron thick, and we wait in it for but a nanosecond of time, in "the twinkling of the eye."

Chapter X:
Our Road Also Turns

*Road Maps: Psalm 2, 110; Isaiah 9, 40; Romans 12-14;
Luke 16; John 18*

Isaiah, the Messianic prophet, foretold Christ's glorious role among men with the promise that "the government shall be upon his shoulder." Then Jesus on trial tells Pilate in John 18:36, "My kingdom is not of this world: if my kingdom were of this world, then would my servants fight, that I should not be delivered to the Jews; but now is my kingdom not from hence." Note that he says three times that his kingdom is not of this world, leaving the casual reader with the notion that men have the power to prevent the governance of God and his Son in this world "to break their bands asunder and cast away their cords," as David puts it in Psalm 2. This is not so. The exact opposite is true, for Christ is ruling this very day, and will tomorrow when the stars begin to fall and the sun finally sets on this Sixth Millennial Day.

Look more closely, as we always must when we read what the Lord of Canon is telling us. In his answer to Pilate, twice Jesus uses the preposition "of," but chooses "from" the third time, thus excluding Israel from his kingdom. After all, they claimed to have no king but Caesar, and then cried out for his crucifixion. Then Pilate, perhaps more sensitive to the royal deportment of his prisoner, asks the broader question, "Are you still a king?" So we plainly see that Pilate was aware that the triple denial was not of his royalty, but only of the source of his royalty and who the citizens were of his kingdom. Jesus still avers his identity, and that he is to reign. Do you notice that Jesus is not asked where his kingdom is? One supposes this would be important to know, like the other question that nobody thought to ask, "Where were you born?" Oftentimes, the questions we do not ask make their answers more heavily freighted with meaning than had we asked them. Jesus assures Pilate that nothing at all has been changed. He is still a king, King of the Three Heavens, the *aer*, the *aithmos* and the *ouranos*—the Kingdom of Everywhere and Always, that is where his kingdom is. Those who are of the truth will receive him as King. Pilate retorts with the dramatic question, the kind that does not want an answer, but is stated as a question to weld the universal hope for truth to the stubborn insistence that no one has it: "What is truth?" then he instantly goes out to the restless throng. He tells them, "I find no fault in him!" Where here is his famous authority? Why doesn't he say, "Innocent! Case closed!" then whirl around and leave as abruptly as he had just left Jesus? He is weakening, you see, and turns to the Barabbas ploy, followed by this, "I will scourge him and let him go." Plainly, he is on the defensive.

The language used in this dialogue was probably Aramaic, though the only record we have of it is in Greek. Remember this as we consider the sentence ending in the middle of verse 37, "You yourself say that a king I am." In Greek, the final word of this sentence is the first half of the holy name God gave to Moses in the burning-bush episode, I AM. Now, the first word of the next sentence (in Greek) is ego, meaning "I." Therefore, if we add it to the end of the sentence, the holy name becomes the same as God used when he spoke to Moses from the burning bush. Jesus used the "I AM" expression when speaking to the clergy about his age, and that is why they attempted to stone him. When he was arrested in the Garden of Gethsemane, he used it once more, at the utterance of which Judas and the soldiers tumbled backward to the ground. Could it be that these words, spoken by Jesus, had such influence over Pilate that he, like Pharaoh, became a servant of God, wholly unable to resist the power of Truth Personified? In this way, Christ moved the absolute authority of

Rome aside, so the Jews could have their own Moriah Test, which they failed. Do not suppose I do violence to Scripture by pirating the first word of one sentence and tacking it onto the word that precedes it. The point is, 1) the sentence would not lose its meaning or lack its subject by my doing so, but 2)there were no punctuation marks, not even word dividers, in the earliest manuscripts—just a steady flow of capital letters! God's word is powerful in the mouths of men and beasts; how much more could it be in the mouth of his Holy Son? Here is how Romans 8:28 would look in English: ANDWEKNOWTHATFORTHOSELOVINGGOD ALLTHINGSWORKTOGETHERFORGOOD. We can see how easily a mistake in copying or translating could happen.

Our task in this chapter is to examine our relationship with our country, especially since the shadows have lengthened with the recently ended second millennium AD. The Scripture clearly states that Jesus is King over his Kingdom of the Heavens, the plural form that means the Kingdom that is everywhere and will never end. This means that Christ is even now walking the marble floors of parliaments and senate chambers, and turning to nothing the boasts of judges who rise up against him and build a high wall between church and state, over which Christ leaps with greater ease than did Milton's Satan as he entered Eden. He descends with a shout, standing beside the seats of monarchs and dignitaries, wielding his mighty scepter against spiritual wickedness in high places. He once stood beside Caesar Augustus and whispered to him, "It is time now for you to take that census of the whole world." So he did, fulfilling God's promise made to that little sheep station six miles south of Jerusalem, as it is written, "But thou Bethlehem . . . though thou be little among the thousands of Judah, yet out of thee shall come forth unto me that is to be ruler in Israel, whose goings forth have been from of old, from everlasting" (Micah 5:2).

So for a short while we, too, walk with Bunyan's Pilgrim through government, the exoskeleton we support to maintain our freedom and the benefits of living in society. Whatever betides, he rules. He advances the programs that proclaim his truth. He turns the work of evil in our midst into a confirmation of truth. Thus glitters the sway of his unseen scepter. His reign will never end, since the kingdoms of this world will surely become the Kingdom of our God and of his Christ. "I THAT I will see to it," says Father Abraham, as he and Isaac watch the flames lick up the sacrificial ram on Mount Moriah.

We who dwell in the lengthening shadow of the Sixth Millennium's sunset have no time to review religious and political systems competing for our loyalty to Jesus Christ and the Holy Bible. We regard them all as inadequate, contradictory schemes born of man's rejection of his Loving Heavenly Father and a desperate hope of finding some other way—perhaps one closer to the desire of the heart, which Scripture reminds us is deceitful and desperately wicked. In the little time remaining, I call upon the Holy Ghost to so emphasize the Good News of Jesus Christ that we will not need to further fortify ourselves against spiritual wickedness in high places.

At the end of this two-thousand-year response to Christ, two extreme religions come to the fore. They are at opposite poles, as climax would suggest. One is physical—Islam—and one makes the intellectual approach—socialism. As history will attest, each in its extreme becomes identical in behavior, with violent opposition to all enemies. It would not take long for anyone to answer the question, who butchered more people, Saddam Hussein or Joseph Stalin?

Scripture has always taught that men are gods and not animals. Three of Jesus' five unique doctrines, The Fatherhood of God, The Importance of the Individual, and The Equality of Men join to present man as a god—in-the-making. Since we are potential inheritors of a holy and royal destiny, we cannot help but conclude that we should be equal in society and government. Now we see clearly the reason behind what I have always said about the Christian and government: the citizens of a spiritual theocracy make the best citizens of a temporal democracy. A nation of laws is what we are, based on those given us by God at the hand of Moses. In essence, we have a Constitution wholly consistent with Holy Scripture. We are not a nation of political thugs, those who claw their way to the top of the heap, where they enjoy the power of life and death over all under their sway. That's what we see in socialism; that's what we have in Islam.

Perhaps some will be confused with my blend of socialism and communism. The only difference between the two is a matter of degree, just like the degree we see in Islam. A communist is no other than a socialist with a machine gun in his hands. You will notice the name, USSR identifies its leaders with socialism. The socialists in America—let us hope, anyway—are mostly of the more benign sort, who believe in social evolution, that socialism is a cultural inevitability. So they vote and wait.

You may wonder, "If they are socialists, why do they call themselves Democrats or Republicans?" This is true. Another truth is that an antichrist would be the last to call himself exactly what he is. Socialists have invaded American politics. They have been elected to the highest offices in American government, and mistake it not, they have made a religion of what they believe. Any value system that makes metaphysical judgments about reality and establishes social values for its adherents is a religion.

Not only are these two religions, Islam and socialism, expressing themselves more intensely than ever, but they will, no doubt, join forces for a time and purpose to defeat that political form based on Sacred Scripture. It is difficult to imagine how the intellectual dream boat of socialism, with Marx, Freud, Darwin and dozens of the world leaders aboard, would cooperate with Islam for a common end, yet it is so. Necessity makes for strange bedfellows. We have seen in history many times that two enemies, when faced with a common foe, often become temporary friends. Yet they two are out there, each with the same dream of replacing The United States of America with a Utopia that never has been, nor ever will exist on the face of this planet. The part of their dream they never share with us is that they see themselves sitting on top of the heap.

Should Christians get involved in political concerns? Of course they should. Scripture says so, and so do our very natures. Has not Solomon said that God has put the world in our heart? I am reminded of an old Irish witticism that I misunderstood for years: "It's a long road that has no turning." I understand now, after a native Irishman told me it is a warning to evildoers that, in a little while, they will get their comeuppance as surely as you can expect an Irish road to turn. I thought it meant that Irish roads were always turning, and that's a good thing because it would be a long, monotonous road indeed that had no turns. I still like my meaning, but maybe both are true—or can be true for the one who uses it.

It is true that we need variety in our lives, especially in our friends and family members. So it is between us and our Divine Lover. Though he is immutable—in him is no shadow of turning—yet he, so wonderfully and mysteriously, is the author of infinite variety. David speaks of his coming Lord as being like his Heavenly Father in this: "In the beauty of holiness, he has the dews of his youth." In one of his several roles, he is the Shepherd, and we are his sheep. He tells us that we go in and out of the fold, and thereby find pasture. We sheep on this difficult road to heaven must take a turn in our road and, lo and behold, we see before us among so many other things, our city and our nation.

For those of us who enjoy living in a free society bought by the precious blood of our men and women, participation in government is not only a source of variety and privilege—it is a necessity. Anyone who holds exemption to this participation enhances the power of enemies who are perennially active in bringing our political freedom to a decisive end.

Still, I seem to hear someone say, "All this may very well be, but how about the straight and narrow way?" So often have we heard this familiar phrase that we surely conclude that it is the Scripture's way of describing the Christian Road. The truth is the Christian Road is neither of these things! It is true that the gate onto the Road is narrow; Jesus says it is so because he alone is the Gate, the only Gate, by which men enter the Eternal City. The Road itself is often spoken of as being "straited," but that is not a synonym for "straight." The word, "strait" is a nautical term, which essentially means that a person has only one way to go; all options are gone. This is what our Beloved said about the imminent Passion before him. No alternate choice was open to him, so ". . . how I am straitened until it be accomplished." He does not mean "anxious," as some have supposed. The word is far more involved than that. Being "straight" as that Irish road that has no turning is not characteristic of the difficult Road ahead of us, which is as varied as it is difficult, both features of which make it an abundant life experience and full of glory.

Another easily misunderstood term used by Jesus—rather by those who translate his words—is his advice to us that we should "make friends with the mammon of unrighteousness." This is indeed a foggy translation.

What he means is plainly "secular society." Read Luke 16 and you will see clearly that the rules of the marketplace are eminently practical and can apply to spiritual living, too. He tells us this sad truth as well, that the children of this world are wiser in managing their lives than are the sons of light! In Romans 12:1ff., Paul tells us to live by the laws of our country, pray for our rulers, honor them especially as well as all others, don't go into debt, treat your neighbor as yourself, love even your enemies and become a peculiar people, zealous of good deeds. "Peculiar" in Elizabethan English means "conspicuously belonging to," not "strange and unusual."

So we sheep must find pasture in the sheepcote, and then go out into the world where we find more pasture. Paul says, "No man liveth to himself. In our final chapters, our Road turns out into society where we must find pasture in society, in government where our witness is publicly examined, and where we in the most meaningful of ways become the epistles known and read of men. We are surely to be careful in our secular lives. John cautions, "Let no man steal thy crown," meaning that we should not put our trust in those he calls false prophets.

There are dangers at every curve in our varied Road. We must resist the temptation of stepping off into the neon brilliance of the "darkness made visible" that hovers over nations. Look! There is the United Church of America, with its message of love—love everybody, love society, love the world. Around the corner is the Theocracy of Hate, whose clergy are the mouthpiece of a strange god who rules with the sword. These represent the two beasts seen by John in his Apocalypse—the State-ruled Church and the Church-ruled State. Then there are the carnival barkers of every pleasure known to man. Hear also the calliope tooting sassy tunes and the sirens singing people to the outer edge of the strait where ruinous rocks are hidden. The kingdoms of this world appear! We must see them as they really are—indeed, become part of the dynamism that makes them, though unseen as such—"the kingdoms of our Lord and of his Christ. And he shall reign forever and ever. Hallelujah!" God has a message directly for them, as fresh and relevant as the day it was written 3,000 years ago. Its author, David, is the world's first and greatest lyric poet, who was a man after God's own heart. He also took an active part in government.

FOR THE RULERS OF PLANET EARTH

Psalms is the hymn book of the Hebrew people, and is the longest book in the Bible. It was completed sometime after the Hebrews returned from their Babylonian Captivity. We know this late date is correct, for one of its most popular poems was written while they were in that captivity—Psalm 137. So here we have what is probably the latest of the psalms placed right next to the one scholars deem the very oldest, composed during the Egyptian Exodus—Psalm 136. By the time Psalms was finished, it had grown into five books, clearly indicated in most of our modern translations. Given the obvious limitations of reading scrolls, we can easily imagine the importance scribes would place on where a psalm would be located. In Book I, for example, there are 41 items. They knew that the nearer a psalm was to the beginning of the scroll, the more often it would be seen. The one most often seen was Psalm 1. Psalms 1 and 2 earned their most conspicuous locations in Scroll I because they were on critically important subjects. Psalm 1 focuses on the isolated individual. It begins like the ministry of Jesus began, with beatitudes. Psalm 2 gives notice to rulers of nations that the Kingdom of God will soon arrive! God's son will sit upon his throne over all peoples, "to the ends of the world," as the psalm puts it. These monarchs have no choice but to bow to Messiah's will, which will prevail. We citizens of the world are invited to listen in. Though the proclamation is not addressed to us, we know instinctively that what our leaders must do, so must we. Could it be that we will be alive—some of us, anyway—at the end of the Millennial Week?

Psalm 2, in keeping with its prominent location in Scroll I, is quoted more often in the New Testament than any other psalm. It is the Great Messianic Psalm and should be related always to Psalm 110, another on the same subject, the Ancient of Days who will take on flesh and visit us. "Who may abide the day of his coming?" asks the prophet. Indeed, the fact that Psalm 2 is where it is also indicates the prominence of Messianic expectancy from the time it was written in about 1,000 BC, a millennium until the time the Messiah would be born in Bethlehem.

You will notice that Psalm 2 indicates no authorship, but Peter tells us in Acts 4:25 that David wrote it. Many modern scholars, for obvious reasons, do not regard the statement of Peter as being anything more than a popular opinion. About half the psalms are ascribed to David in their titles. A few others have other authors indicated, such as Solomon or Moses. Some scholars believe that David wrote many more of them, perhaps 100 in all. The fact that his name does not appear in the heading of a given psalm is no indication that someone else must have written it. Some scholars feel, even if they do not say so, that their greater education and knowledge of Scripture than Peter had on the Day of Pentecost makes their opinion of authorship more reliable than Peter's. Still, Luke's account has Peter attributing it to David. Since Peter was filled with the Holy Spirit, he transcends his own limitations and leaves the opinions of scholars at a lower level. We have no reason whatever to doubt David's authorship of Psalm 2.

As regards the occasion for the psalm, those who see it as written for a historic occasion usually choose the coronation of David, thereby relating it to Psalm 24, which not only suggests the coronation of David, but that it is also applicable to the Advent of Christ. This dual application does not fit Psalm 2, however. There is no reference to David's being anointed or crowned upon God's holy hill of Zion, nor does the title "Son of God" ever apply to David. Indeed, Caesars and Pharaohs may claim to be "living gods," but never would a Hebrew claim such a title. We are told in John 5 that the Jews set out to kill Jesus because he called God his father, thus making himself equal with God. Also foreign to their thinking would be the universal claim of sovereignty over all the kingdoms of the world applied to any King of Israel. No, this is not an occasional psalm; it is not applicable to any event in Hebrew history. Nearly all Christian and Jewish scholars from times past until today consider the subject matter of Psalm 2 applicable to the reign of the Messiah.

The outstanding characteristic of this psalm is its tone. None of the 150 psalms excel it in intensity of emotion. Do we not feel the force of mighty power radiating from it in each image and speaker? Notice the disciplined parallelism. One characteristic of Hebrew poetry is its rhyme of ideas; it frequently says something twice, a first statement followed by an echo line. I envision a sinewy blacksmith pounding mightily upon the metal with each stroke echoing against the hill behind him. You will see these repetitions in all but the last verse. In verse 12 we find a gentle stair step of idea, each line building upon what precedes it. Also, notice how short the lines are—in Hebrew, all but verses 7 and 12 have only five or six inflections. Such shortness adds to the tone of the poem. Five verbs are in the imperative mood. Finally, in this dramatic psalm we have a change of speakers four times, and the use of prosopopoeia twice. This quoting of absent or imaginary persons as though present and speaking adds further vigor to the psalm. It brings the kings front and center with their spiel, followed by God thundering his holy ascription of royalty and holiness to his Only Begotten Son.

The psalm's vigor is so impressive that Handel gave it a conspicuous place in his *Messiah*. Its *bel canto* aria for the bass voice has become one of the most challenging and successful of all great vocal music. Just before Caiaphas called for Jesus' condemnation, he referred to Psalm 2, asking Jesus whether he were the Christ (Greek for Messiah), the Son of the Blessed One. Let us look once more at this familiar prophetic psalm. It will go a long way to get us in the right frame of mind about our beloved country and the world as the shadows lengthen.

Why do the nations rage and the people imagine a vain thing? (Ps. 2:1)

In the KJV, the word to describe the Jewish people is *Israel*, the new name the Pre-incarnate *Logos* gave Jacob after they had wrestled all night. They regard themselves the Family of God, the sanctified race, for they alone are "contenders with God," what their new name means. The rest of mankind would be less than sanctified, or not holy—the *goyim*. This word means "nations," but its connotation to the Hebrew mind was indeed less than desirable. They meant "heathen" every time they said *goyim*. Now you can see why translators have a difficult choice to make. They had to decide on using what the word said, or what it meant to its intended readers.

The KJV translators chose "heathen," as we all know, but most modern translators opt for "nations." The writers of the Hebrew Canon had to call non-Jews something. In Hebrew it was *goyim*. St. Paul and other writers followed suit and chose to identify those who rejected Christ (or those who had not yet had a chance to do so) by using much the same language, calling them "the ungodly." We will admit that it is difficult to keep from clustering negative connotations about the word, since this is a condition that sends men to hell. Let us look at how David used this word. Before we can do this, however, we must decide what kind of question introduces the psalm to us.

What is the motive of this chorus of Jews for asking the question? Is it, like most questions, a quest for knowledge? Of course not, for people wanting knowledge are not "raging." They are humble, treating their auditors with deferential courtesy, hoping to inspire a willingness to fill an intellectual void. No, the seculars, the heathen, the 2-D people, are raging. They are downright unhappy participating in this victory parade because they are not riding in the victory chariot. They are raging and whispering to each other as they walk toward someone else's castle. They definitely are not asking a question of substance.

Is it a rhetorical question, one with so obvious an answer that the speaker lets his hearers answer it for themselves? This could not be so because the answer is not obvious. These kings and counselors are, moreover, "imagining an empty thing." Is it a stylistic question, i.e., stating a subject as a question that you intend to answer, like the opening sentence in my preceding paragraph. Paul asked many such questions, usually those with negative answers, which he immediately answers with, "God forbid!" Here is an unfortunate choice for the KJV translators. Paul says, directly from the Greek, "Not so!" I suppose they did not choose it because it was too informal for proper gentlemen in the court of King James. Please don't think me pedantic, forgetting that I am not in an English literature classroom. Knowing what kind of question is being asked—and there are many of them in Scripture—always aids us in understanding Holy Writ. The answer to the question before us is the only one left—the dramatic question. It is used mostly for expressing agonizing frustration, as though you were sending a question up to heaven for an answer that defies all logic among us earthlings.

Consider an illustration. Johnny is two, and he likes cookies. He knows exactly where Mother keeps them. One day Mother hears a loud crash. She rushes into the kitchen and there on the floor is the shattered cookie jar, cookies scattered all over the floor with Johnny sitting among them eating as fast as he can. She puts her hands on her hips and yells out loud enough to be heard in heaven, "Johnny! Why are you such a bad boy?" She is asking a dramatic question.

Our chorus is expressing painful and perplexing frustration they feel from seeing men mindlessly oppose God Omnipotent. Recall those shepherds on the hillside of Bethlehem. They obeyed the invitation of the angel at once. They were glad to know that God had invaded our space, giving us his choice for our new King. The omnipotence is confirmed by that same panoply of angels in battle gear stretched clear across the midnight sky as Jacob saw a thousand years before David wrote. Here are some kings whose judgment has departed from reality. They reject God and his choice. Why, why do they imagine a vain thing?! Do they not know? Have they not heard? The High and Lofty One who inhabits Eternity will have his way!

Notice that we are not told what they are imagining; it is but a vain thing, an empty thing. Recall another generalization in this vein: "There is a way that seems right unto a man, but the end thereof are the ways of death." The ways may be as many as there are people, but they have one thing in common, a single destiny—death. Their ways are wrong because they emerge from the dungeon of man's imagination.

Do men today worship similar idols of the mind? Just a few years ago we saw the dream of socialism collapse. Man was not evolving into some sort of a social creature after all. Yet in spite of this Russian failure, the dream is still quite alive. There are those among us who saw Russia fail, not communism. They are ready and anxious to give us a Marxist police state and believe they can convince us that a new man is just over the horizon. That is their idol of the mind, their sacred cow. Islam is equally as far-fetched, though less subtle in approach. They must submit themselves to the powers that be because these powers are ordained from above. They can destroy a perceived enemy (i.e., anyone who does not adhere to their brand of religion) at any cost of life because it is Allah's will and he is merciful. The more destructive they are, the greater their reward in heaven. Some "martyrs" who become human bombs are promised no fewer than 70 virgins in Paradise.

Why, why are these so filled with empty dreams? See what they will do next in verse 2.

The kings of the earth set themselves, and the rulers take counsel together against the Lord and against his Christ. (Ps. 2:2)

Let us not suppose these leaders are bravely telling everybody what they think or plan. They want to get rid of God and Jesus Christ once and for all, yet what they say is only window-dressing. They are speaking to each other in private, and are experts in handling political pronouncements. Instead of being "against the Lord and his Christ," they are for "cultural diversity."

The newspapers some time ago featured a story about a local board of education allowing Jews and Muslims to wear religious symbols, but Christians were not allowed to wear the cross of Christ. The reason behind this obvious discrimination was stated to be a desire for the children to experience cultural diversity, so the Christian symbols were not allowed because Christians were in the majority. Herein is a perfect example of the work of an antichrist. Most of us are not aware that the Greek prefix "anti" has two quite different meanings, both of which are used in Scripture. The first, that of being "against," as in anti-aircraft guns, and the other being "instead of." The subtle message of an antichrist is one who is against Christ, or one who advocates someone or something to take Christ's place.

One might wonder why these "rulers" are so daring. Don't they know God is omnipotent? The truth is that they don't know this at all! Rather, they are atheists who would rather proclaim "cultural diversity." They are bold in their stand because they do not believe God exists, or in the supernatural identity of Jesus Christ. One cannot be a socialist and yet be a

Christian. Anyone who believes otherwise is either ignorant of socialism, or Christianity, or both. Take Darwinism for example. A theory—and only a theory—of radical changes apparent and ongoing in all living things. Socialists are wholly devoted to Darwin's concept of evolution, and that is why they are so fascinated with the idea of themselves becoming catalysts of change. They want to speed the process up like the Muslims who wish to help Allah get everybody to bow before him. One cannot believe in the struggle for existence and survival of the fit (which are even biblical doctrines), then also accept the atheistic doctrine of *natural* selection and *random* variation. These last two parts of Darwinism are, of course, based on faith—faith in "missing links."

Let us break their fetters off and cast away their cords from us. (Ps. 2:3)

Here is their real message, their naked objective, which is given here in the form of prosopopoeia—the chorus telling us what they *mean* by what they say. These words raise two conflicting images in my mind. In the preceding verse, we see them in their throne rooms proclaiming their stands to one another, yet in this verse we see them in handcuffs with their necks tied together in a row behind the coronation chariot of God's choice for King. I notice a puzzling choice made by the LX X translators. They substitute "yoke" for "cords." This is quite possibly intended to express the posture and function of these unruly kings in the parade, viz., they are wearing yokes to which chains are attached that lead to the chariot. They, and not beasts of burden, are drawing Christ's victory chariot down the corridors of history! Here we see a kind of conversion—God is converting evil deeds to work for the advancement of God's cause! Time and again this has proved the case. Hence, we are certain that all things work together for good for those who are loving God. When the Supreme Court banned devotional reading of the Bible in public schools, we saw units and entire courses created in high schools, and units of study in the lower grades for teaching the Bible as *literature*. The Bible, after all, doesn't have to be taught as dogma. It is, as one scholar says, in both the indicative and imperative moods—a matter-of-fact presentation that is so powerful of its own accord that it is imperative by implication. I understand that county court houses all over America are now installing the Ten Commandments on their walls.

The parade continues, and God's enemies are doing their part of the pulling. If you listen carefully you may hear God whisper to a wicked Pharaoh, "Harden your heart! Don't let these Hebrew slaves leave the country!" Pharaoh was so fierce an opponent that his chariots, racing toward the Hebrews, were drowned in the same sea the Jews passed through dry shod.

He who sits in the heavens laughs; the Lord makes a mockery of them. (Ps. 2:4)

What else, given the circumstances, could God do but laugh? We all are but grasshoppers before him. Those attempting to overthrow the superstitious beliefs of us miserable failures called "Christians" always blame their own failures on the stupid ignorance of us naïve ones who are incapable of leadership. It is because of us that they fail to advance their cause. They never hear the belly-laugh—the guffaw—of Almighty God. This is similar to the time God spoke audibly from heaven, approving of his Son, and "some said it thundered."

Mistake it not: those who would impose socialism upon us envision themselves as our managers! Socialism, in spite of the suggested meaning of its very name, is wholly dependent on the most obvious elitist philosophy ever conceived. Those who see socialism as the inevitable best solution for our social woes indubitably see themselves as the collectors of the means "from each according to his ability to give, and to give to each according to his need." That phrase sounds good, doesn't it? They want you to overlook the matter, but they are the ones—not you—who determine what your tax will be, and it is they who will determine what is your need. Will we surrender to these elitist enemies within our country? Will they listen to us when we tell them that they are working for God, toward God's ends, which are opposite their own? No, they will not.

As I said before, we cannot take time to present a review of political science or comparative religions—not at this late hour. Still, as I attempt to help you fend off the coming cataclysms that will fall upon this age, there is one thing I must share with you. Strange to say, it is a matter of grammar—imagine that. The ancient Hebrews were most careful about grammar. They used it in a theological way, just as they used history, which they were the first to need and, hence, the first to use. They had the genius to be amazed at the creation because God created it for them and for a purpose. How about the basic unit of language—alphabetic letters? They even celebrated these in acrostic psalms, i.e., the first line began with the first letter of their alphabet, and each thereafter began with the next letter of the alphabet. So at the beginning margin (right side), the first line would begin with *aleph*, comparable to our letter "a." One could read the entire alphabet by looking straight down the column of letters. Psalm 119 is an acrostic psalm with the same number of stanzas as there are letters, each stanza having eight lines beginning with the same letter. There is also an acrostic poem on motherhood at the end of the Book of Proverbs. Yet beyond the alphabet is the matter of lexicography (the science of defining words) and orthography (the spelling of words). Having said this, let me tell you not only that God has no name (the only one who hasn't), but that he, his prophets and all other canonists are always talking about "the name of God." The prohibition of taking God's name in vain is also one of the Ten Commandments. This seeming paradox is solved theologically! The Jews never were so foolish (as some are today) to think that secular and spiritual lives have a high wall between them. This idiocy, this unbiblical and non-constitutional notion, could turn us all into schizophrenics and hypocrites as well. Come November, God and I will go to the voting booth together.

Scripture always stresses what a person is inside—it's character that counts. In fact, good looks and shapely form can actually deceive both the one who has them and those fascinated by them. "Beauty is deceitful and favor is vain, and whosoever is deceived thereby is not wise." In the dictionary there are two kinds of definitions—the denotative and the connotative. Usually, there is only one denotative meaning, and it comes first. The word "name" has the denotative meaning of being a word that distinguishes a person, place or thing from all others. A name is a designator. Then come the connotations, chief of which is "reputation." However, in the Bible's dictionary (which is the Bible itself), the two categories are reversed. The denotative meaning of "name" according to the Bible is "reputation." Consequently, we must compare Scripture with Scripture to determine definition.

One of the first things Moses wanted God to do was to tell him his name, i.e., to give him his designator. Moses was well aware of all the gods of Egypt, and knew them by name. He rightly anticipated the Israelites asking him to give them the name of this particular god. Moses was soon to learn that biblical theology put reputation before designation, and he would never forget that lesson. God said, "I THAT I." If we assume this is in the present tense, and the verb to-be is meant, we have, "I AM WHAT I AM." God continued, "Go tell them that I send you to them, the God of Abraham, the God of Isaac, and the God of Jacob." Christ commented on this designation, when he said, He <u>is</u> the God of Abraham. He <u>is</u> the God of the living." He considers grammar quite important, you see. Secondly, we find more than eternal life in this substitute for a name; we also see history. God identifies himself with great persons, places and happenings in history.

The common name in Hebrew for God is *El,* and we capitalize it out of respect. It almost always occurs in the construct state, i.e., in construction with some other word part. Notice how many Hebrew names begin or end with *El.* Jacob changed the name of Luz to *Beth-el,* which means "house of God." He later changed its name to *El-bethel.* People followed God in this manner. They named the great happenings in their lives after God. His is one of the loveliest and most bountiful names you may take comfort in. I have used it often in my prayers when going through the shadows of some deadly valley in my life. I call God, *El-Shaddai,* which becomes a functional name, one to be used when the occasion calls for it. It has a most wonderful etymology. The word *shad* means "breast," but here it occurs in the dual form, so the meaning is "God-of-the-two-breasts." An incidental blessing herein is that God transcends bisexuality, and so will we all by and by. St. Augustine said in reference to *El-Shaddai*, that God had two breasts, the

Old Testament and the New Testament, and he would suck bountifully at both. The KJV scholars translated it as "Almighty God." So when you need something badly, call your loving Heavenly Father *El-Shaddai*.

How I-THAT-I became *Jehovah* is a long, technical story that requires knowledge of Hebrew, but let me attempt a brief word about it. This expression was regarded by Moses and all the Jews as so holy that none should ever read or say it aloud. Instead, when the reader came to it when reading Scripture, he would instead say *Adonai* or *Elohim*, "Lord" or "God." Later, when vowels were added as little dots and dashes under their large, square letters, nobody knew what to put under the holy name! So they added the vowels for *Adonai* or *Elohim,* and said that word instead when they came across YHWH. Today, some spell it as *Jehovah, Yahweh,* or *Jehve.* I must add that these are all conjectures. It is interesting to note that only three possible vowels can be used with the letters JHWH, so it is possible that, taken as a name, JHWH has nine possible pronunciations.

There is something even more mysterious and wonderful about I-THAT-I, and it involves grammar. Recall that ancient Hebrew, like so many other ancient languages, had no tense. This is not as difficult a matter as one might expect when we consider that much of Hebrew literature is narrative in nature. This makes the matter easier, for much is obviously in the past tense. Context also gives the reader a few clues. What is most important for us to remember is that Hebrew gets the job done. Now we can consider the tense involved with I-THAT-I. We see at once that we are not at all helped by context or narrative. There is nothing in the text to tell us what tense God wants us to use! Every time I came to this passage in my course in the Bible as Literature, I would ask my students which of the following nine versions is best.

> Present: I am what I am. I am what I was. I am what I will be.
>
> Past: I was what I was. I was what I am. I was what I will be.
>
> Future: I will be what I will be. I will be what I was. I will be what I am.

I kept on asking my question for years, never getting the best choice. Finally, one student gave his opinion, which also is mine. "I'll take all nine," he said.

I have one more option to share with you, raising the number to ten! The famous Jewish philosopher and rabbi, Martin Buber, reasoned that, whenever we duplicate a pronoun, as in "*I myself* will wash the dishes," we add emphasis. This is what he does with the two pronouns in the answer God gave Moses. Then Buber opts for the future tense, chooses an alternate meaning for "THAT," and comes up with this glorious news: I MYSELF WILL BE THERE. Which of the ten is your choice?

So you see what I mean when I said that the ancient Hebrews considered that more than the heavens are singing of God's glory. The alphabet, grammar and lexicography do as well, and God revealed to John this orthographic variation of the name of his Son—*Logos*. We learn much from this summary upon the character of Almighty God: "I am . . . ," leaving your need to finish his name. He is whatever you need him to be, so great is his love. We hear from these words that God is greater than time. A thousand years is as yesterday when it is past. God must not be given a name, either, for his omnipotence makes him greater than any one thing we could say of him. Any attribute we would identify him by distorts our understanding of him and neglects what else should be said. Therefore, our solution is to give him who calls himself self-sufficient . . . no name at all. He says exactly this in a remarkable statement found in Deut. 32:39, "It is I, even I, am he, and there is no god with me."

When we understand that Hebrew is a grammar without tense, we can see why some translators vary from others, and yet both are correct. Look at verse 5 below—it uses the future tense. Now look at how the Jerusalem Bible translates the same passage: "Then in his anger he rebukes them, in his rage he strikes them down." It uses the present tense.

The Hebrews usually—though not always—named their children after religious virtues, and more often than not, they would include God in the name. Indeed, so very many Hebrew names begin or end with *El*, and after Moses' time, *Je* or *Ja* was used as either prefix or suffix. The name *Elijah* must surely be the holiest name of all; it means "God-Jehovah."

Joshua truly had a unique name—it not only means "Salvation of Jehovah," but it became the given name of his holy Son Jesus, because he would indeed save his people from their sins.

Then will he speak to them in his wrath, and in his sore displeasure will he trouble them. (Ps. 2:5)

Some scholars envision a parade taking place in this psalm, a victory procession at the end of a fierce battle. Christ is to be crowned as King of Kings. Monarchs defeated in battle are in chains walking behind his chariot. God above sees to it that all these kings keep in place and move at the proper pace as time marches on. It is God's will that the kingdoms of the world are the Kingdoms of Christ, who will reign over them—*Jehovah-jireh* will see to it.

Yet what is this we see? These monarchs are attempting to break rank, and struggle to escape their chains. They defy the Omnipotent God and his holy Son. We in time's balcony gasp, shake our heads and cluck our tongues in disgust at such audacity. Are they insane to oppose God Himself? But we are told by the poet David that God has given them wiggle room in this matter. He exposes to us the meaning of their thinly disguised political speech, which always means exactly the opposite of what they say. They do not want God's Law, nor do they want his son to "tent" among us, as John says in the Prologue of his Gospel. Still, God insists otherwise, and speaks to them in his wrath, warning them sometimes via clouds of witnesses brought before their very eyes. He vexes them with adverse circumstances, or they see their efforts turning out the opposite of what they had planned. Yet God does not destroy them. God is love—he loves the world and wants men to "change their minds about him"—to repent.

They do not see themselves in the chains of God, but as annoyed by the mere cobwebs of an outgrown culture. They see the Bible in the same category as books of popular myths that belong to ancient times. As far as God being a Loving Heavenly Father is concerned, they deny his very existence. Society is their reality, and science is their god. Yet they are loaded down with the chains of the Almighty, being dragged along in the wake of Christ's victory chariot, ever moving down through the few years that remain in this Sixth Millennium, where they will see what has always been the case—Christ sitting on God's holy hill called *Zion*, or "pillar" by translation, being so conspicuous that one would suspect they could feel the chains as chains and not cobwebs. Such is the power of deceiving others—it becomes self-deception, and who can save anyone (even kings) from that?

Another shocking matter in this verse clearly contradicts a popular slogan of modern thought, the "separation of church and state." If this foggy quip were first coined in the Middle Ages, it would more precisely read, "the separation of state *from* church." However, since it came from the mouth of a very liberal justice of the Supreme Court early in the 20th century, I suspect he should have stated, "the separation of church *from* state," because we live now in a secular society that wants its government to escape from the influences of the Church. Be that as it may, it is as foreign to our Constitution as it is to reality itself. In Psalm 2, we see God, ready and able to interfere in all phases of society, politics included. This jingle is indeed a strange idea, for it is not found either in Holy Scripture or anywhere in the courts of heaven, where angels, like the Pony Express, wait anxiously and willingly to post over land and ocean without rest in service to his irresistible will.

At first, "the separation of church and state" seems a commendable venture. As a student of history, I applaud such an objective of government— that is, as I understand it. The twenty centuries behind us have shown that the greatest crimes against mankind take the form of either a state in control of religion, or a church organization in control of the state. The two bloodiest events in human history were Constantine's Edict of Toleration in 313 AD, making the church subordinate to the state, and the crowning of Charlemagne as Holy Roman Emperor on Christmas Day, 800 AD, making the state subservient to the organized church. We must never allow either of these extremes to occur again. It well may be that the two beasts in John's Apocalypse are these two extremes. Though the records are incomplete, estimates have been made that more than 5,000,000 people lost their lives as the result of religious oppression up to the time of the

Renaissance. I would almost suspect our Western ancestors were akin to some contemporary Muslim radicals and not Christians!

To see this issue more clearly, we must distinguish between churches as legal entities, and personal, overt acts of faith—even in public places. Christ told us that being Christian relates more to personal living than belonging to organizations in a legal way. He said that he is the Way, or the Road. Quite plainly, this separation cannot extend to insulating personal expressions of religious life from public living. So the expression, "separation of church and state," to have meaning must refer to church organizations and not to personal acts of faith, public or private.

The First Amendment to the Constitution, which together with freedom of the press and freedom of petition, has limitation of government as regards religion, and not government limiting religion. As we look, let us not read more into it than what is said. First, there are two clauses: The Establishment Clause and The Free Exercise Clause.

The first clause prevents Congress from passing any law that establishes an official church for the United States. There is never to be a Church of America as there is a Church of England. By 1776, six states had already officially adopted their own "state" churches, and they did not want Congress to replace them with the an equivalent of the Church of England.

Now to the almost universally ignored second clause, The Free Exercise Clause. It says that Congress shall pass no laws prohibiting the free exercise of religion. It is here where liberal logic turns fuzzy. As part of the complete man, religion goes with him everywhere, beyond the meeting house and outside the home. In contemplating the variety and extent of religious activity, we are drawn to the conclusion that some matters do not involve law at all, but custom, regarding which no legal restraint is needed. It is a safe rule that any expression of my religion ends where that same freedom in others begins. However, this does not mean that I must restrict my freedom just because someone disapproves of what I do in a free society. One is never guaranteed to be free from exposure to another's exercise of religion.

Offences will continue to occur; living in a free society guarantees it. We all agree that it is wiser to endure the offences of the few than to require restrictions incumbent on us all. By implying the First Amendment proclaims a separation of Christians in general, and the Christian witness in particular from government and even society, is to proclaim one needs to go back to school and learn how to read the Constitution.

During high holy days in biblical times, the population of Jerusalem doubled. That is why Titus in 68 AD, exactly 40 years after the crucifixion of Christ, laid siege to Jerusalem during Passover. On one such occasion, a group of Jews from Greece found it very difficult to see Jesus. In response to hearing of their request, Jesus said, "There will come a time after I am crucified that all men will be drawn to me." With today's universal polarization of ideologies achieving worldwide dimensions, we do not doubt for one minute that the crucifixion of Christ will become visible to all, and with a climax befitting the Holy Son of God. Why? Because God will see to it—his name is *Jehovah-jireh.*

Yet have I set my king upon my holy hill of Zion. (Ps. 2:6)

This is the shortest of the 12 verses in Psalm 2, and yet its content makes the brevity just right. We see the sinewy arm of Almighty God moving against the force of Satan and the overwhelming host of mankind, whom Satan has deceived. The odds are overwhelming, yet God has established Christ on his throne in the holiest place in the universe, his hill, Zion. Note the opening word "yet," an adverb serving as a golden hinge to fuse God's power to his will, which many outside heaven are, to this very day, categorically opposed to.

Another thing about this brevity is that it draws our attention to the end of the human race, man's final battle. Afield are all the kingdoms of this world against Christ and his followers, so few by comparison. Mind not the host of the enemy! The battle will be short and decisive. Death, where is thy sting? Grave, you will be found empty. In a moment, in the twinkling of an eye, he will put to death the battalions of hell and all nations that have forgotten God.

Let the nations hear it often: "Yet have I set my king upon my holy hill of Zion." Once again, God invades history, leaping the high wall that puny men have erected between us pilgrims and our state. You may wonder why

I keep the word "hill" in my translation. The Hebrew text says "mountain." However, we must do as St. Peter says and "compare Scripture with Scripture." Elsewhere we find God's dwelling called "mountain" and "hill" in the same sentence (Isa. 10 and 31), and in three other places the word "hill" is the preferred term (Ps.15, 24, 43). So Zion is either a hill or a mountain.

Is this that earthly place, just to the rear of where the Muslim Dome of the Rock now stands, on the place where Abraham raised a sacrificial altar to offer up Isaac? Or is it the very throne of God, eternal in the heavens, which seems more in keeping with the scenery Ps. 2 sets before us? We must be always aware of two habitations, earth and heaven—the spatial-temporal continuum and the spiritual Eternity. In Psalm 46 we read: "There is a river the streams of which make glad the city of God." Here we have a literary allusion to the unnamed river that divided into four distributaries as it left Eden, and yet here Jerusalem is clearly indicated as the location of that river. Of course, as John says in his Gospel (7:38), this river is the Holy Spirit that will also flow out of our lives. In Psalm 43:3, we find combined "hill" with "tabernacles," which leads us to believe that both are symbols of a higher reality. There are no rivers and tabernacles in Jerusalem. We are the tents of the Lord, and also the temples, as Paul points out. In Psalm 84 we find the tabernacles (tents) actually personified, i.e., spoken of as though they were persons: "How agreeable are thy tabernacles, O Lord of Hosts." It is my view that the KJV translators chose "hill" rather than mountain because the context and treatment suggests a figurative, not literal, Zion, and when any feature of earthly topography is related to God, it seems but a hill! Also, it seems to me that the line reads better with "hill." I see the immensity of God when I read "hill." God needs no more than a hill to raise Christ up high enough so that all men will see him. After all, the Hebrew word, *Zion*, means a promontory or a pedestal.

Here seems the best place to remind ourselves that we must always determine which place God speaks of—the earthly one or heaven's equivalent! Paul reminds us of this when he says in Galatians that there are two Jerusalems—the earthly one and the New Jerusalem, the Church, which Augustine is quite justified in naming for all times henceforth as The City of God.

This dual identity is extremely important when we come to a study of the last things—eschatology. Are not our bodies described as temples? The place near the city of Jerusalem where Christ was crucified, Skull Place, or in Latin *Calvary*—exactly where is it? Also, when John refers to it in symbolic language as *Har Megiddo*, or "Mount Rendezvous," does he mean some exact place near Jerusalem, or perhaps some other place?

Recall the logic problem I used to share with my philosophy students. I asked them to identify the highest mountain in the world. After they had chosen Mt. Everest, I told them that they should have asked me to say what I meant by "highest" in order to determine the intended point of reference. There are at least four possible answers to this question: 1) Everest is the correct choice if I mean highest above sea level; 2) Mona Kea in Hawaii if I mean highest from point of origin; 3) McKinley if I mean panoramic view accessible from sea level; 4) Chimborazo in Ecuador if I mean distance from the center of the earth (hence, nearness to the sun), as it is always at least 100 miles farther than Everest from the center of the earth, and twice a year at the equinoxes one can be closer to the sun at its summit than at any place on earth. Chimborazo also enjoys the distinction of being the largest mountain in the world—a cut halfway through its height would create a plateau of 40 square miles. The lesson in all this is the next time someone asks you to name the world's highest mountain, ask for more information.

Yet when we are in an Einsteinian way, we might convert time to space for one more possible answer. What mountain is the "highest" in the space it occupies on the pages of history? Which has proved to occupy most of your time because of how profoundly it has influenced your life?

It has four names and one nickname in Scripture: the oldest is *Moriah*, meaning "seen of the Lord;" next is *Jehovah-jireh*, the name coined by Abraham meaning "Jehovah will provide;" then *Zion*, which means "pedestal" or "promontory"; in New Testament times it received the nickname of "Skull Place" (*Calvary* in Latin, and *Kronos Topos* in Greek); in the Apocalypse of John we find its final name, *Har Megiddo* in Hebrew, or "Mount of Rendezvous" in English. This mount is beyond all possible equivocation the highest mount in human history, and ours is the double task of keeping it there on the contemporary scene and in our own lives. At less than 3,000 ft. above sea level, it is dwarfed by any of the aforementioned mountains, but in God's orientation with reality, his Holy Hill is spiritually centered upon our globe, before which men are but as grasshoppers.

What's more, Mount Rendezvous continues to grow in spite of the best efforts of God's enemies. Judges of the earth have ordered the Ten Commandments on a granite stone carted off to some basement closet. However, shortly thereafter I read of several counties in Kentucky and elsewhere that are seeking and getting permission to publish the holy document in county court houses, with more to follow. Superintendents have ordered crosses off of necks and lapels, yet yesterday I saw televised one of many young men carrying a life-sized cross on his back, trekking from New York to San Francisco. He is doing it not out of some morbid, masochistic need, but to advertise the cross, to get it into everyday culture. Oh, the heathen are raging, imagining a vain thing! Soon the whole world will be full of the knowledge of the Lord, as the waters cover the sea. God has set his Son on his holy hill of Zion, and that is that. We have no other choice but to join in the celebration.

Now we must prepare ourselves for a glorious song offered by a trio. In verse 7, the pronouns change and thereby convince us that someone else has taken up the message. Christ is the speaker, quoting the Father through the poet David—a trio of voices.

I will proclaim the decree: the Lord has said unto me, Thou art my Son; this day I have begotten thee. (Ps. 2:7)

Not only do we hear these three in their polyphonic voices transcending all time and places, even singing forever as Christ Himself prophesied, but we hear other accompaniment from elsewhere in the golden treasure of Holy Writ. We recall Messiah's proclamation (Ps. 40), his announcement for the world, yet given before its foundations were laid, that he will become God's sacrifice, and then prepares for the plunge downward to desperate men waiting to welcome him as the Lamb of God. There also comes to mind the great metaphysical passage (John 14:23-36) in which Jesus the Messiah and God the Father are proclaimed One, and that they come to dwell in us together with the Holy Spirit. Indeed, we have by promise a Trinity of heaven within us that tunes us to hear this trio sung by Scripture. The Living Word gives us the Spoken Word through the pen of that great sinner David, whose life presents to us in blinding clarity what the "sure mercies of David" really mean.

We hear a variation of this verse, sung in a minor key by someone else who sings slowly, almost hissing out its syllables: "I adjure you by the Living God that you tell us whether you be the Christ, the Son of God!" This is the crux of Caiaphas' attack. He knows that if Jesus of Nazareth thinks he is the Messiah, he will have to answer this command with affirmation, so he will be able to get the Sanhedrin to condemn Jesus for blasphemy. Moreover, above all other Messianic prophecies in the Old Testament, it is this verse in Psalm 2 that comes to Caiaphas' mind, further confirming the popularity of this psalm above all other possible choices. Most of all, this psalm has the unique distinction of being the only Messianic passage that calls Christ the Son of God! Isaiah speaks of him as the Suffering Servant, and even as being "the everlasting father." Yet of the many titles and functional names given the coming Messiah, only Psalm 2 identifies him by the very title he himself preferred. Every time he called God his Father, he implied his sonship, making himself God's equal and worthy of death for blasphemy, according to the "political correctness" of the day (John 5:18).

So Jesus knowingly seals his death warrant, but he and his Father are One; they were in charge on Good Friday, as they have been ever since. For two full millennia now, the kingdoms of this world have become the kingdoms of our Lord and of his Christ. The fact that Caiaphas thought he was in charge, a delusion he shares with nearly all those smeared with the gold of office, is only to be expected. Depravity brings men to believe the exact opposite of what really exists. A phrase used often by psychiatrists in the diagnosis of mental patients with psychosis is "not oriented with reality." As with the mental, so with the spiritual. The spiritual insanity of men is what makes God's Great Symbol of Love, the Cross of Christ, an object of scorn to be hated by them.

Also seen in the expression, "Son of God," is the Fatherhood of God, one of the unique five teachings of Christ. So familiar the term is that we find it difficult to believe that it does not exist in the Old Testament. When Jesus said, "When you pray, say this: Our Father, who is in the heavens . . . ," he spoke of God as having a deifying relationship with those who come to him through Christ. No prayer in the Old Testament ever addressed God that way—none had ever been that personal, that intimate. It is the living and dying of Christ for us that makes this unique doctrine possible. Here it is with the other four teachings that logically devolve from it:

1) The Fatherhood of God
2) The Kingdom of God
3) The Importance of the Individual
4) The Equality of All Men
5) Love Transcends Law

Another point in this brief, heavenly trio is the puzzling, even mysterious term, "this day." Exactly when did Jesus become the Son of God? The text is quite emphatic about the matter, singling that day out from all other days. The date, in fact, is like the doctrine of Christ emptying himself so he could assume the form of limited man. It may be we will have to wait until we shed our natural bodies and assume our heavenly ones before we are able to understand what happened before the foundation of the world was laid, and on what day Christ became God's son. Read Rom. 1:4 and Acts 13:33. They seem to say that "this day" was the day he rose from the dead. Yet from heaven's viewpoint, "this day" may have been more than one diurnal day, involving other events as well. Before his crucifixion, as we have just seen, Jesus claimed to be the Son of God. Luke's Gospel (3:22 and 9:35) tells that the voice of God was heard announcing the Sonship of Christ at his baptism and at his Transfiguration. Comparing these and other pertinent verses, the Church Fathers who composed the Nicene Creed said it this way: "Jesus Christ, the Only Begotten Son of God, born of the Father before all worlds." The sonship of Christ relates quite significantly to what follows it:

Demand of me, and I shall give thee the nations for thine inheritance, and the uttermost parts of the earth for thy possession. (Ps. 2:8)

Notice the powerful climax of this couplet. The thought in the first line is extended to totality in the second. We see here globalism of lands, totalitarianism over peoples and divinity of rule, all in two lines. It is now that we have the third reason why David could not be referring to himself and his kingdom. David was not 1) anointed on God's holy hill of Zion, 2) he would never presume to call himself the son of God, and 3) he would never want the entire world to be his kingdom, nor would his sanctified citizens wish to dilute their holy acres with heathen lands and customs. For these three reasons this prophetic poem is not about David, as some liberal scholars contend, but about Israel's coming Messiah.

But why does our Messiah tell us what God demanded that he ask and then fail to tell us whether he did ask? Moreover, why didn't God just say what he would do? We are fully aware that God will act after the counsel of his own self-determination without inviting anybody to demand that he do it. What is the thinking behind this illogical statement?

Remember that the Old Testament is divided into three segments: Law—Genesis through Esther; Writings—Job through Song of Solomon; the Prophets. When we read law, we are confined to the logical use of language, but when we read in the other two divisions, our imaginations are invited to take part. This is to say that the artistic sensibility of man joins his logic to achieve understanding of what is presented. We know from John 14 as well as from several other proof texts that God is Trinity. However, you will notice that Jesus speaks of himself, the Holy Spirit and the Father as though they were separate. Indeed, what other option was available? We communicate in the ortholinear mode, i.e., in the form of a straight line, as I am using in writing this very sentence. No other option is open to me, for I live in space and time. I speak of my own trichotomy in such a way—body, mind and soul—not knowing where each leaves off or begins. Jesus made certain that he, his Father and the Comforter are

One. They are One in the Eternal world, but must manifest themselves singly to us.

Even so, David sets up the Father, demanding that the Son ask him to give him the entire world for his kingdom. Since God speaks to us by what he does not say as well as what he does say, he leaves unsaid what Christ does about this command. God is saying to us that the answer is so obvious that it need not be given. Love leaves so many things unsaid, things that do not need to be said, some so much so that any attempt at an answer would be less than what the holy silence surrounding it would imply. Will Christ obey his Father? Answer that question for yourself. Then as Isaiah declares, each of us should go up on a high mountain or a housetop and share the Good News everywhere.

You may find it interesting that the literary figure of speech David uses is like the one called personification—likening something other than a man as acting like a human being; it is called an anthropomorphism. Here David is likening God to a human being—the Bible uses many of these.

So the Word is out. The Spoken Word about the Living Word, who is the personification of abstract virtue (I am the light of the world) enfolding himself in anthropomorphic images to the end that the whole world can become his kingdom. This we pray when we say, "Come thy kingdom! Be done thy will, as in heaven, so on earth!" We now live on a visited planet by the Holy One from Eternity pressed into this mere 3D, spatial-temporal world. He was not just a jurist like Moses, not a mere prophet like Isaiah, not just a philosopher like Solomon or the Apostle John, or a literary genius like David or Paul, but God-in-the-Flesh—not a god, but The God. Each who hears is spurred into action—without exception. Either he falls before the Lord of Glory to worship him, or he laughs in faithless incredulity. When he can no longer laugh, he picks up Cain's club and waits for an occasion, or erupts into such vocal blasphemy that David spoke of his halitosis as having the stench of an open sepulcher.

In verse 9, God is still speaking as indicated by the same pronouns found in verse 8:

Thou shalt break them with a rod of iron; thou shalt dash them in pieces like a potter's vessel. (Ps. 2:9)

We must remember how David took comfort, as expressed in Ps. 23, from seeing the "rod" swinging at the shepherd's waist, and the "staff," or crook, with the hook at the upper end, designed to fit around the sheep's neck, catching its skull behind the mastoid bones, and then pulling the sheep out of some horrible pit. The "rod," or club, is for driving away predators. Comfort and confidence is a constant benefit for being led by such a shepherd, especially as the shadows lengthen and darken on this waning sixth day of the Millennium Week.

This shepherd has a special "rod of iron," an offensive weapon used to destroy. A wooden club would not last long if it were used to break imperfect pots from the day's firing. This rod of iron is designed for destruction, not correction. So Christ, by whom the worlds were made, has two opposite functions—to save and to destroy. There is no social gospel to help improve the world, no siphoning off of redeemable features to blend with the latest scientific achievement, no catalyst to speed things up—no, none of these things. He has come from the Omniscient Father with salvation for a lost world, and for the world itself, a rod of iron. We should not be troubled by this commingling of two opposites in the bosom of our Lord. Love cannot exist without hate—both are two sides of the same coin. The more we love, the more we hate that which would destroy what we love. There is no doubt that the ungodly fail to see either his saving or destroying work as he traverses the chapters of history, moving us all closer to the Day of Judgment.

History is always an interpretation of the past, and never a disinterested description of it. No two writers will present the same period with exactly the same effect. We are also not surprised to see attempts at rewriting history, so its narrative will present the past according to some pattern invented by men. It is now too late for them to present their propaganda of a preferred past. The Book has been given, inerrant in its impression upon us all. It was inspired by the Lord of Canon, who saw to it that how he handles history is expressed so clearly that it is more than a presentation of truth that all men can understand—it is also so powerful that they cannot misunderstand.

What of the great divisions among so many churches? Their dividing points build up walls of pride, soon to be beaten to shards with Christ's iron rod. Read Scriptural history and you will see clearly the pattern of God, the central structure in place. It was St. Augustine who gave us insight into Judeo-Christian historiography (how history happens). The first of four principles of St. Augustine that make up a biblically historical foundation is that history is *universal*. It involves all persons, places and events. It begins where no other history can begin (at the beginning), and it ends where none other can end (at the very end). What a history! One would think all would rush to read such divinely inspired pages. Second, history is *providential*. God is *anti facto, de facto* and *post facto* to all that happens because he is accessory before the fact, to the fact, and after the fact. All things are a product of his active or permissive will. Third, history is *apocalyptic,* or revelatory. What Augustine means, stated as briefly as possible, is that the world is comprised of two kinds of people—the saved and the lost. There is only one way the lost can be saved—for God to reveal himself and control his Holy Scripture. The fourth and final principle of Augustine's historiography is that history is *periodic.* God has divided man's history into seven periods, certainly redolent of the Great Millennial Week. God makes his will known to man through a person who is the epic figure of that age. These persons are as follows: Patriarchal Age—Abraham; Judicial Age—Moses; Monarchial Age—David; Prophetic Age—Elijah; Incantatory Age—Christ Himself; Ecclesiastical Age—Holy Spirit; Eternal Age. These seven periods are parallel to the seven millennia I use as a frame for this book.

We come now to the final segment of Psalm 2. As this psalm figured into public worship, I imagine a chorus singing the opening and final parts. Perhaps soloists sang the parts designated to God and his Messiah. So the chorus now sings:

Be wise now, therefore, O ye kings; be instructed, ye judges of the earth. Serve the Lord with fear, and rejoice with trembling. Kiss the

Son, lest he be angry and ye perish from the way, when his wrath is kindled but a little. Blessed are all they who put their trust in him. (Ps. 2:10-12)

We must never lose sight of the fact that David, himself a king, is the one singing of an even greater king. How often men fondly conclude within themselves that no entity in the entire universe is their master. Man is the final authority. If the barber and baker muse thus, how much more those who are kings and dictators! Indeed, they will all be tempted to hold Nebuchadnezzar's view of their persons—not so with David. He saw himself a conduit of mercy through which God flowed, and he wholly believed in the supernatural origin of the Law. He saw the Law as an unsearchable deep. You can be sure he was positively impressed by the way knowledge of the Messiah came to Abraham during his Moriah Test. He knew how God, via strange circumstances, paralleled events in the Patriarch's life to the future of Israel's Anointed King, his own Son, who would die for the sins of his people. He no doubt marveled over the rabbinical teaching that Abraham had to believe God would have raised Isaac from the dead.

The revelations continue. In Genesis 49, David observed the blessing Jacob pronounced upon each of his 12 sons. He saw the unexpected rejection of Reuben his firstborn son for becoming intimate with his father's concubine. Then came Simeon and Levi, who murdered all the men in a certain town, stole their wealth, and made slaves of the wives and children. Both were soundly rebuked and rejected by the Holy Spirit speaking through Jacob. The next in line was Judah, David's own grandfather several generations before. He must have pondered quite keenly Jacob's notable addition to the growing prophecy of Messiah himself, who was to come as a descendent of Judah, through David himself and his single dynasty "until Shiloh come."

There was surely a time when a seeming inconsistency in the prophecy occurred to David, one that would trouble him for years. How could Messiah be king forever and yet die for the sins of the people, like the ram that Abraham sacrificed on Mount Moriah? When in his very eventful life did he, like Abraham before him, see Christ's day and rejoice? See the whole of it, the crowning events? What womb of circumstance swelled mightily toward the greatest advent of prescient knowledge yet given to man, the climaxing events of Messiah's life? We are never told, just as we lack biblical guidance as regards the time when Abraham arrived at his contribution to the glorious reign of the Messiah.

It is my personal view (part of my gospel, if you will) that David's restoration after the defeat of Absalom was about the time when God brought circumstances parallel to Christ's resurrection to him. This may be why the great Psalm 42 is placed as the first psalm of the Second Division of that book. In addition, we see a significant and also subtle application of the glorious idiom of kings, "the sure mercies of David" in Acts 13:34. I had always associated "the sure mercies of David" as being most associated with his summary forgiveness pronounced by Nathan the prophet following his scathing public denouncement of David for the sin of adultery, of the multiple murders of Uriah and his men, and for abetting the complicity of Joab. This was one of the worst crimes recorded in Scripture, achieving its seriousness not for the complexity of the crime, but especially for who committed it. I concluded that if God would forgive David, he will forgive anyone. I continued to think that "the sure mercies of David" referred to the forgiveness freely given to David. Yet Paul relates this passage from Acts to the resurrection of Christ. So my search continued. I finally came to see that nothing in David's life could be more parallel to Christ's resurrection from the dead than his own restoration to the very throne to which Messiah was to come. This restoration edged him over the holy threshold where cognition took place. Messiah would die, but he will also rise from the dead and ascend up to the right hand of God, where his kingdom will have no end. This is exactly what David said in Psalms 16 and 22. It was David who supplied Paul with a subtle reference to the resurrection, and everlasting rule of Messiah by likening him to Melchizedek.

Only one more major Messianic prophet remains—Isaiah. He gives us the most voluminous treatment of all, but most of his volume relates to the message of the Messiah. Toward the end of his prophecy, he stresses the universality of his message: "The Gentiles shall come to thy light . . . the isles shall be waiting for thee . . . Of the increase of his government there will be no end . . . he is the everlasting father." Such quotations imply the extent and eternity of his rule.

Then come with me to the New Testament and its three Synoptic Gospels, followed by John's unusual Gospel, which seems to be a thematic, rather than chronological, treatment. It is almost impossible to dovetail his narrative into the Synoptics. Yet I would not want to part with a syllable of it. Think of it—95% of John's Gospel is unique! Maybe it is the result of instructions from the resurrected Christ. Recall that Jesus was with his disciples for 40 days before his Ascension. During this silent period is when Jesus might have sketched out what he wanted John to say.

Of course, there are many other gospels. Paul speaks twice about his gospel. We are all members of the cloud of witnesses, each with his own story of the life of Christ living within, each a unique message that nobody else could write. Our task is to see to it that Christ is placed squarely before the whole of mankind. He must stay on the front page of human consciousness until the end of time.

CONCLUSION

We Christians must never be naïve about government, lest we become discouraged, even despondent about the governance of God. We must remember always that God rules from his holy hill of Zion with Jesus our Messiah at his right hand. His scepter sways over the entire globe of our little planet. Even now God and Christ are moving all things toward the end of this space-time continuum. Remember also that you live by faith, without which it is impossible to please God. If his scepter were seen, his rod laid to the backs of violent, atheistic men, and our deserts were blossoming like the rose—why would we have need of faith any longer if we already had the proof? Remember that faith is conviction about reality. This the world does not have, being convinced that reality is understood by the working of the cerebral cortex of the human brain. So for us to see God's fingerprints on the ambiguities of life, and to hear his footfalls on the senate floors, courtrooms, battlefields and brothels of this world will take, at times, all the faith we can summon up. To worry is to doubt the omnipotence of God and his control of your destiny. So have faith. He tells us of a final battlefield where all nations will unite to make war on Christ and his saints. Then in the presence of stupefying odds against us, fire will come down from heaven and consume Christ's enemies.

Another thing we must not be naïve about is the nature of salvation. I say this against the current backdrop of something called the "electronic church," whose telemongers proclaim a prosperity theology (first introduced by the "friends" of Job) to receptive crowds, and affront the nation's airways with such a description of Divine Providence that will cripple souls, make it impossible for them to meet the challenges of the future, and bring them to the conclusion that God has deserted them. Christ came to save us from the world, from hell, and mostly from ourselves. He did not come to make life easier; he came to make it better. Jesus warns us that persecution, the cares of the age, and the deception of riches will destroy many. What happened to Judas, and what of Demas, the close companion of Paul?

How do we escape being naïve?—by recognizing the danger and the imminence of the sunset ahead of us, whether it takes the form of a body raging against its dying in some hospital bed, or a field of battle where blood flows up to the horses' thighs, or even some subtle rendezvous where men cry out for peace and safety after all the accouterments of warfare have been tossed into a bonfire, as Isaiah saw it, and the clanging of swords is no longer heard, nor the screams of the dying, but only snores of those long spent in the sleep of some false hope.

Above all, continue singing those Songs in the Night, especially the one called the *Shir Hasharim*, "My Beloved is mine, and I am his. He feeds among the lilies," and dance the *Mahanaim*, "between the rows," as Jacob did. While you sing, please avoid singing as the world does, for how can you sing the Lord's song in a foreign land? As you dance, be sure about how and where you do it. Make sure the Holy Spirit sparks your heels, and calls the step. Do not dance as Israel once did, drunk and naked before a calf of gold. Join David, as he brought the Ark of God toward its holy place. He danced outside the gate with the unseen Christ at his side. You will please God if you do—and you will also thereby participate in the saving of your soul during the hour of greatest trial.

FOR THE SUITCASE

1. God and his Christ now rule the nations.
2. It is Almighty God, with the total cooperation of his Holy Son, who was primarily responsible for the events of Good Friday.
3. The Fatherhood of God, The Importance of the Individual, The Equality of All Men—these unique teachings of Christ establish the foundation for representative government.
4. Islam and socialism are the religions, though opposite in nature, that rise up together to overthrow Christ and God. Ridiculous, isn't it?
5. It is our duty to be involved in our government as much as possible.
6. For the past two millennia, Christians have lived between two bloody enemies, the State controlling the Church, and the Church controlling the State.
7. The term "antichrist" has two meanings in Scripture: "against Christ" and "instead of Christ."
8. God has no name—since he is the only One, he needs no name. His reputation is his name. He identifies himself with the great persons, places and events of history.
9. There is no call for the separation of church and state in either the Bible or the Constitution of the United States. In fact, the Bible is obviously against such a notion.
10. David was the first person to foresee the Resurrection and Ascension of Christ.

Chapter XI:
Over High Mountains And Deep Valleys

Road Maps: Psalm 139; Ecclesiastes 7-8; I Timothy 6;
Hebrews 11

Now that the 20th century is over, it is possible to gather material for a definitive summary. What we want, of course, is more than a mere summary; we want an evaluation. Yet history itself reveals that this must wait until we learn exactly where this present century has led us and what in the past influenced our getting there. Still, one thing is so obvious about this last century that we can identify it now without any disagreement. The 1900s comprised the most eventful century in recorded history, a fitting climax to the sixth millennium since the creation of Adam and Eve. More people were born then than in all preceding centuries, more scientific knowledge was discovered, and more technology was invented than in all previous centuries combined. It is estimated that 90% of all scientists are alive today, and moreover, 90% of our medical knowledge was developed since 1900. From these advances come the good news that anyone alive today has an average life expectancy of over 65 years, the highest ever achieved. So exponential has this century climaxed that we seem to hear the haunting words of Yeats: "Surely, the Second Coming is at hand."

In light of the little I have just said about the 20th century, we find it almost impossible to believe that someone would be naïve enough as was the Director of the Office of Patents in 1889, when he wrote President McKinley, recommending that the office be closed because it would soon run out of business! Just 14 years later, in 1903, the Wright Brothers flew the first heavier-than-air craft at Kitty Hawk, and in 1969 man first set foot on the moon. By that time we were already well into the Atomic Age. Max Planck gave us a more precise math for the world of the very small, called quantum mechanics, and Albert Einstein said that, in the world of the very large, parallel lines actually do meet.

If we look a little more closely at the last century, we will see it dominated by science, engineering and technology; however, such a rapid burgeoning of knowledge would not have been possible without the transistor. It was hardly any time after it appeared until engineers, using the binary system of numbers, developed a hand-held calculator with transistors that made obsolete the 30-pound mechanical calculator that cost almost $1,000. Transistors replaced vacuum tubes, making radios and television sets smaller and cheaper, and thus affordable for all. There is a microchip on the market about the size of a period on this page that can do the work once requiring 10,000 vacuum tubes. What's more, I saw a photograph the other day of a computer the size of a small room that does the work of one using vacuum tubes that would require the entire floor space of the Empire State Building, and all the water of the Niagara Falls to cool its circuits. "It is a long way," said a computer scientist who attends my church, "from the chisel and mallet that first carved the Decalogue in stone to the complete Bible contained on a computer chip the size of a thumbnail." It seems to me, then, that the 20th century may be known to future times as the Communication Renaissance.

In our preceding chapter we saw that the Pilgrim's Road could not avoid the political world. We noted that some social scientists waxed religious by claiming more for their discipline than the facts justified. So it is as regards the professionals who study the natural world. I suppose it is best to concede that they are in a higher category than politicians are, since our world is dominated by things scientific. Moreover, we all regard scientific truth as more certain than social truth. This is so because things can be more precisely measured than human behavior. Yes, we are rising to higher ground, where the chasms are deeper and the air is rarer, making shadows darker and outlines more precise. Scientists justly take pride in showing us admiring laymen their amazing experiments with unerring predictability. Day in, day out, a whole lifetime long, the calipers and chemicals do their work.

Then what happens? Some scientists—indeed, some estimates say 60%—have come to believe that only things which can be objectively measured and publicly shared exist! This atheism is, you see, an occupational hazard among scientists and academicians, as a matter of fact. Many of those who have not been infected with atheism are content with deism, some sort of pantheism, or what I call religion by accommodation, a spare-tire approach that says with jesting Spinoza "There is no God, and Mary is His mother." Such views are even worse than atheism to those who have experienced the awesome God who "tented" among us, as John's Gospel says, and became the Road, the Truth, even the Life. All believe Copernicus was correct in exchanging the medieval concept of a geocentric solar system for the heliocentric one. Yet rarely do we find among the professionals, especially in science, those who have forsaken the egocentric universe they were born with for the theocentric one they meet in Genesis 1 and in the Prologue to John's Gospel. Hear with awe and adoration the activity of the Pre-incarnate Christ as he creates: "All things through him were created, and without him was created not one thing . . . . In the world he was, and the world was made by him, yet the world knew him not. To his own he came, and his own received him not. But to as many as did receive him, to them he gave authority to become children of God, to those who have faith in his name [Being], to those who, not of the blood, not of the will of the flesh, nor of the will of man, but of God have been born."

I call this chapter on science, which I write in the twilight of the Sixth Millennium, "Over High Mountains and Deep Valleys" to suggest the elevation of the human intellect to its highest achievements by obeying God in bringing the natural world within man's power, yet at the same time the creation of deeper valleys of ignorance. The higher the one, the deeper the other. All serious thinkers see all avenues of intellectual inquiry ending in a cul-de-sac. From each achievement in the natural world rise several new questions, questions at least one step ahead of the present sophistication of our tools for investigation. Hence, we have more questions than ever, and they are more difficult to answer. Since this is so, it must also be that we end up with more of the unexplored than we have discoveries, and that the greatest contribution of science to this or any age is a more accurate measurement of the height, depth and breadth of human ignorance! This no doubt is what Solomon meant when he said that with the increase of knowledge is also an increase of sorrow. We increase the penetration of our telescopes by tenfold, and increase the size of the unknown dimensions of the heavens by an easy hundredfold.

EVERYBODY HAS TO LIVE BY FAITH

Faith, with the imagination it stimulates and the intuition it sharpens, is a universal tool in the workplace and in our lives in general. We would be lost without it. Yet some of our scientists, while lauding the intellectual aeration of induction, which is the very mode of science in general, slam the door on all metaphysical considerations. They bravely assume the posture called logical positivism, the philosophy that says only what can be objectively measured and publicly shared exists. Yet they do not—indeed cannot—live consistently in such a box. Later in this chapter, we will look at the environment in which this philosophy exists, but I must begin by assuming the universal need of faith in all professions and in all personal lives. We Christians believe, moreover, that it is impossible to please God without faith. Indeed, we are saved by faith. Without faith it is possible to be lost by having faith in science instead of God. An overwhelming segment of scientific discovery is by trial and error. That faith is inherent in such effort is obvious.

We learn early in life to accept certain things as self-obvious. They are irreducible truths, foundational truths that must be accepted by faith before we can proceed with our work. For example, we cannot study geometry without first accepting Euclid's famous ten rules. They are presented first as so basic that we cannot prove them. We call these *a priori* truths. Here is where faith begins because people sometimes include certain errors in their thinking, like the medieval Schoolmen. Scientists, to be true to "the scientific method," will have to keep their theses open wide for modification in the future. It is intellectually sloppy to keep the thesis open on the missing links in Darwinism, for example, then close it against God, who is obviously the Creator of the world and everything in it.

We must have faith in our sense organs that they are free enough from illusion to interpret phenomena adequately, and in the reliability of our selective perception that it will not exclude vital phenomena. Then consider our tools. The numerals we use, are they adequate to measure the task at hand? Do our words deliver the proper meaning? It may be that formulas and scientific models lack necessary precision. We must have faith in the universality of law and, above all, faith in the ability to express ideas to others, and for others to comprehend what we have to say. There are even times when faith must be blind, though thankfully enough these times are rare. From the Bible we recall the ascent up Mount Moriah. Here Abraham was called by God to do what was absolutely contrary to everything he knew about God. The logical positivists must believe that we are apes. Also, they must—absolutely must—not only deny the existence of God, but endorse spontaneous generation. But where is the proof? There is none. Logical positivists believe these matters solely by faith!

Fellow pilgrims on God's Holy Road, keep in mind that everybody has faith in something or someone, even those who may stoutly deny that they do. There is a degree of irrationality in us all, a symptom of which in many of our scientific minds is to deny this very irrationality. Never be discouraged about the overwhelming numbers who choose faith in themselves, and inadvertently fulfill the prophecy of Christ about them, viz., few there are who will be able to find the difficult road and the narrow gate that leads to our Eternal Home.

THE ROLE OF NATURE

Nature is not deceptive. This is the most problematic matter before us. The wickedness of persons and governments we can expect. After all, we shrug our shoulders and say, "Man has fallen from the grace of God. What else can we expect?" But nature, too? Then what else is there? It would then seem that everything in the universe works adversely in our lives. People who spend too much of their time thinking and talking about evil have even been driven to suicide. What makes matters worse is that modern media bring before our very eyes any and all calamities caused in the natural world—not a single earthquake, hurricane, famine or plague goes unnoticed. History, too, joins our contemporary scene with the message that nature has always been violent. One event comes to my mind that seems especially provocative, an earthquake in Portugal in the 18th century, which occurred on a religious holiday. As soon as the cathedral in Lisbon was full of worshippers, the earthquake came upon them, causing the house of worship to collapse and crush them all, much like the ten children of Job. Such an ironic face did nature wear that day that Voltaire said that no Loving Heavenly Father would ever have allowed such an event to occur. He became a bitter skeptic and remained so until the end of his life. Some believe, though, that he converted on his deathbed. One witness said his last words were, "I die adoring God, loving my friends, not hating my enemies and an avowed enemy of all superstition whatever."

When this frowning countenance of nature comes upon us, plus the wickedness of human nature, we are tempted to cry out with Job, "I know you hate me, God. I know you do!" Yet when we see the whole picture— yes, though only through the eye of faith—we stand upon a foundation that cannot be shaken; we see with equal clarity both the smiles and frowns of nature from the vantage point of Sacred Scripture.

Here is the best place to dispel the popular notion that science and nature are at odds with each other. This is not so. They both give us the same message, provided that we excavate a grand canyon between scientific fact and theory. When we do, we will see that science and nature tell us the same thing about subjects they have in common. How could life be otherwise? God created the universe. What kind of a monster would he be if the laws of science led us logically to conclude atheism? There is no such message to be found. Let Darwin, Freud, Einstein and all atheists in the scientific community prate what they will. Their exposure to nature and science is just as limited as everyone else's when the full human scope of reality is involved. The lowly beggar is just as equipped as Dr. Einstein to answer questions about such matters. In fact, let us call upon Einstein himself to identify science with nature. He tells us in such stately prose that nobody has been able to say it better: "Science is the posterior recapitulation of nature through conceptualization." In more familiar words, he means that the scientist looks upon a nature already complete. He goes back over this reality and writes sentences about it. Then science is no more than sentences written about nature, or the physical universe, i.e., every physical datum from the respiration going on in one of the 100 trillion cells in your body to the spectrographic analysis of a galaxy located 14 billion light-years away!

Scientific statements and the beautiful, though tooth-and-fang, witness of nature are a wholly correct and a consistent reflection of our Loving Heavenly Father. This is why John's Apocalypse (Rev. 4-5) puts nature's praise of God as second in a descending order of believability:

1. Twenty-four Elders (Old and New Testaments)
2. Four Living Beings (Nature/science)
3. 108 of Angels (personal experience)
4. An Infinity of Saints (history, biography, etc.)

This paradigm, worthy of at least four full chapters of explanation, must always be kept in mind and always in this correct order. Twenty—four Elders represent one of the key tasks of Hebrew sanctification, the preservation of the written Word of God, identified as the twelve tribes established by Moses, plus the twelve apostles of Jesus Christ. I call the second order "Beings" because that is exactly what they are called. They are not "beasts" or even "creatures," but "Beings," as identified with *Zoe*, the highest kind of life in the Greek language. The message is clear, viz., everything that Scripture and nature say about reality is infallible (logically excluding the theories of scientists, of course). However, nature is limited, as we soon shall see, by only faintly giving us what we need to know about the Creator of both nature and Scripture.

Scripture is not deceptive. Science is the abstract of nature; nature is the creation of the Pre-incarnate Christ, who loves us; Scripture preserves for us its message from God, the Lord of Canon. Note also that there are two separate creations. Of the first John's Prologue says, "Everything through Him was created, and without Him was created not one thing." Paul also writes, "Christ, who is the image of the invisible God . . . created all things in the heavens and upon the earth, things visible and things invisible" (Col. 1:16ff). So we see two creations—a visible and an invisible—which the Nicene Creed also includes. From Hebrews this: ". . . through whom he [Christ] made the ages . . . and when he had made purification of sins, sat down at the right hand of the Majesty on high . . ." (Heb. 1). In this last quotation is the statement of the two creations, the one before time began and the one at Skull Place. It is there that I see the hands that hold the pen, and he sketches me into his plans for the universe. He forms me in my mother's womb, entering me into the battle of the genes. He then opens his hands to receive the spikes that impale them to a wooden cross. That is the Creator I speak of! This is my Beloved and Friend, O fellow lovers of Christ!

So from a Gospel written in the blood of our Creator, who also became our Savior, we see with categorical certitude and urgency that he is the origin of the human species. We come before him, our mallet and chisel in hand, engrave in stone and fill the engraving with lead so it will last forever, this conclusion written to the Roman Christians: If God gave up his son to die for us while we were yet his enemies, how much more readily would he be, with Christ now sitting at his side, to give us all things? This logic is blindingly clear. Logicians call it the *argumentum a fortiori.*

Then how is it that so many with scientific educations are atheists? If we give thought to the matter, we can clearly see the answer. Because we all are spiritual beings and take pleasure in conceptual thought, which most conspicuously expresses itself in choice-making, our scientists find it difficult to "shift gears" when they leave the laboratory. They fail to separate the laboratory from the living room. They cannot seem to keep universal causation exclusively confined to the laboratory, and pride and imagination out of it. Atheism, I repeat, is the occupational hazard of scientific professions.

It is ridiculous for so many of our scientists to posture science and religion in opposite corners of the boxing ring. Indeed, they have many concerns in common, one of which is to be mutually beneficial. Let me give you two examples. When geologists discovered that uranium degenerates into helium and lead at an unvarying rate, they measured the depth of the lead encrustation and determined that some rocks in Southeastern Canada had to be 4.5 billion years old. Many Bible students saw that they must reexamine what the Hebrew word *yom* meant in the Creation Hymn. They soon saw that it means the same as its English equivalent, usually a twenty-four hour period, but could also mean any longer period of time the writer wished to indicate. Science had made a contribution to biblical scholarship—no contradiction. Thanks to science, we now see that Moses must have meant a period of time longer than a diurnal day.

Just after the French Revolution, scientists were anxious to disprove the existence of God, and tried to do so by proving spontaneous generation— that life springs into being without help from any outside intelligence—in other words, that there is no Creator. One experiment they were fond of performing was putting hay emulsion in a test tube, which was then heated to boiling, then plugged and left to incubate. After a proper waiting period, they examined the emulsion under the microscope and, lo and behold—amoebae appeared! They boldly proclaimed as part of a new Year One this proof that there is no God. They were correct, I suppose, in saying that spontaneous generation proves that the elements can generate life without any outside help—truly a giant step toward atheism! It was not long, however, until a flaw was discovered. They had overlooked the fact that amoebae can be airborne. One clever scientist plugged the test tube before the emulsion was boiled, and no amoebae were found from that day on. The Bible tells us that God created life, but some scientists who would rather deny the existence of God, have blind faith in the sentiment that someday scientists will prove spontaneous generation.

Nature does not reveal God. Of course, one can logically prove the existence of God by recapitulating universal causation to its beginning. Surely it must be true that, if for every effect there is an antecedent cause, there must also be a first cause, and that cause is God. This is all we know by our logic—First Cause or Prime Mover. Still, we crave far more than that. We want no intellectual construct, a link in a logical chain. Even the primitive religions of the jungle offer more than that. Some of the great classical religions of the past at least offered a Righteous Judge at the end of life. Even "old Zeus the Deceiver" was more than this deistic god. According to James, the devils have faith that God exists, and they tremble (James 2:19).

God does not reveal himself through nature because nature does not say enough about him. What nature gives is unsatisfying because it is like Adamic nature's predicament—an experience of good and evil. In addition, nature's god would elevate human intellect to an idolatrous level and would obviate faith, which is love's greatest activity. Most of all, God does not use nature to reveal himself because he does not need nature, angels, or anything else to reveal him. Just like any lover, he prefers to press his suit of love himself.

At the heart of the Christian faith is a personal relationship with God Himself. Jesus teaches his disciples to do what had never been done before by any Hebrew worshipper—to address God in a familiar way. He tells us to say, "Our Father, who is in the heavens." Examine all the prayers in the Old Testament—none addresses God as Father. Jesus brings God into our personal lives, and the Kingdom of God at the level of our daily threshold.

We must not regard nature as a source of revelation. God does not want a proxy to press his suit of love. This is why it is called "Gospel" or "Good News" or "Great Proclamation." God comes himself, suffering from the limitation of human nature and enduring the depravity of man, staggering down the *Via Dolorosa* "with the government upon his shoulder" (Isa.9:6), the shoulder carrying the cross. What's more, he requires us all to join him in carrying our own crosses out of town to our own personal

Skull Place. Hear him once more as he gives out a singular invitation that climaxes in a threefold categorical demand: "If anyone wants to come after me [the invitation], he must deny himself [command], even he must take up his cross [second command] and he must follow me [third command]." Gently introduced in the indicative mood in the Greek is, "If anyone wants to come after me," but the three conditions are in the imperative mood: Deny! Take up! Follow!

Nature's true function. No sooner have proofs for the existence of God been formulated than opponents rise up with arguments for rejecting them. This is as it should be in the wisdom of God, who is far more interested in the heart than the head. God wants to reveal himself to those he wants to love him. He is love, and what we know chiefly about love is his determination to have no competitors whatever! "For I the Lord am a jealous God!" This is the greatest compliment God has ever given to man!

We examine the four classical proofs for God's existence, and the logical flaws they contain, then see that we are left with no more than the conviction that we cannot prove the existence of God, nor can men prove he does not exist. This is just as God would have it. It is one's faith that must weigh these ambiguities in favor of affirmation. God forces men to seek him by faith, a faith which grows in the soil of ambiguity. We saw in our study of Abraham that ambiguity makes faith grow.

However, growth comes to us intermittently. Between these periods of increasing our faith, we need sustaining power to develop deeper roots and wider foundations. This is precisely the role of nature in our lives. Nature is constantly confirming our faith. She echoes it from the vast expanse above us. Her message is contemporaneous, and loudly she proclaims Him who is the Absolute of quality, the Infinite of degree, hence the Ultimate of value. What a lavish hand that has strewn across the heavens our Milky Way! We are aware that science-nature has told us of the age of these glittering masses of stars, speaking all day long, all night long of the Ancient of Days and the Eternal Rock who is our home. Little wonder Sir James Jeans said, "Among us astronomers there are no atheists." True of 19th century astronomers, though not so today. Atheists now look at the heavens and see no God. The heavens that are continuously singing, as the psalm says, day and night, yet their Good News is not heard by those who set themselves up as their own gods. It seems that the poet David is saying that the message is implied and received by those who know the God who made these heavens. Atheists see the same skies, yet do not hear the message. It is not intended for them.

We pilgrims on Jesus' Road are born again, so all things are new because they are newly seen, newly heard. Nature lavishly displays motifs of our Mighty God, perhaps even somewhat different to each of us, and they grow in number and intensity. When one converts to Christ, nature converts from the neutral to a confirmatory force, from a thing of beauty to a message from God.

Yet what about the other side of nature, when the blessing of rain becomes the curse of flood, or when the absence of rain brings drought? Nature might not cause as many premature deaths as human nature, but she runs a close second. Jesus said that God causes the rain to fall on us all, so we are not able to see any pattern emerging from where and when it rains. We must never forget that the whole of life, nature included, is in the unknown bundle we place before the Lord, at his throne of mercy. Also, we can never forget that our lives pursue a future divinity that has gained victory over all things that come our way, bane and blessing, adversity and prosperity. Not a hair falls uncounted from our heads, no sparrow falls unnoticed—and God participates as well as counts. He may send a young man baldness without ever telling him why. Nature, too, is a significant part of heaven's plans. Life transcends our full understanding of its gifts and powers. We must remember that we know about more adversity than we ever experience, beholding example rather than having experience. It may be that we see ten thousand fall, and even a thousand at our side, as a way of glorifying our marginal experience—though we are scarcely saved, we are indeed saved. So that which is adversity is turned to advantage, and all things work together for good for those who are loving God, who are called according to his purpose. To our expectant ear Christ Himself triumphantly shouts, "Yea, yea," and nature echoes, "Amen!"

DARWIN & COMPANY

Never has a book been more cursed or blessed than Darwin's *On the Origin of Species*. It came into print in 1859, in the midst of the pomp and circumstance of Victorian England. Its red-hot effect was due to the plain fact that never before in the history of printing had such an elaborate and eloquent defense of atheism found its way into print. It is true that it is a book about biology, yet its very title implied a more inclusive scope than mere biology. It was a book, not on the *variety* in species or the *development* of species, but on the *origin* of species. Certainly, Victorian eyebrows arched at this puzzling, extravagant title that seemed to include a study of the Creator as well as what he created. The reader was soon to learn that the Creator was not to be included; instead, the message began the long and fully developed account of a biology that more resembled Topsy, by just springing up, than by the fiat of any intelligent being whatever. Atheists saw Darwin as the final word in their apologia, and all followers of Jesus Christ saw that he had categorically rejected the Holy Scripture. Yet all would soon come to see that the *Origin of Species* was also a superb example of didactic prose. They were correct about that feature of his controversial work, for Darwin proved to be among the very best stylists of the English language.

However, the beauty of what Darwin was saying tended to disguise the fact that it was a scheme for what one wished were true, being presented as scientific fact. The situation is like the popular notion of "progress" in human culture: We want so much to believe the best of human nature that we often confuse technological proliferation with progress. Yet when we think more factually about the matter, we see people are no better in the 21st century than they were in the 18th century—perhaps better off, but not better. Even so, Darwin's book was overwhelmingly accepted by scientists and other highly literate people, and they regarded Darwin as their emancipator, who let them "out of the closet." They proclaimed man as a happenstance of the forces of nature. Quite soon they came to regard as intellectually dishonest, or even ignorant, those who still held God as their Creator, even those who held the less radical form of evolution within species, as a means whereby he brought about comparatively minor changes to adjust to changes in the environment. This attitude prevailed so extensively that in collegiate teaching, those who held to the view of theistic evolution were soon put into the very closets the atheists so recently had vacated.

From its entrance into human culture 150 years ago, Darwinism has known no successful challenges until quite recently. Atheists are beginning to see what has always been the case: because they have ignored the "missing links" in Darwin's work, they cannot escape the accusation of their critics that Darwinism has in it elements of religion—a faith in the unknown. Therefore, they have accepted Darwin's "origin" by faith, and faith, they have always maintained, has no place in scientific understanding! One might ask how it could be possible that Darwinism would so quickly and so enduringly take root in people known for their intelligence. Before I attempt to answer that question, let's consider an even more perplexing one—how could Darwin have deceived himself?

Consider the following illustration. A bank clerk is asked to count 20 banded packets of 100 $100 bills. It is late in the afternoon, so he begins at once, not wanting to miss the first train home. He works fast and accurately. He is quite weary when he has completed 15 of those packets. Every single one of those already counted has 100 bills in it. He is sure—justifiably sure—that the remaining 5 packets will be the same as well, but it is almost quitting time, so he hurries. While counting the 16th bundle, he comes to the 90th bill and it looks as though what remains appears to be ten more bills. So he doesn't count them. He assumes on good, sound judgment that all 100 are there. In stack 17, he comes to the 75th bill, and he estimates again. He uses the same method for stacks 18 and 19, and since its only two minutes until closing time, he doesn't even count the 20th stack at all. He initials all the packets quickly and runs to catch the train home.

The bank teller probably escaped detection of his superficial job. He knew positively that most of his task was completed, and the reputations of his fellow workers gave him confidence that all $100 bills were there.

So he starts his task with pure science, or mathematics, and ends it with faith in his own judgment.

This is exactly what Darwin did. Look again at the title of his famous book—the complete title: *On the Origin of Species by Means of Natural Selection, on the Preservation of Favored Races in the Struggle for Life.* This long title anticipates all four parts of his famous paradigm:

1. Natural Selection
2. Random Variation
3. Struggle for Existence
4. Survival of the Fit (not "fittest")

Since Darwin had no room for God as Creator, you might be surprised to know that he studied theology at Cambridge for one year. One might rightly conclude from this that at some time during his collegiate education, he had a change of heart about the Christian faith and the Bible that teaches it. His title is quite reactionary, for it states his belief that the forces of nature (and not God) were the origin of all species. The second mode is random variation, the belief that environment changes our design (and not God). Nothing could be more contrary to the Genesis account of creation. As regards the final two modes in the paradigm, Darwin seemed to agree with biblical teaching, for the Judeo-Christian ethic expresses life as a struggle, and only those who endure to the end will be saved. Both Darwin and the canonists looked out upon nature and saw these same two parallels in nature and in human culture. So Darwinians are half right, but since we all concede these two common features of life, viability demands far more than a grade of 50%.

It is evident that Darwin intended his "scientific" work to refute the Christian faith. Otherwise, he would have limited his scope and titled his work to read, *The Development of Species,* or *Variety in Species.* He rather did as so many of his followers today do in that he let his enthusiasm for his private, egocentric universe lead him across the metaphysical barrier, from the laboratory to the chapel. It is no wonder those who reject Darwinism say its advocates practice the religion of scientism. Since Darwin offers no laboratory proof for the transmigration of species, how does he arrive at this conclusion about the roles of nature and her variation? By the same approach used by our bank teller—by having faith in his own judgment, which essentially means his own opinion. Whether it is said in eloquent prose, or more fully satisfies the yearnings of Darwin's fellow atheists does not enter into the argument.

We might well ask why Darwin completely ignored other theories that suit all the facts in his complex scheme of things. The Threshold Theory states that God created all species, but made them subject to changes in design as they were exposed to significant variations in their environments. This theory agrees with all Darwin has to offer except the common origin of all species. The Recapitulation Theory describes God as recreating six different times, each time varying his species to meet new environmental challenges. This theory agrees with all the evidence available to Darwin. Finally, The Gap Theory extends the period of creation over the entire duration of the ages involved. Why would none of these theories suit Darwin and his followers? It is plain that these theories plus Darwin's theory are equally from the evidence we do have that may lead to evolution within species as a dynamic force in pre-historic times. Darwin ignores them because he is an atheist.

We now begin to see the enemy of our faith emerge from the camouflage of scientific maneuvering. It is not evolution at all! Evolution means nothing more than change. For example, French-Canadians are taller in stature than their relatives are back home. The closer races live to the equator, the darker are their complexions. Then there is the matter of genetic vigor, expressed when an offspring has features superior to those of either parent. There is nothing in Scripture that speaks against variation within species. However, we are told that God made all species bear offspring "after their own kind." Darwin goes far beyond development within species, and traces all species to a common ancestor, presumably a one-celled creature living around 600,000,000 years ago. The point he stresses is that life began without a creator; it just happened as a chemical compound, and that being an environmental accident to boot—spontaneous generation.

This happenstance beginning is the crown jewel of modern Western philosophy, called logical positivism, the belief that only what can be objectively demonstrated and publicly examined exists. Here is the

Christian's chief cultural enemy. Ironically enough, those who hold it must do so on the grounds of faith, for it is a position based on metaphysics, the study of what exists. One has faith in himself, and how stubborn and proud he is determines how strong his defenses are against any changing of his mind. Logical positivism—what a momentous ring to these words! How attractive it sounds—indeed, how positive. One can muse, "Why wouldn't I take a positive stand about reality, and what stand could be more salutary than positivism?" Yet nothing could be more denigrating to the Lord of Creation and man himself, in whom wells all the attributes of God.

Look for a moment at how this enemy of faith measures against the *tour de force* of God's creation—man himself. Consider the protein molecule. It is comprised of some 20 amino acids in a complicated array of nearly 100 atoms. I saw a model of one made of colored ping-pong balls joined by plastic straws, placed on the wall above a biology professor's fireplace. Some of these acids have been synthetically constructed by using the Urey-Miller experiment of passing electric sparks through a mixture of water plus methane and hydrogen gases. Though a long way from creating a cell, this is by no means an insignificant achievement.

But what are the chances that life could generate spontaneously? Early in the last century, a biologist of considerable reputation determined the time it would take, given the size of the known universe and the estimated atoms in it in the year 1935 (it is known to be much larger now!). He said for all the atoms in one highly complicated protein molecule to arrive randomly at the same place so spontaneous generation could take place would require 10243 years. Recall that this is 10 followed by 242 zeroes. I have never seen a number larger than this, not even one representing the number of atoms in the universe, which has been estimated at 3 x 10100. It is beyond comprehension. Hence, it is very clear that not only the Bible refutes spontaneous generation, but so does the law of probability.

We have only begun to describe our complexity. We will forego a description on the forming of these molecules into a complete cell. Let's consider the DNA double helix. One such strand is wadded up into a compact ball inside of every one of the 100 trillion cells in your body. Unwrapped and extended, the DNA is about 6 ft. long. Over this length are 3 billion nucleotides carrying the genetic message using an alphabet of only 4 letters. All these strands in your body placed end to end would reach 113.6 billion miles! "I am fearfully and wonderfully made . . . that my soul knoweth, and that right well" (Ps. 139:14). Yes, David, it is so!

If Darwin's theory be true, surely there has been some proof come forth to be—as the Darwinians themselves say—"objectively designed" and "publicly evaluated." Microbiologists have peered deeply into the wonders of the microscopic world via the electron microscope, but they have found no indication of alteration in the genetic code or through some other variation suggesting natural selection or random variation—not a glimmer of evidence. Paleontologists have unearthed quite a heap of bones, but they will tell you the going is rough for them, given the deterioration of their significant fossils. Not only has not one missing link been found, but erosion of landscapes and a myriad of other natural enemies of their science make research quite limited. Too few bones, they say, to tell the story of all too many millennia of time. What of chemistry and other cognate sciences? No, there is no proof of Darwin's thesis.

Atheists, scientific and otherwise, still live by faith in spontaneous generation. The restrictions of their logical positivism have closed the door to any other option. Scientists are mostly honest; they have to be because their work is constantly evaluated by their peers. So why not extend that honesty to evaluate Darwinism as well? Why not admit and teach others that the common origin of species is, as it has been since the day of its insinuation into human culture, no more than a theory. Darwinians do not know the origin of species from science. As a man of faith, I find it one of the most caustic of ironies that men will extend to Charles Darwin the faith they will not extend to Almighty God and his Holy Word! Some cling with blind faith to the atheism of Darwin and attempt to argue God out of existence. Scripture says it twice, "The fool hath said in his heart, there is no God."

VERY GOOD BUT NOT PERFECT

You will remember how pleased God was at the climax of his creation. He created man last, then said, "Very good!" Nowhere else in the entire Bible will he say again exactly that. Then we hear several times that he changed his mind—yes, even repented. How does such a seeming reversal square with the immutability or eternity of God? Thinking about these two attributes for a few minutes will make you conclude that he cannot be eternal without being immutable, too. What's more, he cannot be eternal unless he does not change; he is "the same yesterday, today and forever."

Let us lay aside our contemplation of what is perfect in order to deal with the imperfections about us. Consider our surest mode of natural knowledge, the "scientific method." Every branch of science has its unanswered questions and is trammeled by the limitations of its tools. Recall Einstein's definition of science, which I paraphrase as "writing sentences about nature," simply that. Since God is perfect, we might naively suppose that nature would reflect his perfection, which it does. Yet we must realize that reflections are always less distinct than the real thing, and their quality is limited by our ability to see. God said his creation was very good, which implies a higher possible level of perfection. In the Love Chapter of the Bible, I Cor. 13, Paul tells us that we see, as it were, by using a mirror (in his day no more than a sheet of burnished copper), so we see only poorly, but then face to face in heaven. There is a Hebrew word for "perfection," but it occurs only rarely in the Old Testament. The word is used in Psalm 50:2, in which the poet Asaph speaks of God's eternal Zion as perfect, the perfection of beauty. Eden and its residents were less than that, for they were created only as being "very good."

We are told of a better inheritance, something beyond "very good." We aid our inadequate power of description sometimes by a literary device called *negative affirmation*. We speak of the ideal hero by juxtaposing him alongside someone who is only average or even opposite in character. The glory of Christ was thus enhanced on every page of the Gospel, reaching its height as we see Judas identifying him to the temple guard by kissing him. Then come the three hours of midnight at high noon when even nature shuts down the light of day, lest the Lord of Glory be seen dying in great pain, naked and wanting so little as a cup of water, which man denies him. Petition Five of the Paternoster is the most often used example of negative affirmation: "And lead us not into temptation [because we know you will not do so], but deliver us from evil." So we express the sanctification of our lives for another day by reminding ourselves negatively of what now becomes the more certain to us, viz., we will not ever be tempted by God, but rather delivered from what is evil. For all of us who fall short, there is this awaiting our aching heart: "And forgive us since we have forgiven those who sin against us."

Let us turn for a moment to the most exact of the sciences, which some have called "the queen of the sciences"—mathematics. If anywhere, we would expect it is in math that we would find perfection, or at least fewer imperfections than in the other sciences. I am not qualified to speak on this matter, but I suspect the mathematician will say there are several imperfections rising from the task of measuring, the most conspicuous of which is so often used that it is given a special name—*pi*—the ratio between the diameter and circumference of a circle. It is an irrational number that is so famous and so challenging that mathematicians have worked it out to the 2,600,000,000th decimal, and still no end in sight. Pascal, one of the world's greatest mathematicians, and also often cited with C. S. Lewis as one of the world's greatest Christian apologists, guessed that the 1,000,000[th] decimal of *pi* would be a 5, and he was proved right a short time ago when modern computers could handle the math required to find it. Of course, Pascal's choice was only a guess. The ratio *pi* usually stops at 3.14159, quite adequate for almost all our purposes.

The most fascinating ratio of them all is a three-way cross, where science, the arts and social studies meet. The Greeks as far back as Pythagoras debated over the most aesthetically pleasing place to divide a line. They settled on what has been named the Golden Section. They said the line should be divided at that place where the shorter segment (A) would be in the same ratio to the longer segment (B), as (B) would be to the entire line (C), or A : B :: B : C. This is not some opinion, some arbitrary choice, but conformity to something deep inside us all that is as certain in aesthetic judgment as the octave sequence in music is to the human ear. What is that ratio? We call it *phi*, but the answer is as remote as that of *pi*. It also is an irrational number. We may know it someday, but not until the eternal day breaks and the shadows flee away, and we behold our Loving Heavenly Father, the Omniscient One, who himself is the Perfection of Beauty. We may be so amazed at the beauty of effulgence and glory we behold in him that we will forget, just like Job, to ask the question. *Phi* has a working ratio of 1.61803. Its most fully developed form was set on a large computer for the 10,000,000th decimal place. The computer worked only 30 minutes to arrive at a series of ten million numerals with no resolution or discernible pattern.

Let us look to the heavens for a moment. One of the dearest of verses in the Bible involves something God made that is, according to our measurement, quite imperfect. "This is the day the Lord has made; we will rejoice and be glad in it" (Ps. 118:24). God has made it, and yet God's day, according to sidereal measurement, i.e., according to the position of the heavenly bodies, is not 24 hours long, but 23 hours, 56 minutes and 4.09 seconds long. In addition, the year ends about 6 hours late, and even that is not exactly right. It comes to 6 hours, 9 minutes and 9.54 seconds. Since we now have the use of radar and laser light, we have been able to discover something even more amazing; our sunrise is early or late by 0.07 of a nanosecond every day. Some are of the opinion that the earth trembles as it rotates on its axis.

Yet the most abundant and even most conspicuous "shortcoming" of nature occurs in the world of atoms. We have found that the nearer we get to this ultimate detail of nature, the less conformity to law we discover. Have you ever experienced static in your radio reception while driving alongside a row of electrical pylons? This static is caused by some of the units of electricity disobeying the law—a very small percentage, but enough to make you want to change stations. Or have you noticed how a spotlight in a dark room tends to become less distinct as its source moves away from the wall it shines upon? We see at once that the beam of light ought to grow dimmer and fainter. But what causes its border to become less distinct? The answer is that some of the phota are not following the path toward which they are directed, so they strike the surface beyond the edge of the beam. A final example involves another of Newton's famous Laws of Motion—the one that says the angle of reflection equals the angle of incidence. That is to say, if a cue ball strikes the bumper on a pool table at 30o, it will also take a path of 30o away from the bumper. Simple enough and quite amenable to all. But what happens when a stream of atoms is hurled at a surface at such an angle? An overwhelming number of them will obey this law of motion—but not all. Some shoot straight up into the air, some scoot along the surface, some veer off at an angle, some bounce backward in the direction they came from, and some stop dead in their tracks—all this without any discernable cause.

GOD'S TWO DAYS

Long before the birth of Christ, men imagined the universe was comprised of atoms, but it was not until the 20th century that they were able to know anything about them. What they found was so bizarre that any attempt to describe what they learned in the ortholinear mode, i.e., traditional writing such as I am using now, did more to distort than to clarify what they saw. Scientists found that mathematics was the only mode possible, so they developed a new language of mathematics called quantum mechanics.

Before long, philosophers and theologians saw that the behavior of atoms had a connection to their value systems. Atoms (called "quanta") were seen disobeying the Laws of Motion; they were behaving irrationally. Meanwhile, atheists took comfort in the doctrine of universal causation; for every effect there is a cause, and without exception. Naturally, they established unwavering faith in scientists, who would in time solve this puzzle. Causal patterns would be found. Theologians were also troubled. They feared that relativity in natural law argued for relativity in moral law as well. Still, some were quick to see a difference between the two kinds of laws, possibly for the first time. The Laws of Moses and the Laws of Newton were radically different from each other. It was argued that nature's laws were really rules because they cannot be broken. No one, they were to point out, ever broke the law of gravity and lived to talk about it. On the other hand, moral law was, as the great jurist Blackstone said, "the abstract of human conscience."

We who have faith in our Heavenly Father are not troubled by the irrational behavior of atoms; we see no spiritual significance in their behavior. We have learned to live with irrational behavior in our own lives and in God's relationships with us. Without faith we cannot please God, and he sees to it that we experience from him those irrational inclusions and exclusions, even to the point of denying us logical justification for their existence. This irrational part of life takes on the impossibility of God's being able to reduce his plans to our level. He will never tell us why because he cannot, so we accept him initially and always by faith. We see the imperfect measurements in nature as enhancements of his greatness; they are like a beauty-mark on a beautiful face. Indeed, what better way is there than to show the perfection of God made by using imperfect tools? Sunrise comes .07 of a nanosecond early or late, and our day is not quite 24 hours long; yet in the long run, all averages out to the perfect day.

We also see in the imperfections the beauty (glory) of God, such as we would like to experience in the lives of those we love. We call such "infinite variety." So it is with God after 2.6 billion patternless decimals of *pi*. We see this amazing number as an example of the eternity of God, for the number seems to be without ending or pattern. We see most clearly the omniscience of God exhibited by his ability to avoid pattern in so large a number. Indeed, so complex is this number that it is almost impossible to avoid inadvertently creating some kind of pattern. So God gives us ratios to discover, then to use such answers that lead to his fingerprints upon our conclusions. After dizzying calculations and countless hours of toil, we arrive at an answer that causes me to recall Professor Buber's tenth possible meaning for God's great name, I-THAT-I, given to his servant Moses. Hear and rejoice, you aging comrades, as we hear it from the ever faithful caverns of our memories, redoubling its echoes against the Great White Throne of God's Judgment: I MYSELF WILL BE THERE. So go on to 10 billion decimal points of *pi* and see what you will find there. Imagine yourself in heaven. God asks you to work toward the perfect ending.

This will take a great deal of time, but time is not among the furniture of Eternity. Nevertheless, when you finish, God asks you to see if any pattern has finally emerged. You see none and say so. He tells you that there is one more, the infinite number to be placed. He writes it there, then tells you the pattern is complete, but you see it only after he explains it to you.

The irrationality of *pi* or *phi* exerts no imminent influence on your life, but you do have irrationalities, and God deliberately made his tools imperfect so the perfection of his artistry would be a reflection of what he intends for all of us who love his appearing. God transcends his creation in beauty, and he waits to work out for each of us a more perfect self than we bring to him. We are a tattered tent. We can hardly imagine what the next decimal of *pi* is, or in the least item of those things eye has not yet seen, nor ear heard, nor yet entered into the heart of man.

MY TWO DAYS

On this subject, I am more comfortable speaking of "my," rather than "our" because I feel a need of reminding us that no two Christians will see things exactly alike or rank all priorities in the same order. Paul spoke of <u>his</u> gospel occasionally, by which he meant his presentation of the Gospel, exhorting all to follow him—but only as he followed Christ. He hoped, as do I, that in critical matters the Holy Spirit will keep us all as parallel as possible. Perhaps this needed and unavoidable variation among unique persons acts as a catalyst, a quickener, and yet a unifier, to the end that our experiences will be enough alike to fortify us against all enemies without, and to be different enough to stimulate our quest for further understanding. With such differences as we do experience, Phillips Brooks, who is probably better known to most of us as the author of the Christmas carol, "O Little Town of Bethlehem," defined preaching as "truth through personality." I am sure that the way in which we differ from each other makes us all preachers; God chooses for us audiences and occasions, too.

There is one thing I am sure we will agree on, and that is we can't find pattern or resolution in the ratio of *pi*. Another is we do not know what its next decimal will be, or what tomorrow will bring forth, no matter how perfectly we understand the past. Our tomorrow is a mystery. Still, we do know that, "for those loving God, all things work together for good: for those according to his purpose, called, they indeed are" (Rom. 8:28).

Yet how do we know this greatest of all promises? By faith, of course, a faith that weighs all ambiguities in favor of God. True, some of these ambiguities are more difficult to nudge in the right direction than others. At times they may appear unnamed, unknown, and look quite human. They serve a purpose in your life. If it be a good deed, it is easy to see they were from heaven. However, what would you say of a dozen or so who drive you to your knees with the overwhelming conviction that you had no place else to go? Are these enemies? If so, what bad thing did they do to you? Strange enemies if they improve your prayer life! It is better to go to the house of mourning than to the house of mirth, says the wise King Solomon. He also robs death of its seeming tragic role by the assurance that the day of one's death is better than the day of his birth. Paul concurs with this attitude by seeing death as the door to eternal life, with Christ waiting just beyond that door.

Imagine a house of mourning in your neighborhood. A mother of four young children has just died in childbirth, and the father is of limited means. Help is needed now, and a lot of it. So you and your spouse take on the demanding chores of cooking, cleaning, child care and shopping for several weeks until relatives arrive from out of town—all this without reward. Or say you are a member of A A and become a buddy for a recovering alcoholic. There are evenings when his need preempts your social events, or even just a comfortable evening at home. Sometimes you are with your needy friend all night. Time passes, and one day you are burdened with the puzzling need of taking on an additional member of the local A A—no, let's put it another way. You are also in need—you need to be needed, so you seem to be losing yourself and some of your life as well. In an earlier chapter, I spoke of two "Als"—alchemy (turning lead to gold) and altruism (losing yourself in a higher cause than yourself). Now I want to share with you a secret power I have tapped that has made me a rich man (Rev. 2:9). One day I realized the medieval chemists' dream of changing lead to gold. It came to me suddenly, like E = mc2 came to

Einstein, as a supernatural flash of intuition. I saw a subtle relationship between altruism and alchemy, I saw that I was enlarging my life by giving it away. Whatever value dwells in me now is from God, and God is love. And love is the one thing that grows as you give it away. That is exactly why it is more blessed to give than to receive.

All this reinterpretation of values, this total reversal of values, is foolishness to the ungodly, even as is the sacrifice that Christ made is foolishness. Men will say—with their lives, if not with their mouths—that Christ died for nothing. He wasted his life, which is downright foolishness. They are among the hordes of mankind who go on the wide and easy way to hell. They are quite adequately represented during the ministry of Christ by the Rich Young Ruler, who sadly walked away when Jesus told him he would have to forsake his wealth and follow him if he wanted to have eternal life. Later on, he must have recalled this meeting with Jesus as nothing but foolishness. I wonder how he cast his vote when the Sanhedrin met to decide the fate of Jesus. He just had to be overwhelmed by his version of the world, which demanded that he join the preachers, professors and politicians of his day in condemning Jesus.

Let us briefly return to Eden. Recall Moses' teaching about sin as having three parts: lust of the flesh, lust of the eyes, even the pride of life (*bios*, not *zoe*). This kind of life is flesh and eye. Yet nothing is said about these two gods in the making, these *theoi ex machina*, these "gods in machines," nothing more than "flesh" and "eyes." In saying this, Moses is anticipating Paul by well over 2000 years: "For to be carnally minded is death," says Paul. Moses saw the choice of Adam and Eve relating to the flesh and eyes as bypassing the soul on their way to the mind, hence degenerating into carnal mindedness—here is a closed loop. But when the soul, the holistic you, symbolized as the "heart," welcomes God into the loop, the body henceforth becomes a battlefield because the soul gladly welcomes God, and not his own ego, as Lord and Master.

When I say that our Commander-in-Chief tells us that the most potent weapon is love, and that we are to love all men, take up our own crosses and follow him, he is plainly advocating altruism. I hear someone say, "If altruism is what Jesus meant by cross-carrying, why didn't he say so?"

Because the word had not been invented yet. It first occurred in French during the Middle Ages. Monastic writings used this new word to mean the commandment to take up our cross and follow him. We must lose our lives in something greater than our lives if we want to live forever. So my answer is that Jesus would have used this word if it had been available to the culture of his time. The cross is a symbol of the dedicated life. We will spend our entire lives developing the full meaning of what this means, but one thing becomes immediately evident—we must subordinate our natural selves to eternal purposes. We are well acquainted with the lust of the flesh and the eyes. As we age, these lusts tend to migrate into the memory where they are nurtured by the imagination and natural environments. Still, the pride of choosing, the thrill of self-determination abides and grows stronger with age. It seeks confirmation among the many philosophies of life, all of which have one thing in common: they make you the righteous one, the one who excludes our Loving Heavenly Father, and is ruled by whispers from what Martin Luther called "that whore, reason." Reason, or the logic of the mind, coupled with pride is our most formidable enemy.

The mode whereby lead (horizontal, secular living) is changed into gold (ultimate value) is altruism (giving yourself in a cause that is greater than yourself). Note that the ultimate expression of altruism is the cross. However, when Jesus commanded us to take up our cross and follow him, he used an anachronism. That is, he gave the command several months before his own death by crucifixion; carrying his own cross was at this time a future event. Christ as Priest and King here became Prophet of this future event. We also know he takes all of his followers down through the ages as members of his audience. His command to us all includes an audience in all times and places.

I suppose we all might logically agree that an excellent time and place for talking about the significance of the cross would be the Last Word from the Cross. Yet he says it is not then, but now—today. So what added meaning might we infer from this *ante facto* location of his most expansive commandment to his followers? It is to start today, regardless of time; there is no more convenient occasion. Today stresses that we must love Christ as we love ourselves, for love is the gold-from-lead we clothe ourselves with when we arrive at our predestined home, and the longer the time available to start weaving its threads, the better. This commandment stresses the Golden Rule that we Western Christians take from the Sermon on the Mount, which generates from his motive for carrying the cross—to love each of us as he does himself. The Golden Rule is not a biblical name, though not an objectionable one. Still, there is an even greater commandment which we must find another name for—I call it the Platinum Rule. So loving your neighbor as yourself gives way to loving your neighbor as God loves you.

We are staggering under our altruistic cross, and now we wrinkle our brows at this even more demanding command and ask, "Just how much does God love us?" I answer with the Bible's Golden Verse, "For God so loved the world that he gave his son, his only begotten, that the one who is having faith in him should not perish but have life everlasting" (John 3:16). There could not be a more important verse in the entire Bible than this, and yet we do not know who said it, Christ or John. It could go either way, as Christ still speaking to Nicodemus or as John speaking directly to us. Maybe part of its message is for all of us to say it to a universe of men in love with themselves, so a few of them will hear its life-saving message. In addition, we must be sure to give precedence to the message lived over the one spoken as we are exhorted to do by Jesus' natural brother James. Then the godless man may see your life, even though you may not have occasion to give him the spoken message of John 3:16. He may be convinced by your holy love for others, as though you were already living in the future City of God, just as Jesus lived by the ultimate expression of God's love, dying on the cross, before he actually experienced it. Indeed, the *ante facto* reality is why the Heavenly City is of transparent gold, a poignant metaphor with the meaning that the highest value (gold) is spiritual (transparent). We citizens of Eternity must act as though we are already there; we must overcome time and space. Listen to Paul's version of God's living beyond place and time. "He who spared not his own son, but freely gave him up for all of us, how shall he not with him [now seated on the throne beside him] freely give us all things?" (Rom. 8:32).

Christ proclaimed love as the crowning part of God's reputation. Recall that the duty of the Christian is to advertise the Good Proclamation (Gospel). How carefully David guarded his steps: "He leads me in the right paths for his reputation's sake." Hence, we are obligated to advertise God's reputation, more precious than rubies. Now read again Commandment III: "Thou shalt not advertise the Lord's reputation in a reckless way." Another way to say it is, "Thou shalt not trivialize God's reputation." See where Jesus puts God's reputation, as the First Petition of the Lord's Prayer: "Be your name holy." Satan, being in some ways more knowledgeable than we are of heaven's priorities, busies himself as *Diabolos*, a blend of two Greek words: *dia*, meaning "across," and *bolos,* meaning "to throw," which carries the idea of crossing out someone's name. He is the defamer, the false accuser. What is the reason so often given by the ungodly for rejecting God and his church? The negative quality of the people in it. Their hypocritical reputation! The bad elder! The money-hungry preacher! The church is full of hypocrites—all of them! *Diabolos* is quite successful in drawing away so many. Each of us does well to beware, lest someone steals our crown. In the Prologue of Job, Satan shows his nature as *Diabolos* when he accuses Job of opportunism, i.e., being good toward God because God has been good to him. What's more, Satan gets double purchase from this accusation. He not only accuses Job of falling short of disinterested virtue, but scorns God as failing to make a creature capable of loving him.

This gold of ours, surrounded still by its matrix of lead, our bodies (our vessels of clay, as Paul puts it), this gold can become more visible and attractive because of—not in spite of—its clay container. Recall the great words of David: "Out of the mouths of babes and sucklings hast thou ordained strength because of the enemy" (Ps. 8:2). This is so because the enemy is deceived by the clay or lead. The jeweler does not put the diamond he wants you to buy in a tray among many sparkling stones, but on black velvet all by itself. In a similar manner, the enemy always underestimates his foe even as he overestimates himself, a fault always attending the pride of life.

THE WORLD'S TWO DAYS

It seems that the stronger an enemy is, the more of its badness God converts into blessing. It is something like what a great preacher once shocked his congregation by saying, "Let the power of sin pass into you." What he meant is, when we resist sin, we rob it of its power, so the stronger that sin's temptation is, the greater strength you will have gained from resisting it.

Jesus Christ, who never yielded to sin, came into the world to save his own from the tragedy of death, the consequence of sin. His quality of life and stated purpose—coming to save his people from their sin—must have inspired all the powers of hell to do him battle. From his initial temptations in the wilderness just after his baptism, he returned to the haunts of men— this Lion-Lamb of God was indeed full of grace and power. He had taken the power of sin away from sin and was fully equipped to give the world the narrative of God-With-Us.

This Gospel, this Great Proclamation (as I prefer to call it) of Emmanuel, had another superlative characteristic that often goes unnoticed by the world. Christ's life and work among men, recorded in four short pamphlets, proved to contain the briefest message given by any founder of a major religion. Yet Christianity, by one recent count, has the largest number of followers.

One biblical scholar confirmed this quantitative comparison by writing a harmony of the Gospels featuring only the known sayings of Jesus, omitting all repetition. He timed himself reading this harmony aloud—it took him only 45 minutes! At an average delivery speed, this could be contained in an 18-page, typewritten manuscript using double spacing. Many short stories are longer than that. However, one interesting fact ameliorates this brevity. The world's religions—all the major ones—are one of two kinds. They are based on either the life of the founder or his teachings, but never both. Only with Christ are both equally significant. As God-Among-Us, the life he led is as admissive of theological interpretation as is the message he delivered. The Gospels give us double purchase from their contents.

Jesus knew he would be captured and executed as quickly as men could get their violent hands on him. Hardly had his public ministry begun until men sought means to kill him (Mark 3). To forestall the inevitable, Jesus used several delay tactics. He never in public spoke of himself as the Messiah, but rather as the "son of man," which in Aramaic and Hebrew is expressed as "son of Adam," as we find in the Old Testament books of Daniel and Ezekiel. Not only is this a frustrating generality (for which man is not a "son of Adam"?), but he often requested that the people he healed keep their healings secret. In addition, he explained that one of the reasons he taught in parables was to frustrate his opponents by using symbolic language. Recall that his own townspeople took him by force and headed for a high cliff to push him over it just because he read a few verses from Isaiah and concluded with one sentence: "This day is this Scripture fulfilled in your sight." When we think about the matter, it is amazing that his brief ministry lasted as long as it did.

The brevity of his miraculous ministry among men was a matter known to biblical writers before Isaiah. Moses' description of the Passover meal made haste a conspicuous part of the ritual. The lamb was to have its throat cut and the blood drained out, then roasted with hide and entrails intact. All participants were to be fully clothed. The men were also to eat with their heads covered and their staves in hand. The bones of the lamb were not to be broken, i.e., to take time to eat the marrow, and they were to eat this roasted lamb with their fingers. They were allowed no time to let the bread dough rise before baking it—they were to eat only unleavened bread. Vegetables were not to be roasted, but eaten raw. All these things suggested that God would make a short matter of slaying the Egyptian firstborn. The Passover Lamb, of course, was a type of Christ.

In Isaiah 53, we see the Messiah camouflaged. He will look like an average person, as common as an annual weed or a root protruding from the ground; he will not be good-looking or have an exceptionally impressive physique. Isaiah, like Moses, speaks of haste. Christ is cut off out of the land of the living. He is tried before a hasty judge, then executed so quickly that they must put him in a borrowed grave, probably because he does not live nearby. To Isaiah, the reference to a rich man's grave probably meant the practice (even today) of a rich man having a sarcophagus prepared long before his death. Isaiah also tells us that he is so young that he does not even have a wife and children. This ending remark closes this remarkable passage: "He was numbered *with* the transgressors," meaning two, rather than *among,* which is more appropriate for three or more.

There is another matter, somewhat obscured by a cultural practice almost universally accepted as fact. I refer to the practice of having a Communion service on Maundy Thursday, as Jesus did. This is correct, but the name is misleading. Since the Hebrew day begins at sunset, even as day began in darkness as recorded in Genesis 1:5, our Thursday evening is already Friday as the Jews reckon time. This means that all the events of Christ's Passion occurred on Good Friday, Hebrew time. The world managed to rid itself of our Beloved Christ in one primary unit of time, a diurnal day, on Day Six of the seven-day week—on the same day that God created man. This day God ordained because he loved mankind, the crowning achievement of his creative powers. He so loved the world of men that he gave his son, his only begotten, to show how far divine love will go. In addition, he did it on Friday, the very day when man was created. Listen to how the great Westminster Confession answers the question, "What is the purpose of man?"—". . . to glorify God and to enjoy him forever."

The study of the haploid number that answers the question about the world's incomplete day brings us to the subject of Hebrew numerology— the use of numbers to express ideas. All languages until the Middle Ages used the letters of their alphabets to express numbers. We are well acquainted with "Roman numerals," which do exactly that. However, Greek and Hebrew, as well as nearly all other languages of that time, used letters for numbers, and in logical succession, i.e., a = 1, b = 2, c = 3, etc. We can see that sometimes a number could coincidentally spell a word, and eventually numbers were used for secret communication, which may indeed explain the extensive use of numerology in John's Apocalypse.

As fascinating as the subject is, we have no opportunity to do more than give enough background to understand what John is saying with his mysterious haploid number—half of the number 7, or 3 ½. Notice that we have seven orifices in our head, and it is through these orifices that all our knowledge of the physical universe enters. That the number 7 means totality—infinity—is seen in an early vision of the Apocalypse. After promising us a vision of the Lion of the Tribe of Judah, John shows a lamb with its breast imbrued with its own blood, as though his throat has been cut in preparation for a sacrifice. This surprising vision presents us with a *prima facie* oxymoron. Yet as we look more closely, this lamb has 7 horns (omnipotence), 7 eyes (omniscience) and 7 spirits (omnipresence). We are given the message that love is the greatest power in the universe. There can be no naïveté in the Christ who carries our sins out to Skull Place. Fully restored to his former glory, which he left in heaven when he came to earth, he knows all that these "omni" attributes involve. It is knowing who died for us—only this—that convinces us he means exactly what he says in our behalf, so for us to doubt is to be damned.

The number 7 is not only the most powerful number in Hebrew numerology, but it is also the one most often used. What we must consider is the length of the week, universally accepted as 7 days long by cultures today. We noted in the Introduction that the book of Enoch exhibited a week of millennia, the greatest unit of time concerning man, a symbolic week of 1,000 years for each day. A justification for this is found in II Peter 3:8, "one day with the Lord is a thousand years, and a thousand years is as one day."

Another number in Hebrew numerology that pertains to the subject at hand is 40. Since 4 is the number of earth and 10 the number of the complete man (body plus soul) we get the esoteric message, "all that the earth can do to your body and soul," or simply stated, "a period of trial." Check out the number 40 in a concordance, and you will find this interpretation is applicable to its context in every citation. You will also find that the event most frequently cited is the length of time the Hebrews spent in their exodus to the Promised Land. Scholars, however, have come to the conclusion that the time spent was factually only 38 years and not 40. So what are we to say about this? The writer (probably Moses) felt the sojourn in the desert had a more significant meaning by using 40. He is using the round figure for the sake of including the numerological message. I seem to hear Moses say, "It's close enough," while Paul smiles and says, "After all, the letter killeth, but the spirit maketh alive."

The last number we shall look at is even more mysterious, the number 42, for John blends Hebrew numerology with Roman time. Incidentally, that is why his time for our Lord's Passion differs from that in the Synoptic accounts. The number 42 is used several times in chapters 11-13 of the Apocalypse. The special reference is made by expressing it in three different yet equal forms: 1) time, times and half a time, or 3 ½ years; 2) 42 months; 3) 1,260 days. Again returning to the Introduction, you will recall how St. Augustine also holds this millennial-week interpretation:

Adam to Abraham	1,000 years
Abraham to Moses	1,000 years
Moses to David	1,000 years
David to Christ	1,000 years
Christ to his Parousia	2,000 years
Parousia to Eternity	—

The 6th millennium since the creation of Adam (which is also the second millennium since the birth of Christ) reached modern times around the year 1995. Nobody seemed to notice the year, and obviously it had no eschatological significance since Christ did not return then. However, ahead of us is the second millennial anniversary of Christ's dying for the sins of the world. This will reach us in 2028 or thereabouts. I have no doubt but that the haploid number in question refers to the length of Jesus ministry. Luke lets us know the ages of John the Baptist and Jesus when their public ministries began. He says they were about 30 years of age. In John's Gospel only is the information that Jesus spent three consecutive Passovers in Jerusalem. If we measure the beginning of his ministry, as most scholars do, it had to last about half a week (3 ½) of years, or 42 months, or 1,260 days.

John was not the only Canonist who used 42 in a symbolic way. Observe the genealogical chart in the first chapter of Matthew. Verse 17 makes a conspicuous use of 42 by dividing the list into three sections, 14 generations each, a total of 42 generations. Three interesting features are: 1) the list is taken from the LX X and not the Hebrew version of the genealogy in I Chron. 1-3; 2) a few of the minor kings were omitted to make the total come to the desired number of 14; 3) only 13 generations make the total in the third group, which nevertheless is represented with a 14. The omission of a few names and the shortage of one king in the last section clearly indicate the nature of biblical error, viz., scribal omissions and statistical irregularities, like the two versions of lepers healed on one particular occasion. One account speaks of ten and another speaks of two. We find human fingerprints elsewhere in both testaments, but there are no theological errors to be found at all. Pascal makes the point that there is just enough error in Scripture to challenge the faith of the believer, and just enough for the ungodly to damn himself.

The question before us is what is John saying when he uses this haploid number? Surely it is of major importance, for it is a summary upon the space-time sojourn of God-With-Us. This half-number must have two answers, one on each side of the "half"—God's side and man's side.

God was totally in charge at Skull Place. He creates an environment in which Cain comes close enough to God as possible, "within striking distance," to use military language. Our Commander-in-Chief, the Lord of Hosts, brings man and Satan to such an environment that gives them no choice, precisely because the choice is totally theirs, and they seize it with passionate intensity. Perhaps the middle word of the Seven Words uttered by King Jesus as his 1,260 days of ministry draws to its end will shed some light on the matter.

The curtain of God's great sanctuary falls at noon as a cosmic cloud sweeps across this sinful planet. What is it that Jesus says? *"Eli, Eli, lama sabachthani?"* Why, he is quoting Scripture! He has not energy enough, moisture enough to lubricate his tongue and lips—even his vocal chords need moistened breath to vibrate. They have taken everything away. Naked he is, of course. There is no place for him to stand on this huge globe. He dies lifted up above our real estate. The water, though it covers more than three times as much area as the land, and miles deep in many places—yet for him there is not a drop to drink. So he quotes just the first line of Psalm 22—what is he saying? He is telling us that the Hebrew sanctification has come to its end. The veil of God's sanctuary has closed them out—now they are with the rest of humanity. He says, "Eli, Eli," probably with a failing voice, but they hear "Eliya, Eliya"—that is not what he is saying. They incorrectly assume that he is calling for Elijah. He is actually saying, "Go read Psalm 22 and you will see the significance of what you have done!"

In the Garden of Eden, God taught the silent, hiding Adam what he should be doing, even asking himself, "Where am I?" Even so, Christ is putting in man's mouth what he should be saying. Those fall into deep theological trouble who say Christ is asking this question, seemingly bewildered over what has happened to him. Then God forsakes him, turning his back on him because he becomes sin for us. I ask such people: Is not Christ at this very moment showing men how far love will go? He has not taken on the substance of sin, but the power of it, robbing it of its power. Will God turn from him at this show of his own mighty power? Why is it that we constantly turn to the Savior of our lives by returning fondly to Skull Place, there to see the Eternal Eden established forever by virtue personified? God was never *nearer* to Christ than then. "He who has seen me has seen the Father," was never truer than then. Indeed, who is turning his back on Christ is not God, but man. I am moved to ask which of these damned personae I most resemble. Which might I have become had he not stopped me in my downward slide to my own egocentric hell?

For three and one-half years, he raised the dead, opened blind eyes, and healed everyone who came to him. Was there a family in all Israel that had not felt his healing hand? For 1,260 days he taught with such authority that soldiers sent to arrest him were paralyzed by the power of his teaching, and angels leaned over the banisters of heaven to hear him. For 42 months he endured the insults of men, and in turn rebuked them for their heresy and hypocrisy. Then after time, times and half a time, they endured his glory no longer. They cut him off, out of the land of the living. They rid themselves of what he said, burned what they could, martyred his witnesses, jailed or exiled his preachers—and they continue doing it even today. His brief ministry condemns mankind for doing their best to get rid of God, to erase his fingerprints from the pages of history. That is the world's day—its part of the haploid message.

The other half of the haploid week is our half; we are to complete the ministry of Jesus Christ, and that is why Paul called us "workers together with God." The Christian Way is the Divine-human synergism that for 42 months presents the contemporaneous Christ to each generation of mankind until time shall be no more. For 1,260 days we take his place; we are the body of Christ dragging our own crosses down the *Via Dolorosa* in our city, the light of the world upon a candlestick and not under a bushel basket, a city built on a hill. Can any Christian deny this is our mission? We must accept it from Christ for a time, times and half a time, if we would join him in the Eternal City. Listen to Paul in his letter to the church in Philippi: ". . . that I may know him, and the power of his resurrection, and the fellowship of his sufferings, being made conformable unto his death; if by any means I might attain unto the resurrection of the dead" (Phil. 3:10-11). Listen to Peter in his first epistle, "Christ also suffered for us, leaving us an example, that ye should follow in his steps" (I Pet. 2:21). Hear John in his first epistle, "Hereby perceive we the love of God, because as he laid down his life for us, and we ought to lay down our lives for the brethren" (I John 3:16).

Who can deny that we are the world's psychodrama? We speak out to the world the words of the Great Proclamation, while because of it the world spontaneously afflicts us as it did him, and inadvertently brings to view its only hope of salvation. As it is in a psychodrama, we the afflicted gain insight into the dimensions of his love and the certitude of our own salvation.

In such a way, his 3 ½ years complete 7 through us! We add our pages to his Gospel. As Paul said, "We are the epistles known and read of men." Jesus himself prophesied that we would do even greater works than he did—greater in quantity, of course, not quality! One preacher can reach more via our modern media in just one sermon than God-With-Us did in his brief tenure among us. The Lord gave the light, and great was the company of the preachers. He also said that these preachers would encircle the globe before he returns. His greater achievement in the second half of his haploid tenure of a mere 42 months is a synergistic venture; God and we are workers together.

See Simon of Cyrene exit the Beautiful Gate on Good Friday? He is the first to carry his proxy cross down through the centuries. Two millennia lay before our Lord as he forced these brutish men to impale him, the Commander-in-Chief (Lord of Hosts) of Heaven's Army affixed to this bizarre Roman "signboard" designed to induce obedience from all enemies of the State. Yet before this is John the Baptist, who gave this advertisement: "Look! The Lamb of God, who is bearing away the sins of the world!" We are instructed at this very moment by the silence of Christ, for that message belongs in our mouths. He never called himself the Lamb of God. Paul and Peter did, and all the enlightened ones since continue to do so. Above all lesser sign posts of history rises the Lamb of God. The four Gospels and our everyday gospels hemorrhage across the 20 centuries to follow, drenching human culture with a bloodbath of love-hate—love of mankind, hatred of sin—from the Lion-Lamb of God.

CONCLUSION

So you are to take up your cross and follow him if you expect to reach his destination. You are to complete his haploid week by keeping his Passion before the faces of doubting men and women, by letting him wear your shoes and gloves before all saints, and thereby, to the degree you accomplish your own Passion, the world will hate you, and will help you find your cross and guide you to your own *Via Dolorosa*. Jesus said this will happen. You may say, "What is this cross I am to carry?" It may take a long time to find it. We Christians have the reputation of being wrong about this matter, and the cross might change over the years—but be patient. Paul said, "Work out your own salvation with fear and trembling." Apparently, God wants you to make a critical evaluation of yourself. You are unique, so your cross will be different from mine and everyone else's. Don't let anyone else prescribe the dimensions of your cross—only God and you can tend to this matter. Besides, he wants to help you because he loves you. Through Paul he says, "Work it out," but note in the quote one of those words with two unrelated meanings, and both are often used in Scripture. The word "fear" depends heavily on context. Sometimes it means worry and suspicion about a formidable foe who intends to do you harm, or it means to be awe-struck. Since we know that perfect love casts out the first kind of fear, Paul must mean the latter in this context.

I am working out my salvation, awe-struck and trembling in anticipation of my nearness to heaven. I am amazed at the near-disasters and tragedies I have passed through. How narrowly saved am I—yet saved! I am awe—struck at the way God has kept his Romans 8:28 promise to me. All things have worked for my good—I have no doubt about this. It is true that I did not sit down at one particular time and think of everything of an adverse nature that has happened to me, but as they have come to me from time to time. Yet the answer is always the same. God has kept that promise to me; all things have worked for my good. Oh, they may have come in disguise, like some Halloween villain. I have torn away the mask and seen them defeated in time to save me from harm. Still others were like the pattern of contrary effects that Job experienced all on a given day, as Jesus also had hurled at him in one 24-hour day. A short time ago, I discovered a secret about me revealed by the Holy Ghost—I have often been my own worst enemy. Not my heart, but the part of me in control, perhaps best called the pride of living, a witch's brew of "cares of this world" and "the deceitfulness of riches" preempting the whole of me, dragging my soul along, yielding—reluctantly, but yielding. Too much of this carnal-minded intercourse with good and evil. Too much fruit from the wrong tree.

I suspect that you, too, have been drawn aside. Recall what Paul said in his first letter to Timothy. He gave us a "saying," and then went on to say it ought to be accepted by everybody, viz., "that Jesus Christ came into the world to save sinners, chief of whom I myself am!" (I Tim. 1:15). In the light of who said it, it seems as though everybody ought to climb aboard. I am of the growing opinion that every Christian is his own worst enemy—perhaps not always, but overall. William James made a very provocative statement in this vein of thought. He said there are two kinds of religion—the religion of the healthy soul and the religion of the sick soul. It was his view that Christ focused on the sick soul.

You may recall the incident in Jesus' life that seemed to lean toward that conclusion quite forcefully. He was invited to dinner, and by his accepting the invitation, the clergy felt he had compromised his religion by eating with tax collectors and prostitutes. Jesus said he was sent to heal the sick, and that the healthy people did not need a physician. Of course, we know that there were only two kinds of people that day—those who were spiritually sick and knew it, and those who were sick but did not know it.

There are people successfully adjusted to this world. Each is adequately endowed with a good mind, attractive personality, sound body, and a comfortable living. The fruit of the interdicted tree tastes just fine to them; they accept the challenge of knowing good and evil, and the last thing they would want is for someone to come along and confront them with the Grand Proclamation of God-With-Us. Jesus speaks first of the "poor in spirit," then follows with "those who mourn." His whole Gestalt of the Redeemed (the name I give the Beatitudes) seems to present salvation as being desirable for the sick soul, those living on the verge.

Consider one obscure verse of Scripture. It is so hauntingly beautiful and yet so very simple. Matthew had just finished presenting the baptism of Jesus, and his 40 days in the wilderness being tempted by Satan. Now he announces the ministry that will change the course of history—he simply says in Matt. 4:17, "From that time Jesus began to preach and to say, Repent, for the Kingdom of the heavens is at hand."

It is little wonder King Herod and his court (and all Jerusalem, too) were troubled at the announcement of the magi. They must have thought something like this: "Why hadn't God told us first that a new king of us Jews had been born? Why must we be told by these Persian astrologers?" Jonah told the very ancestors of these magi to repent, and they did so immediately. Repentance is the word that epitomized the preaching of John the Baptist, and repentance is the message of Jesus.

Repentance is the first move toward salvation. It is far more than sorrow for sins, but a categorical repudiation of a life that has admitted anything that supplants the Divine Lover of our lives. The word itself suggests more than some emotional upheaval, *metanoia*, to turn the mind around. It is an admission of being totally wrong about life. This is tantamount to an insult to one's system of values, ranking of priorities, choice of lifestyles. Recall the Mosaic trilogy of sin—the lust of the flesh, the lust of the eyes, even the pride of living. The fault with some Christians is their misunderstanding about the scope of repentance. It is an ongoing activity; it's our logical response to sin. As long as we have sin, there is something in the mind that must be changed. We also must consider the elaborate causal pattern leading to sin. A causes B, B causes C, C causes D, and D causes E—the sin itself. We must repent not only of sin, but of the causal pattern that leads to sin—every rung of the ladder.

In considering man's nigh universal rejection of repentance, let us look at the Jews' four reasons given for rejecting Jesus as their Messiah. They are four: he came at the wrong time; he did not look the part; he was not a military leader; he died in an unthinkable way. They are fully convinced that God would never allow his Son to be crucified—it is unthinkable. You see, it is mostly the offence of the cross that makes the Messiahship of Jesus unthinkable.

So Christ's life ended in the most unconvincing, unthinkable way! Through the eyes of faith, it could not have been otherwise. If it is unthinkable that God would allow his Anointed Son to die this way, then it is also unthinkable that God would make it possible for the 99-year-old Abraham to sire a child, the 90-year-old Sarah to conceive and bear a son, and then to require Abraham to slit that son's throat, drain out his life's blood, disembowel his body, quarter it and stack the parts on the logs, then burn it all to ashes. This from the God of Love? Unthinkable. Unthinkable, too, the virgin birth. Unthinkable that Christ Triumphant will split the heavens and appear amidst a host of brilliant angels before the sight of all living on planet earth.

The unthinkable religion is God's answer to what Luther called, "that whore, reason." That is what transcendence means, beyond the reach of man's thinking power. As he watched the flames consume the sacrifice God had provided instead of Isaac, Abraham came to see how he would become a blessing to men of all nations. He had shown us what faith is—the conviction about reality that God is Love, and that Love has the power to help us endure whatever contradictions occur to challenge it, including, yes, the unthinkable.

FOR THE SUITCASE

1. The trial and error method of science must rely on faith in the human mind.

2. Nature and science do not lead us to atheism.

3. Science, religion and nature are in harmony regarding subjects they hold in common.

4. God does not use nature to reveal himself to men; he handles that matter for himself.

5. All proofs for God's existence have been neutralized by logical argument.

6. Nature may confirm the faith of Christians—but not always.

7. Theistic evolution is not denounced by Scripture, but Darwinism is.

8. Logical positivism and spontaneous generation are theories contrary to biblical theology.

9. The laws of human conduct can be broken, but not the laws (rules) of nature.

10. Irregularities in nature, science and Scripture not only challenge faith, but add to the glory of God.

11. Repentance involves more than sins. Repentance is an ongoing reality in the Christian life.